U·X·L ENCYCLOPEDIA OF

NATIVE
AMERICAN
TRIBES

U·X·L ENCYCLOPEDIA OF

NATIVE AMERICAN TRIBES

VOLUME

3

Arctic & Subarctic
Great Plains
Plateau

Sharon Malinowski, Anna Sheets
& Linda Schmittroth, *Editors*

U·X·L®

AN IMPRINT OF THE GALE GROUP

DETROIT · SAN FRANCISCO · LONDON
BOSTON · WOODBRIDGE, CT

U•X•L Encyclopedia of Native American Tribes

Sharon Malinowski, Anna Sheets, and Linda Schmittroth, *Editors*

Staff

Sonia Benson, *U•X•L Senior Editor*
Carol DeKane Nagel, *U•X•L Managing Editor*
Thomas L. Romig, *U•X•L Publisher*
Jeffrey Lehman, *Editor*
Melissa Walsh Doig, *Editor*
Dorothy Maki, *Manufacturing Manager*
Evi Seoud, *Assistant Production Manager*
Rita Wimberley, *Senior Buyer*
Cynthia Baldwin, *Product Design Manager*
Barbara Yarrow, *Graphic Services Director*
Michelle DiMercurio, *Senior Art Director*
Keasha Jack-Lyles, *Permissions Associate*
LM Design, *Typesetter*

Library of Congress Cataloging-in-Publication Data

U•X•L Encyclopedia of Native American Tribes / Sharon Malinowski, Anna Sheets, and Linda Schmittroth, editors

p. cm.

Includes bibliographical references.

Contents: v. 1. The Northeast and Southeast – v. 2. The Great Basin and Southwest – v. 3. The Arctic, Subarctic, Great Plains, and Plateau – v. 4. California and the Pacific Northwest.

ISBN 0-7876-2838-7 (set).

ISBN 0-7876-2839-5 (volume 1)   ISBN 0-7876-2841-7 (volume 3)

ISBN 0-7876-2840-9 (volume 2)   ISBN 0-7876-2842-5 (volume 4)

1. Indians of North America – Encyclopedias, Juvenile. [1. Indians of North America – Encyclopedias.] I. Malinowski, Sharon. II. Sheets, Anna J. (Anna Jean), 1970– . III. Schmittroth, Linda. IV. Title: Encyclopedia of Native American tribes.

E76.2.U85 1999

970'.003—dc21

98-54353
CIP
AC

Copyright © 1999
U•X•L, An Imprint of the Gale Group
DETROIT•SAN FRANCISCO•LONDON•BOSTON•WOODBRIDGE, CT

Contents

VOLUME 2

The Great Basin

Southwest

VOLUME 3

VOLUME 4

Tribes Alphabetically

First numeral signifies volume number. The numeral after the colon signifies page number. For example, **3:871** means Volume 3, page 871.

Reader's Guide

Long before the Vikings, Spaniards, and Portuguese made land-fall on North American shores, the continent already had a rich history of human settlement. The *U•X•L Encyclopedia of Native American Tribes* opens up for students the array of tribal ways in the United States and Canada past and present. Included in these volumes, readers will find the stories of:

- the well-known nineteenth century Lakota hunting the buffalo on the Great Plains

- the contemporary Inuit of the Arctic, who have recently won their battle for Nunavut, a vast, self-governing territory in Canada

- the Seminole in Florida, drawing tourists with their alligator wrestling shows

- the Haida of the Pacific Northwest, whose totem poles have become a familiar adornment of the landscape

- the Anasazi in the Southwest, who were building spectacular cities long before Europeans arrived

- the Mohawk men in the Northeast who made such a name for themselves as ironworkers on skyscrapers and bridges that they have long been in demand for such projects as the World Trade Center and the Golden Gate Bridge

- the Yahi of California, who became extinct when their last member Ishi died in 1916.

The *U•X•L Encyclopedia of Native American Tribes* presents eighty tribes, confederacies, and Native American groups. Among the tribes included are large and well-known nations, smaller communities with their own fascinating stories, and prehistoric peoples. The tribes are grouped in the ten major geographical/cultural areas of North America in which tribes shared environmental and cultural connections. The ten sections, each beginning with an introductory essay on the geographical area and the shared history and culture within it, are arranged in the volumes as follows:

- Volume 1: Northeast and Southeast

- Volume 2: The Great Basin and Southwest

- Volume 3: Arctic, Subarctic, Great Plains, and Plateau

- Volume 4: California and Pacific Northwest

The *U•X•L Encyclopedia of Native American Tribes* provides the history of each of the tribes featured and a fascinating look at their ways of life: how families lived in centuries past and today, what people ate and wore, what their homes were like, how they worshiped, celebrated, governed themselves, and much more. A student can learn in depth about one tribe or compare aspects of many tribes. Each detailed entry is presented in consistent rubrics that allow for easy access and comparison, as follows:

- History

- Religion

- Language

- Government

- Economy

- Daily Life

- Arts

- Customs

- Current Tribal Issues

- Notable People

Each entry begins with vital data on the tribe: name, location, population, language family, origins and group affiliations. A locator map follows, showing the traditional homelands and contemporary communities of the group; regional and migration maps throughout aid in locating the many groups and at different times in history. Brief timelines in each entry chronicle important dates of the tribe's history, while an overall timeline at the beginning of all the volumes outlines key events in history pertinent to all Native Americans. Other sidebars present recipes, oral literature or stories, population statistics, language keys, and background material on the tribe. Black-and-white photographs and illustrations, further reading sections, a thorough subject index, and a glossary are special features that make the volumes easy, fun, and informative to use.

A note on terminology

Throughout the *U•X•L Encyclopedia of Native American Tribes* various terms are used for Native North Americans, such as *Indian, American Indian, Native,* and *aboriginal.* The Native peoples of the Americas have the unfortunate distinction of having been given the wrong name by the Europeans who first arrived on the continent, mistakenly thinking they had arrived in India. The search for a single name, however, has never been entirely successful. The best way to characterize Native North Americans is by recognizing their specific tribal or community identities. In compiling this book, every effort has been made to keep Native tribal and community identities distinct, but by necessity, inclusive terminology is often used. We do not wish to offend anyone, but rather than favor one term for Native North American people, the editors have used a variety of terminology, trying always to use the most appropriate term in the particular context.

Europeans also had a hand in giving names to tribes, often misunderstanding their languages and the relations between different Native communities. Most tribes have their own names for themselves, and many have succeeded in gaining public acceptance of traditional names. The Inuit, for example, objected to the name Eskimo, which means "eaters of raw meat," and in time their name for themselves was accepted. In the interest of clarity the editors of this book have used the currently accepted terms, while acknowledging the traditional ones or the outmoded ones at the beginning of each entry.

The term *tribe* itself is not accepted by all Native groups. The people living in North America before the Europeans arrived had many different ways of organizing themselves politically and relating to other groups around them—from complex confederacies and powerful unified nations to isolated villages with little need for political structure. Groups divided, absorbed each other, intermarried, allied, and dissolved. The epidemics and wars that came with non-Native expansion into North America created a demographic catastrophe to many Native groups and greatly affected tribal affiliations. Although in modern times there are actual rules about what comprises a tribe (federal requirements for recognition of tribes are specific, complicated, and often difficult to fulfill), the hundreds of groups living in the Americas in early times did not have any one way of categorizing themselves. Some Native American peoples today find the word *tribe* misleading. In a study of Indian peoples, it can also be an elusive defining term. But in facing the challenges of maintaining traditions and heritage in modern times, tribal or community identity is acutely important to many Native Americans. Tremendous efforts have been undertaken to preserve native languages, oral traditions, religions, ceremonies, and traditional arts and economies— the things that, put together, make a tribe a cultural and political unit.

Advisors and contributors

For the invaluable contributions, suggestions, and advice on the *U•X•L Encyclopedia of Native American Tribes,* special thanks are due to: Edward D. Castillo, (Cahuilla-Luiseño), Director, Native American Studies Program, Sonoma State University, California; Ned Blackhawk; Elizabeth Hanson, Ph.D., Research Associate to the Dean, The College of Charleston, South Carolina; Daniel Boxberger, Department of Anthropology, Western Washington University; John H. Moore, Ph.D., Anthropology Department, University of Florida, Gainesville; Amanda Beresford McCarthy; George Cornell, Ph.D., Associate Professor, History and American Studies, Michigan State University; Brian Wescott, Athabascan/Yup'ik; Gordon L. Pullar, Director, Department of Alaska Native and Rural Development, College of Rural Alaska,UAF; and Barbara Bigelow.

Comments and suggestions

In this first edition of the *U•X•L Encyclopedia of Native American Tribes* we have presented in-depth information on eighty of the hundreds of tribes of North America. While every attempt was made to include a wide representation of groups, many historically important and interesting tribes are not covered in these volumes. We welcome your suggestions for tribes to be featured in future editions, as well as any other comments you may have on this set. Please write: Editors, *U•X•L Encyclopedia of Native American Tribes,* U•X•L, 27500 Drake Road, Farmington Hills, Michigan 48331–3535; call toll-free 1-800-347-4253; or fax: 313-699-8066; or send e-mail via http://www.galegroup.com.

Words to Know

A

Aboriginal: native, or relating to the first or earliest group living in a particular area.

Activism: taking action for or against a controversial issue; political and social activists may organize or take part in protest demonstrations, rallies, petitioning the government, sit-ins, civil disobedience, and many other forms of activities that draw attention to an issue and/or challenge the authorities to make a change.

Adobe: (pronounced *uh-DOE-bee*) a brick or other building material made from sun-dried mud, a mixture of clay, sand, and sometimes ashes, rocks, or straw.

Alaska Native Claims Settlement Act (ANCSA): an act of Congress passed in 1971 that gave Alaska Natives 44 million acres of land and $962.5 million. In exchange, Alaska Natives gave up all claim to other lands in Alaska. The ANCSA also resulted in the formation of 12 regional corporations in Alaska in charge of Native communities' economic development and land use.

Allotment: the practice of dividing and distributing something into individual lots. In 1887 the U.S. Congress passed the Dawes Act, or the General Allotment Act, which divided Indian reservations into privately owned parcels (pieces) of land. Under allotment, tribes could no longer own their lands in common (as a group) in the traditional way. Instead, the head of a family received a lot, generally 160 acres. Land not allotted was sold to non-Natives.

American Indian Movement (AIM): an activist movement founded in 1966 to aggressively press for Indian rights. The movement was formed to improve federal, state, and local social services to Native Americans in urban neighborhoods. AIM sought the reorganization of the Bureau of Indian Affairs to make it more responsive to Native

American needs and fought for the return of Indian lands illegally taken from them.

Anthropology: the study of human beings in terms of their populations, cultures, social relations, ethnic characteristics, customs, and adaptation to their environment.

Archaeology: the study of the remains of past human life, such as fossil relics, artifacts, and monuments, in order to understand earlier human cultures.

Arctic: relating to the area surrounding the North Pole.

Assimilate: to absorb, or to be absorbed, into the dominant society (those in power, or in the majority). U.S. assimilation policies were directed at causing Native Americans to become like European-Americans in terms of jobs and economics, religion, customs, language, education, family life, and dress.

B

Band: a small, loosely organized social group composed of several families. In Canada, the word *band* originally referred to a social unit of nomadic (those who moved from place to place) hunting peoples, but now refers to a community of Indians registered with the government.

Boarding school: a live-in school.

Breechcloth: a garment with front and back flaps that hang from the waist. *Breechcloths* were one of the most common articles of clothing worn by many Native American men and sometimes women in pre-European/American settlement times.

Bureau of Indian Affairs (BIA): the U.S. government agency that oversees tribal lands, education, and other aspects of Indian life.

C

Census: a count of the population.

Ceremony: a special act or set of acts (such as a wedding or a funeral) performed by members of a group on important occasions, usually organized according to the group's traditions and beliefs.

Clan: a group of related house groups and families that trace back to a common ancestor or a common symbol or totem, usually an animal such as the bear or the turtle. The *clan* forms the basic social and political unit for many Indian societies.

Colonialism: a state or nation's control over a foreign territory.

Colonize: to establish a group of people from a mother country or state in a foreign territory; the colonists set up a community that remains tied to the mother country.

Confederacy: a group of people, states, or nations joined together for mutual support or for a special purpose.

Convert: (as verb) to cause a person or group to change their beliefs or practices. A *convert* (noun) is a person who has been *converted* to a new belief or practice.

Coup: (pronounced *COO*) a feat of bravery, especially the touching of an enemy's body during battle without causing or receiving injury. To *count coup* is to count the number of such feats of bravery.

Cradleboard: a board or frame on which an infant was bound or wrapped by some Native American peoples. It was used as a portable carrier or for carrying an infant on the back.

Creation stories: sacred myths or stories that explain how the Earth and its beings were created.

Culture: the set of beliefs, social habits, and ways of surviving in the environment that are held by a particular social group.

D

Dentalium: (pronounced *den-TAIL-ee-um*; from the Latin word for tooth). Dentalia (plural) are the tooth-like shells that some tribes used as money. The shells were rubbed smooth and strung like beads on strands of animal skin.

Depletion: decreasing the amount of something; *depletion* of resources such as animals or minerals through overuse reduces essential elements from the environment.

Dialect: (pronounced *DY-uh-lect*) a local variety of a particular language, with unique differences in words, grammar, and pronunciation.

E

Economy: the way a group obtains, produces, and distributes the goods it needs; the overall system by which it supports itself and accumulates its wealth.

Ecosystem: the overall way that a community and its surrounding environment function together in nature.

Epidemic: the rapid spread of a disease so that many people in an area have it at the same time.

Ethnic group: a group of people who are classed according to certain aspects of their common background, usually by tribal, racial, national, cultural, and language origins.

Extended family: a family group that includes close relatives such as mother, father, and children, plus grandparents, aunts and uncles, and cousins.

F

Federally recognized tribes: tribes with which the U.S. government maintains official relations as established by treaty, executive order, or act of Congress.

First Nations: one of Canada's terms for its Indian nations.

Five Civilized Tribes: a name given to the Cherokee, Choctaw, Chickasaw, Creek, and Seminole during the mid-1800s. The tribes were given this name by non-Natives because they had democratic constitutional governments, a high literacy rate (many people who could read and write), and ran effective schools.

Formal education: structured learning that takes place in a school or college under the supervision of trained teachers.

G

Ghost Dance: a revitalization (renewal or rebirth) movement that arose in the 1870s after many tribes moved to reservations and were being encouraged to give up their traditional beliefs. Many Native Americans hoped that, if they performed it earnestly, the Ghost Dance would bring back traditional Native lifestyles and values, and that the buffalo and Indian ancestors would return to the Earth as in the days before the white settlers.

Great Basin: an elevated region in the western United States in which all water drains toward the center. The *Great Basin* covers part of Nevada, California, Colorado, Utah, Oregon, and Wyoming.

Guardian spirit: a sacred power, usually embodied in an animal such as a hawk, deer, or turtle, that reveals itself to an individual, offering help throughout the person's lifetime in important matters such as hunting or healing the sick.

H

Haudenosaunee: (pronounced *hoo-dee-noh-SHAW-nee*) the name of the people often called Iroquois or Five Nations. It means "People of the Longhouse."

Head flattening: a practice in which a baby was placed in a cradle, and a padded board was tied to its forehead to mold the head into a desired shape. Sometimes the effect of flattening the back of the head was achieved by binding the infant tightly to a cradleboard.

I

Immunity: resistance to disease; the ability to be exposed to a disease with less chance of getting it, and less severe effects if infected.

Indian Territory: an area in present-day Kansas and Oklahoma where the U.S. government once planned to move all Indians, and, eventually, to allow them to run their own province or state. In 1880 nearly one-third of all U.S. Indians lived there, but with the formation of the state of Oklahoma in 1906, the promise of an Indian state dissolved.

Indigenous: (pronounced *in-DIJ-uh-nus*) native, or first, in a specific area. Native Americans are often referred to as *indigenous* peoples of North America.

Intermarriage: marriage between people of different groups, as between a Native American and a non-Native, or between people from two different tribes.

K

Kachina: (pronounced *kuh-CHEE-nuh*) a group of spirits celebrated by the Pueblo Indians; the word also refers to dolls made in the image of *kachina* spirits.

Kiva: (pronounced *KEE-va*) among the Pueblo, a circular (sometimes rectangular) underground room used for religious ceremonies.

L

Lacrosse: a game of Native American origin in which players use a long stick with a webbed pouch at the end for catching and throwing a ball.

Language family: a group of languages that are different from one another but are related. These languages share similar words, sounds, or word structures. The languages are alike either because they have borrowed words from each other or because they originally came from the same parent language.

Legend: a story or folktale that tells about people or events in the past.

Life expectancy: the average number of years a person may expect to live.

Linguistics: the study of human speech and language.

Literacy: the state of being able to read and write.

Longhouse: a large, long building in which several families live together; usually found among Northwest Coast and Iroquois peoples.

Long Walk of the Navajo: the enforced 300-mile walk of the Navajo people in 1864, when they were being removed from their homelands to the Bosque Redondo Reservation in New Mexico.

M

Matrilineal: tracing family relations through the mother; in a *matrilineal* society, names and inheritances are passed down through the mother's side of the family.

Medicine bundle: a pouch in which were kept sacred objects believed to have powers that would protect and aid an individual, a clan or family, or a community.

Midewiwin Society: the Medicine Lodge Religion, whose main purpose was to prolong life. The society taught morality, proper conduct, and a knowledge of plants and herbs for healing.

Migration: movement from one place to another. The *migrations* of Native peoples were often done by the group, with whole nations moving from one area to another.

Mission: an organized effort by a religious group to spread its beliefs to other parts of the world; *mission* refers either to the project of spreading a belief system or to the building(s)—such as a church—in which this takes place.

Mission school: a school established by missionaries to teach people religious beliefs, as well as other subjects.

Myth: a story passed down through generations, often involving supernatural beings. *Myths* often express religious beliefs or the values of a people. They may attempt to explain how the Earth and its beings were created, or why things are as they are. They are not always meant to be taken as factual.

N

Natural resources: the sources of supplies provided by the environment for survival and enrichment, such as animals to be hunted, land for farming, minerals, and timber.

Neophyte: (pronounced *NEE-oh-fite*) beginner; often used to mean a new convert to a religion.

Nomadic: traveling and relocating often, usually in search of food and other resources or a better climate.

Nunavut: a new territory in Canada as of April 1, 1999, with the status of a province and an Inuit majority. It is a huge area, covering most of Canada north of the treeline. *Nunavut* means "Our Land" in Inukitut (the Inuit language).

O

Oral literature: oral traditions that are written down after enjoying a long life in spoken form among a people.

Oral traditions: history, mythology, folklore, and other foundations of a culture that have been passed by spoken word, often in the form of stories, from generation to generation within a culture group.

P

Parent language: a language that is the common source of two or more languages that came into being at a later time.

Per capita income: *per capita* is a Latin phrase that means "for each person." Per capita income is the average personal income per person.

Petroglyph: a carving or engraving on rock; a common form of ancient art.

Peyote: (pronounced *pay-OH-tee*) a substance obtained from cactus that some Indian groups use as part of their religious practice. After eating the substance, which stimulates the nervous system, a person may go into a trance state and see visions. The Peyote Religion features the use of this substance.

Pictograph: a simple picture representing a historical event.

Policy: the overall plan or course of action issued by the government, establishing how it will handle certain situations or people and what its goals are.

Post-European contact: relating to the time and state of Native Americans and their lands after the Europeans arrived. Depending on the part of the country in which they lived, Native groups experienced contact at differing times in the history of white expansion into the West.

Potlatch: a feast or ceremony, commonly held among Northwest Coast groups; also called a "giveaway." During a *potlatch,* goods are given to guests to show the host's generosity and wealth. Potlatches are used to celebrate major life events such as birth, death, or marriage.

Powwow: a celebration at which the main activity is traditional singing and dancing. In modern times, the singers and dancers at powwows come from many different tribes.

Province: a district or division of a country (like a state in the United States).

R

Raiding: entering into another tribe or community's territory, usually by stealth or force, and stealing their livestock and supplies.

Rancheria: a small Indian reservation, usually in California.

Ratify: to approve or confirm. In the United States, the U.S. Senate *ratified* treaties with the Indians.

Red Power: a term used to describe the Native American activism movement of the 1960s, in which people from many tribes came together to protest the injustices of American policies toward Native Americans.

Removal Act: an act passed by the U.S. Congress in 1830 that directed all Indians to be moved to Indian Territory, west of the Mississippi River.

Removal Period: the time, mostly between 1830 and 1860, when most Indians of the eastern United States were forced to leave their homelands and relocate west of the Mississippi River.

Reservation: land set aside by the U.S. government for the use of a group or groups of Indians.

Reserve: in Canada, lands set aside for specific Indian bands. *Reserve* means in Canada approximately what *reservation* means in the United States.

Revitalization: the feeling or movement in which something seems to come back to life after having been quiet or inactive for a period of time.

Ritual: a formal act that is performed in basically the same way each time; rituals are often performed as part of a ceremony.

Rural: having to do with the country; opposite of urban.

S

Sachem: the chief of a confederation of tribes.

Shaman: (can be pronounced either *SHAY-mun* or *SHAH-mun*) a priest or medicine person in many Native American groups who understands and works with supernatural matters. *Shamans* traditionally performed in rituals and were expected to cure the sick, see the future, and obtain supernatural help with hunting and other economic activities.

Smallpox: a very contagious disease that spread across North America and killed many thousands of Indians. Survivors had skin that was badly scarred.

Subsistence economy: an economic system in which people provide themselves with the things they need for survival and their way of life rather than working for money or making a surplus of goods for trade.

Sun Dance: a renewal and purification (cleansing) ceremony performed by many Plains Indians such as the Sioux and Cheyenne. A striking aspect of the ceremony was the personal sacrifice made by some men. They undertook self-torture in order to gain a vision that might provide spiritual insight and knowledge beneficial to the community.

Sweat lodge: an airtight hut containing hot stones that were sprinkled with water to make them steam. A person remained inside until he or she was perspiring. The person then usually rushed out and plunged into a cold stream. This treatment was used before a ceremony or for the healing of physical or spiritual ailments. *Sweat lodge* is also the name of a sacred Native American ceremony involving the building of the lodge and the pouring of water on the stones, usually by a medicine person, accompanied by praying and singing. The ceremony has many purposes, including spiritual cleansing and healing.

T

Taboo: a forbidden thing or action. Many Indians believe that the sacred order of the world must be maintained if one is to avoid illness or other misfortunes. This is accomplished, in part, by observing a large assortment of taboos.

Termination: the policy of the U.S. government during the 1950s and 1960s to end the relationships set up by treaties with Indian nations.

Toloache: a substance obtained from a plant called jimsonweed. When consumed, the drug causes a person to go into a trance and see visions. It is used in some religious ceremonies.

Totem: an object that serves as an emblem or represents a family or clan, usually in the form of an animal, bird, fish, plant, or other natural object. A *totem pole* is a pillar built in front of the homes of Natives in the Northwest. It is painted and carved with a series of totems that show the family background and either mythical or historical events.

Trail of Tears: a series of forced marches of Native Americans of the Southeast in the 1830s, causing the deaths of thousands. The marches were the result of the U.S. government's removal policy, which ordered Native Americans to be moved to Indian Territory (now Oklahoma).

Treaty: an agreement between two parties or two nations, signed by both, usually defining the benefits to both parties that will result from one side giving up title to a territory of land.

Tribe: a group of Natives who share a name, language, culture, and ancestors; in Canada, called a band.

Tribelet: a community within an organization of communities in which one main settlement was surrounded by a few minor outlying settlements.

Trickster: a common culture hero in Indian myth and legend. *Tricksters* generally have supernatural powers that can be used to do good or harm, and stories about them take into account the different forces of the universe, such as good and evil or night and day. The Trickster takes different forms among various groups; for example, Coyote in the Southwest; Ikhtomi Spider in the High Plains, and Jay or Wolverine in Canada.

Trust: a relationship between two parties (or groups) in which one is responsible for acting in the other's best interests. The U.S. government has a *trust* relationship with tribal nations. Many tribes do not own their lands outright; according to treaty, the government owns the land "in trust" and tribes are given the use of it.

U

Unemployment rate: the percentage of the population that is looking for work but unable to find any. (People who have quit looking for work are not included in *unemployment* rates.)

Urban: having to do with cities and towns; the opposite of rural.

V

Values: the ideals that a community of people shares.

Vision quest: a sacred ceremony in which a person (often a teenage boy) goes off alone and fasts, living without food or water for a period of days. During that time, he hopes to learn about his spiritual side and to have a vision of a guardian spirit who will give him help and strength throughout his life.

W

Wampum: small cylinder-shaped beads cut from shells. Long strings of *wampum* were used for many different purposes. Indians believed that the exchange of wampum and other goods established a friendship, not just a profit-making relationship.

Wampum belt: a broad woven belt of wampum used to record history, treaties among the tribes, or treaties with colonists or governments.

Weir: a barricade used to funnel fish toward people who wait to catch them.

Timeline

25,000–11,000 B.C.E. Groups of hunters cross from Asia to Alaska on the Bering Sea Land Bridge, which was formed when lands now under the waters of the Bering Strait were exposed for periods of time, according to scientists.

1400 B.C.E. People who live along the lower Mississippi River are building large burial mounds and living in planned communities.

1 C.E. Small, permanent villages of the Hohokam tradition emerge in the Southwest.

400 Anasazi communities emerge in the Four Corners region of the Southwest. Anasazi eventually design communities in large multiroomed apartment buildings, some with more than 1,200 rooms. The Anasazi are farmers and skilled potters.

900 The Mississippian mound-building groups form complex political and social systems, and participate in long-distance trade and an elaborate and widespread religion.

1000–1350 The Iroquois Confederacy is formed among the Mohawk, Oneida, Onondaga, Cayuga, and Seneca nations. The Five Nations of the Haudenosaunee are from this time governed by chiefs from the 49 families who were present at the origin of the confederation.

Anasazi ruins at Pueblo del Arroyo, Chaco Canyon, New Mexico.

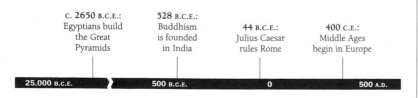

c. **2650** B.C.E.:
Egyptians build
the Great
Pyramids

528 B.C.E.:
Buddhism
is founded
in India

44 B.C.E.:
Julius Caesar
rules Rome

400 C.E.:
Middle Ages
begin in Europe

| 25,000 B.C.E. | 500 B.C.E. | 0 | 500 A.D. |

1040: Pueblos (towns) are flourishing in New Mexico's Chaco Canyon. The pueblos are connected by an extensive road system that stretches many miles across the desert.

1350 Moundville, in present-day Alabama, one of the largest ceremonial centers of the Mound Builders, thrives. With 20 great mounds and a village, it is probably the center of a chiefdom that includes several other related communities.

1494: Christopher Columbus begins the enslavement of American Indians, capturing over 500 Taino of San Salvador and sending them to Spain to be sold.

1503 French explorer Jacques Cartier begins trading with Native Americans along the East Coast.

1539–43 Spanish explorers Hernando de Soto and Francisco Coronado traverse the Southeast and Southwest, bringing with them disease epidemics that kill thousands of Native Americans.

1609 The fur trade begins when British explorer Henry Hudson, sailing for the Netherlands, opens trade in New Netherland (present-day New York) with several Northeast tribes.

1634–37 An army of Puritans, Pilgrims, Mohican, and Narragansett attacks and sets fire to the Pequot fort, killing as many as 700 Pequot men, women, and children.

1648–51 The Iroquois, having exhausted the fur supply in their area, attack other tribes in order to get a new supply. The Beaver Wars begin, and many Northeast tribes are forced to move west toward the Great Lakes area.

1660 The Ojibway, pushed west by settlers and Iroquois expansion, invade Sioux territory in Minnesota. After fighting the Ojibway, many Sioux groups move to the Great Plains.

1760–63 The Delaware Prophet tells Native Americans in the Northeast that they must drive Europeans out of North America and return to the customs of their ancestors. His message influences the Ottawa leader Pontiac, who uses it to unite many tribes against the British.

The attack on the Pequot fort in 1637.

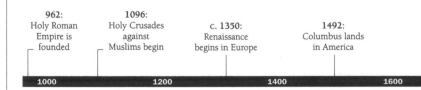

962:
Holy Roman
Empire is
founded

1096:
Holy Crusades
against
Muslims begin

c. 1350:
Renaissance
begins in Europe

1492:
Columbus lands
in America

1000   1200   1400   1600

1763 England issues the Proclamation of 1763, which assigns all lands west of the Appalachian Mountains to Native Americans, while colonists are allowed to settle all land to the east. The document respects the aboriginal land rights of Native Americans. It is not popular with colonists who want to move onto Indian lands and becomes one of the conflicts between England and the colonies leading to the American Revolution.

1769 The Spanish build their first mission in California. There will be 23 Spanish missions in California, which are used to convert Native Californians to Christianity, but also reduces them to slave labor.

c. 1770 Horses, brought to the continent by the Spanish in the sixteenth century, spread onto the Great Plains and lead to the development of a new High Plains Culture.

1778 The treaty-making period begins, when the first of 370 treaties between Indian nations and the U.S. government is signed. The treaty-making period ends in 1871.

1786 The first federal Indian reservations are established.

1789 The Spanish establish a post at Nootka Sound on Vancouver Island, the first permanent European establishment in the territory of the Pacific Northwest Coast tribes.

1805–06 Explorers Meriwether Lewis and William Clark, led by Sacajawea, travel through the Plateau area, encountering the Cayuse, Nez Perce, Walla Walla, Wishram, and Yakima.

1830 The removal period begins when the U.S. Congress passes the Indian Removal Act. Over the course of the next 30 years many tribes from the Northeast and Southeast are removed to Indian Territory in present-day Oklahoma and Kansas, often forcibly and at great expense in human lives.

Franciscan priest with an Indian child at a Spanish mission, California.

Sacajawea points out the way to Lewis and Clark.

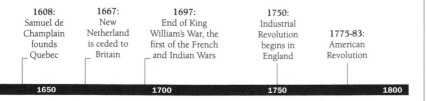

1608:
Samuel de Champlain founds Quebec

1667:
New Netherland is ceded to Britain

1697:
End of King William's War, the first of the French and Indian Wars

1750:
Industrial Revolution begins in England

1775-83:
American Revolution

1650   1700   1750   1800

1851 Early reservations are created in California to protect the Native population from the violence of U.S. citizens. These reservations are inadequate and serve only a small portion of the Native Californians, while others endure continued violence and hardship.

1870 The First Ghost Dance Movement begins when Wodzibwob, a Paiute, learns in a vision that a great earthquake will swallow the Earth, and that all Indians will be spared or resurrected within three days of the disaster. Thus, their world will return to its state before the Europeans had arrived.

1870–90 The Peyote Religion spreads through the Great Plains. Peyote (obtained from a cactus plant) brings on a dreamlike feeling that followers believe moves them closer to the spirit world. Tribes develop their own ceremonies, songs, and symbolism, and vow to be trustworthy, honorable, and community-oriented and to follow the Peyote Road.

1876 The Indian Act in Canada establishes an Indian reserve system, in which reserves were governed by voluntary elected band councils. The Act does not recognize Canadian Indians' right to self-government. With the passage of the act, Canadian peoples in Canada are divided into three groups: status Indian, treaty Indian, and non-status Indian. The categories affect the benefits and rights Indians are given by the government.

1880s The buffalo on the Great Plains are slaughtered until there are almost none left. Without adequate supplies of buffalo for food, the Plains Indians cannot survive. Many move to reservations.

1884 Potlatches are banned by the Canadian government. The elaborate gift-giving ceremonies have long been a vital part of Pacific Northwest Indian culture.

1887 The Dawes Act, or the General Allotment Act, is passed by Congress. The act calls for the allotment (or parceling out) of tribal lands. Tribes are no longer to own their lands in common in the traditional way. Instead, the land is to be assigned to

*Preparing for a potlatch
ceremony in the
Pacific Northwest.*

1812:
The War
of 1812

1861-65:
American
Civil War

1867:
Russia sells
Alaska to the
United States

1870:
The Fifteenth
Amendment guarantees
male citizens the vote

1850   1860   1870   1880

individuals. The head of a family receives 160 acres, and other family members get smaller pieces of land. Many Native Americans, unable to make a living from their land, end up having to sell their parcels. All Indian lands that are not allotted are sold to settlers. Millions of acres of Indian lands are lost.

1889 The Oklahoma Land Runs open Indian Territory to non-Natives. (Indian Territory had been set aside solely for Indian use.) At noon on April 22, an estimated 50,000 people line up at the boundaries of Indian Territory. They claim two million acres of land. By nightfall, tent cities, banks, and stores are doing business there.

1890 The second Ghost Dance movement is initiated by Wovoka, a Paiute. It includes many Paiute traditions. In some versions, the dance is performed in order to help bring back to Earth many dead ancestors and exterminated game. Ghost Dance practitioners hope the rituals in the movement will restore Indians to their former state, before the arrival of the non-Native settlers.

1912 The Alaska Native Brotherhood is formed to promote civil rights issues, such as the right to vote, access to public education, and civil rights in public places. The organization also fights court battles to win land rights.

1920 The Canadian government amends the Indian Act to allow for compulsory, or forced, enfranchisement, the process by which Indians have to give up their tribal loyalties to become Canadian citizens. Only 250 Indians had voluntarily become enfranchised between 1857 and 1920.

1924 All Indians are granted U.S. citizenship. This act does not take away rights that Native Americans had by treaty or the Constitution.

1928 Lewis Meriam is hired to investigate the status of Indian economies, health, and education, and the federal adminis-

The day school at the Sac and Fox Agency in Indian Territory, between 1876 and 1896.

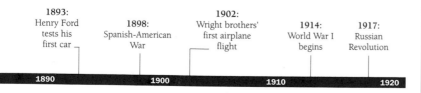

1893:
Henry Ford
tests his
first car

1898:
Spanish-American
War

1902:
Wright brothers'
first airplane
flight

1914:
World War I
begins

1917:
Russian
Revolution

1890   1900   1910   1920

Timeline **xxxiii**

tration of Indian affairs. His report describes the terrible conditions under which Indians are forced to live, listing problems with health care, education, poverty, malnutrition, and land ownership.

1934 U.S. Congress passes the Indian Reorganization Act (IRA), which ends allotment policies and restores some land to Native Americans. The IRA encourages tribes to govern themselves and set up tribal economic corporations, but with the government overseeing their decisions. The IRA also provides more funding to the reservations.

1946 The Indian Lands Commission (ICC) is created to decide land claims filed by Indian nations. Many tribes expect the ICC to return lost lands, but the ICC chooses to award money instead, and at the value of the land at the time it was lost.

1951 A new Indian Act in Canada reduces the power of the Indian Affairs Office, makes it easier for Indians to gain the right to vote, and helps Indian children enter public schools. It also removes the ban on potlatch and Sun Dance ceremonies.

1952 In an all out effort to make Native Americans "blend in" or assimilate with the rest of society, the U.S. government begins a policy of moving Indians from reservations to cities. The government hopes that Native Americans will find jobs in the city and adopt an "American" lifestyle. Then the government will be able to "terminate" the tribes and eliminate the reservations.

1954–62 The U.S. Congress carries out its policy of "termination." At the same time laws are passed giving states and local governments control over tribal members, taking away the tribes' authority to govern themselves. Under the policy of termination, Indians lose their special privileges and are treated as any other U.S. citizens. The tribes that are terminated face extreme poverty and the threat of loss of their

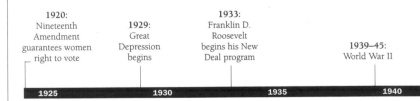

1920: Nineteenth Amendment guarantees women right to vote

1929: Great Depression begins

1933: Franklin D. Roosevelt begins his New Deal program

1939–45: World War II

1925   1930   1935   1940

community and traditions. By 1961 the government begins rethinking this policy because of the damage it is causing.

1955 The Indian Health Service (IHS) assumes responsibility for Native American health care. The IHS operates hospitals, health centers, health stations, clinics, and community service centers.

1960 The queen of England approves a law giving status Indians the right to vote in Canada.

The Menominee tribe was terminated by the U.S. government but after much protest, won back federal recognition.

1965 Under the new U. S. government policy, the Self-Determination policy, federal aid to reservations is given directly to Indian tribes and not funneled through the Bureau of Indian Affairs.

1968 The American Indian Movement (AIM) is founded in Minneapolis, Minnesota, by Dennis Banks (Ojibway) and Russell Means (Lakota). AIM is formed to improve federal, state, and local social services to urban neighborhoods and to prevent harassment of Indians by the local police.

1969 Eighty-nine Native Americans land on Alcatraz Island, a former penitentiary in San Francisco Bay in California. The group, calling itself "Indians of All Tribes," claims possession of the island under an 1868 treaty that gave Indians the right to unused federal property on Indian land. Indians of All Tribes occupies the island for 19 months while negotiating with federal officials. They do not win their claim to the island but draw public attention to their cause.

1971 The Alaska Native Claims Settlement Act (ANCSA) is signed into law. With the act, Alaska Natives give up any claim to nine-tenths of Alaska. In return, they are given $962 million and clear title to 44 million acres of land.

1972 Five hundred Indians arrive in Washington, D.C., on a march called the Trail of Broken Treaties to protest the government's policies toward Native Americans. The protestors occupy the Bureau of Indian Affairs building for a week,

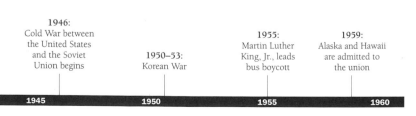

1946:
Cold War between
the United States
and the Soviet
Union begins

1950–53:
Korean War

1955:
Martin Luther
King, Jr., leads
bus boycott

1959:
Alaska and Hawaii
are admitted to
the union

1945   1950   1955   1960

The armed takeover of Wounded Knee in 1973.

causing considerable damage. They present the government with a list of reforms, but the administration rejects their demands.

1973   After a dispute over Oglala Sioux (Lakota) tribal chair Robert Wilson and his strong-arm tactics at Pine Ridge Reservation, AIM leaders are called in. Wilson's supporters and local authorities arm themselves against protestors, who are also armed, and a ten-week siege begins in which hundreds of federal marshals and Federal Bureau of Investigation (FBI) agents surround the Indian protestors. Two Native American men are shot and killed.

1974   After strong protests and "fish-ins" bring attention to the restrictions on Native American fishing rights in the Pacific Northwest, the U.S. Supreme Court restores Native fishing rights in the case *Department of Game of Washington v. Puyallup Tribe et al.*

1978   U.S. Congress passes legislation providing support for additional tribal colleges, schools of higher education designed to help Native American students achieve academic success and eventually transfer to four-year colleges and universities. Tribal colleges also work with tribal elders and cultural leaders to record languages, oral traditions, and arts in an effort to preserve cultural traditions.

1978   The American Religious Freedom Act is signed. Its stated purpose is to "protect and preserve for American Indians their inherent right of freedom to believe, express, and exercise their traditional religions."

1978   The Bureau of Indian Affairs publishes regulations for the new Federal Acknowledgment Program. This program is responsible for producing a set of "procedures for establishing that an American Indian group exists as an Indian tribe." Many tribes will later discover that these requirements are complicated and difficult to establish.

1965:
U.S. troops take part in Vietnam war

1968:
Student protest demonstrations hit U.S. campuses

1974:
Richard Nixon resigns the U.S. Presidency

1975:
Bill Gates cofounds Microsoft

1981:
AIDS is first recognized

| 1965 | 1970 | 1975 | 1980 |

1982 Canada constitutionally recognizes aboriginal peoples in its new Constitution and Charter of Rights and Freedoms. The Constitution officially divides Canada's aboriginal nations into three designations: the Indian, the Inuit, and the Métis peoples. Native groups feel that the new Constitution does not adequately protect their rights, nor does it give them the right to govern themselves.

1988 The Federal Indian Gambling Regulatory Act of 1988 allows any tribe recognized by the U.S. government to engage in gambling activities. With proceeds from gaming casinos, some tribes pay for health care, support of the elderly and sick, housing, and other improvements, while other tribes buy back homelands, establish scholarship funds, and create new jobs.

1989 U.S. Congress approves a bill to establish a National Museum of the American Indian under the administration of the Smithsonian Institution in Washington, D.C. (As of 1999, the Museum has not been built.)

1990 Two important acts are passed by U.S. Congress. The Native American Languages Act is designed to preserve, protect, and promote the practice and development of Indian languages. The Graves Protection and Repatriation Act provides for the protection of American Indian grave sites and the repatriation (return) of Indian remains and cultural artifacts to tribes.

1992 Canadians vote against a new Constitution (the Charlotte-town Accord) that contains provisions for aboriginal self-government.

1999 A new territory called Nunavut enters the federation of Canada. Nunavut is comprised of vast areas taken from the Northwest Territories and is populated by an Inuit majority. The largest Native land claim in Canadian history, Nunavut is one-fifth of the landmass of Canada, or the size of the combined states of Alaska and Texas. Meaning "Our Land" in the Inukitut (Inuit) language, Nunavut will be primarily governed by the Inuit.

Chinook Winds Casino, Oregon, 1997.

After many years of struggle, the Inuit celebrate the establishment of a new Canadian territory, Nunavut, or "Our Land," in 1999.

1983: The Internet is born	1989: The Berlin Wall is destroyed	1993: Apartheid is outlawed in South Africa	1999: NATO forces bomb Serbian military sites

1985   1990   1995   2000

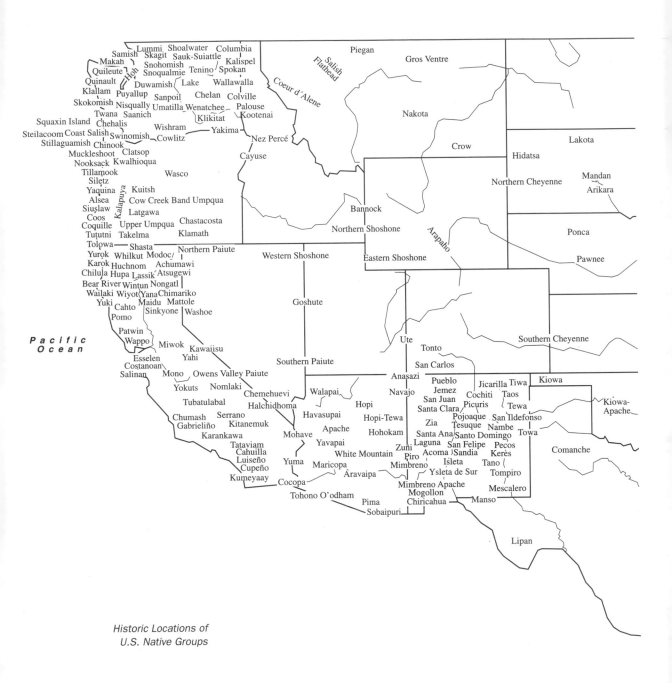

Historic Locations of
U.S. Native Groups

Dakota

Menominee

Sauk

Fox

Omaha

Kickapoo

Winnebago

Oto

Iowa

Peoria

Potawatomi

Kaw (Kansa)

Illinois

Cahokia

Miami

Erie

Adena

Hopewell

Missouri

Kaskaskia

Mississippian

Shawnee

Osage

Tutelo

Tonkawa

Koasati

Waco

Cherokee

Tawakoni

Quapaw

Wichita

Chickasaw

Etowah

Caddo

Hasinai

Kichai

Choctaw

Creek

Tunica

Hitchiti

Natchez

Yuchi

Alabama

Houma

Biloxi

Mobile

Coushatta

Apalachicola

Chitimacha

Apalachee

Yamasee

Yazoo

Guale

Seminole

Timucua

Miccosukee

Calusa

Gulf
of
Mexico

Abenaki

Penobscot

Pennacook

Mohawk

Onondaga

Manhattan

Iroquois

Tuscarora

Oneida

Cayuga

Mohegan

Seneca

Munsee

Mahican

Wappinger

Nipmuk

Massachuset

Stockbridge

Unami

Schaghticoke

Susquehanna

Brothertown

Narraganset

Pequot

Podunk

Wampanoag

Delaware

Nanticoke

Montauk

Shinnecock

Paugussett

Piscataway

Mattaponi

Pamunkey

Monacan

Powhatan

Chickahominy

Saponi

Rappahannock

Nansemond

Meherrin

Lumbee

Pamlico

Catawba

Cheraw

Waccamaw

Pedee

Coharie

Santee

Edisto

Cusabo

Atlantic
Ocean

Maps | **xxxix**

Historic Locations of
Canadian Native Groups

Inuit

Inuit

Inuit

Inuit

Inuit

Inuit

Inuit

Inuit

Inuit

Inuit

Inuit

Inuit

Intuit

Inuit

Inuit

Beothuk

Naskapi

Innu

Montagnais

Cree

Maliseet

Micmac

Ojibwa

Passamaquoddy

Algonkin

Ottawa

Nippissing

Huron

Tobacco

Wenrohronon

Nuctral

Wyandotte

Arctic

Arctic

It is difficult to define the indigenous (native) peoples of Arctic North America by the recognized boundaries of the modern political world because the geographical context in which they live goes beyond the borders of countries. While the United States (Alaska) and Canada make up the Arctic region of North America, indigenous peoples of these two countries occupy areas that extend across international boundaries. Alaska's Siberian Yup'ik (pronounced *YOO-pik*) peoples, for example, are also found on the Siberian side of the Bering Straits, and the Inupiat (pronounced *in-NOO-pee-aht*) people of Alaska's Arctic slope also reside on the Canadian side of the border. In Alaska's northern interior, the Gwich'in (pronounced *GWITCH-in*) Athabascan Indians (Kutchin) live in both Alaska and in Canada's Yukon territory. All the indigenous people of Arctic North America therefore belong to a larger community of peoples who live in the Circumpolar North (the area surrounding the North Pole).

The people of the Arctic region belong to one of two major cultural and linguistic divisions, Aleut and Eskimo. While the Aleut have traditionally occupied Alaska's Aleutian Islands, the Eskimo, who are further divided into the Yup'ik and Inupiat/Inuit language groups, live from Alaska to Greenland. Despite the vast territory separating Arctic peoples, which also includes many different groups in Arctic Siberia and the Sami people of northern Scandinavia, they remain united both culturally and politically. As Inuit Circumpolar Conference President Caleb Pungowiyi, a Siberian Yup'ik, proclaimed in 1995, "While we are divided by four political boundaries, our common languages, traditions, and ancestry give us common bond and strength to work together."

History

Most archaeologists believe that the Arctic region of North America has been populated only within the last 11,000 to 14,000 years. These scientists base their estimates on the theory that a bridge they call the Bering Land Bridge, or Beringia, once spanned the distance from Asia to Alaska with lands that are now under the waters of the

Bering Strait. While this land bridge existed, they say, hunters from Asia gradually migrated into Alaska and from there, they and their descendants spread throughout North and South America. Scientists believe that this bridge became submerged by about 12,000 B.C.E. The Beringia argument is hotly contested by some Native Americans, however.

The more recent history of the Arctic is well documented. European contact with the Inuit of Arctic Quebec began in the late sixteenth century as the British, French, and Danish all sent ships in search of a Northwest Passage to China (a water route along the northern coast of North America extending between the Atlantic and Pacific oceans). The British Hudson's Bay Company was founded in 1667, beginning a long period of trade among Arctic indigenous peoples. By the nineteenth century, the Hudson's Bay Company had expanded westward and was trading with Athabascan Indians in what is now interior Alaska. A colonization process began in what would later be Canada on the margins of Inuit territory in the mid-eighteenth century, as Europeans, particularly the English and French, began to form settlements. This process included the establishment of trading posts, missions, and whaling stations.

THE RUSSIANS RULE ALASKA The first European contact in Alaska came from the opposite direction, Russia, when Vitus Bering, a Dane serving in the Russian Navy, landed in Prince William Sound in 1741. Over the following decades, the Russians made attempts at establishing outposts in the Aleutian Islands and on Kodiak Island but were rebuffed by the Unangan (pronounced *oo-NUNG-an,* also know as Aleut; pronounced *AHL-lee-ay-LOOT*) and the Sugpiat (Alutiiq; pronounced *ahl-loo-TEEK*). The Aleut destroyed four Russian sea vessels in 1763, but paid dearly in the savage retaliation by the Russians. The Sugpiat were able to hold off the Russians for over 20 years, beginning with their first landing attempt in 1761. In 1784, however, Russian vessels headed by Grigorii Shelikhov made a brutal assault on Kodiak Island that ended with the massacre of many Sugpiaq people at a refuge rock near the present day village of Old Harbor.

The early years of Russian rule in this part of Alaska were marked by the enslavement of Native men, who were forced to hunt sea otters for the Russians. The absence of these men from their communities caused great hardships, as they were not there to provide food and shelter when needed. The Russian Orthodox church halted many of the atrocities as the clergy complained to the Tsar (ruler of Russia) of the mistreatment of the Native peoples at the hands of the Russian

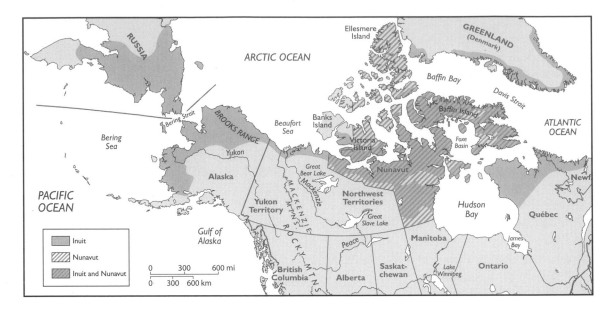

A map of the Arctic Region.

American Company personnel. The Natives then became employees of the Russians and began adapting to Russian culture. Even today, Russian influence is evident in Aleut and Alutiiq villages as many people have Russian surnames, prepare Russian food dishes (thought of as Native food), and maintain the Russian Orthodox Church as the center of village social life.

AMERICANS MOVE INTO ALASKA By the mid-nineteenth century hundreds of American whaling ships were operating off the Arctic coasts, severely depleting the population of walruses and bowhead whales, which affected the Native residents considerably. In addition to supplying food, the bowhead is crucial to Inupiat culture and identity. The Yankee whalers also brought new diseases and alcohol. In 1867 the Treaty of Cession transferred control of Alaska from Russia to the United States. Before the end of the century, American Christian missionaries had established themselves in all corners of Alaska, including the Arctic—a region which, for the most part, had been left alone by the Russians. While most Alaska Natives are now members of Christian churches, mixed feelings remain for many. "Christianity saved our souls but indeed left deep psychological scars in our hearts," Caleb Pungowiyi lamented.

With the firm establishment of the U.S. government in Alaska came the American education system. Under this system, children were often required to leave their villages to attend boarding schools where they were punished if they spoke in their Native language. One result has been the severe eroding of indigenous languages. The state of language preservation varies greatly throughout Alaska; some villages still speak their language on a daily basis while in others only a few Native-speaking elders remain. A cultural revitalization movement has been taking place in Alaska for the past decade or two in which the restoration and protection of languages is a high priority.

The American government unwittingly caused new and severe problems in the North. While attempting to provide services to Alaska Natives in every aspect of their lives, they created a "culture of dependency." This system replaced proud Native identities with an epidemic of self-destructive behavior. "For many Natives, the sense of personal, familial and cultural identity that is a prerequisite to healthy and productive life is being lost in a haze of alcohol-induced despair that not infrequently results in violence perpetrated upon self and family," the Alaska Federation of Natives stated in its 1989 report called *The AFN Report on the Status of Alaska Natives: A Call for Action.* This report revealed such grim statistics as the fact that Alaska Native males between the ages of 20 and 24 were committing suicide at 14 times the national average and that the homicide rate among Alaska Natives was four times the national average. Conditions worsened even as the federal and state governments were spending millions of dollars on Native services. "Rather than feeling comfort in government-built homes and contentment in government-funded food supplies, Alaska Natives felt instead, emptiness and an overwhelming sense of loss," concluded the final report of the Alaska Natives Commission, published in 1994, adding that "the spiritually and psychologically debilitating intervention of government services . . . has created a culture of dependency."

CANADIAN GOVERNMENT AND THE INUIT In Canada the situation of indigenous peoples became similar to the one in Alaska. Jack Hicks, the director of research for the Nunavut Implementation Commission found that "European and Canadian explorers, traders, missionaries, police, soldiers and administrators brought many things with them to Nunavut—some good and some not so good. Suffice it to say that, as late as the early 1970s, the Inuit of Canada were a thoroughly colonized and economically dependent people." (See below for more information on Nunavut.)

Culture

If one is to begin in Alaska and trace the geographical areas of the various cultures in the North, a logical place to begin would be Prince

William Sound, the westernmost home of the Alutiit (plural for Alutiiq) people. The Alutiit also live on the lower Kenai Peninsula, the Kodiak Island archipelago, and the lower Alaska Peninsula. The traditional name for Alutiiq is *Sugpiaq,* meaning "a real human being." The plural is *Sugpiat,* meaning "the real people." The Alutiit are classified as Pacific Eskimo by anthropologists, but most strenuously object to that label. They are, however, closely related linguistically (by the language they speak) to all the Inuit peoples of the Arctic.

Beginning at the tip of the Alaska Peninsula and stretching out the Aleutian Island Chain and into Russia are the Aleut, or as they call themselves, Unangan. The name Aleut was applied to them by the Russian explorers and fur traders of the eighteenth century. The name was also used by the Russians to identify the Sugpiat, thus the name Alutiiq, which is simply the word Aleut in the language of the Sugpiat.

Beginning at the northern edge of the Alaska peninsula and continuing through Bristol Bay, through the Yukon-Kuskokwim River Delta, and north to the village of Unalakleet are the Central Yup'ik, or Yupiaq, people. The words *Yup'ik* and *Yupiaq* translate to "a real person." The plural is *Yupiit,* meaning "the real people." The Central Yup'ik language is very close to Alutiiq, such that speakers of the two languages can usually carry on a conversation. Both differ substantially from the Aleut language, however. Another Yup'ik language is Siberian Yup'ik, spoken on St. Lawrence Island and the Chukchi Peninsula of Siberia. The relationship of what are usually referred to as Eskimo languages is quite apparent when one compares a single word, such as the one for "person." The Alutiit say *suk,* the Yupiit say *yuk,* or in some areas, *cuk.* The Inupiat of Arctic Alaska, the Inuvialuk of Northwest Canada, and the Iglulik of Eastern Canada all use the term *inuk* for "person." Another major indigenous group of the Arctic is the Athabaskan Indians. The Athabaskans, who call themselves Den'a (Dene), live in vast areas of the interior of Alaska and Northern Canada. They are made up of numerous subgroups who speak eleven different languages.

Subsistence

"Subsistence is a word that means . . . my way of life," Moses Toyukuk of Manokotak, Alaska, told the Alaska Native Review Commission in 1985. "Our subsistence way of life is especially important to us. Among other needs it is our greatest. We are desperate to keep it," Paul John of Tununak, Alaska, told the same commission. In the Alaska Native Claims Settlement Act of 1971 (ANCSA; see below for more information), all aboriginal hunting and fishing rights were abolished, which created a dilemma for remote Alaska Native villages dependent on such resources for their livelihood. Efforts were made to restore these rights with moderate success. The Marine Mammal Protection Act of 1972 enables coastal Alaska Natives to take marine mammals for food and for use in arts and crafts. In 1980 the Alaska National Interest Lands Conservation Act (ANILCA) provided a subsistence preference for rural residents. As the majority of rural residents in Alaska are Natives, this essentially restored Alaska Natives' right to hunt and fish for subsistence. After the state's implementation of the ANILCA's subsistence provision was thrown out by the Alaska Supreme Court in 1985, the Alaska state legislature, in 1986, passed its own law, which is consistent with federal law. In 1989, however, the Alaska Supreme Court ruled that the state law confirming a preference for rural residents to hunt and fish for subsistence is unconstitutional because it discriminates against urban residents. This action resulted in the U.S. Government takeover of fish and game on federal lands in Alaska in 1990 in order to guarantee subsistence rights to rural residents. The debate over subsistence continues in Alaska with no end in sight. Dr. Angayuqaq Oscar Kawagley, a Yupiaq educator, has summed up the meaning of subsistence for most Alaska Native people: "Alaska Native peoples have traditionally tried to live in harmony with the world around them. This has required the construction of an intricate subsistence-based worldview, a complex way of life with specific cultural mandates regarding the ways in which the human being is to relate to other human relatives and the natural and spiritual worlds."

Current tribal issues

In 1971 the U.S. Congress passed the Alaska Native Claims Settlement Act (ANCSA), starting a controversy that continues today. ANCSA resulted from a drive for settlement from a variety of interests: business and government interests in the oil source, the state of Alaska's desire to develop land, the conservationists' desire to preserve wilderness areas, and the Alaska Natives' wish for their land. Twelve regional profit-making corporations were established that were responsible for distributing money to village corporations and individuals, controlling the subsurface resources, promoting economic development in the region, and supporting the village corporations within the region. Where past agreements had been made only between the federal government and individual Indian tribes, ANCSA was an agreement made with these newly created Alaska

Native regional associations, which were charged with the responsibility of establishing for-profit business corporations to receive a cash settlement and perhaps more importantly, legal title to the land. Under ANCSA, the corporations received title to 44 million acres of land and a cash settlement of $962.5 million for land lost. This amounted to about three dollars an acre. As discontent mounted in many areas of Alaska with ANCSA, a number of studies were carried out to assess its effectiveness and its legality.

A 1984–85 study conducted by the Alaska Native Review Commission, under the auspices of the Inuit Circumpolar Conference (ICC)—an international organization founded in 1977 to represent the Inuit or Eskimo peoples of the United States, Canada, Greenland, and Russia—recommended that title to land owned by Alaska Native corporations be transferred to village tribal governments. "A corporation cannot take from the rich and give to the poor without facing a shareholders' suit," claimed Thomas Berger, a former Supreme Court justice of Canada who headed the study. "A tribal government can implement measures designed to achieve social justice." Berger also recommended that Alaska Native villages assert their sovereignty (self-rule) as tribal governments, concluding "Tribal governments established in all of Alaska's Native villages should assert their Native sovereignty."

Many legal scholars believed that under the American legal system, land owned and controlled by Alaska Native village tribal governments would take on the legal status of "Indian Country." According to federal law and the terms of over four hundred treaties, Indian tribes have sovereign power—the power to act as independent nations. Although most Native governments are based on reservations, sovereignty can extend beyond reservation boundaries by the terms of the definition of "Indian Country," which includes reservations, scattered Indian home sites, and sometimes areas near reservations as well. By law, tribal governments in Indian Country have the authority to make and enforce their own laws and to enter into agreements with the United States, just as foreign governments can. The legal debate over whether village-owned land in Alaska was indeed Indian Country, as it would be if located in the 48 contiguous states, raged for well over a decade. Then, in 1996, the U.S. Ninth Circuit Court of Appeals ruled that there is Indian Country in Alaska, a ruling strongly opposed by the state of Alaska, which appealed to the U.S. Supreme Court. In 1998, the Supreme Court overturned the Court of Appeals in what is known as the "Venetie Decision," ruling that the Alaska Native Claims Settlement Act abolished Indian Country status.

Another political issue that has become very emotional, both within Alaska Native communities and within the general Alaska population, has to do with the potential opening of the Arctic National Wildlife Refuge to oil development. U.S. law currently prohibits oil development within a federal wildlife refuge unless Congress votes to open it and the president concurs by signing the legislation. The Arctic National Wildlife Refuge, or ANWR, as it is usually referred to in Alaska, covers about 19 million acres of remote northeast Alaska. Geologists believe that ANWR contains vast deposits of oil and the state of Alaska has pursued opening the area to oil development for more than a decade. ANWR is also the spring calving grounds for the Porcupine caribou herd that resides in the Canadian Arctic during the winter months. The Gwich'in Athabaskan Indians of both Alaska and Canada depend heavily on the Porcupine caribou herd for subsistence and cultural identity. At the same time, the Inupiat of the North Slope are in favor of opening ANWR for oil development.

The indigenous people of the Canadian Arctic have pursued a different, but similar, path to that of Alaska Natives in terms of their aboriginal land claims. In 1975 a negotiated agreement was reached between the Inuit and Cree Indians of northern Quebec and the Canadian government after the James Bay Hydroelectric Project nearly flooded a large area of traditional hunting lands. The agreement, called the James Bay and Northern Quebec Agreement, conveyed title to 5,250 acres of hunting grounds, confirmed exclusive hunting and fishing rights on another 60,000 square miles, provided for local administrative control, established autonomy in education decisions for villages, verified control of local justice systems, and supplied a $90 million monetary settlement. In return, the indigenous peoples were required to give up any further aboriginal rights. The settlement was not embraced by all aboriginal people involved, and considerable dissent was voiced. However, in 1984, the Inuvialuit of the northwesternmost portion of the Northwest Territories entered into a similar agreement.

The Inuit Tapirisat, an indigenous Canadian political organization formed in the 1960s, actively pursued a land settlement with the Canadian government. The Nunavut, or "Our Land" movement, began in 1974 and ended in 1992 with the signing of Nunavut Land Claim Agreement. The Nunavut agreement involved 18,000 Inuit living in the northeastern portion of the Northwest Territories. Under the agreement, the Inuit gained legal title to the surface of 353,610 square kilometers of land, or about 18 percent of the settlement area, in addition to priority hunting and fishing rights throughout the Nunavut settlement area. They also received subsurface rights to oil, gas, and minerals on 36,257 square kilometers, or about 10 percent of the settlement area, as well as a cash settlement of $1.148 billion (Canadian) to be paid by the Canadian government to the Inuit over a period of 14 years. In addition, the Canadian government must pay the Inuit 50 percent of the first $2 million of royalties from oil, gas, or mineral development. The Inuit were required to give up all rights and claims to land and waters elsewhere in Canada, but will keep all other constitutional rights, including continued recognition as aboriginal people by the Canadian government. An especially important part of the agreement calls for the government of Canada to set up a Nunavut Territory by the year 2000. This will mean that the Inuit, who make up about 85 percent of the population, will have self-government in their homelands. The election of the first Nunavut Legislative Assembly will take place in 1999.

Perhaps the largest issue facing the indigenous people of the Arctic is one of self-determination. They want to control their own affairs and chart their own destinies. They want meaningful input into decisions being made by the governments of the United States and Canada on issues that will impact their ways of life. Over recent decades they have become more vocal in pursuing these rights. The United Nations Draft Declaration on the Rights of Indigenous Peoples clearly summarizes their pursuits: "Indigenous peoples have the right of self-determination. By virtue of that right they freely determine their political status and freely pursue their economic, social and cultural development."

Gordon L. Pullar
Director, Department of Alaska Native and
Rural Development
College of Rural Alaska, UAF, Anchorage, Alaska

FURTHER READING

Berger, Thomas R. *Village Journey: The Report of the Alaska Native Review Commission.* New York: Wang and Hill, 1985.

Burger, Julian. *The GAIA Atlas of First Peoples: A Future for the Indigenous World.* New York: Anchor Books, 1990.

Chaussonnet, Valerie, ed. *Crossroads Alaska: Native Cultures of Alaska and Siberia.* Washington, DC: Arctic Studies Center, National

Museum of Natural History, Smithsonian Institution, 1995.

Damas, David, ed. *Handbook of North American Indians,* Vol. 5: *Arctic.* Washington, DC: Smithsonian Institution, 1984.

Fitzhugh, William W., and Aron Crowell, eds. *Crossroads of Continents: Cultures of Siberia and Alaska.* Washington: Smithsonian Institution, 1988.

Kawagley, A. Oscar. *A Yupiaq Worldview: A Pathway to Ecology and Spirit.* Prospect Heights, Illinois: Waveland Press, 1995.

Inuit

Name

Inuit (pronounced *IN-yoo-it*) is the Inuit's name for themselves and means "people." The Inuit are sometimes called Eskimo, which means "eaters of raw meat" in the Algonquian language, but they prefer to be called Inuit.

Location

The Inuit inhabit the area around the Arctic Circle, including Greenland, northern Canada, Alaska, and the Chukokta region of Russia.

Population

There were approximately 127,000 Inuit in the mid-1990s, including 44,000 in Alaska, 32,000 in Canada, 49,000 in Greenland, and 2,000 in Russia.

Language family

Eskimoan or Eskimaleut.

Origins and group affiliations

Inuit creation stories say that at the time the world began, the Earth was covered by the waters of a great flood. In time the waters receded, leaving the Earth exposed and surrounded by large oceans. Then human beings were created out of nothing and inhabited the Earth.

Scientists have theorized that the Inuit migrated from Asia on foot and by dogsled perhaps as long as 10,000 years ago, by crossing the Bering Land Bridge that once connected Siberia to Alaska. From there, some groups continued eastward through northern Canada and into Greenland. Today, the Inuit inhabit a 5,000-mile stretch of territory around the Arctic Circle.

The Inuit are generally divided into three major groups: the Alaskan Inuit, including those living in Chukotka, Russia; the Central Inuit, which encompasses the groups in northern Canada, including those in Labrador and on Baffin Island; and the Greenland Inuit.

INUIT

Inuit Territories today

The Inuit occupy a 5,000-mile stretch of territory around the Arctic Circle.

(Also see map of Nunavut.)

Shaded area: Traditional Inuit lands encompassing present-day Alaska, Siberia, the Northwest Territories, Canada, and Greenland.

The Inuit are a people of great ingenuity and endurance who, over thousands of years, have managed to survive and thrive in the harsh and icy environment of the Arctic. Modern times have forced them to become much more involved with the economic and political structures of the countries in which they live. As a result, they are trying to preserve the best of their old ways as well as adopt the best of the new.

HISTORY

Inuit migrate from Asia—one theory

The Inuit were probably among the last of the Native groups to migrate to North America by crossing a land bridge across the Bering Straits between Siberia and Alaska, according to many scientists. Scholars disagree as to just when the crossings occurred. The earliest evidence of Inuit civilization remains hidden, because a great deal of the land that they would have crossed in Alaska and northern Canada now lies underwater. The Aleut, who now occupy the border islands of western Alaska probably split off from the Inuit earliest, while other bands of Inuit continued wandering eastward into Greenland.

Evidence supports the theory that the Inuit migrated eastward from Asia. For example, despite being spread over 5,000 miles, all of the Inuit people speak varieties of the same language. They also have similar customs and share the same physical characteristics. They are generally short and stocky, with oval-shaped faces and dark complexions.

Some anthropologists (people who study the cultures of different peoples) think that Inuits first lived in eastern Alaska, long before western Alaska and the Canadian Arctic were inhabited. They believe that by around 4000 B.C.E., Inuit people had reached the coast of Alaska; some even ventured into the interior. By about 1200 B.C.E., the entire Arctic was inhabited from the western coast of Alaska to the eastern part of northern Canada. Permanent coastal settlement existed in Alaska by around 1600 B.C.E., and by 600 C.E. the settlements had grown larger and more stable. From about 600 C.E. through around 1800, people lived in coastal and inland villages and developed more sophisticated tools and more complex ways of life. Contact with whites, beginning around 1800, brought tremendous changes to the lives of the Native people.

First white-Inuit encounters

Because of the remote location of their homelands, most Inuit people had very little early contact with Europeans. The Inuit of Greenland were the first Native group in the Western Hemisphere to encounter white men when the Vikings, under Eric the Red, traveled to their territory in the year 984. Six centuries were to pass before English explorer Martin Frobisher (c. 1535–1594) came into contact with the Inuit of Greenland and northern Canada during his unsuccessful searches for the Northwest Passage—a water route that was believed to connect the Atlantic to the Pacific.

In 1741, the Russian explorer Vitus Bering, for whom the Bering Strait was named, was the first European to meet the Inuit of Alaska. Bering was sent to Alaska by the Russian emperor Peter the Great

IMPORTANT DATES

984: The Vikings under Eric the Red first encounter the Inuit of Greenland.

1576: English explorer Martin Frobisher first comes into contact with the Central Inuit of northern Canada.

1741: Russian explorer Vitus Bering becomes the first European to reach the Inuit of Alaska.

1867: United States purchased the Alaska Territory from Russia.

1971: Through the Alaska Native Claims Settlement Act (ANCSA), the Inuit and other Alaska Natives receive $962 million and 44 million acres in exchange for giving up claims to another 335 million acres.

1999: The Canadian government transfers control of a newly formed province, Nunavut, to the Inuit. At 818,962 square miles, Nunavut will cover one-fifth of the total landmass of Canada.

(1728–1762) to establish Russian settlements. Soon Russian fur traders began traveling to the area.

Samuel Hearne, a representative of the Hudson's Bay Company, a wealthy English trading firm, reached the Inuit of northern Canada over land in the late 1700s. But the Inuit in Canada did not have major dealings with whites until the coming of the nineteenth-century whaling fleets and the development of the fur trade there.

Contact with whites causes lifestyle changes

From the seventeenth to the early nineteenth century, hundreds of Scottish, English, and American whale fishermen came to the Arctic shores. The Inuit supplied them with oil, blubber, whalebone, and furs. In return the Inuit received tea, tobacco, flour, crackers, matches, lead, molasses, brandy, rifles, and ammunition. In the early 1800s, some Inuit people began replacing some of their Native culture with the use of European goods, such as metal knives, kettles, lamps, guns, cloth, and alcohol.

In the 1800s, whale fishermen from New England sailed to the Arctic, where they spent the winters living ashore. Come spring, they returned to their ships; the Inuit would take their places in the winter dwellings. The Natives and whites worked together hunting sea mammals, and in time their cultures began to blend. Many of the white men took Inuit women as temporary wives and the children from these unions were raised as Inuit.

Also during the 1800s, Russian fur hunters and traders began to move in on western Alaska. In time the Russian-American Company completely controlled the fur trade in Alaska and the Aleutian Islands. About that same time, on the peninsula of Labrador in the northeast corner of Canada's mainland, German missionaries established missions to try and convert the Inuit to Christianity. The Germans traded the Inuit practical goods for furs, introduced seal nets to Native hunters, and encouraged them to produce baskets, carvings, and other crafts. For the most part, the Inuit had friendly relations with the white traders, for whom they served as guides and interpreters.

Whites bring new technology and diseases to Alaska

The mid-1800s saw the end of the large-scale trading, fishing, and whaling industries on the coast of Alaska. By 1850 seals, salmon, bears, and walruses had grown scarce, and by 1860 whales were no longer plentiful either. In search of better supplies of wildlife, white hunters

spread further north and west. The Inuit by then were very dependent on the white-produced goods for which they traded their furs.

After the United States purchased the Alaska Territory from Russia in 1867, there was much greater contact between the Inuit of Alaska and Americans, who established fur-trapping, gold-mining, and commercial whaling operations in Inuit territory. But despite the ever-growing number of white explorers and settlers, several Inuit bands managed to avoid all contact with non-Native peoples into the early 1900s.

The whites brought something terrible to the Inuit: diseases for which the Natives had no immunity. Epidemics of smallpox, influenza, measles, and scarlet fever killed great numbers of Native

Group of Inuit in Port Clarence, Alaska, 1894.

people in the Arctic. Before coming into contact with non-Native peoples, the Inuit population was estimated at approximately 60,000. The introduction of white diseases cut their numbers in half by 1900.

Inuit-white relations in Canada

After the decline of whaling in the late 1800s, three main groups managed the central and northern Arctic: traders, missionaries, and the Canadian police. They tried to find new occupations for the Inuit to replace some of the old ones.

The Canadian government-run Hudson's Bay Company ran all the trading posts in the region. In the 1920s the company imported reindeer from Norway and tried to turn the Inuit into herders. But the poorly trained Inuit failed in these efforts. Attempts to move some Inuit away from their families to new hunting and trapping grounds did not succeed either, as the people were heartsick to be separated from their relatives. Then Anglican and Roman Catholic missionaries established schools for the Inuit and stayed in charge of education and health in the Arctic until 1945, when the Canadian government took over. Beginning in the 1900s, the Royal Canadian Mounted Police (the "Mounties") traveled to Canada's western provinces to keep peace among both the whites and the Inuit. This was difficult for the Inuit, who were used to policing themselves.

During World War II (1939–45), interaction between the Inuit and other Canadians grew rapidly as airfields, weather stations, and a radar line were built across Canada's North. Soon, mining exploration and development increased. More recently, discoveries of large oil and gas reserves brought thousands of people from the south into the land of the Inuit.

In recent decades, the Canadian government recognized the need to provide education, health services, and other social services to the Inuit. As a result, the government presence grew and the Inuit moved to a smaller number of large, more stable communities.

Land claim disputes in Alaska

Over the years, the Inuit have been involved in many land-claims issues, but major ones were not settled until the last half of the twentieth century. In 1971 Alaska Natives reached an agreement with the U.S. government called the Alaska Native Claims Settlement Act (ANCSA). Alaska Natives, including tribal members, received $962.5 million and 44 million acres in exchange for giving up their claims to another 335 million acres. The agreement came about mainly because

the government wanted to build the Alaskan Pipeline through Alaska to transport oil from north to south across the state.

From ANCSA, the Inuit and other Native groups received legal ownership of 12 percent of the total lands of Alaska. The agreement has provided them with much-needed funds for economic growth. They developed local corporations to manage their land and money, and invested in businesses such as oil fields, mining operations, hotels, and shipping companies. In 1980 ANCSA was amended to restore Native hunting and fishing rights.

Major land claims of Inuit and other Native groups in Canada were finally successful in 1982, when legislation was passed calling for the formation of a new territory called Nunavut in the Northwest Territories. Nunavut was scheduled to enter the federation of Canada as a new territory on April, 1, 1999. (See Nunavut map and "Current tribal issues.")

The Inuit in modern times

By the end of the twentieth century, the Inuit population had recovered to its earlier peak levels. But increasingly, traditional ways are being exchanged for those of modern life. Many Inuit have been forced by necessity to adopt aspects of white culture, including guns, knives, clothes made of modern fabrics, sewing machines, boats with motors, snowmobiles rather than dog sleds, and wooden houses, which have made their traditional ways seem obsolete. The environmental impact of oil-drilling, mining, commercial fishing and whaling, and military activities in the Arctic regions have greatly lessened the numbers of sea mammals and land animals available to Inuit hunters. And anti-sealing, anti-trapping, and anti-whaling movements have lessened the value of these Inuit industries.

In recent years, some Inuit bands have settled down in one place to grow crops or herd reindeer and cattle. In Alaska, the Inuit people have been moving into urban areas. In 1960, 12 percent of Inuit people lived in cities, but by 1990 the number had grown to 44 percent.

RELIGION

The Inuit believed that all aspects of nature—including animals and natural occurrences like the weather—had a spirit. Among their gods were Sedna, who lived at the bottom of the ocean and controlled the year's supply of sea mammals, and the guardian of the caribou who controlled caribou numbers during their migration across the Arctic.

Human beings had two types of souls: the "breath of life" was what disappeared when a person died; the "soul" separated from the body but continued to exist after death. In the afterworld, most souls went into the Earth, while those of women who died giving birth or people who perished in a violent way or through suicide went to the sky.

The Inuit also believed in evil spirits that sometimes disrupted people's lives. They used several methods to try and eliminate the influence of evil spirits. For example, individuals who had suffered from bad fortune would wander away from the tribe and spend several days alone. They would make contact with the good spirits of their dead ancestors to help reverse their situation.

Religious rituals were used to appeal to the elements of nature for good weather or success in hunting. Sometimes carved decorative objects of wood, bone, or ivory, with attached feathers or fur, were used in rituals to summon the attention of the spirits. During ceremonial dances, Inuit men often wore masks on their faces, while women wore tiny masks on their fingers, often fashioned to resemble animals or other spirits in nature.

By the end of the twentieth century, most of the Inuit had converted to Christianity, but they continued to be somewhat superstitious. For example, a common Inuit belief is that showing contentment during good times invites bad times to return. So, people tend to avoid boasting and instead will complain about their good fortune.

LANGUAGE

The language of the Inuit is called Inuktitut. Despite being scattered over great distances, all of the Inuit bands speak closely related dialects (varieties) of the Eskimoan or Eskimaleut language family. Only two different linguistic groups are found among the Inuit: the Pacific or Alaskan group, which includes the Yup'ik of Siberia; and the Canadian or Northern group, which includes the Inuit of Greenland.

Since around 1900, Inuit contacts with whites resulted in the creation of a special mixed language of from 300 to 600 words, based on their language, Inuktitut as well as on English and other languages. This mixed language has sometimes been mistaken for Inuktitut, the actual Inuit language.

Inuit languages make great use of body signals, such as squinting. In addition, they are extremely rich in specific words. For example, language experts say that in some bands there are more than fifty words that mean snow, and indicate the various types of snow, a distinction that was vital to survival in the frigid North.

INUIT WORDS

Many Inuit words have gained wide usage in English, including *kayak, parka, igloo, husky,* and *malamute*, the name of a variety of dog. The common Inuit expression *Ajurnamat*, which means "It cannot be helped" demonstrates the calm and stoic approach toward life that is typical of the Inuit.

GOVERNMENT

The Inuit put so much time and effort into hunting and protecting themselves from the harsh environment that there was little social or political organization. The Inuit did not have chiefs who ran the tribe. But there were unofficial leaders, usually the strongest hunters, who were consulted on matters that involved the whole tribe. Still, each man was in charge of himself.

The cooperative spirit of the Inuit caused them serious problems in their dealings with Europeans. For instance, the Inuit found it difficult to organize themselves to form relationships with other nations' governments. As a result, dishonest traders often took advantage of them.

Today, Inuit people are very involved in political activities at the local, national, and international levels. International organizations allow the Inuit of different countries to work together on matters of economic, social, and cultural importance. Inuit are also taking greater part in the policy-making of the various governments under which they live. Inuit villages in Alaska are governed by various elective systems. In Canada, most Inuit communities are governed by

NUNAVUT

Shaded area: The new territory of Nunavut, in the Northwest Territories, Canada.

Nunavut 1999: "Our Land"

On April 1, 1999, Nunavut became a new Canadian province, governed by the Inuit.

It is the largest Native land claim settlement in Canadian history.

In area, Nunavut is one-fifth of the landmass of Canada, or the size of the combined states of Alaska and Texas.

elected councils. Inuit members now sit in both houses of Canada's governmental body, the Parliament.

ECONOMY

In early times, the Inuit did not have a money economy, and people had very few possessions. Families had their dogs, their dwelling, and a few hand-made items that may have included tools, sleds, weapons, and kayaks, and an occasional piece of craftwork, such as a whalebone carving.

Many of the basic materials needed for survival were freely shared among members of the community and the land was considered to belong to all the people. Getting food by fishing and hunting could be undependable, but no one was allowed to go without food. Successful hunters regarded it as an honor to share the fish they caught with others. Sod homes that were abandoned by one group as it moved to other areas in pursuit of game, were available for the people who came along later.

No part of the animals caught by the Inuit went to waste. They made tools out of bones and teeth, melted down fat into oil that was burned for light, heat, and cooking, and fashioned clothing or coverings for boats and tents from the skin. Because few trees grow in the Arctic, the Inuit had to rely on stones, driftwood, bones, and antlers to make tools. Sometimes they traveled hundreds of miles just to find the right type of stones for making knives. This way of life went on century after century.

Today, the economic base has expanded. Artistic products by the Inuit, such as carvings and paintings, are in demand on the world art market and provide a steady source of income. The growth of Inuit communities has provided the people with jobs in community services, industry, and government.

DAILY LIFE

Adapting to an extreme environment

Over thousands of years, the lives of the Inuit were regulated by the seasons. In their land, the sun never rises between October and February and the temperature can reach -80 degrees Fahrenheit. The short, wide bodies of the Inuit conserve heat and they have many more blood vessels in their hands and feet than other people, allowing them to stay warm enough to use even in very cold weather.

Because the Arctic region has few edible plants, the Inuit learned to live almost entirely by hunting and fishing. In order to kill enough game to feed and clothe their families, Inuit men spent a large portion of their time hunting.

Inuit harpooning a whale in Point Barrow, Alaska.

The hunting cycle

In winter, about a dozen families would live together in small communities. Each day, hunters crawled over the ice to net or harpoon seals on the surface of the water. Sometimes they waited patiently by holes in the ice for hours on end until the seals came up for air. It was easy for the hunter to fall asleep and he had to make efforts to concentrate and stay awake.

In spring, the communities broke up. Some families went off to hunt seals on the water in kayaks (skin-covered one-person boats). Sometimes seals were captured using rawhide nets. Walruses and sea lions were also available in the summertime, but unlike seals they migrated south for the winter. Occasionally the Inuit hunted whales. They used boats to herd them close to shore and then struck them with harpoons attached to floats. When the whale was exhausted from dragging a float, the hunters would haul it ashore with their boats.

Pursuing caribou as the herd made its way back north was the main summer activity. Hunters crept up on the caribou or hid in a pit until the animals approached, then killed them using spears or bows and arrows. Sometimes they drove the caribou in the water to capture them. Various Inuit bands, depending on their geographic region, hunted a wide range of other game as well—including musk oxen, mountain sheep, wolves, wolverines, foxes, hares, marmots, squirrels, and birds. They hunted the animals from blinds, caught them in traps, or entangled them in weighted nets called *bolas*. As colder weather approached, the families joined together again.

The Inuit used teams of trained dogs to hunt polar bears, cornering the bears then killing them with spears. This type of hunting took place at night and was extremely dangerous because spears had to be thrown from close range.

Families

Faced with the task of surviving in the Arctic, the Inuit developed a cooperative culture, and the extended family was the most important unit in society. (Extended families consist of parents, children, aunts, uncles, cousins, and grandparents.) Often two or more related families lived together in one house, working, traveling, and eating together. The oldest man was usually in charge of a household, but he had to display hunting skills, and be generous and reasonable.

People depended on their relatives to help them accomplish everyday tasks, especially in times of trouble. People unable to feed themselves were "adopted" by families.

Men were expected to hunt and build homes, while women had the duties of preparing food, working on skins, and making the clothing. Women were not permitted to hunt; in fact, it was considered bad luck for a woman to touch a harpoon or a bow.

Buildings

IGLOOS AND OTHER EARLY STRUCTURES

The term *igloo* is a Native word that refers to any type of dwelling, but it will be used here in its popular meaning of an ice house. Not all Inuit lived in igloos, though they were highly practical in the Arctic environment. Igloos were a common type of dwelling for some bands in northern Canada, where snow was plentiful. The circular, dome-shaped structures were made out of blocks of hard-packed snow cut with long knives of bone, metal, or ivory. The inside walls were melted with the heat of a blubber lamp and then quickly refrozen to make a solid, windproof barrier. The outside walls were covered with a layer of soft snow for insulation.

Inuit woman at her summer skin tent, Point Barrow, Alaska, 1935.

Most igloos featured a hole at the top to let smoke and air escape. Some had a clear block of ice for a window, and some had skylights. To enter an igloo, a person had to crawl through a long, low tunnel. Inside, people slept on a low platform of snow covered with twigs and caribou furs. Sometimes several igloos were linked together to provide separate living, sleeping, and storage facilities. A simple igloo could be built in about one hour.

The Inuit of Alaska and Greenland more commonly lived in a *karmat*, a cabin that was made out of stones or logs and covered with sod. These rectangular houses were usually low to the ground and set over a shallow pit. As with igloos, the entrance consisted of a long tunnel to keep out the cold air. Windows were sometimes fashioned by stretching transparent animal intestines over small openings. Inside the karmat, people burned animal fat in shallow, saucer-shaped soapstone lamps over which fish and meat could be cooked. In warmer weather, when the Inuit traveled frequently in pursuit of game, many bands made tents out of driftwood or whalebones covered with sealskin or caribou hides.

MODERN HOUSING In modern times, government officials complained that the traditional Inuit sod houses were damp, smelly, and unsanitary, and they decided to do something about it. Now most Inuit live in prefabricated (already put together) houses supplied by the government; they are shipped on barges during warmer months. The wood houses are set on stilts or gravel pads to insulate them from the earth beneath, which stays permanently frozen. Although they arrive painted, the paint soon wears away and is seldom reapplied. Most such houses have front doors that open out, making them a problem when winter snow piles up. The freezing and thawing cycle the houses undergo causes them to warp, and many have leaky windows and are often drafty.

Inside, the house is one large room with dividers separating the eating and sleeping areas. Few communities have indoor plumbing, so a five-gallon bucket often serves as the toilet, and bathtubs are used for storing dirty clothes. Most families use the front porch to store freezers or other appliances when not in use. Despite their problems, the houses are appreciated by many because they provide more space than the traditional dwellings.

Transportation

The Inuit built kayaks and *umiaks*—large, deep boats that were rowed with conventional oars; umiaks were often rowed by women. The vessels were made of wooden or whalebone frames covered with sealskin.

They also built sleds, called *komatiks,* by tying a platform onto wooden or bone runners. The surface of the runners was often rubbed with mud, then brushed with water that froze to a smooth, slippery finish. The sleds were usually drawn across the snow and ice by a team of sturdy northern dogs called huskies.

Today, Inuit travel by four-wheel drive vehicles, airplanes, motor boats, and snowmobiles, although dog sleds and kayaks remain important vehicles.

Clothing and adornment

Inuit clothing was well adapted to the extreme cold of the Arctic. Clothing had to allow a person to sleep out in the open in temperatures reaching -60 degrees Fahrenheit. In very cold weather two of each garment were worn, with the fur side facing the body.

Basic apparel for men and women consisted of a hooded parka, pants, stockings, boots, and mittens. Mittens were made of waterproof sealskin for the summer or warm, light-weight caribou skin for the winter. The Inuit also made clothing from the hides of polar bears, wolves, foxes, dogs, marmots, squirrels, and birds.

Parkas were usually worn with the fur facing the body and were made to fit snugly around the wrists, neck, and waist to keep cold air out. Women's parkas sometimes featured large, fur-lined hoods that were handy for carrying babies. Inuit boots, or *mukluks,* were crafted from four layers of sealskin, with moss and down placed between the layers for insulation. Women's boots came all the way up the leg, while men's boots were usually shorter. Snow goggles with narrow eyeholes helped to cut down the glare of the bright snow.

Special occasions called for clothing deco-rated with fur borders or embroidered designs. Some Inuit bands wore earrings, nose rings, or lip plugs made of ivory, shell, sandstone, or wood.

Inuit mother and child in furs, c. 1915.

The importance of dry clothing

It was the duty of Inuit women to make and maintain all the clothing. As young girls they learned how to sew waterproof seams with thread made of tendons. They were also in charge of drying the men's clothing when they returned from hunting. This was a very important task. Wet clothes could freeze and quickly become stiff, making them no longer able to provide adequate protection from the frigid weather.

Bone or wood scrapers were placed in the tunnel entrances of Inuit homes to remove some of the ice crystals that formed on cloth-ing. Upon entering the home, the men took off their clothing—since it was usually warm enough to go naked inside. Women would chew the fabric to make it soft again, then hang the clothing on a special rack over a blubber lamp to dry.

Food

The major food source for the most northern Inuit were sea mam-mals, especially seals, and sometimes walruses, as well as the few land animals of the Arctic. The most common fish the people consumed were salmon, trout, and smelt. In summer, they built dams to trap the salmon that swam upstream from the sea. The Inuit waded waist-deep into the water to spear them with three-pronged harpoons.

The Inuit who lived below the Arctic Circle had wider food choices than did their neighbors farther north. They also hunted birds, fished in rivers, collected clams, and ate berries and other edible plants. Cranberries, blueberries, and young willow root were especially prized.

The people believed that if they offended the spirits of game animals, they could bring on sickness or famine. For this reason, there were complicated rules about food preparation. Products of the sea and products of the land were kept separated so as to maintain harmony between the Inuit and the environment. They also had strict rules about how meat was distributed. For example, the head, eyes, front legs, and heart were given to women, while the backbones went to the men. The hunter who captured the prey received the ribs, breastbone, and attached meat, while everyone shared other parts of the mammal.

Most meat was eaten raw, and only the toughest parts were cooked by boiling. The caribou and polar bear were hunted primarily for their fur, rather than for whatever meat they provided, but the antler tips of the caribou provided a crunchy snack. In times when food was in short supply, the Inuit might have to eat their clothing, sleds, or even their dogs. But during periods of plenty, they enjoyed big feasts.

Experts examine the Inuit diet

The question is often asked: Can a diet such as the one consumed by the Inuit, based from 40 to 70 percent on meat, be healthy? At one time, the Canadian government tried to get the Inuit to consume mostly powdered milk, cereals, and grains, but the food made many of them sick and they returned to eating frozen meat known as *quaq*. Most raw meat is eaten soon after it is killed, when it tastes best. Quaq is easy to eat because the ice crystals in the meat and the blood help in the chewing process.

Medical research has shown that in eating animals raw, the Inuit absorbed vast quantities of vitamins and minerals that were stored up in the animals' tissues, and the vitamins counteracted the onset of heart disease. For example, the skin of the white whale was rich in vitamin C; raw liver, another staple item, had plenty of vitamin A and D.

Recent studies seem to show too that fat from wild animals is easily converted into energy, and provides a rush of rapid body heat, important for people in frigid climates.

Inuit people who eat the traditional diet have been shown to have low rates of diet-linked diseases such as heart disease. Today, the real threat of the traditional Inuit diet seems to be the amount of concentrated pollutants that have shown up in foods such as the whale and the seal. Unfortunately, Inuit who come to live in the south often have problems adjusting to the more common American ways of eating.

Education

Inuit children learned the importance of friendliness and cooperation, most often by being treated that way by their parents and extended families. Children received much attention and affection in the culture. They learned by the example and encouragement of their playful parents, rather than through being punished.

At about age eight, boys received their first training to become hunters. They learned how to build an igloo, track game, and make weapons. A feast was held after a boy had captured his first seal or caribou. Girls were taught how to trap animals, care for stone lamps, and make and repair clothing. Handling dogs, driving a sled, and assessing the environment and weather, were skills taught to both sexes. They learned how to estimate the thickness of ice and figure out where animals were most likely to be found.

In the 1940s and 1950s, Christian missionaries started the first Inuit schools to teach reading and mathematics. They tried to teach the Native people to assimilate—live according to white ways. Lessons were taught in English to force students to learn English by the "sink or swim" method. Inuit children were forbidden to use their own language, a rule they found very frustrating. Because there were relatively few missionaries, though, schools were mostly located in larger communities in Alaska and Canada. Parents in remote locations were encouraged to send their children to these faraway boarding schools. Many did, and the separation proved painful for both children and parents, who were concerned that their sons and daughters would forget their Native way of life.

Today most Inuit children are required to attend elementary school, and most have to leave their home communities to attend high schools or trade schools. Schools in Canada conduct many classes for elementary-school children in their native language.

Adult education centers help older people to qualify for jobs in industry and government.

Healing practices

When an Inuit person's life was in peril due to illness, a healer called a shaman (pronounced *SHAY-mun*) or an *angakok* might be called in to help. A shaman often put himself into a trance in order to study the problem and develop a solution. The shaman tried to contact the spirits by singing, dancing, and beating on drums. When the spirits entered the shaman's body, he rolled around on the floor or suddenly began to speak a strange language. The patient took comfort in having the shaman intercede with the spirits on his or her behalf.

Today, Inuit have access to medical personnel who visit their communities. Those who live in remote places are flown to bigger cities that have hospitals.

ARTS

Ancient Inuit made ivory carvings of people, bears, birds, seals, whales, walruses, and caribou. They also made masks for dancing that depicted various human expressions. Later, their materials were expanded to include antlers, bone, stone, and wood.

Modern Inuit artists continue the tradition by carving animal and human figures of soapstone and ivory. They also create paintings and embroidered clothing and tapestries that are sold throughout the world. All of these items are displayed at the annual Great Northern Art Festival in Northern Canada. The event also features music, dance, storytelling, and fashion shows.

Oral literature

Storytelling was a favorite form of entertainment during harsh winters. The Inuit culture was preserved by passing down stories, songs, and poems from one generation to the next. Often the songs and stories were about nature and the spirit world. They explained how the world worked and taught the values of the people. Sometimes the storyteller would illustrate a tale by using a knife to draw pictures in the snow. Scholars point out that often the stories illustrated the tension between opposite ideas—such as male/female, land/sea, winter/summer, or dark/light.

CUSTOMS

Names

The Inuit were superstitious about names. After a person's death, it was considered bad luck to mention his name out loud until a baby received the same name and brought the spirit back to life. The baby was thought to inherit all the good qualities of the deceased person. It was also considered bad luck for a person to say their own name aloud; instead, a visitor might announce his presence by saying, "Someone is here."

Feasting customs

Since the Inuit people were constantly on the move and might not see their relatives for months on end, they took advantage of all opportunities to visit and feast. Most feasts were held in fall, when food was plentiful and winter supplies of it were already stored. Inuit people gathered at a family home or at a big snow house, to dance to the music of drums, dine, tell stories, and practice religious rites.

When a successful hunter hosted a feast, he invited his friends and neighbors to the meat rack outside to help him fetch the main course. All the while, he apologized for the sorry quality of what he had to offer, even though he was secretly proud of it. As they helped their host haul the meat into the house, the guests complained loudly about how heavy it was, at the same time complimenting their host on his great skills as a hunter. At the end of the feast, the well-fed guests fell asleep. When they awakened, it was time to dine once again.

Games and celebrations

The Inuit held two annual ceremonies to give thanks to the natural world that supported them. The Bladder Dance was intended to set free the spirits of sea mammals that had been killed during the year's hunt. The Inuit believed that the animals' spirits resided in their bladders, so they saved the bladders and inflated them with air. After several days of dancing and rituals, the Inuit returned the bladders to the sea. Another annual ceremony took place in the spring, when the Sun rose again over the Arctic after several months of darkness. The Inuit welcomed the return of the Sun with special dances; they dressed in costumes that represented both men and women to symbolize creation.

Today, Arctic villages hold special celebrations to welcome the New Year, or for such occasions as the beginning or end of summer.

Most celebrations involve sharing food and feature games such as dogsled races, wrestling, a form of baseball, and the "twokick" game, where a player jumps up and kicks an object as far as possible, using both feet at the same time, then landing on the floor on both feet.

The Inuit were fond of games, including one resembling soccer that was played without goals. Two teams would kick a caribou-skin ball around in the snow, competing to see which team could keep possession of the ball for a longer period of time. Children also enjoyed jumping trampoline-style on the stretched-out walrus skins in a game called "skin toss."

Today, basketball has become a central part of Inuit culture. High school basketball occupies the young people during the long, dark winters, and team rivalries instill pride in the communities. Because villages may be hundreds of miles apart, young basketball players travel to their games by plane and ferryboat.

War and hunting rituals

Before departing the village, Inuit hunters performed special ceremonies, spoke prayers, and sang songs to guarantee a successful catch. Through prayers and offerings of fish, the Inuit sought the help of the Sea Mother, who lived in land and sea animals, and the Raven Father, who was associated with storms, thunder, and lightening. Hunters had faith in charms fashioned in the shape of ravens. When a hunter caught a polar bear he usually ate a small portion of the meat, not only for survival, but also to show reverence for the beast.

Courtship and marriage

Inuit men married when they were able to support a family. Women usually married shortly after their first menstruation. Courtship customs varied. Sometimes children were pledged to one another from birth. Other times a man asked another for permission to marry his daughter. Occasionally a man would simply take a woman from her house and ask her to live with him. Successful hunters often had more than one wife, and women sometimes had more than one husband. Wife exchange was common. People were so dependent on one another that no one remained unmarried.

A hunter setting off on a large trip might "borrow" the wife of another, if his wife was unable to go. Partnerships among hunters were sometimes strengthened in this way. Men were expected to be prepared to "lend" their wives, but the women were not asked about their feelings in the matter.

In the Inuit culture newly married couples usually lived in the house of the man's parents for a while. During that time the man worked hard to show that he would be a good provider. Among the Inuit, plumpness was considered a sign of beauty and plenty, and men preferred plump wives.

Death

It was common for an old person who could no longer contribute to the community to stay behind when the family moved, thereby sealing his or her own fate. The souls of the dead were thought to join the world of the spirits, and could become hostile to their surviving relatives or others.

CURRENT TRIBAL ISSUES

April 1, 1999, was the date set for Nunavut to become a new Canadian province, governed by the Inuit. Nunavut, meaning "Our Land," is made up of land taken from eastern and northern sections of the Northwest Territories. Under the terms of the agreement establishing the new province, the Inuit will receive a financial settlement of $1.14 billion and 818,962 square miles of land. This is equivalent to one-fifth of the landmass of Canada, or the size of the combined states of Alaska and Texas. In exchange, the Inuit will give up any claims to other lands in Canada.

In modern times, Inuit people throughout the Arctic are concerned about numerous issues affecting their economic and physical health. These include interference by animal rights' activists in Inuit efforts to protect their own land and animal populations; pollutants found in their food sources; global warming that could increase temperatures in the Arctic regions; and the social effects of high rates of alcohol and substance abuse, and suicide.

NOTABLE PEOPLE

Kenojuak (1927–) is one of the best-known Inuit artists in Canada. Her stone-block prints of her drawings of birds and human beings often involve intertwined figures and fantasies. They are strong, colorful, richly composed and designed, and were almost immediately recognized as unique and valuable in the art community. They continue to be sought after by national and international collectors and museums. Kenojuak also carves and sculpts soapstone and other material. The National Film Board of Canada produced a film about Kenojuak's work in 1962 and her work was featured in a limited edition book published in 1981.

Another notable Inuit is Alaska State Senator and co-founder of the Alaska Federation of Natives William J. Hensley (1941–).

FURTHER READING

Bonvillain, Nancy. *The Inuit*. New York: Chelsea House, 1995.

Fleischner, Jennifer. *The Inuit: People of the Arctic*.Brookfield, CT: The Millbrook Press, 1995.

Subarctic

Subarctic

The Subarctic region covers the vast interior of what is now Alaska and Canada, stretching some 3,000 miles from the Yukon River to the coast of Labrador. To the north it borders the Arctic tundra, treeless plains around the Arctic Circle that remain frozen most of the year, with the subsoil never having a chance to thaw. To the south it runs along the temperate rainforests (woodlands that get a great deal of rain, in which broad-leaved evergreen trees often grow so thick as to create a tent over the forest) of the Northwest coast, the mountain forests of the Plateau, the grasslands of the Plains, and the woodlands of the Northeast. Though there is tundra in the northern parts and at higher elevations of the Subarctic area, it consists mainly of *taiga*—a Russian word meaning "land of little sticks,"a good description of the scraggly spruce trees that often characterize the region.

Two broad cultural groups are usually included as part of the Subarctic region, the Dene (also known as Athabaskan) in Alaska and western Canada and the Algonquin-speakers in central and eastern Canada (Cree, Anishinaubeg, Métis, and Innu). *Athabaskan*, a Cree term, is still in use in Alaska but frowned upon in Canada. *Anishinaubeg* is how the Ojibway often refer to themselves, while *Innu* is the preferred term for those formerly known as Montagnais and Naskapi. Though Dene and Algonquin communities are separated by different languages both within and between themselves, the fairly consistent nature of the forest across the Subarctic leads to certain similarities in lifestyle among them, especially their reliance on caribou and moose as primary subsistence animals.

Living inland in a challenging climate, the relatively scattered, nomadic peoples of the Subarctic region tended to experience the arrival of non-Natives later than did other tribal nations. The early non-Natives arriving in the region were mostly fur trappers, followed by missionaries and miners. While the Subarctic groups were left somewhat more alone than other groups, in the latter half of the twentieth century their mineral, timber, and hydroelectric (producing electricity from water) wealth caught the attention of the industrial world. In response, they have asserted their sovereignty (self-rule) in an effort to have a say in the future.

Origins

The Dene Nation in the Dehcho (Mackenzie River) delta of Canada dates its existence to at least 30,000 years ago. Subarctic oral literature is full of creation stories set in a mythic time when people and animals could talk to each other, an era in which tricksters like Raven and Wolverine (Dene), Nanabush (Anishinaubeg), and Wesucechak (Cree) had many adventures that helped shape the world. These characters, however, are not always confined to particular areas or groups. The stories are told to entertain and to convey fundamental attitudes about the Earth and its creatures. The Koyukon in Alaska have a lovely story in which Dotson'Sa (The Great Raven) creates the world. As retold by John Smelcer, it tells of a place full of giant animals, many that no longer exist, and of a great flood that drowns the Earth. Dotson'Sa tells Raven to save animals aboard a big boat. One of the rescued animals, Muskrat, swims below and brings up mud to rebuild the Earth. Dotson'Sa populates the new land with people made from clay. Versions of this story are widespread in Dene country.

Archaeologists (people who study the artifacts, or things left behind by ancient civilizations, to try to learn more about the ways that people once lived), for their part, have only sketchy information on how or when human beings came to inhabit the Subarctic. Most believe that ice-age migrations over the Bering Strait Land Bridge were involved. (Many scientists believe that sometime about 25 to 15 thousand years ago, a land bridge formed from lands that are now under the waters of the Bering Strait. They believe that over a period of years, small groups of hunters crossed the land bridge from Asia to Alaska. Eventually these people and their descendants spread throughout North and South America.) The archaeologists' uncertainty about when human beings inhabited the Subarctic region is due to scarce digging sites, acidic soils, erosion, and the nomadic lifeways of inhabitants who traveled lightly and left few artifacts of metal, bone, or stone.

As summarized by John W. Ives, here is how scientists apparently think the Na-Dene people (whose language covers the largest territory in the Subarctic) came to be: as early as 10,000 years ago, following an original migration over the Bering Strait, proto-Dene (the earliest to be identified as a group) people began to develop their own identity. The locale of this genetic (relating to biological hereditary traits) and cultural birth seems to have been in the northwestern section of the Subarctic. Later periods saw a movement of

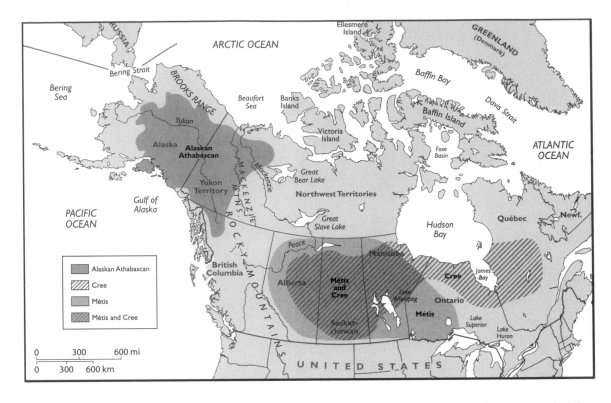

A map of the Subarctic region and the lands of some contemporary Subarctic groups.

Dene-speakers westward into the Dehcho (Mackenzie River) delta; another southward into the Northwest Coast and Northern California (the Tlingit, Haida, Eyak, and Hupa tribes); and a recent split perhaps just prior to European contact took the Dine (Navajo) and Apache peoples into the Southwest. As Kerry Abel has pointed out, oral history and scientific evidence suggest that a natural disaster (maybe a volcanic eruption) motivated the dispersal (the group's breaking up and spreading out). To the dispersal we can add the Tsuu T'ina (Sarsi), a group of Dene-speakers who joined the Blackfoot Confederacy on the northern Plains.

Meanwhile, Algonquin speakers came to inhabit the central and eastern parts of the boreal (northern) forest: the Innu in Labrador, the Cree around Hudson Bay, the Anishinaubeg (Ojibway) just south of the Cree, and finally the recent mixed Indian-white population known as Métis. Two linguists, Richard A. Rhodes and Evelyn M. Todd, reported that proto-Algonquin people may have originated in southern Ontario and spread out into Cree and Anishinaubeg lands from there. Archaeologist James V. Wright has asserted that the caribou-hunting way of life remained more or less unchanged in Algonquin country for over 7,000 years.

Relations between scientists and Native people have not always been happy. Many local people are skeptical of the Bering Strait Land Bridge theory. Writer Vine Deloria, Jr., in his spirited critique, has pointed out the scarcity of physical evidence, the daunting mountain ranges on either side of the land bridge, and the lack of oral history about crossing a land bridge. He also points out the political motivations involved in suggesting that if Native Americans are merely immigrants then perhaps their claims to the land are not so deep after all. On the other hand, cooperative ventures between archaeologists and Native elders began in the 1980s in several places in both Alaska and Canada. These studies have incorporated such elements as oral history and traditional place names, thus giving elders a new sense of purpose and younger people employment and a chance to learn about their past. In some cases commissioned by tribes themselves, such work draws upon the depth, richness, and complexity of traditional knowledge about the land.

Living from the land

Generally speaking, life in the Subarctic follows the rhythm of the seasons. Though there are significant differences within and between groups, the boreal forest and nearby tundra have produced a subsistence lifestyle (a way of life in which people work to hunt or gather the things they need to survive) that transcends many boundaries. Students are encouraged to research particular groups thoroughly to discern how people live in their time and place.

During the Subarctic's long winter, when temperatures can drop to minus-50 degrees F. or below, snow blankets the ground and ice locks up rivers and lakes. In the summer, when temperatures can top the 90s, animals and people move around more freely but forest fires become a threat and in boggy areas clouds of mosquitoes harass anything that moves. The Sun ebbs and flows throughout the year, barely rising at the winter solstice but virtually not setting at high summer. In-between there are two short but vivid seasons, autumn and spring, which usher in the ice and break it up, respectively. Autumn and spring also set the stage for annual migrations of caribou, geese, ducks, and salmon.

The two most important animals across the Subarctic are caribou and moose, whose meat, hide, bone, and sinew traditionally went into clothing, tents, tools, and, in some places, moose skin-covered boats. Caribou tend to migrate in herds between summer calving grounds and winter ranges, while moose tend to be solitary and to migrate within smaller areas. In pre-contact times, bands that stressed moose hunting had to remain small, perhaps the size of an extended family, at least until summer fish camps could support larger populations. Caribou-hunting groups could be somewhat larger and had to travel farther. The extra hunters probably were needed to deal with herds. Some peoples hunted (and still hunt) both animals, though now with rifles instead of spears.

The Gwich'in (Kutchin) in northern Alaska and the adjacent Yukon Territory depend on the Porcupine caribou herd, some 160,000 animals that each spring migrate north from the boreal forests, across the Porcupine River, and onto the Arctic plains where calves are born. In the fall they return inland. Up until the turn of the century Gwich'in hunters were known to build fences to corral some of the animals. Slobodin has documented that, because the Gwich'in and the caribou were closely related in early times described by Gwich'in mythology, the human heart still has a piece of caribou heart in it, and vice versa; they can share each other's thoughts.

When caribou and moose are not available, smaller game like snowshoe hare, beaver, muskrat, otter, porcupine, squirrel, migratory geese, and grouse are hunted. Animals that are taken rarely, or only in limited places, include bear, musk-ox, elk, Dall sheep on some mountains, bison in lands bordering the Great Plains, and sea mammals in coastal areas. Many rivers provide salmon in the summer, while other waterways offer pike, whitefish, and grayling. Dried fish sustains both people and sled dogs during colder months. Forests and tundra yield bark for baskets and firewood and wood for snowshoes and spears, as well as Labrador tea, medicines, berries, roots, greens, and, in pre-contact times, seeds that were used for beadwork. The trapping of animals for the fur trade, a development of the past two hundred years, has also become an essential part of the economy throughout the Subarctic; pelts are most valuable when trapped in fall and winter.

The annual migrations between summer fish camps and winter hunting and trapping ranges still occur throughout most of the boreal forest, though most people now have permanent homes. Old-time housing might vary from semi-subterranean (partly underground) structures and temporary double lean-tos in Alaska to oval or conical tents in Canada; most were home to multiple families. In traditional times government generally operated on a consensus (general agreement amongst the group) model, with headmen of extended families making decisions based on discussions with elders and other members of the family. At summer camps, or among larger caribou-hunting communities, consensus had to be reached among more people. Relations with other groups could alternate between warfare and trading, and even intermarriage, depending on circumstances. This complexity continued when non-Native people started coming into the north country.

Tribal distribution

Though Subarctic peoples have many similarities in their lifestyles, they do see themselves as belonging to bands and nations. Rivers are a typical focal point for organizing the landscape and distinguishing where people come from. One of the biggest, the Yukon, flows almost 1,900 miles from the upper Yukon Territory in Canada, through interior Alaska, to Norton Sound; its major tributaries include the Porcupine (which also begins in Canada), the Koyokuk, and the Tanana. The Yukon, along with the Kuskokwim River, is a defining feature of interior Alaska, the westernmost geographical and cultural region in the Subarctic. The Dene peoples here include the Koyukon around the Koyokuk and Yukon Rivers; the Tanana around the Tanana River; the Deg Hit'an (formerly known as Ingalik) in west-central Alaska around the lower Yukon and Kuskokwim Rivers; the Dena'ina in south-central Alaska around Tikahtnu (Cook Inlet) and Yaghanen (the Kenai Peninsula); the Ahtna around Ts'itu (the Copper River) just east of the Dena'ina; and the Eyak in the Copper River delta, a Dene-derived people who developed close ties with the coastal Tlingit.

The section immediately to the east of interior and south central Alaska is known as the Cordillera, a series of roughly connected mountain ranges between the Yukon River to the west and Dehcho (the Mackenzie River) to the east. Its northern part includes much of the Brooks Range around the Alaska/Yukon Territory border, home to the Gwich'in people and the Han just below them, while farther south it reaches into the Rocky Mountains in interior British Columbia and northwest Alberta, making homelands for the Kaska, Tahltan, Sekani, Carrier, and Chilcotin. The cultures and subsistence practices of those closer to the Northwest Coast and the Plateau reflect ties with those tribes.

The Dehcho (Mackenzie River) Delta to the east of the Rocky Mountains, unlike the Yukon, drains into the Beaufort Sea instead of the Pacific. This area is Denedeh, homeland of the Dene Nation of Canada, which is situated between the Cordillera and Hudson Bay. Although its formal membership has been evolving, in the mid-1980s the Nation listed the following constituents: the Dinjii Zhuh (Gwich'in or Locheux) in the north; the K'ashot'ine (Hareskin) northwest of Sahtú (Great Bear Lake); the Tlicho (Dogrib) between Sahtú and Tucho (Great Slave Lake); the Deh Gàh Got'ine (Slavey or Dene Dhá) along Dehcho and south of Tucho; the Shihts Got'ine (Mountain People), who live a little farther downriver; the Denesoliné (Chipewyan), the largest group whose area extends between the big lakes, Hudson Bay, and as far north as the Arctic coast; and some Cree and Métis immigrants, discussed below. In the 1990s, when some of the Dene land claims were finally settled with Canada, one tribal government, Inuvialuit, consisted of both Dene and Inuit peoples.

Geographically, the Dehcho area overlaps the western side of the Canadian Shield, a massive plate of bedrock that was scraped by glaciers and erosion during the last ice age, leaving lowlands around both Dehcho and Hudson Bay, along with great mineral wealth underground. The relatively low elevations make for some enormous lakes, which aside from Sahtú (Great Bear Lake) and Tucho (Great Slave Lake) include Lake Athabasca, Reindeer Lake, and Lake Winnipeg. Because the Shield wraps around Hudson and James Bays all the way into Labrador, it makes up about half of Canada.

To the south of Denedeh, around the Peace River, live the Dene-speaking Beaver people; they are not members of the Nation but are related culturally. Their immediate neighbors to the east are the Cree, Algonquin-speakers whose language comes from an entirely separate family. (Some Cree fled into Northern Alberta in the late 1780s during a smallpox epidemic; their descendants became members of Denedeh.) Bands of Cree extend from the western forests all the way around Hudson and James Bays well into Labrador. The easternmost of these bands, the Innu, call their homeland in eastern Quebec and Labrador *Nitassinan*.

Other speakers of Algonquin dialects live in the southern reaches of the Subarctic. Some Anishinaubeg live in Manitoba and Ontario, along rivers that drain into the Hudson and James Bays. (Most live in the Great Lakes area, not in the Subarctic.) In the area around lower Lake Winnipeg live a people known as Saulteaux, cousins of the Anishinaubeg. Also south of Dehcho, in parts of Alberta, Saskatchewan, and Manitoba, live the Métis, descendants of unions between European fur trappers and Cree, Anishinaubeg, and Saulteaux women. In their 200 years of existence the Métis have maintained the subsistence lifestyle of their Indian ancestors, hunting, trapping, and fishing in the boreal forest, although their proximity to the Great Plains introduced an element of the bison-hunting lifestyle as well.

Historical changes

It is tempting to idealize traditional time as static and unchanging, as if the historical clock began ticking only with the arrival of non-Native immigrants. The truth is that people adapted to Europeans, as they did to other tribal nations, within their own ongoing processes. Indeed, European goods and diseases worked their way through aboriginal (native) trading networks in the Subarctic region well before actual explorers and fur traders started building forts there in the late eighteenth century. Russian trade goods came into interior Alaska via annual Inuit trade fairs in the mid- to late-eighteenth century. The French and English came into the Subarctic from the east and southeast, allowing Algonquin middlemen to trade firearms and other items for western furs. Coastal Tlingit traders used Russian goods to bolster their business dealings with Dene in the southern Cordillera.

Relations with non-Natives involved less warfare than farther south, because fur traders generally were more interested in a supply of pelts than in stealing land. However, increasing dependence on outside goods did affect subsistence practices and occasionally resulted in violence. For example, the people on what is now Newfoundland, the Beothuk, got into real trouble by misunderstanding the private property concepts of French and English fishermen. Branded as thieves, they were hunted down for a scalp bounty and died out by the early nineteenth century.

In Alaska, where Russians brutally enslaved coastal tribes for the fur trade, the Ahtna, who lived in upper Ts'itu (the Copper River) repelled more than one party of Russians in the early colonial period. In one harrowing account told by Katie and Fred John, a party of Russians, apparently in the winter of 1794–95, drove the men out of a village to freeze to death and conscripted the women to tan hides. The Russians' Dena'ina guide purposely mistranslated certain dialogue in order to give the Ahtna men time to retaliate, which they did, killing the entire party. No white people lived among the Upper Ahtna until after the Klondike gold rush of 1898, in part because the coastal Tlingit discouraged outsiders from disrupting their own trade relations with the interior.

In most parts of the Subarctic, where violent confrontations with outsiders did not occur, fur traders did establish posts that by degrees greatly affected the patterns of Native people. The introduction of sled dogs enabled more trapping to be done but also increased pressure on summer fish camps to produce food. Tending trap lines affected the location and duration of winter camps, lessening mobility. Intermarriage was not uncommon and had far-ranging effects. The Métis nation, which grew out of mixed-race marriages, included both fur-trapping people in the north and buffalo-hunting people on the prairies. The dominant fur company, the Hudson's Bay Company, controlled forts and land from Hudson Bay to the Yukon until 1869, when it sold its huge territory to Canada. Conflicts between the Métis and Canada led to the only armed conflicts on the western Canadian frontier. These ended with the Second Riel Rebellion in 1885 near the Saskatchewan River, when Métis patriot Louis Riel and Cree compatriots finally were defeated militarily. Tensions between the Métis and the government over land and sovereignty continue to this day.

Other contacts between Natives and fur traders demonstrated the creativity and adaptability of Subarctic peoples. The introduction of trade beads, the fur trade, and missionary instruction led to the blossoming of Dene beadwork, which formerly had been done with quills and seeds. Floral embroidery was introduced in the eastern Dene region in the nineteenth century and spread as far as Alaska. Kate C. Duncan has documented the long history of ornamented Dene art on such items as clothing, mittens, moccasins, baby-carrying straps, and dog blankets. Similarly, early contacts with Europeans led the Algonquin-speaking Innu to develop a tradition of painted caribou-skin coats that echoed the garments worn by Europeans. As documented by Dorothy K. Burnham, the coats were in use for well over two centuries, ending in the early twentieth century. These Dene and Innu developments show how outside materials and ideas breathed new life into long-standing traditions.

As with clothing and embroidery, Native people responded enthusiastically to new songs and dances. The Hudson's Bay Company established a post at Fort Yukon in 1847, where men from Scotland, France, Canada, and the Orkney Islands introduced fiddle music to the Gwich'in and Han peoples. The locals loved fiddling so much that, even after the fort closed twenty years later, they kept on playing at social gatherings. Tribes farther south, such as the Tanana, learned of fiddling from Americans, and they incorporated it into ceremonial potlatches (feasts celebrating major life events such as birth, death, or marriage, in which goods are given away to show the host's wealth and generosity) and a big celebration known as Nuchalawoya in late spring. Native people were often excluded from dance halls, where non-Natives enjoyed such music, so the Native people incorporated fiddling into their own events. Starting in 1983 the Athabascan Old-Time Fiddling Festival became an annual attraction in Fairbanks, Alaska. There, audiences experience nineteenth-century Orkney Island fiddling, jigs, and reels while Dene people, some who cannot understand each other's dialects, have an art form that all can appreciate.

While these gradual adaptations were taking place, the superpowers of Canada and the United States were preparing to exert their authority over the Subarctic. The United States bought Alaska from Russia in 1867, but it was not until Alaska approached statehood in the late 1950s that the Native people realized the enormity of their potential land loss. Neither treaties nor reservations had been established in the American Subarctic, as had been done in the lower 48 states. Desire to build the Trans-Alaska Oil Pipeline led the government in 1971 to enact the Alaska Native Claims Settlement Act (ANCSA), which assigned to the Natives some 40 million acres of land and almost $1 billion in exchange for relinquishing their aboriginal claims in the rest of Alaska. The land was divided among thirteen regional corporations, the largest of which is Doyon, Limited, representing most of the Dene peoples of interior Alaska.

Meanwhile, tribal councils still exist, which leads to some confusion about who truly represents the future of the people. The village of Venetie in the 1990s sued the state, insisting that despite ANCSA their village fits the definition of "Indian country" as exhibited in the rest of the states. (Indian Country is a term used in federal law that includes reservations, scattered Indian home sites, and sometimes areas near reservations as well. By law, tribal governments in Indian Country have the authority to make and enforce their own laws and negotiate government-to-government with the United States.) In any case, the challenge for Doyon, as well as for the other corporations and tribal councils, is to navigate the modern capitalist economy without losing sight of basic cultural values.

Ancient subsistence practices and modern industries often do conflict. The Gwich'in, who number from 5,000 to 7,000 people in both Alaska and Canada, have been resisting the efforts of the U.S. Congress and the coastal Inuit to develop an oil field in the Arctic National Wildlife Refuge. Though they live inland, the Gwich'in depend on the Porcupine Caribou herd whose calving ground is in the Refuge. They fear that oil development in the delicate tundra environment will threaten the survival of the herd. The presence of Inuit people on the other side of the question prevents a simplistic Native versus non-Native interpretation of this conflict.

Canadian peoples face similar dilemmas, as the industrial world has taken a great interest in their oil, mineral, timber, and hydroelectric resources. Like the United States, Canada never bothered to make treaties in most of its northern reaches, so the late twentieth century witnessed a flurry of efforts to settle the land claims of the various nations, an agonizing process for the aboriginal people. The Innu, for example, have resisted efforts to develop resources in Nitassinan until their land rights are settled, knowing full well that such development is already happening. They have been negotiating directly with mining and timber companies in an effort to provide economic benefit for the people while protecting their subsistence base in the ecosystem (the way that a community and the environment work together).

Since it is unlikely that anyone in the Subarctic lives totally outside the cash economy, villages and towns across Alaska and Canada are attempting to balance the creation of jobs with the well-being of the land and people. This is a daunting challenge, but the various Dene and Algonquin nations certainly have long traditions of survival in their favor.

Brian Wescott
(Athabaskan/Yup'ik)

FURTHER READING

Many of the nations in the Subarctic now have websites. Students are encouraged to search for these on the Internet.

Abel, Kerry. *Drum Songs: Glimpses of Dene History.* Montreal: McGill-Queen's University Press, 1993.

Cruikshank, Julie, with Angela Sidney, Kitty Smith, and Annie Ned. *Life Lived Like a Story: Life Stories of Three Yukon Native Elders.* Lincoln: University of Nebraska Press, 1990.

Cruikshank, Moses. *The Life I've Been Living.* Fairbanks: University of Alaska Press, 1986.

Deloria, Vine, Jr. *Red Earth, White Lies: Native Americans and the Myth of Scientific Fact.* New York: Scribner, 1995.

Duncan, Kate C. *Northern Athapaskan Art: A Beadwork Tradition.* Seattle: University of Washington Press, 1989.

Handbook of North American Indians, Vol. 6: *Subarctic.* Ed. June Helm.

Washington, DC: Smithsonian Institution, 1981.

Ives, John W. "Sketch of Athapaskan Prehistory." *A Theory of Northern Athapaskan Prehistory.* Boulder: Westview Press, 1990: p. 52-55.

Mishler, Craig. *The Crooked Stovepipe: Athapaskan Fiddle Music and Square Dancing in Northeast Alaska and Northwest Canada.* Urbana: University of Illinois Press, 1993.

Moore, Patrick, and Angela Wheelock, eds. *Wolverine Myths and Visions: Dene Traditions from Northern Alberta,* comp. Dene Wodih Society. Edmonton: University of Alberta Press, 1990.

VanStone, James W. *Athapaskan Adaptations: Hunters and Fishermen of the Subarctic Forests.* Chicago: Aldine Publishing, 1974.

Vaudrin, Bill. *Tanaina Tales from Alaska.* Norman: University of Oklahoma Press, 1969.

Watkins, Mel, ed. *Dene Nation: The Colony Within.* Toronto: University of Toronto Press, 1977.

Wiggins, Linda E., ed. *Dena—The People: The Way of Life of the Alaskan Athabascans Described in Nonfiction Stories, Biographies, and Impressions from All Over the Interior of Alaska.* Fairbanks: Theata Magazine, University of Alaska, 1978.

Alaskan Athabaskan

Name

Alaskan Athabaskan (pronounced *uh-LAS-ken ath-uh-PAS-ken*; also spelled "Athapascan"). The name refers to the language spoken by eleven groups of Alaska Natives. The call themselves Dene, (or *Dinnie*, meaning "the People."

Location

The Alaskan Athabaskan are a Subarctic people who live in an area directly south of the true Arctic regions. It stretches from the border of the Canadian Yukon Territory to just beyond the Arctic Circle. They once wandered throughout a vast region, but after Europeans came, they built villages of 50 to 500 people along the Yukon, Koyuckuk, Tanana, and Copper rivers. Most of them still live in those areas today. Few villages have roads leading into them and are reached by boat, snowmobile, or plane.

Population

In the 1850s, there were more than 10,000 Alaskan Athabaskans. In a census (count of the population) done in 1990 by the U.S. Bureau of the Census, 14,198 people identified themselves as Alaskan Athabaskans, making the tribe the nineteenth largest in the United States (see box).

Language family

Athabaskan.

Origins and group affiliations

The Athabaskan were among the first people to arrive in North America. According to scientists, they crossed a land bridge that linked Siberia and Alaska as many as 40,000 years ago (it no longer exists). The term "Athabaskan" is commonly associated with the language family. There are the Southern Athabaskan—the Apache and Navajo—and the Northern Athabaskan in Alaska. Eleven groups of Athabaskan-language speakers now live in the interior of Alaska. They are the Ahtna (also called Ahtena), Han, Holikachuk, Ingalik, Koyukon, Kutchin, Tanacross, Tanaina, Tanana, Upper Tanana, and Upper Kuskokwim peoples.

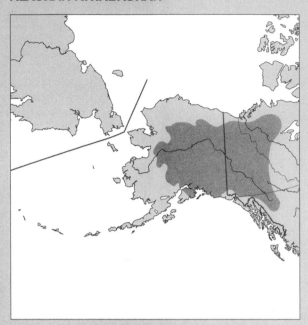

ALASKAN ATHABASKAN

Contemporary Communities

Alaskan Athabaskan communities abound throughout Alaska.

Shaded area: Traditional lands of the Alaskan Athabaskan in present-day Alaska and Canada.

The Dene, as the Alaskan Athabaskan people prefer to be called, have lived for centuries in a vast, awe-inspiring, and sometimes forbidding wilderness of rolling, ice-covered hills and evergreen forests of the Subarctic region. There, short summers of twenty-four-hour sunlit days are followed by long, often brutal winters with heavy snowfalls. The people share a feeling of kinship with the animals on which they once depended for their whole existence. Their relations with the U.S. government have been unusual compared to those of many Native Americans, because they were not torn from their homelands and forced onto reservations. Living in remote locations where roads are few, these hardy people have managed to retain many of their old ways, while adopting useful elements of modern culture.

HISTORY

Explorers unwelcome

Shortly after 500 C.E., Athabaskan speakers split into three major divisions: the Alaskan, who remained in the cold northwest; and the

Plains and Southwestern branches, who moved south and east. Athabaskan became the most widespread language family in North America. The Alaskan Athabaskan settled in an area to the east of their current territory, but were pushed out by the Tlingit (see entry) in prehistoric times. In their new territory, they battled neighboring Eskimos (Inuit) and won, laying claim to the subarctic interior of Alaska.

The Alaskan Athabaskan pursued a nomadic (wandering) existence based mostly on hunting until the arrival of whites in the late 1700s. Because of the vast area in which they lived, the various groups met white people at different times. Some had already heard how Russian fur traders were enslaving the Eyak people of Prince William Sound, forcing them to hunt and trap for Russian gain. Even though some groups did not see their first white men until well into the 1800s, they spoke of a new race of people who would come and try to kill all the Natives and take away their hunting grounds.

The Russians, English, and Americans appreciated the high quality of furs available throughout Alaska, and hastened to set up trading posts. Conflicts arose. On four separate occasions, Russian explorers were massacred during expeditions within Alaskan Athabaskan territory. In 1796 and 1818, three different Russian exploring teams were killed by the Ahtna and neighboring tribes as they attempted to locate the source of the Copper River. In 1847 another group met the same fate. One early explorer wrote about the Tanana: "They are always opposed to any exploration of their country."

Those whites who managed to establish relations among the Alaskan Athabaskan fell victim to their wars with other tribes—wars in which they sought revenge for trespassing or wars that happened simply because a group was suspicious of and hostile to anyone who was different. In 1851 a group of Koyukon descended upon the town of Nulato, killing the Native inhabitants as well as the Russian traders in residence. The unfriendly reputation of the Alaskan Athabaskan, combined with the unwelcoming nature of their territory, kept white immigration to a minimum during this period.

IMPORTANT DATES

1769–83: Samuel Hearne and Alexander Mackenzie are the first explorers to penetrate Alaskan Athabaskan territory, looking for furs and a route to the Pacific Ocean. Russian fur traders are not far behind.

1818–19: Two separate Russian expeditions are massacred by the Ahtna while exploring the Copper River.

1896: Discovery of gold brings hordes of miners and settlers to Alaska.

1962: The Tanana Chiefs Conference is formed to pursue land claims for the Alaskan Athabaskan people.

1971: Alaska Native Claims Settlement Act is passed, awarding 40 million acres of land and more than $960 million to Alaskan Natives.

A delivery of furs during the Klondike Gold Rush in Alaska, a time that changed the lives of Alaskan Athabaskans forever.

Missionaries and miners

The discovery of gold in 1896 in Yukon Territory in northwest Canada, just above the Alaska border, began the ten-year Klondike Gold Rush, changing the Native way of life in Alaska forever. For the first time since the United States bought Alaska from the Russians in 1867, Americans began to see Alaska as a valuable addition to American territory. The stampede for gold between 1898 and 1900 brought thousands of whites through Alaskan Athabaskan territory. The Natives had little interest in gold, but watched as their lands were taken over by whites, who introduced alcohol and harmful hunting practices to the region (like hunting for trophy heads, not food). This created a feeling of mistrust between Alaskan Natives and whites that persists today.

Christian missionaries coming into Alaska at the same time also changed the Native life. Settlers and priests demanded conformity to white culture, to the extent that Native languages, ceremonies, and healing rites were often abandoned. Still, some Alaskan Athabaskans were protected from efforts to change their culture by the size of Alaska and their remote locations. Some did not come into any regular contact with whites until World War II (1939–45), when the U.S. military built the Alaska Highway (which opened up the territory for later settlement), established air strips for landing planes, and stationed troops there.

Natives organize against oppression

Throughout the early 1900s, plans were made for major projects on or near Native Alaskan lands, often without consulting the people. Natives protests began with the formation of the Alaskan Native Brotherhood in 1912. It was not until 1962, however, that the Alaskan Athabaskan established their own organization, called the Tanana Chiefs Conference, to address land issues. Land rights had become increasingly important for the Alaskan Athabaskan as whites fished, hunted, and trapped wherever they wished throughout Native territory. The issue came to a head when an oil pipeline was proposed across Native lands. The Tanana Chiefs Conference and other Alaskan Native organizations won a victory when the Alaska Native Claims Settlement Act (ANCSA) was passed in 1971.

ANCSA awarded the Natives 40 million acres of land and more than $960 million, in return for them giving up their rights to the rest of Alaska. The ANCSA also resulted in the formation of 12 regional corporations in Alaska to be in charge of economic development and land use. A path was cleared for the construction of the pipeline, and millions of acres were set aside for parks and wilderness areas. Still, hunting rights remain a problem. The Natives object to white trophy hunters, who kill moose for the antlers and allow the meat to rot. Furthermore, as sports hunters use modern technology to track their game, Alaskan Athabaskan hunters using ancient hunting techniques cannot compete.

RELIGION

The Alaskan Athabaskan lived a life in close harmony with nature. Their religious belief system was based on their relationships with the supernatural spirits in plants, animals, and natural occurrences. The spirit world included both well-meaning and evil characters who had to be kept happy with songs, dances, and charms. One of the most feared spirits among the Alaskan Athabaskan was known as *Nakhani* or the "Bush Indian." In the summer, the Nakhani loitered around the camps at night, waiting to steal children and attack hunters.

Probably the most important aspect of their belief system was the relationship they had with the animals on which they depended for their very existence. The Athabaskan considered animals equal to them and believed people would be reborn after death as animals.

In the 1800s Russian Orthodox missionaries reached the Alaskan Athabaskans, but their numbers were few and the territory they had to cover was vast. Sometimes their only contact was brief, when they

came to a village and baptized everyone in it at the same time, then moved on. The Natives did not object, and may even have thought the ritual was part of the trading process.

Some Russian missionaries remained after the sale of Alaska, and their influence increased and can still be seen in Alaska. The Russians were followed by Protestant, Episcopalian, and Catholic missionaries. They helped the Natives in their fight to keep their land but discouraged many elements of Native beliefs. They especially disapproved of the gift-giving ceremonies called potlatches, which the missionaries saw as wasteful. The Natives were willing to listen to the words of the missionaries, but they ignored their attempts to do away with the potlatch. Today, nearly all Alaskan Athabaskans profess to be Christians.

LANGUAGE

The term "Athabaskan" refers to a language family spoken by the Southern Athabaskan—Apache and Navajo—and the Northern Athabaskan in Alaska. Generally, the term is used to refer to the Athabaskan speakers of Alaska.

Today, eleven different Alaskan Athabaskan languages are spoken. Although figures vary from group to group, it is estimated that about 21 percent of Alaskan Athabaskan peoples still speak their Native language. Borrowing from other languages has occurred throughout Alaska, where a mix of Inuit, Russian, and Athabaskan people still live side by side.

GOVERNMENT

In the days before Europeans came into their lands, Athabaskan leaders were only needed when several families came together and formed bands, usually to hunt and gather. Then they chose as their leader or "boss" a person with the qualities best suited for the task at hand. When the band broke up, his position of leadership was over.

A man who wished to be a leader had to give frequent potlatches (gift-giving ceremonies). This was the major way to gain the respect of his own and neighboring groups. With increased contact with white people, the band leader's role expanded. He became the middleman between the Natives and white traders. By 1906, Americans had introduced to Native villages the concept of elected chiefs and village councils.

This system of government—elected chiefs and tribal councils— remains in place, but Native villages were made "corporations" with the 1971 passage of the Alaska Native Claims Settlement Act (ANCSA). The act placed twelve large regional corporations in charge of the economic development and land use of the many villages, which also incorporated. It was assumed that these profit-making corporations would lead to improved lives for Alaskan Natives, although many Native groups felt that this manner of governing conflicted strongly with their traditions. Disagreement has arisen among the corporations, the traditional village leaders, and the state of Alaska. The state would prefer that the Native lands be developed in the usual way of American cities, but the Natives want to use it in ways more in keeping with their traditions. Some Natives believe land ownership should be transferred from the corporations to the traditional tribal governments.

ECONOMY

Since prehistoric times the Athabaskan economy has been based on hunting. During the period of fur trading with the Russians, a money-based economy began to develop, and it became firmly established during the Klondike Gold Rush. Great profits were made by supplying meat, furs, and labor to whites. The Athabaskan people developed a liking for the tobacco, tea, and other luxuries they bought from whites, and soon they looked upon the luxuries as

POPULATION OF ALASKAN ATHABASKAN GROUPS: 1990

According to the 1990 census, 14,198 people identified themselves as Alaskan Athabaskans. Some identified themselves more specifically as follows:

Group	Population
Ahtna	205
Alaskan Athabaskan	13,192
Doyon	265
Tanaina	536
Total	14,198

necessities. Their hunting was made much easier with the white man's guns. As they came to depend on manufactured goods, they gave up wandering in small groups and settled down in villages near trading posts. Some continued old practices in a new way: they set off in the summer for fish camps but used the villages as a winter base while they trapped animals. As they killed more and more caribou with American rifles, the number of caribou fell. Overhunting reduced the supply of furs, and hunting became an occupation only for the most skilled and efficient men.

Twentieth-century economy

With American troops stationed in Alaska during World War II (1939–45), the Natives' wage economy boomed as they helped supply military installations with food. A decline set in after the war when the posts closed down and the soldiers left.

In the twentieth century, Alaskan Athabaskans depended on the earning money in the economy for survival, although some people still trap, hunt, and fish for part of the year. Some Native men have to leave their villages to work as laborers at white-owned fish canneries and mines. Since the 1960s, many have been employed as summer forest firefighters for the U.S. Department of the Interior. Today, the major employers in the region are the mining, fishing, lumbering, and oil industries, but the best jobs go to educated workers from outside the state. Most jobs available to the Natives are at the lower-paying levels.

The Alaskan Athabaskan are striving for economic independence. With the award they received under the Alaska Native Claims Settlement Act of 1971, they have established Native-run businesses that are prospering. For example, Ahtna, Inc., a regional corporation, engages in construction work, oil pipeline maintenance, and other profitable ventures. Still, many people are unemployed or underemployed, and many families depend on wage labor supplemented by government welfare and food stamps to survive.

DAILY LIFE

Families

Athabaskan families were made up of a mother, father, their children, and grandparents. Households might contain two families who shared tasks, and winter villages might consist of five households. Athabaskans spent almost all their time preparing to hunt, hunting,

then drying and processing the products of a successful hunt. Famine was a constant threat, and the only way to endure it was to be prepared. The people were generous in good times and bad, sharing what they had with others.

Education

For Athabaskans childhood was short, and they believed it should be filled with freedom and joy because adult life would be

very hard. Children were rarely spanked and heard few harsh words. Childhood ended at puberty, when boys and girls were kept apart from one another in special huts for at least a year and learned from their elders all the skills they needed to know to survive. Afterwards, they were ready to marry.

Christian missionaries first introduced formal, Western-style schooling in the 1800s. They set up boarding schools, which allowed them more control over childrens' lives. They discouraged children from speaking their Native language, causing tension when the children returned to their families. Some families simply kept their children at home, but in the 1930s the government declared that all of them had to attend schools. This had the effect of breaking up families, as mothers lived with their children near the schools, while the men departed to hunt. Some young men dropped out of school during hunting season.

In spite of the difficulties, literacy (the ability to read and write) increased, along with an awareness of and involvement in the outside world. Today, more and more Alaska Natives are attending college.

Buildings

Summer dwellings were rectangular bark houses that were easy to set up and offered protection from the rain. During the spring and fall hunting seasons, the Alaskan Athabaskans constructed skin-covered tepees or brush lean-tos set up face to face, a structure known as the double lean-to. After Europeans came, the people began to use canvas instead of skins for tepees.

Winter houses varied from wooden log cabins to round buildings covered with hide and sunk partly underground. Smoke houses and underground bark- and earth-covered sheds that acted as freezers were also typical. Common to all Alaskan Athabaskan was a specially built house for the potlatch ceremony.

As their lifestyles changed, and more Natives began to live year-round near trading posts, permanent log cabins became the preferred architectural style.

Food

The harsh climate and the scattering of food resources over large areas required almost constant wandering in search of food for the Athabaskans. Fruits and vegetables were scarce or non-existent, and the coming of cranberry, blueberry, and salmonberry seasons was cause for much rejoicing. The main staple in the Alaskan Athabaskan diet was caribou, supplemented by moose and mountain goat when they were available.

A delicacy among the Alaskan Athabaskan was roasted young caribou antler. The antler was cooked over the fire and the charred velvet peeled back to reveal a tender, tasty inside. Small game, including rabbit, ground squirrel, and porcupine, provided additional variety.

Fishing, especially for salmon and whitefish, was long considered to be of secondary importance. It became more important when sled dogs were introduced; they were fed fish. White traders introduced the Alaskan Athabaskan to tea, alcohol, and tobacco, three products now in widespread use.

Travel

In the warmer months the Alaskan Athabaskan traveled by boat or raft because the spring thaw left large amounts of standing water over the landscape. Winter travel was by snowshoe, with sleds and toboggans to carry heavy loads.

Today, four-fifths of Alaska cannot be reached by roads and is seldom visited. Yet Alaska Natives still live there. In addition to the old ways of getting around, they also use snowmobiles, airplanes, and boats powered by motors.

Clothing and adornment

Any differences in clothing among the Alaskan Athabaskan groups were in the decorative details. Caribou was the skin of choice for clothing. In the winter, tanned hides with the hair left on were worn as capes. Summer capes were similar but the hair was removed. Winter clothing was bulky to protect against the elements: rabbit, sheep, and deerskin robes were worn over fringed, hooded shirts and pants with moccasins attached. Mittens were attached to a string that hung around the neck.

The Alaskan Athabaskan were accomplished embroiderers, and used quills, beads, and colored threads to brighten their wardrobes. Face painting, tattooing, ear and nose piercing, and feather adornments were popular, as were necklaces and hair ornaments made of teeth, claws, stones, ivory, and bone.

Healing practices

The Athabaskan believed that supernatural spirits bestowed power upon men and women who were to become healers, called shamans (pronounced *SHAY-muns*). Healing power came to shamans in dreams and visions, when the spirit taught the dreamer the songs and dances that would help cure sicknesses. Shamans sang the songs and performed the dances over a patient while sucking, massaging, or blowing on the afflicted area.

Plants were also used for curing by experts who were not shamans. These included potions of cottonwood for curing colds, juniper berries for internal ailments, and spruce needles for stomachaches. Blood-letting—the removing of blood from a vein—and daily baths in a sweat house were also common practices.

Christian missionaries discouraged belief in shamans, and by the 1930s few shamans would admit to their skills. White people brought new diseases and alcoholic beverages to Alaska Natives, and by the 1950s, tuberculosis, an infectious lung disease, had become widespread. The United States government responded to the problem by building modern hospitals in Native villages, and by introducing better health and dental care practices. Current health problems that plague the Alaskan Athabaskan people include extremely high rates of teen suicide and alcoholism. Babies of heavy drinkers can be born with mental and developmental damage.

CUSTOMS

Marriage

Marriages were arranged by the parents. A girl was considered ready to marry soon after she reached puberty, and a slightly older husband was chosen. Preference was given to young men who had demonstrated hunting skills. The couple usually moved into the home of the bride's family. For a year or two, the young man worked for his in-laws before setting up his own home. By then, he had mastered two hunting territories—those of his family and his wife's family; this was useful knowledge during lean times.

The partner system

Men chose male partners to be their close friends for life. The two agreed to help each other when help was needed, to offer hospitality to one another, and to always respect one another.

Hunting rituals

In keeping with their belief that animals had souls, Alaskan Athabaskan hunters observed many prohibitions, such as never killing a dog, wolf, or raven. Ravens were spared because they might be the spirits of dead people; killing them would bring bad luck in hunting. Hunters carried medicine bags that contained lucky objects such as animals' teeth and claws. If a woman touched his medicine bag, a hunter would lose his power.

Tom Kizzia, a newspaper reporter who spent two years visiting remote areas of Alaska and interviewing the people he encountered, wrote a book in which he described how early Native Alaskans killed a bear using only a spear. They would "walk right up to the bear, stare him in the eye, let him know you're going to kill him. Then show a sudden flash of fear, to make the bear drop his guard, and that's when you make your thrust. Hunters wrapped leather around the spear handle at a bear's arm's length from the point, so they would know not to let their hand slip too close."

Ceremonies, potlatches, and games

Winter was the time for celebrating, and there was much feasting, dancing, singing, reciting of myths, and speech making; all of this activity helped groups maintain contact with other groups. Since the coming of Christian missionaries, these winter festivities have been joined to the celebration of Christmas.

Two major celebrations that are still held by Alaskan Athabaskans are the potlatch and the stick dance. Both are week-long, gift-giving ceremonies that honor the dead. Potlatches originated in the Pacific Northwest (see Haida entry). In the old times, the Alaskan Athabaskan potlatch might also be held to celebrate a girl's reaching puberty or to call attention to a man's wealth. During the ceremony, tribal members perform their spirit songs and dances, feast, and receive the plentiful gifts distributed by the hosts.

The stick dance is held in March and is hosted by a widow to honor her dead husband. Men carry a fifteen-foot-long pole into the village hall on the fifth evening of the ceremony, and women decorate it with ribbons and furs. Thirteen dances are held with the stick as a focal point. There is much feasting and distributing of gifts. Sometimes the event takes years to plan and save for.

The Athabaskan people were extremely fond of games, especially a ball game using animal bladders that were either inflated or stuffed with grass. Today, softball is popular, and organized teams often travel by boat to compete with rival teams.

Death and burial

Russian Orthodox missionaries introduced the concept of burying the dead, instead of cremating or exposing dead bodies to the elements as they had done before. Funerals were usually arranged by old men of another family group, who prepared the body while younger men dug the grave. They were thanked for their services at a potlatch and were given gifts of guns, blankets, eagle feathers, and digging tools. The Athabaskan believed that the life spirit left the body of the dead person while the potlatch feast was going on.

CURRENT TRIBAL ISSUES

In modern times the tribe has problems with alcoholism, overdependence on government welfare payments for survival, and hunting rights issues. Trying to solve their common problems has unified the people, who now call themselves the Dene Nation.

Other issues of concern for the Athabaskans are the sale, by the state of Alaska, of surrounding lands for development and hunting rights.

NOTABLE PEOPLE

Velma Wallis (1960–) is an Athabaskan writer who has written several stories about her people's struggle to survive in a harsh environment. Among her works are *Bird Girl and the Man Who Followed the Sun: An Athabascan Indian Legend from Alaska* (1996), and *Two Old Women: An Alaskan Legend of Betrayal, Courage and Survival* (1994), which tells the shocking but uplifting story of two elderly women who are abandoned by their starving tribe.

Moses Cruikshank (1906–) is an Athabaskan storyteller whose stories convey moral messages and share personal experiences of his life and family. His book *The life I've been living* was published in 1986.

FURTHER READING

"Frequently Asked Questions About Alaska" [Online] http://sled.alaska.edu/akfaq/akancsa.html

Griese, Arnold A. *Anna's Athabaskan Summer.* Boyds Mills Press, 1997.

Kizzia, Tom. *The Wake of the Unseen Object: Among the Native Cultures of Bush Alaska.* Holt, 1991.

Younkin, Paula. *Indians of the Arctic and Subarctic.* Facts on File, 1992.

Cree

Name

Cree (*kree*). Cree groups in different regions refer to themselves by various names, and only use the term "Cree" when speaking or writing in English. The French called the people *Kristineaux,* which became shortened to "Kri," spelled "Cree" in English.

Location

Canada's Cree live in areas spanning the nation's provinces from Quebec in the east to Alberta in the west. The group called Plains Cree live in the parklands and plains of Alberta and Saskatchewan, and the group called Woodland Cree live in the forests of Saskatchewan and Manitoba. A small group of Woodland Cree known as the Swampy Cree lives in Manitoba, Ontario, and Quebec. American Cree are scattered throughout many states, and several hundred share the Rocky Boy's Reservation in Montana with the Ojibway and other tribes.

Population

In the 1600s, three were an estimated 30,000 Cree. In Canada, in 1995, there were at least 76,000 Cree. In the United States, in 1990, 8,467 people identified themselves as Cree.

Language family

Algonquian.

Origins and group affiliations

For more than 6,000 years, the ancestors of the Cree lived near the Arctic Circle. Some of the Plains Cree intermarried with French people, creating the unique Métis culture (see next entry) of the Red River Valley. At various times, enemies of the Cree were the Blackfeet, the Nakota, the Ojibway, and the Athabaskans (see entries). The Assiniboin (*uh-SIN-uh-boin* people were their major ally.

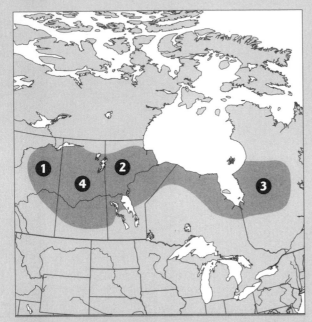

CREE

Contemporary Communities

1. *Alberta* more than 25 Cree reserves
2. *Manitoba* more than 20 Cree reserves
3. *Quebec* more than 9 Cree reserves
4. *Saskatchewan* more than 40 Cree reserves

Shaded area: Traditional lands of the Cree in present-day northwestern Manitoba, Saskatchewan, Alberta, and northern Quebec.

The early Cree lived among the lakes, rivers, and spruce forests of eastern Canada, where the winters were long, the summers were short, and their lives were regulated by the seasons. In all their activities, they showed respect for animals and the land that supplied their needs, and many of their customs were developed to ensure the success of tribal hunters. Their gradual movement over an immense area made the Cree perhaps the most widespread of the Indian peoples.

HISTORY

Changes come

The Cree, who occupied lands in eastern Canada for thousands of years, have a complicated history. Before they had contact with Europeans, the Cree lived south and southwest of the Hudson Bay in northern Quebec, where they were able to make all the tools, weapons, and warm clothing they needed to survive from materials found nearby. They used parts of trees and animals to fashion tents, spears, bows and arrows, cooking equipment, boats, sleds, and snowshoes.

When English explorer Henry Hudson came into the Cree homelands in 1611, trade relations began between the Cree people and whites. During the mid- to late 1600s, the Cree carried on a thriving trade in animal pelts, primarily beaver. They had an advantage in the new trade because their traditions gave them experience in hunting and gathering over vast areas and they were already greatly feared and respected by other Indians.

Middlemen in the fur trade

Between 1668 and 1688, Hudson's Bay Company, the rich and powerful English trading company, set up posts at the mouths of various rivers in Cree territory. Before long, the Cree were serving as middlemen in trade, bringing European goods to more remote inland tribes and returning with fine furs for European traders. The Cree were well adapted to the demands of a trapper's life. They used canoes, which allowed them to take advantage of the waterways, and they quickly became familiar with white ways. They used guns to hunt, to control access to the trading posts, and to turn away their enemies and rivals.

Over time, the Cree experienced many cultural changes because of the fur trade. They gave up their traditional tools for those of the whites, and replaced their clothing of fur and animal skins for wool and cloth garments. The Cree swapped their furs with whites for knives, axes, metal scrapers for preparing animal skins, fishhooks, brass kettles, rifles, blankets, and steel animal traps.

The Cree traded at English posts to the north and French posts to the south. For a while, their part in the fur trade helped them become the wealthiest and most powerful tribe in the region, but soon there was a terrible price to pay, when they were exposed to white diseases to which they had no immunity, and to the use of liquor. Some estimates indicate that two-thirds of the Cree were wiped out by epidemics brought by Europeans. But unlike other Native groups, the tribe's population seemed to increase anyway,

IMPORTANT DATES

1668–88: The Cree become middlemen in trade and the chief consumers of European trade goods.

1885: Along with the Métis, the Cree in the Saskatchewan River area fight against Canadian forces in the Northwest Rebellion.

1905: Treaty No. 9 is signed at Hudson's Bay Company's Moose Factory. For $8 upon signing and $4 a year thereafter, each Cree gives up all rights to his or her land.

1971: Quebec government unveils plans for the James Bay I hydroelectric project. Cree and Inuit protest the action in Quebec courts.

1994: James Bay II project is put on hold indefinitely, largely due to the Quebec Cree's successful legal efforts.

probably because the Cree were able to move out of the disease-infested areas when necessary.

Many Cree move west

By the 1730s, wanting to escape disease epidemics and explore new fur-hunting areas, a large portion of the Woodland Cree had relocated to the Great Plains region of western Canada. Some settled as far west as the Canadian Rocky Mountains. This relocation made them far less dependent on the trading posts, and allowed them to live in larger tribal groups. When the supply of beaver for furs was depleted from over-hunting, the Cree helped keep the trading system going by simply substituting buffalo for beaver. They were able to get or make most of the items they needed to survive from various parts of the buffalo.

Alliance with Blackfeet

For a time, the Woodland Cree made use of the resources of both the woodlands and Canada's Great Plains further west. They formed an alliance with the Blackfeet on the Great Plains in what would soon become the United States, trading furs for weapons. The Cree visited the Blackfeet in spring and obtained furs from them, trapped for their own, then returned east to trade the furs. Then they hunted in the province of Saskatchewan before again visiting the Blackfeet. The Cree supplied the Blackfeet with weapons to drive back their enemies.

Between 1790 and 1810, the Cree-Blackfeet alliance fell apart and the trading system disappeared. By then the Cree were making wide use of horses (introduced to North America by the Spanish). Horses became so important to Cree society that a person's status was measured by the type and number of horses he owned.

Life on the Plains grows difficult

By the mid-nineteenth century, the Plains Cree had settled in and were battling for control of land and resources. They based their tribal movements on the migrations of the buffalo herd. They often intruded on the territory of their opponents, which then included their former partners the Blackfeet, as well as the Nakota, the Crow, the Cheyenne, the Nez Perce (see entries), and the Flathead tribes.

In 1870, buffalo were plentiful on the Great Plains. But within ten years, after widespread slaughter by whites, only a small number remained. With the buffalo gone, the tribe faced constant starvation. The epidemics weakened or killed many, and most Cree people, after all that had happened, could not find their way back to the traditional

Cree ways of life. Some believed that their god, the *Great Manito,* had delivered them over to the Evil Spirit for their wickedness.

Attempt to become farmers

In the 1870s, while negotiating treaties with the Canadian government, the Plains Cree sought help to make the change to a farming-based economy. The government promised them tools and livestock but was slow to provide them. They gave the Cree poor quality grain and plows and wagons barely fit for use, as well as wild cattle that were not used to farm work and could not be hitched to the plow. In addition, the wheat given the Cree was useless, as there were no facilities for grinding the grain near their reserve (the Canadian term for reservation). In spite of these obstacles, the Cree began to make a success of farming, and soon were seen as a threat to area whites, who argued that government assistance gave the Indians an unfair advantage.

The Métis rebellions

In 1885, the Plains Cree joined their relatives the Métis (see entry) in the Second Riel Rebellion to protect their land rights from the whites. The Riel Rebellions were among the few wars that took place between First Nations (Canadian Natives) and the Canadian government. The Cree chiefs Poundmaker and Big Bear led warriors against the Northwest Mounted Police ("Mounties"), who patrolled Canada's western wilderness, and an army sent from Eastern Canada to put down the uprising. After two major battles, the Métis gave up the fight; Cree leaders eventually turned themselves in and served prison terms.

Following the conflict, a group of Cree left Canada and settled in the United States in northern Montana. They later joined with a group of landless Ojibway, and in 1915 the homeless Indians were granted the Rocky Boy's Reservation, fifty miles south of the Canadian border, where Cree people still live today.

Many Plains Cree give up farming

In 1889, the Commission of Indian Affairs in Saskatchewan, a province where many Cree lived on Canada's Great Plains, began a new farming system. It reduced each Indian farmer's area of cultivation to one acre of wheat and a garden of roots and vegetables. The provincial government also insisted that the people use only simple tools and that they manufacture at home any items they needed for farming, such as hay forks or carts.

In part because of these new restrictions, many Plains Cree decided to give up farming entirely. They soon fell behind in their technology and were never able to catch up. Many ended up living on Indian reserves and scratched out a meager living through farming, ranching, and manual labor.

Ontario Cree

While the disappearance of buffalo caused the Plains Cree to face starvation, the Cree in the East encountered different challenges. In 1905, faced with increasing numbers of white settlements, and with mining activities and railway construction that threatened their way of life, the Woodland Cree signed Treaty No. 9 at Hudson's Bay Company's Moose Factory. The Cree who signed were to be granted a sum of $8 upon signing and a payment every year after of $4 in "treaty money." In return, the Cree gave up all rights to their former land. It remains unclear whether the Indians understood the treaty, which many of them signed by using Native picture symbols.

Between 1920 and 1940, hundreds of Cree in Ontario died from tuberculosis, flu, measles, whooping cough, and bronchitis that they had gotten from whites. Starvation was widespread due to a dramatic decline in the beaver and caribou they hunted for food. In addition, the provincial government began strict enforcement of its wild game laws, which limited when people could hunt and how much game they could take.

During the 1940s, immunization and medicines were made available to the Ontario Cree. Still, their health care and educational services remained poor.

Twentieth-century challenges

In 1971 the Cree in the Province of Quebec were faced with a new threat. The Canadian government planned to begin work on the James Bay hydroelectric project, which would dam the La Grande River and build several generating stations along the rapids to produce electricity. The electricity was to be transmitted south to Montreal and to cities in the United States. At that time, fifty Cree and Inuit (see entry) hunters protested this proposed action in Quebec courts, arguing that the project would threaten their way of life. The protestors won their case, but the decision was overturned and the conflict continues (see box).

In 1975, the Cree signed the James Bay and Northern Quebec Agreement. This document recognized that the Cree had the same rights to health care and education as other Canadians, and that the way their lands were to be used should be the decision of the Cree themselves.

Today, life for the Cree on the reserves remains difficult, and many residents live on government welfare payments. They send their children to a school on the reserve, and get health care when needed from a government nursing station. This way of living can result in what has been called a "forced and numbing idleness," in the words of Rupert Ross in *Dancing with a Ghost; Exploring Indian Reality.* On top of a harsh economic situation, the Cree face racial discrimination from many of their neighbors.

RELIGION

For the Cree, the life force, similar to the Christian notion of the soul, resided in all living beings. They also believed in spirits, ghosts, and demons, which sometimes revealed themselves in dreams.

The Plains Cree honored one powerful creator—the *Great Manito,* who controlled all things in the universe. Manito was considered too powerful to be approached directly for blessings. Instead, he was approached by go-betweens, spirit powers called *atayohkanak.* All unpleasantness, disease, and wickedness in life came from the Evil Manito.

With sorrowful voices, the Cree repeated long prayers asking for help from the kind and caring gods. They used objects such as eagle

THE JAMES BAY PROJECT

In 1971 the head of the Province of Quebec unveiled the James Bay Project. This $6 million hydroelectric project (a plant that generates electricity from water power) to be built near Cree lands promised to create 125,000 new jobs for Canadians. It would also flood the rivers where the Cree hunted and trapped. For several decades, the Cree and the Inuit fought the project.

In opposing the James Bay project, it was up to the Cree, among other tribes, to prove they had rights in the territory, that the project would do harm to these rights, and that the harm would be irreversible. When opposition to the project began, the Cree tribe of northern Quebec was made up of eight separate communities scattered across 150,000 square miles of forest. They had no regional unity or organizational structure, which made a fight against the government more difficult. Still, they won a favorable court decision in 1973, when a lower court ruled that the Cree and Inuit had title to their lands and that hunting was important to their way of life. Work on the James Bay Project was therefore to cease immediately.

Later that same year, a higher court ruled that because the project was too far along to stop, the work on it should go on. In 1975, the Cree gave up rights to the lands affected by the power project. In return they received a cash settlement of more than $300 million. They also received hunting and fishing rights on 29,000 square miles of land and the right to have a say in future projects.

The first phase of the hydroelectric project was completed in 1991. By then, one-third of the best Cree lands lay under water because of the project. Before work could begin on the next stage of the project, the Grand Council of the Cree of Quebec sued Hydro-Quebec (who ran the project). The project was put on hold so experts could study the environmental impact.

The Cree and their supporters went to work to influence public opinion against the project, using videos, concerts, displays of traditional culture, and other effective techniques. In the summer of 1994, the project was put on hold indefinitely.

Several research projects have been done to examine the impact of the projects on the area where the Cree reside. The studies found unhealthy levels of mercury in the blood of the people resulting from the building of reservoirs that affected the water supply and the fish.

The grand chief of the Quebec Cree, Matthew Coon-Come, explained what the James Bay Project has meant for his people: "[The dream of the hydroelectric project] has become our nightmare. It has contaminated our fish with mercury. It has destroyed the spawning grounds. It has destroyed the nesting grounds of the waterfowl. It has displaced and dislocated our people and broken the fabric of our society. And we have decided, knowing the behavior of the animals, that we will not be like the fox, who, when he sees danger, crawls back to his hole. We have come out to stop the destruction of our land."

feathers and eagle wings during these rituals, and many wore amulets (small objects encased in a beaded envelope) to keep evil away.

Christianity

During times of near starvation, the Cree occasionally were forced to resort to cannibalism (eating the bodies of other humans). However, they viewed cannibalism with horror and greatly feared the *windigos*, human beings who had eaten human flesh and been transformed into supernatural man-eating giants.

In the late 1880s, missionaries converted a number of the Cree to Christian religions. The missionaries burned the drums of Cree people, because they hoped their actions would lead to the end of many traditional Cree beliefs and practices. But many Cree retain their traditional beliefs.

LANGUAGE

The Cree are an Algonquian-speaking people. Today, children on most Cree reservations speak their native language for the first years of elementary school, adding English a few years later. The Cree language is written using a series of symbols called syllabics.

GOVERNMENT

The Cree government was based on a system in which chiefs, councils, leaders, elders, women, and youth all participated in group decision-making, and all voices were heard.

Today, Canadian Cree villages are still headed by chiefs, and a grand chief presides over the Grand Council of the Cree, which was founded in 1974. The Cree hold a general assembly for all Cree people in a different community each year. There, leaders report on events of the past year, and the people discuss the course of Cree affairs in the year ahead.

ECONOMY

The Woodland Cree were hunters and fishermen who trapped in winter, hunted goose in spring, and fished in summer. They used bows and arrows, clubs, spears, and snares of various kinds to capture large and small game. These highly adaptable people later served as middlemen in the prosperous fur trade, trading goods with the French, then the British.

The buffalo supplied many needs of the Cree other than food. The bones were used to make arrowheads; the skull provided a kind of lamp in wet weather; the tail served as a fly swatter; the hair was twisted into ropes; tendons were used for bowstrings and sewing thread; boiled bones made a glue; teeth were fashioned into ornaments and necklaces; the hooves were employed as ladles and spoons; and waste material, in the form of dried dung, was burned for fuel.

DAILY LIFE

Families

For the Woodland Cree, life in the forest required flexibility. Men and women shared the work, and both sexes knew how to perform the duties of the other. Men usually hunted, conducted raids and warfare, and protected their families. Women were responsible for preparing meat, tanning, netting fish, and killing beaver, as well as watching over the children and tending to the fire.

Buildings

The Woodland Cree lived in both cone-shaped and dome-shaped wigwams covered with birch bark, pine bark, or caribou skins. For the Plains Cree, a hide-covered tepee that held between ten and twelve people was the main dwelling. It had a three-pole foundation, a central fireplace with a smoke hole, and was covered with a flap made of twelve to twenty buffalo hides.

Women made the tepees, assembled them, and owned them. Inside each tepee were beds made of bundles of dried grass or rushes, with buffalo robes placed over them for warmth. Pillows consisted of rawhide sacks filled with duck feathers.

Today, most Cree live in homes with modern conveniences. But at their winter camps, woodland hunters live in *muhtukan*, rectangular-shaped houses made of logs and sod. They also build tepee-shaped structures called *michwaup*, which are made of logs and spruce boughs.

Clothing

Until about the age of five, most children wore little or no clothing. Babies were carried about in sacks lined with soft moss that cushioned them and also served as a diaper material.

During summer, men wore leather breechcloths (flaps that hung from the waist and covered the front and back). Leggings decorated with quill and beadwork were worn in winter. Except when the men wore buffalo robes, they usually left the upper body uncovered. They wore a type of poncho, often heavily quilled or beaded, but only for ceremonial occasions such as dances.

Women wore buffalo robes in all seasons. They also wore dresses made of two oblong pieces of cloth or hide, placed one on top of the other, that were sewn or laced together lengthwise, and worn with a fancy belt. The dresses were decorated with elk tusks and bear claws, as well as much quillwork, beadwork, and painting. The Plains Cree made use of beadwork with elaborate floral designs. Painting on garments usually appeared in geometric designs of red and blue.

Cree summer moccasins were usually made of one piece of hide sewn around the outside of the foot. Winter moccasins were made of buffalo skin with hair on the inside for warmth, and often were stuffed with dried grass for more insulation. The Plains Cree wore snowshoes to gain an advantage over other tribes during winter warfare.

Adornments, hairstyles, and body painting

The various types of Cree headgear included a ring of buffalo hide with the hair on the outside, rectangular summer visors made of hide, and ceremonial headdresses such as eagle feather bonnets and buffalo horn caps. Sometimes people made ceremonial head coverings from entire skins of birds, especially the raven.

Popular jewelry included disc earrings made of mussel shells that hung from the ears by short thongs; necklaces made of buffalo teeth, elk tusks, or bear claws hung on tendons; and mussel shell necklaces fastened about the throat by a leather thong. Over time, beads and

"A Cree Woman," photograph by Edward S. Curtis, 1926.

spangles purchased through the Hudson's Bay Company replaced these items.

Men plucked their facial hair. Both men and women parted their hair in the center, and formed two braids. Women tied the two plaits together in back, while men tied them together in front. Some people lengthened their hair by weaving in additional horsehair. Warriors cut bangs into the front of their hair, stiffened it with grease, and combed it up into an erect wave. They brushed their hair with the rough side of a buffalo tongue, and smeared red paint along the middle part.

Both genders created tattoos by working a charcoal paste into punctures in the skin made by needles. While men painted their arms and chests, women generally painted only their chins, cheeks, and foreheads. Face painting was accomplished by first greasing the face, then applying pigment. To make the paint, colored clays were crushed, mixed with water, and baked into small cakes. The pigment was scraped off the cake and combined with hot grease. Before entering battle, warriors often covered themselves with white clay over which wet charcoal was laid. When they returned from war, warriors blackened their faces.

Food

The Plains Cree regarded fishing as an undignified activity for a hunter and only ate fish when hunting was poor. Buffalo was their main staple, but they also hunted moose, caribou, musk ox, elk, deer, and other game.

Their most important root food was turnips, which they ate raw, roasted, boiled, or dried into a powder for soup. They also added berries to dried meat, especially in August when buffalo meat had a poor taste. The first berries of the season were eaten only after each family had held its own ritual feast. The berries were cooked and an elderly man was asked to bless them. In spring, the people collected maple sugar and built fish traps.

When food was in short supply, the people gathered algae, fungus, and caribou dung, which they then boiled and ate. Although the Woodland Indians ate dog meat, the practice was less common among the Plains tribes.

Education

Cree children were allowed a great deal of freedom. They were never beaten and rarely scolded. They usually spent more time with their grandparents than they did with their parents, so grandparent-grandchild ties were very close. Elders were expected to help them learn to make important decisions regarding personal, family, community, and tribal matters.

During the early twentieth century, the Anglican Church in Canada ran elementary schools at various Cree communities that were supported by the federal government. Experts reported severe adjustment problems among Cree children, who were educated in their early years at home. At Canadian boarding schools they were expected to adopt white ways and keep from speaking their native language.

The Cree School Board was created in the late 1970s to help reclaim an education based on Cree values and needs. Today, each Cree community in Quebec runs its own school under the management of the Cree School Board, working along with the Quebec provincial department of education. Many children study the Cree language at school.

Healing practices

Healers called shamans (pronounced *SHAY-mens*) had much authority within the tribe. They were considered links between the human and animal worlds, and could cure illnesses and perform magic. Shamans cured by singing, blowing on the patient, and sucking out the disease. They made use of tobacco and small charms for healing.

Often a tribe had several shamans. Some Woodland Cree shamans practiced sorcery, but the Plains Cree rarely did. Shamans used dreams and rituals to make contact with the spirit world. The Cree believed that evil shamans could bring disease or misfortune upon victims if they chose.

The Cree practiced bloodletting (opening a vein to drain blood) to cure the sick and were able to set broken bones. The knowledge of how to use plant medicines was usually passed down through families or purchased from other informed Indians. Entire plants, or just the root, stem, and bark, were used to cure ailments ranging from headaches to sexually transmitted diseases. Raw buffalo liver was used to treat tuberculosis, and various teas were used to relieve coughs or to clean out the system. Frostbite was treated by pricking frostbitten hands or feet with a sharp bone and rubbing salt or snow around or into the frozen part.

Oral literature

The Cree god of campfire tales was called *Wisagatcak,* the Trickster. The people told a favorite story about a great flood that had taken place in the past. When the flood came, the Trickster constructed a raft to save the animals. He then used his magic to call upon the wolf to run about the raft with a ball of moss in his mouth, forming a new world where the Cree could once again hunt in peace.

CUSTOMS

Naming

Children were named at around age one by a shaman, who chose a name based on an incident or a character in one of his visions. During the child-naming ceremony, the baby was passed around the tepee from person to person; each one addressed the child by its new name and wished it future happiness. Children were often given nicknames for special incidents in their own lives. For example, a mother once left her baby girl unattended for a few minutes and returned to find the cradle surrounded by dozens of birds. From that point onward, she called her baby "Many-birds."

Vision quests

During puberty, a Cree boy took part in the most important rite of initiation into the tribe, the vision quest. This rite put him in touch with the spirit who would guide him through life, and during the rite he was taught a special song. The boy traveled with his father to a secluded spot—a bear's den, or out on a raft in water, or on an unsaddled horse—for the duration of the quest. Wearing nothing but his breechcloth, the boy covered himself with white clay and built a brush shelter with his father. Then the father made a pipe offering to the spirits and left the boy alone to pray and fast. The boy often undertook various feats of endurance in hopes of encouraging a vision. Sometime after returning to camp, he described his vision to others.

Female coming of age ceremony

At the time of a Cree girl's first menstruation, she was secluded for four nights in a small tepee at a distance from the village. An old woman stayed with her, telling her stories and teaching her about the duties of an adult woman. The girl was kept very busy during this time—chopping wood, sewing, and preparing hides. It was then that a girl was most likely to receive a vision from a spirit. After the fourth and final night in seclusion, a feast was held in her honor in her father's tepee.

Festivals

THE SUN DANCE The most important of the Plains Indian ceremonies, the Sun Dance, was called the All-Night-Thirst-Dance by the Plains Cree. During the entire course of the four-day ceremony, participants drank nothing. They made offerings of cloth tied to poles to the gods.

Long ago, Sun Dancers engaged in a bloody rite in which they pierced their skin with a sharp buffalo horn threaded with a leather thong. The thong was tied to a pole or the rafters of a building. As they danced, they tore themselves free from the poles, and offered pieces of their flesh to the god Manito. They hoped to be blessed with a vision, to gain the gods' acceptance, or to give thanks for help they received in battle or in sickness.

Some groups did not practice the self-torture ritual, but danced without food or water for four days, gazing at the Sun, and swaying back and forth until they fainted from exhaustion. In a modern form of the ritual, dancers stand behind green foliage, and bend their knees while blowing on a whistle. As the Sun's rays beat down on them, they fasten their gaze on one spot on the center pole, and refrain from eating or drinking.

SHAKING TENT CEREMONY Another important ceremony was the Shaking Tent Ceremony (also called the Divining Booth), in which spirits were summoned to a tent by a Shaking Tent shaman. After praying, fasting, and purifying himself in a sweat lodge, the shaman stripped to his breechcloth, was bound with leather thongs, and was suspended inside the tent (the spirits were supposed to free him). Outside were onlookers and drummers.

When the spirits arrived, the tent began to shake. Voices and animal sounds could be heard coming from inside. Listeners could hear a conversation taking place between the spirits and the shaman, with the shaman asking questions. Then the leather thongs binding the shaman would shoot out of the top of the tent. The last Shaking Tent Ceremony took place in 1962.

WALKING OUT CEREMONY Young Cree children were not allowed to cross the threshold of their home by themselves until they had taken part in a Walking Out ceremony. At dawn on the day of the ritual, family and friends gathered with the village toddlers in a large tent, forming a circle around the children. Then, each child crossed the threshold with its parents or grandparents, went outside, and followed a path littered with fir branches to a tree about twenty feet away that symbolized nature. The child made a circle around the tree and returned to the tent to be congratulated by the village elders on becoming an official member of the tribe. A feast followed. This ceremony is still practiced.

THE GRASS DANCE The most common ceremonial activity on the Cree reservations today is the Grass Dance, also called the Warriors Dance. Bundles of braided grass are tied to the dancers' belts; the bundles symbolize scalps. In the 1940s, when many Cree men were away fighting in World War II (1939–45), women kept the dance alive. After the war, the women continued to participate by dancing with the men who had returned home from battle.

SWEAT BATHS AND PASSING PIPES Sweat baths in a sweat lodge were used for ceremonial cleansing and for pleasure. Inside the lodge, sweetgrass was burned, a pipe was shared, and water was poured on hot stones to produce a refreshing steam.

All Cree rituals and social occasions were begun by sharing a pipe. Men passed the pipe in a clockwise direction. They believed that the gods smoked along with the men and listened to any requests made during the ceremony. Grasses were braided together in long strands, and during the ritual, pieces were broken off the strands and thrown onto live coals. The fragrant smoke that resulted was thought to be a purifying agent.

Hunting rituals

For the Cree, the hunt was not simply a source of food, but a great mystery. In their view, the gods had given animals to them, and each animal had its own way of thinking and living. Animals made their own decision to participate in the hunt, and in return, hunters made sure animals could grow and survive on the Earth.

Buffalo were hunted by driving them into places where they would stumble—snowdrifts in winter, marshes in summer. Then the herd was stampeded into a corral-type structure called a pound, where they were shot with arrows. Before the beasts were butchered, shamans climbed the wall of the pound and sang power songs. During the butchering, young boys undressed, climbed inside the pound, then threw buffalo intestines over the branches of a tree.

War rituals and raids

A Cree man gained respect in one of three ways: through warfare and raiding, by accumulating wealth, or by being generous. There was much social pressure on young men to participate in warfare, and those who did not were publicly shamed. When he took to the warpath, a man gave up his rights to material possessions. He took with him a sacred bundle containing a single article of war equipment; the bundles were believed to have magical properties. Often a warrior was stripped of his belongings when he returned to the village; even the horses he took in raids were given to relatives and friends.

For the Plains Cree, war was like a tournament. The objective was not to kill or to conquer other tribes, but to gain honors by "counting coup" (pronounced *COO*). Counting coup involved riding up to a live, armed enemy, and touching him with a lance or coup stick. Four coups were enough to make someone a chief.

Raiding another tribe for their horses was considered a warlike undertaking. The object of the raids was to steal as many horses as possible. Raiders did not wish to engage the enemy in battle. But if battles took place, a warrior rose in the ranks depending on the degree of danger involved. For example, a man who shot an enemy while he himself was under fire, outranked one who killed an enemy during an ambush.

The more danger the warrior exposed himself to, the higher the merit he received. If a Cree male performed an act of bravery during his first raid, he was named a "Worthy Young Man." His next step was to join a warrior society, and from there he might be made a chief. The position of chief was often hereditary (passed down from father to son), but if the chief's son was deemed incompetent, another man could be given the position of chief. Ranking among chiefs depended upon their war exploits.

Courtship and marriage

The Cree did not place a high value on virginity, and it was common for unmarried couples to have sexual relations. Women usually married three or four years after their first menstruation. Men married at around age twenty-five. High-ranking men often had two or more wives, and wives often had sexual relations with men other than their husbands.

Parents usually selected their children's mates. The father of a marriageable daughter would present a gift to the young man he considered a good match. If the young man's parents approved, they set up a new tepee for the couple. The bride sat inside, and then the groom entered the tent and sat down beside her. The bride offered him a new pair of moccasins, and if he accepted them, the marriage was sealed.

Funerals

Among the Cree, mourning was very dramatic. Close relatives dressed only in robes, let loose their hair, and cut gashes in their forearms and legs as a sign of their grief. The property of the deceased was given away but usually not to family members. It was believed that giving it to relatives would only lengthen the mourning period. Most dead Cree were then placed in a grave dug about five feet deep and lined with a robe. Tepee poles were fitted over the body, a robe was placed over the poles, and a partially tanned cattle hide was fastened down over the area that had been dug; then earth was placed over the rawhide to keep animals from disturbing the body.

CURRENT TRIBAL ISSUES

Modern Cree face many problems. They have adopted many of the European American ways and have lost many of their traditional beliefs and customs. The incidence of alcoholism, suicide, vandalism, and family violence has increased.

Several matters concerning their relations with the Quebec government occupied the Cree in the 1990s. They have discussed forestry development and its impact on the environment of the Cree. Tribal people sought protection for their way of life, and the opportunity to dispose of the resources of their traditional territory as they saw fit. The Cree continued to express their opposition to Quebec's attempts to break off from Canada and become an independent nation.

NOTABLE PEOPLE

Buffy Sainte-Marie (c. 1942–) is a well-known folk singer and Academy Award-winning songwriter, as well as an advocate for Indian rights. She has written about North American Indian music and Indian affairs and is the author of *Nokosis and the Magic Hat* (1986), a children's adventure book set on an Indian reservation. Sainte-Marie lives in Hilo, Hawaii.

Chief Poundmaker (c. 1842–1886) was adopted as a boy by Blackfeet Chief Crowfoot and given the Blackfeet name, *Makoyi-koh-kin* (Wolf Thin Legs). In 1876 Poundmaker unsuccessfully sought better conditions for his people in treaty talks with the Canadian government. With his followers, he participated in the Métis rebellion against the Canadian government in 1885, supporting the Métis' attempt to form a Native government in Saskatchewan. As a result, he was convicted of treason, served a term in prison, and died shortly after his release.

Other notable Cree include: head chief and resistance leader Big Bear (c. 1825–1888); Payepot, nineteenth-century leader of the Western Canadian Plains Cree; painter and illustrator Jackson Beardy (1944–1984); tribal leader Harold Cardinal (1945–); Jean Cutland Goodwill, editor of *Tawow,* the first Canadian Indian cultural magazine; playwright, director, and producer Thomson Highway (1951–); Plains Cree artist George Littlechild; recording artist Morley Loon; and twentieth-century teacher and missionary Ahab Spence.

FURTHER READING

Erdoes, Richard. *The Sun Dance People: The Plains Indians, Their Past and Present.* New York: Random House, 1972.

Flannery, Regina. *Ellen Smallboy: Glimpses of a Cree Woman's Life.* Montreal: McGill-Queen's University Press, 1995.

Grand Council of the Cree Web site:[Online] http://gcc.ca/

Métis

Name

The word Métis (pronounced *MAY-tee* or *MEH-tis*) comes from the Latin verb *miscere,* which means to mix. The name was used by the French to refer to a group of Canadian mixed-race people. The Métis were also sometimes called half-breeds, mixed-bloods, or *Bois Brules*—a French term meaning "burnt wood," referring to skin color.

Location

The Métis originally wandered throughout modern-day Alberta, Saskatchewan, and along the North Dakota border in the present-day United States. After 1885, the Métis could be found from Lake Superior to Alberta. Today they are mostly located in western Canada along the Manitoba and North Dakota border, in southeastern Alberta, and Saskatchewan. Two groups of about 5,000 people each live in Ontario and Labrador.

Population

In 1821, there were about 500 Métis. Ten years later, in 1831, there were 1,300; in 1843, there were 2,600; in 1870, there were 12,000. No one identified themselves as Métis to U.S. census takers in 1990. In 1991, 135,285 people identified themselves to Canadian census takers as Métis.

Language family

The Métis speak a unique combination of Native languages and French *patois* (pronounced *PAT-wah*; a version of French the English sometimes call "Country French"), with occasional Scottish and Gaelic expressions. Gaelic is a language of Scotland and Ireland.

Origins and group affiliations

The Métis are a group of Native North American people whose origins date back only a few hundred years. They are biracial descendants of Indian women and European settlers. The majority share French and either Cree, Ojibway (see entries), or Assiniboin (pronounced *uh-SIN-uh-boin*) blood, but some trace their European origins to English, Scottish, Irish, or Scandinavian settlers and their Native origins to Inuit (see entry) women. There were many such offspring during the early years of the fur trade in Canada and the Great Lakes region.

MÉTIS

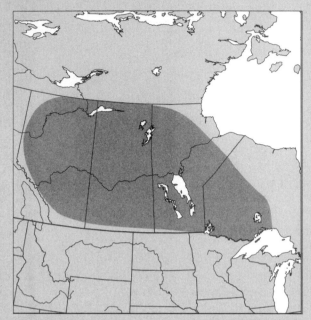

Contemporary Communities

Métis today live in communities scattered throughout Alberta, Saskatchewan, Manitoba, and the Northwest Territories.

Shaded area: Traditional lands of the Métis in Canada, in the prairie provinces of Alberta, Saskatchewan, Manitoba, and the Northwest Territories.

The history of the Métis began with adventurous French fur traders who ventured into the woods and prairies of western Canada during the 1600s. Finding conditions there harsh and wild, the Frenchmen turned to the Native population for instruction. Far from home and lonely, they chose Indian women as mates. The descendants of these couples, caught between two worlds, formed their own communities and developed their own culture. Once united, they played an important role in the settlement of western Canada and in the formation of the new nation. Today they struggle to assert their rights to land and respect.

HISTORY

Birth of a nation

French fur traders known as *voyageurs* came to Canada in the 1600s and were welcomed by Indians—Cree, Ojibwa, and Assiniboin. The Indians supplied them with goods and services of all kinds. They acted as guides, interpreters, canoemen, trappers, and hunters. They supplied the voyageurs with pemmican (see "Food"), buffalo tongue, clothing, and women. The Frenchmen learned much about survival from the Natives. The demand for furs among fashionable Europeans continued throughout the late seventeenth and early eighteenth centuries, bringing more French fur traders, who spent long days and nights in the wilderness trapping fur-bearing animals.

Most of the early traders supplied the Hudson's Bay Company, an English trading company located on the shores of the Hudson Bay. The Métis people were born of the unions between the French fur-trading men and the Native women who became their mates. Some of their sons grew up to became employees of trading companies, serving as trappers, hunters, guides, paddlers, and interpreters. Other boys grew up to become skilled buffalo hunters, who supplied the trading posts with pemmican, a longlasting food that kept trappers going through the winter months.

By the mid-1700s, a large "mixed blood" population had settled around the Great Lakes. Fairly large communities of log cabins emerged at Sault Sainte Marie and other locations. As fur-bearing animals became scarce and settlers moved in from the East, many of these mixed blood people moved westward to the Plains, where the distinctive Métis culture emerged.

Battle of Seven Oaks

Until 1780, the Hudson's Bay Company had enjoyed complete control of trade in Canada. The company depended on the food supplies and know-how of the Métis for its survival. Then the rival North West Company set up a trading post of its own west of Lake Superior. The North West Company saw in the Métis people an excellent source of supplies and labor and lured them into their employ. With this new competition, the Hudson's Bay Company began to suffer heavy losses of money and supplies.

In 1811, the Hudson's Bay traders established a post at the point where the Red and Assiniboine rivers joined (near present-day Winnipeg, Manitoba) called the Red River Settlement. It lay directly on

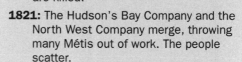

IMPORTANT DATES

1816: Violence erupts during a Métis protest over the Pemmican Proclamation of 1814, and twenty-one Hudson's Bay Company employees are killed.

1821: The Hudson's Bay Company and the North West Company merge, throwing many Métis out of work. The people scatter.

1869: The First Riel Rebellion takes place.

1870: The Manitoba Act allots 1.4 million acres of land to the Métis. Much of it is lost through trickery and misunderstanding.

1885: The Northwest Rebellion takes place.

1983: The Métis National Council is founded.

the preferred trading route of the North West Company. The Hudson's Bay Company encouraged the Métis population to move to this settlement. The nomadic Métis obliged by forming a community there, but to the dismay of the Hudson's Bay Company, the people continued to work for both companies.

Because they wanted sole rights to the pemmican supplied by the Métis, the Hudson's Bay Company passed the Pemmican Proclamation of 1814. Under this law, the Métis were prohibited from trading pemmican with anyone but the Hudson's Bay Company. Since their economy depended heavily on the sale of pemmican—and two good customers were better than one—the Métis chose to ignore the law.

The situation erupted in violence in 1816, and twenty-one traders at the Hudson's Bay Company headquarters at Red River Settlement were killed, including the author of the Pemmican Proclamation. This episode was known as the Battle of Seven Oaks.

Years of changes and rebellion

Five years later, the Hudson's Bay Company and the North West Company merged, and life changed forever for many Métis. Many were forced to find other ways of supporting themselves as excess trading posts were abandoned. Some Métis retained their strips of land along the Red River and farmed, forming the nucleus of what would later become the city of Winnipeg, Manitoba. Others took to the plains and became wandering, year-round buffalo hunters. Still others adopted a combined lifestyle; during the winter months they established temporary settlements in the plains, returning to their more permanent Red River community for the rest of the year.

In 1867 the Canadian colonies united and formed the newly independent Dominion of Canada. Two years later, the Hudson's Bay Company sold its land holdings to the new government. The Canadian government encouraged white Protestants to quickly settle the new territory and sent surveyors to the Métis' Red River Settlement to map out square plots of land to sell to pioneering colonists. They did not consult with or notify the locals, who found out their land was being sold by reading the newspaper. The surveyors completely disregarded the French-style settlement patterns of the Métis, whereby farms were built on long strips of land on the riverbanks. As English Protestant settlers poured into their territory, the Métis saw clearly what the new English-speaking government had in store for them. More settlers would come, take over Métis lands, drive away the buffalo, and Catholicism and the French language would be scorned.

Louis David Riel, Jr., hanged in 1885 for his part as leader of the Métis rebellion, is still considered a martyr and a hero by many French-speaking Canadians. Calls for his posthumous pardon continue to this day.

Furious, the Métis formed a resistance movement and asked the young and well-educated Louis Riel to head it up. Riel and his supporters—who included a gang of rough-and-tumble buffalo hunters and several sympathetic Catholic priests, set up an independent government at the Red River Settlement. They then bloodlessly took over a government fort near Winnipeg and sent a list of demands to Canada's prime minister. The demands included land rights, freedom of language and religion, representation in the Canadian government, and assurance that the Métis would be consulted on decisions about the Red River country. These actions became known as the First Riel Rebellion.

While Riel and his new provisional (temporary) government negotiated with the central government, a local militia was formed to oppose his rule in Red River. Learning of the plans to overthrow the new government, the Métis fought the militia and forced them to surrender. One member of the militia, however, planned another attack, and the Métis arrested him, tried him, and sentenced him to death. His execution turned public opinion in Canada against Riel and his new government.

Although the National Committee of the Métis of the Red River only lasted a year, it had one success—or so they thought at the time: it negotiated the Manitoba Act of 1870 with the Canadian government. The Manitoba Act set aside 1.4 million acres of land for the Métis. The government promised to control the flood of white Protestant settlers and to protect the French language and Catholic faith. The Red River Settlement became the center of what would now be called Manitoba. The government did not keep its end of the agreement. It would not pardon Riel for his part in the execution of the militia member, and sent in troops to control the Métis. Louis Riel fled Manitoba for the United States.

The Northwest Rebellion of 1885

As the Métis expected, their lands were taken over and the government refused to recognize their land claims. In 1885, Riel returned to lead the Northwest Rebellion of 1885. Fired up by pride and a desire to form a new French Catholic nation in western Canada, a Métis army began to fight on March 26, 1885. The government sent thousands of troops to subdue the Métis, and defeated them in the Battle of Batoche on May 12, 1885. Riel voluntarily surrendered to the authorities three days later.

Riel's trial for treason (betraying his country) became a political issue between French-speaking people in Quebec, who favored him, and the English-speaking people of Ontario, the seat of the government, that opposed him. Historians say Riel could have pleaded insanity and probably have gone free. He had spent some time in a mental institution, believed he was on a mission from God, and was known to behave and speak oddly at times. But Riel refused to plead, saying: "What belongs to us ought to be ours." He was found guilty of treason and hanged on November 16, 1885. The hanging caused something of a sensation worldwide. A Philadelphia newspaper predicted: "The ghost of Louis Riel will haunt Canadian statesmen for many a day." (More than a century later, in 1992, the Canadian House of Commons approved a motion recognizing Louis Riel's "unique and historic role as a founder of Manitoba".)

The scrip program

The constant battling over the land along the Red River finally forced the Canadian government to step in. In 1885 a commission was appointed to oversee land distribution to the Métis. This was to be accomplished through a system known as the scrip program. A scrip was a government certificate that could be exchanged for money or land. Dishonest men cheated some Métis people out of their land. Some who did purchase land with scrip found the land was far from their existing community, no good for farming but too small to hunt game. Some Métis took money instead of scrip. While some spent it and became instantly poverty-stricken and landless, others saw the money as a golden opportunity to move to the United States, Saskatchewan, and Alberta to start new lives.

The scrip program caused long-term problems between the Métis and other Native groups in Canada. While the Métis received only land or money, full-blooded Natives were offered treaties that granted land and brought them under the protection of the government. They were able to remain united and receive benefits such as schooling and health care. The scrip program proved nearly fatal to Métis society, and the mistrust created between people who got scrip and people who got treaty settlements still exists today.

Modern times

Ever since the scrip program, Métis history has been marked by bleakness and filled with tales of land grabs and a complete disregard by the government for their unique society. In the 1930s several Métis leaders emerged, and the Métis Association of Alberta was formed. Political pressure on the Alberta government led to the passage of the Métis Betterment Act in 1938, which set aside lands for Métis settlements. However, restoration of land has been slow in coming, and the only Canadian lands held in common by Métis people today are eight settlements in Alberta.

In the 1960s, when the rights of minorities became a worldwide issue, the Métis people began to forcibly reassert the claims made by Métis leader Louis Riel in the 1880s and continue to do so. In an effort to rekindle cultural pride, the Métis uphold Riel as a hero. To them, Riel is a symbol of the independent minds of western peoples who seek control over their own communities.

RELIGION

The first Catholic missionaries arrived in Métis lands in 1818 and were quickly followed by Anglicans and Presbyterians. Catholic missionaries enjoyed success among French speakers, while the Anglicans were more successful among English-speaking Métis. The Métis had part of their origins in France, Scotland, and other European countries, and the European Christian religions were in many cases brought to the Americas by the original trappers and traders. The large population of French trappers brought Catholicism to many Métis settlements in the group's early days. As the Europeans married Native women, the Christian religions gained some Native elements. Organized religion served as a source of support and unity for the Métis and strengthened their sense of community..

LANGUAGE

Language has been a dividing factor throughout the history of the Métis. Some Métis speak Cree, others Assiniboin, and still others Ojibway or any of several other languages, blended with French to create new local languages. The languages spoken by the Métis are a combination of Native tongues and French *patois,* with occasional Scotch and Gaelic expressions thrown in.

Because of the unusual nature of the languages, the Cree of the area created a new name for the Métis—*O-tee-paym-soo-wuk*—"their-own-boss." Métis scholar Marcel Giraud wrote in his 1945 book *The Métis in the Canadian West* that "the language . . . normally alternated between the Indian dialects [varieties] habitually used in the families, and the French of Quebec, modified by expressions from the Indian tongues . . . and modulated by singsong intonations that recalled the accents of the Natives and even today remain very characteristic." Currently, Métis language classes are offered and books and dictionaries on the different dialects are available.

GOVERNMENT

From 1670 to 1857, the Hudson's Bay Company had complete authority over western and northern Canada, and its only interest was in trading furs and making money. Nearly all Métis people were employees of the Hudson's Bay Company, which appointed a governor and a governing council to oversee the Red River settlement (population 10,000 in 1867). Although this was not a democratic way of doing things, the Red River community generally supported it. An exception to this style of government were buffalo hunters, who had leaders like Gabriel Dumont (see "Notable People").

In 1868 the territory was handed over to the Canadian government. The Métis worried that their entire way of life might soon vanish under the influence of an indifferent, faraway, English-speaking governing body. This situation led to their organization of a resistance movement under Louis Riel. For one year Riel oversaw the only legal government the Métis Nation has ever had.

The Métis continue to have no legal rights as a nation and no legal form of self-government. In the 1960s, the Métis began to organize themselves into groups such as the Manitoba Métis Federation, the Métis Association of Saskatchewan, and the Canadian Métis Society. But it still proved difficult for the Métis to have their issues heard by the Canadian government. Many Métis organizations allied themselves with the broader Indian organization known as the Native Council, which speaks to the government on behalf of the Métis and other Indian groups.

Dissatisfied with efforts of the Native Council on their behalf, in 1983 the Métis formed an organization that would address their claims on their terms. The Métis National Council petitions the government for land claims under the Manitoba Act of 1870, for inclusion of Métis texts and courses in Canadian schools, and for self-government. In 1985, the Canadian government set aside all discussion on Métis claims, deciding that a definition of Métis must be agreed upon first. Who is a Métis? After four centuries, that question is still open to debate, and unfortunately, this hinders their unification and attempts to negotiate with the government as a sovereign people.

ECONOMY

The Métis began as suppliers or wage earners for the Hudson's Bay Company. Suppliers hunted buffalo, which provided food, shelter, and clothing for the Métis people and was also used to make pemmican for sale to the company. Historians say that without the dependable supply of meat for the pemmican provided by the Métis, there would have been no food to keep the trappers going in winter and the fur trade would have failed. The Métis conducted communal buffalo hunts. Large parties would set out on the hunt in their two-wheeled Red River carts pulled by horse or oxen.

Wage earners worked as fur trappers, in supervisory positions at the trading posts, as pilots and crew of the boats that carried furs up and down the Canadian waterways, as interpreters, and guides.

When the Hudson's Bay Company left in 1868, Europeans attempted to convert the Métis at Red River Settlement to farming, but it did not suit the nomadic lifestyle of many. The work was not as reliable as the buffalo hunt. Soon the buffalo disappeared, so some people turned to farming. Others continued to trap, but that industry declined after World War II (1939–45).

Living conditions for the Métis after the buffalo were gone were miserable. In an effort to escape poverty and discrimination, many enlisted in the armed forces during World War I (1914–18), World War II (1939–45), and the Korean War (1950–53).

The great central plains area of Canada, where many Métis live, is a vast place of farmlands and ranches and a widely scattered population. Since the 1950s, Métis families have tended to settle in the prairie towns that began to spring up, places where jobs in construction and the low-paying service industries are available. Today many depend on such wage labor and government welfare payments to survive. However, there are still people who live in isolated areas and maintain a version of the hunting-gathering lifestyle.

DAILY LIFE

Families

Métis families usually lived in nuclear families, with a mother, father, and children forming a household. Many families spent their days on the move, especially during the great buffalo hunt. Because of this, a married couple usually did not live near other family members.

Education

When the missionaries settled among the Métis in the early 1800s, many people had their first chance at a formal education. Mission schools for both boys and girls emphasized religious instruction and taught them European culture and ideas. For example, young Métis girls learned to bead and embroider in the European style, causing an evolution of Métis clothing and decorative style that still exists. By the mid-1800s, the Red River settlement where many Métis lived was a sophisticated and wealthy community. Some parents sent their boys off to be educated in Montreal, but an advanced education for girls was not considered important by the Métis or any society of the time.

Today, children attend public schools in the communities that have grown up since the 1950s.

Buildings

The Métis often built homesteads on long strips of land, preferably near a water source. The breadth of their land was measured by sight, with a plot "extending back from the river as far as one might distinguish a horse from a man . . . this was taken to be about four miles," explained Fraser Symington in *The Canadian Indian*. Their homes were simple log structures over which a buffalo hide was stretched taut; this covering offered protection from the elements while allowing sunlight to stream through. Descriptions of typical Métis homes illustrate their preference for simplicity, with furnishings often serving more than one use. The lack of furniture also made it easier to host large gatherings, an important advantage as Métis homes were the usual setting for fiddling and dancing parties.

Large groups of buffalo hunters established temporary winter encampments so that families could more easily follow the roaming beasts. These people were known as *hiverants* and lived in houses similar to those described above but simpler. As settlers began streaming into their lands in the nineteenth century, some Métis chose to live permanently at their winter homes and those structures became more sophisticated. By this time, Catholicism had become firmly rooted in Métis society and a large structure was often erected to house the local church and priest.

Transportation

The supply and demand of pemmican in the Western Canadian fur trade was so crucial that the Métis created a new vehicle to transport large loads more easily. The ox-driven Red River carts enabled the Métis to travel thousands of miles over land and through marsh; they floated on logs across rivers and were used as sleighs in the winter. Most important, they were able to carry tons of pemmican to the trading posts. As a matter of family pride, the Red River carts were lavishly decorated.

Food

Twice a year, once in the spring and again on a smaller scale in the winter, entire Métis communities would set off to hunt buffalo. The great buffalo hunt was a cornerstone of Métis existence.

When the men came back from a successful hunt, the Métis women would start preparing the pemmican. This process began with skinning and cutting the meat into thin strips, which were then hung out to dry. Once it was dried, the women pounded the meat, mixed it with berries and fat, and stored it in a huge sack made of buffalo hide. In this way, the Métis produced a highly nutritional, nonperishable food that was edible for years.

Three Métis trappers.

Today, many Métis meals include fish and game they have caught themselves, just as they have always done.

Clothing and adornment

The Métis are famous for their embroidery and beading skills, so much so that the Sioux and Cree called them the flower beadwork people. They created elaborate decorations for their homes, Red River carts, moccasins, and leggings. Young girls learned European decorative styles in the mission schools, resulting in fashions that combined European tailoring with Native fringe and decoration. The Métis also liked European hats. While women favored a scarf or shawl draped about the head, men wore top hats adorned with ribbons, fur caps made from a variety of pelts, broad-brimmed felt hats or a type of tam (a round, flat hat). The most distinctive accessory was a sash called a l'Assomption, which was borrowed from the French voyageurs of the sixteenth century. Even today, some Métis don this sash to display pride in their heritage.

Healing practices

Métis healing practices used elements of both European and Native traditions. This made for a generally healthier race than either the purely Native or European peoples in western Canada at the time. Still, they suffered diseases along with the rest of the population. Despite vaccination efforts on the part of the Hudson's Bay Company, tuberculosis, measles, smallpox, and influenza had a terrible effect on the Métis in the nineteenth century.

CUSTOMS

Courtship, love, and marriage

In the early days, marriages were arranged by the family, and a person was usually wed to someone outside the community. Married life could be very lonely for wives, who were often left behind when their mates were off for long periods working. Couples maintained a far-flung social network, though, connected by letter writing, message and gift exchanges, and gossip.

The Métis tended to be a romantic people, believing in passionate love and sometimes engaging in stormy, passionate affairs that could lead to violence, abandonment of a spouse, or other sorts of trouble.

Celebrating the great buffalo hunt

The majority of Métis customs were related to the great buffalo hunt, though they celebrated in a European rather than Native style. Their social gatherings tended to be casual and spontaneous, instead of formal. The Métis were famous for their parties; upon returning from the spring hunt, they would host a homecoming gala consisting of a feast and dancing. They danced a unique step called a Red River jig. This was always to the accompaniment of a fiddle, another custom adopted from their European ancestors.

Along with eating and dancing, the Métis enjoyed card playing, drinking, and smoking. In fact, tobacco smoking was so popular among the Métis that when they canoed long distances, they would measure the journey by the number of pipes that were smoked along the way. Today the descendants of many of these Métis travelers are trappers in the northern regions of Canada, and they still measure their traplines in "pipes."

The boatman culture

Métis rivermen, while carrying furs up and down Canadian waterways, developed a culture of their own with singing as its core. They composed work songs, drinking songs, and love songs. When a fleet of boats approached a settlement, the boatmen put on their most festive clothing—including the Assomption sash, colorful leggings, and feather-trimmed hats.

Sundays and feast days

Reflecting the influence of the Catholic church on Métis society, the Métis were strict observers of the Sabbath (the holy day). While worship did occur, most Sundays were spent socializing, gambling, and dancing. The Métis also observed French religious holidays, such as St. Jean Baptiste Day on June 24, featuring organized sporting events and a feast. This observance is still maintained today, although it is primarily a day dedicated to celebrating French-Canadian pride.

CURRENT TRIBAL ISSUES

Because they have roots in two continents and because the exact mix of nationalities or ethnicities that makes up a Métis has never been agreed upon, the Métis have always had a difficult time getting recognition as a Native group in Canada. They found some success in this in 1982, when the Constitution Act divided Canada's Native peoples into three groups: the Indian, the Inuit, and the Métis, with rights accorded to all three groups. But the government does not treat the Métis as it does other aboriginal (native) peoples. The Métis continue to be plagued by issues of group identity. The question is, Who is a Métis? Would, in fact, anyone with mixed blood qualify as Métis, or do only the descendants of the particular groups of people who formed the distinct Métis culture in the last century qualify?

The Métis' uncertain status has led to problems with the government over land use and development. For example, government-sponsored water projects have resulted in the flooding and destruction of adjacent Métis trapping territories. The Métis complain that they are not consulted about such projects, nor are they compensated for their losses. These problems have led to arrests and mayhem. In 1996, the Labrador Métis staged a peaceful demonstration to protest the government issuing a sports fishing lodge license on the sacred Eagle River; they claimed the river and its salmon would be damaged by such activities. Forty-seven Métis were arrested in the demonstration. One Labrador Métis stated: "My family can't even fish for some food for the table [because of government regulations] while foreigners and rich political types fly in to the Eagle River for their leisurely weekend fly fishing."

NOTABLE PEOPLE

Gabriel Dumont (c. 1837–1906) was a Métis buffalo hunter and military leader, the son of a Frenchman and a woman of the Sarcee tribe. He fired his first shot in a battle against the Sioux when he was twelve, and by the time he was twenty-five, he was elected chief of the buffalo hunt, in charge of about 300 Métis followers. Buffalo hunts were highly organized affairs and required firm, intelligent leadership. Dumont excelled at the task. It was Dumont who traveled to Montana to ask Louis Riel to head the Northwest Rebellion of 1885, and Dumont served as Riel's second-in-command. He survived the battle, fled to Montana, and later traveled with William "Buffalo Bill" Cody's Wild West Show, billed as the "Hero of the Halfbreed Rebellion."

Tantoo Cardinal (1950–) is an actress who has appeared in plays, television programs, and films, including the American movies *Dances with Wolves* and *Legends of the Fall* and the Canadian picture *Black Robe*. She was born in Anzac, Alberta, to a Cree mother and a white father. Her feelings of responsibility to the Indian world, coupled with her realization that through acting she could best reach people, induced Cardinal to become a professional actress. Cardinal was awarded the Eagle Spirit Award in 1990.

FURTHER READING

Brown, Brian M., "Riel, Dumont, and the 1885 Rebellion." Account of the Métis side of the 1885 Rebellion. 1997. [Online] http://www.tcel.com/ ~brownb/

Eckert, Allan W. *Return to Hawk's Hill* (fiction) Boston: Little, Brown, 1998. Sequel to *Incident at Hawk's Hill* (Little, Brown, 1971).

Labrador Métis Nation Home page: [Online] http://www.labmetis.org

Great Plains

Great Plains

The stereotyped image of North America's Native population as warriors on horseback who hunt buffalo and live in tepees is just one view of one Native American culture—the classic Great Plains culture. This classic culture began emerging around 1700 C.E. and lasted for nearly two hundred years. It was not wholly native to the Plains, but developed around the interactions between the Plains environment and the different groups who lived there. Before the arrival of Europeans, the peoples of the Great Plains were a mixture of semi-sedentary horticulturists (farmers who stayed in one place for enough of the year to be able to plant and harvest the food they grew) and nomadic hunters (people who moved from place to place seeking animals to hunt). To these peoples, Europeans introduced horses, guns, diseases, and territorial pressures. These changed the ecology, tribal relationships, cultures, and populations of the Great Plains.

The Great Plains culture stretched from Alberta and Saskatchewan in Canada to Central Texas, and from east of the Rocky Mountains to west of the Mississippi, corresponding to the grasslands ranged by the buffalo before their wholesale destruction at the end of the nineteenth century. The Great Plains are characterized by relatively low precipitation. There was enough moisture to enable prehistoric farming activity around the Missouri and its tributaries. To the west, though, where annual rainfall levels generally fall below 20 inches, a nomadic hunting lifestyle prevailed.

Some features of life on the Great Plains united the tribes culturally, but beneath the similarities that arose from adapting to similar conditions, the tribes displayed great differences. Although the tribes shared buffalo hunting, the construction of tepees, and other elements of material culture, they demonstrated a diversity of languages, regional, and cultural backgrounds. Neither was the Great Plains culture unchanging: nomadic tribes were constantly moving, adapting to their new environment, and absorbing new cultural influences.

Prehistoric occupation of the Great Plains

The Great Plains have been inhabited for thousands of years, although there is disagreement among archaeologists (people who

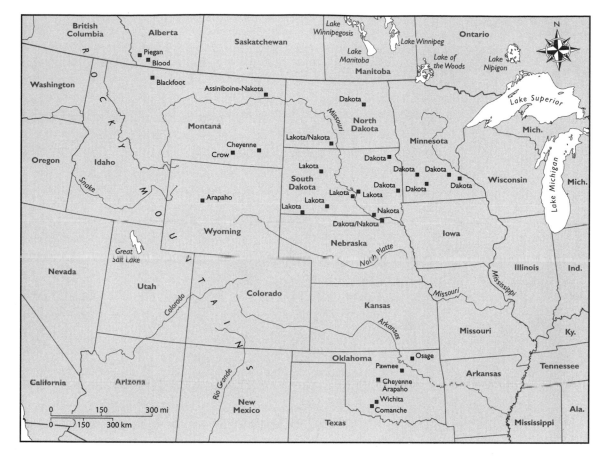

A map of some contemporary Native American communities in the Great Plains region.

study the things left behind by past civilizations) with regard to how many people lived there and for how long. Nineteenth century scientists and historians argued that the Great Plains had no human habitation before the introduction of horses, viewing the region as a vast, empty wilderness. This opinion was dispelled in the twentieth century. Archaeological evidence was found at Head-Smashed-In, Alberta, of buffalo hunting dating back 5,500 years. Still, researchers disagree on how many people lived in the Great Plains, and for what lengths of time, particularly in the years preceding European contact. Frances Haines in *The Plains Indians*, asserted that the Plains population never exceeded 10,000 and that the Plains were virtually empty for some period before 1200 because of drought conditions. However, Karl Schlesier in *Plains Indians*, A.D. *500–1500*, suggested a "reasonable" population estimate of "at least two million" for the early sixteenth century for the Great Plains and adjacent areas, implying a significantly higher population on the Plains than earlier researchers have estimated.

By the seventeenth century, six language families (a group of related languages that are all thought to have arisen from the same base language) were represented on the Great Plains: Siouan, Caddoan, Algonquian, Uto-Aztecan, Athabascan, and Kiowa Tanoan, in addition to the isolated language of the Tonkawa. Although historically the Siouan tribes (see entries on Dakota, Lakota, and Nakota) were a powerful force on the Great Plains, many Siouan speakers were living in the woodlands of Minnesota and Wisconsin at the time of European contact. For example, the Lakota and Nakota moved into the Great Plains in the eighteenth century. Other peoples were present on the Great Plains for hundreds, if not thousands, of years before European contact. The Siouan-speaking Mandan and Hidatsa inhabited the Missouri River region as early as 900 C.E. Archaeological evidence indicates that some Caddoan speakers may have occupied the Great Plains for several thousand years. Most researchers agree that the Kiowa are the descendants of ancient inhabitants of the Northern Plains.

General cultural features

The people of the Plains developed two types of lifestyles based on subsistence patterns: semi-sedentary horticulture and nomadic hunting. These two types of subsistence were interdependent; farmers acquired goods from hunters and hunters from farmers through trade. Around 1700 the nomadic tribes included the Arapaho, Assiniboin, Blackfoot, Blood, Cheyenne, Comanche, Crow, Gros Ventre, Kiowa, Kiowa Apache, Piegan, Sarsi, and Tonkawa. The semi-sedentary tribes included the Arikara, Dakota, Hidatsa, Iowa, Kansa, Lakota, Mandan, Missouri, Nakota, Omaha, Osage, Oto, Pawnee, Ponca, Quapaw, Tawakoni, Waco, and Wichita. However, some tribes do not fit easily in one category. For example, some Siouan peoples, such as the Dakota, originated as semi-sedentary horticulturists in Minnesota, gradually evolving into more nomadic hunters as they migrated westwards.

BUFFALO Despite the diverse cultural and linguistic origins of Plains tribes, the buffalo were fundamental to the development of the classic Great Plains culture. The annual migrations of the buffalo were the most important element in the lives of the nomadic hunters and determined their seasonal activities. Nomadic hunters had roamed the Plains for thousands of years. Before the Europeans brought horses, a pedestrian (on foot) buffalo culture existed. The communal spring and fall hunts brought in most of their subsistence needs in terms of food, clothing, and shelter. The tribe remained together during the summer months, roaming with the herds and observing its most important ceremonies. Historically, the buffalo hunting lifestyle brought a greater level of material conformity to these people.

The semi-sedentary Plains peoples, some of whom were direct ancestors of historic Plains peoples, began moving onto the Plains as early as 900 C.E., where the land was more fertile and precipitation higher. They lived in permanent villages near water courses, dwelling in earth, bark, and grass covered homes. They cultivated maize, beans, squash, and other crops. The buffalo were also important to their subsistence economies, although they were less dependent on the animal than wholly nomadic groups. For example, the Pawnee left their villages in mid-June for the summer hunt and returned in September to harvest their crops. Once their crops were stored around the end of October, they departed until early April to hunt, returning to sow their new crops. Following the buffalo on their long hunting quests, these peoples lived in skin tepees, akin to the nomadic hunters. Sedentary for part of the year, these groups were able to produce goods absent among the nomadic societies, such as pottery. Village life also enabled them to develop elaborate religious rituals.

WARFARE ON THE PLAINS Warfare among tribes influenced the region since pre-history. Societies rewarded brave, successful warriors with prestige, respect, and wealth. Many tribes had separate war and peace leaders, and very often the war chief held sway over his peacetime counterpart. In many societies, men could only marry after proving themselves in conflict. Young men acquired glory by achieving such feats as a "counting coup," which meant touching a live enemy during battle. Tribes of the Great Plains practiced scalping as well, although the prestige gained by such an act varied greatly from tribe to tribe. Supernatural forces guided war efforts. Not only were war leaders assumed to have divine guidance in deciding whether or not to attack, but a successful war leader could also endow shields and other elements of war with good war medicine.

These beliefs about warfare overlap with other religious beliefs. The tribes were pantheistic, believing in spirits existing in natural features and events. One of the most important religious ceremonies to develop among the peoples of the Great Plains was the Sun Dance. The ceremony served as an annual initiation rite for young men. The ceremony also reaffirmed relationships and signaled the renewal of the tribe and its physical environment.

At the heart of the Great Plains religion lay sacred medicine bundles. Collected in these bundles were sacred items such as medicine pipes. The people believed the items in the bundle held the power to improve hunting and other activities. Some would even pay the equivalent of substantial sums of money to view the contents of the bundles.

Post-European contact

The vast size of the Great Plains meant that in some regions tribes made contact with Europeans much sooner than in others. In the Southern Plains, Francisco Vàsquez de Coronado's expedition of 1540 probably interacted with the Wichita. Although the Europeans established a physical presence in the South earlier than in the North, some historians speculate that the diseases that devastated the South made their way to the North long before any European adventurers had arrived there. Devastation to Great Plains Indian society from these diseases stands out as one of the most important features of this early interaction. The 1780 to 1781 smallpox epidemic destroyed half of the Great Plains population.

The first record of European contact in the northern region of the Great Plains comes from Henry Kelsey, a fur trader and explorer who documented his contact with the Assiniboin and Gros Ventre he encountered between 1690 and 1691. The fur trade profoundly affected the destinies of tribes on the Great Plains. The new commerce surrounding fur enabled the flow of guns, alcohol, and other European-style commodities into the region.

Warfare with guns

The presence of guns produced dramatic swings in power among the region's peoples. For example, the Shoshone stood as one of the most powerful tribes on the Northern Plains around 1700; however, when their rivals, the Blackfoot, Cree, and Assiniboin acquired guns from traders, the newly empowered groups drove the Shoshone from the Plains by the end of the eighteenth century. Among the European powers, it was the Spanish who traded with the Shoshone, and they refused to trade for weapons. As a result, the Shoshone found themselves at an insurmountable disadvantage.

Intertribal warfare had been part of life on the Plains long before guns were introduced by Europeans. Undeniably, though, interaction with Europeans changed the nature of warfare. Of course, the appearance of guns increased the damage that one warrior could do, but the introduction of the horse had at least an equally profound effect on the way the tribes fought. Success in battle had always brought glory, but with horses, hunting became easier. With the extra time thus allowed, tribes turned their attentions to political struggles more than previously. Warriors could move across distances more easily and more quickly than ever, thus putting more foes within reach. Also, whereas before horses most tribes fought in pitched battles, after the advent of the horse, raiding parties and attacks on population centers became easier and more common.

European and American settlement also intensified warfare by simply displacing Native peoples. As the white settlers moved west, tribes retreated still further west onto territory used by other tribes. Formal acts of law speeded up this movement occasionally. For example, the 1830 Indian Removal Act generated increased hostility as more tribes vied for an ever decreasing area of land. Under this act the U.S. government relocated the "Five Civilized Tribes" of the Southeast (the Choctaw, Chickasaw, Cherokee, Creek, and Seminole) to the Great Plains. These five tribes left their Native lands on a government-enforced march to the West called the "Trail of Tears," often to find themselves unwelcome on land that Plains Indians had long used for survival.

Horses on the Plains

The introduction of the horse on the Great Plains was revolutionary. Horses began spreading through the peoples of the Great Plains in the middle of the seventeenth century, until all tribes had access to horses by 1800. Besides its influence on warfare, the horse brought other advantages of mobility to the Great Plains tribes. Buffalo hunting became much easier. Not only could the Great Plains hunters kill more buffalo in less time, but they suddenly could carry their prey over great distances. This, in turn, encouraged the commercial use of buffalo. Horses could carry heavier gear than pedestrians or dogs, so the Great Plains peoples built taller moveable tepees. With horses, Great Plains tribes could afford to carry the sick or wounded, whereas before immobilized members of the tribe often had to be left behind. Horses shifted the balance of power somewhat toward the nomadic tribes. The new speeds with which the tribes moved made it nearly impossible to track or catch nomadic tribes. The presence of the horse prompted all of these changes, and the fundamental dynamics of the culture changed forever.

White settlers on the Plains

European and American contact had many incidental effects, but in many cases, direct conflict with whites had an impact just as powerful. The opening of the Oregon Trail in the 1840s brought many whites through the Great Plains, increasing friction with Native Americans. The situation worsened when gold was discovered in California in 1849. As white travelers moved through the area, conflict ensued. In some cases, whites simply came between warring tribes, but in other cases, whites and Natives attacked one another deliberately. The U.S. government sought to ease the situation and enable white travelers to use the Oregon Trail through the Great Council of Fort Laramie in 1851. Although the council gathered members of many tribes, the government's intention had little to do with Native rights and aimed mainly to make travel safe for white settlers. The agreement sought to demarcate specific areas for Native groups so that white settlers could rely on certain areas being free of conflict or hostile parties.

Flaws in the treaty soon began to show as some on both sides violated its terms. Through a series of agreements at Fort Laramie the government agreed to give the Sioux permanent rights to their Dakota lands including the Black Hills, but non-Natives began encroaching on this territory as early as the 1860s. The Sioux, who had been driven from their lands in Minnesota, felt threatened and took a stance against the intruders. When prospectors discovered gold in the Black Hills, the government tried to renegotiate the Sioux possession of the Black Hills, but the Sioux would not negotiate. This tension coincided with the end of the American Civil War, which led to a dramatic increase in people emigrating west. The U.S. government began to take a more direct hand in local politics.

Battling U.S. military and commercial forces

The Sioux were at that time gaining the upper hand on their tribal rivals. In some cases, the Sioux formed alliances; along with the Cheyenne and the Arapaho, they controlled the Northern Plains by 1870. In response to Sioux aggression some groups, such as the Mandan and Hidatsa, sought alliances with whites. A general warfare prevailed in this period. The hostilities reached a peak in the Battle of Little Bighorn on June 25, 1876, where the Sioux and the Cheyenne defeated Lieutenant Colonel George Custer and the U.S. cavalry. This victory stiffened the American government's resolve in battling the tribe. By 1877 the Sioux had lost many military encounters with the U.S. forces and many of the tribes had moved to reservations.

By the 1870s commercial white hunters were slaughtering three million buffalo a year, driving them to near extinction. The completion of the transcontinental railroads divided the buffalo's grazing lands and disrupted their migratory habits. As the white population expanded into the land, the buffalo populations diminished further. Without the buffalo, many Great Plains tribes faced terrible poverty and were forced to turn to the U.S. government.

The confinement of the Great Plains peoples on reservations and the interaction of the U.S. government has been very destructive to their indigenous (native) culture. Although many tribes currently face enormous issues, such as unemployment, the second half of the twentieth century has seen a revival of Native American pride and the renewal of ancient cultural traditions.

Amanda Beresford McCarthy

FURTHER READING

Haines, Francis. *The Plains Indians: Their Origins, Migrations, and Cultural Development.* New York, NY: Thomas Y. Crowell Company, 1976.

Lowie, Robert H. *Indians of the Plains.* Garden City, NY: Natural History Press, 1963.

Mails, Thomas E. *Peoples of the Plains.* Tulsa, OK: Council Oak Books, 1997.

Marriott, Alice, and Carol K. Rachlin. *Plains Indian Mythology.* New York, NY: Thomas Y. Crowell, 1975.

McGinnis, Anthony. *Counting Coup and Cutting Horses: Intertribal Warfare on the Northern Plains 1738–1889.* Evergreen, CO: Cordillera Press, 1990.

Arapaho

Name

The Arapaho (pronounced *uh-RAP-uh-ho*) called themselves *Inuna-ina* or *Hinono'eno*, which might mean "our people," "sky people," or "roaming people." The name Arapaho may have been derived from the Pawnee word *tirapihu,* meaning "trader"; the Kiowa name for the tribe, *Ahyato*; or the Crow name for the tribe, *Alappaho*.

Location

In the 1700s, the Northern Arapaho occupied the plains of southern Wyoming and northern Colorado. The Southern Arapaho occupied the plains of west-central Oklahoma and southern Kansas. Today, the Northern Arapaho share the Wind River Reservation in Wyoming with the Shoshone. The Southern Arapaho live on the Cheyenne-Arapaho Reservation in western Oklahoma.

Population

The Arapaho population was approximately 3,000 in pre-reservation days. By 1861 the numbers had fallen to 750 (Northern) and 1,500 (Southern). In a census (count of the population) done in 1990 by the U.S. Bureau of the Census, 5,585 people identified themselves as Arapaho; 1,319 people said they were Northern Arapaho; and 14 people said they were Southern Arapaho.

Language family

Algonquian.

Origins and group affiliations

The Arapaho probably originated in the Great Lakes region—perhaps in Minnesota or Canada. One group of Arapaho were called Gros Ventre (pronounced *grow VAHNT*) by the French. The reason for the name, which means "Big Bellies," is unknown, but it has stuck. The Gros Ventre settled on Fort Belknap Reservation in northern Montana in 1878; they are not covered in this profile.

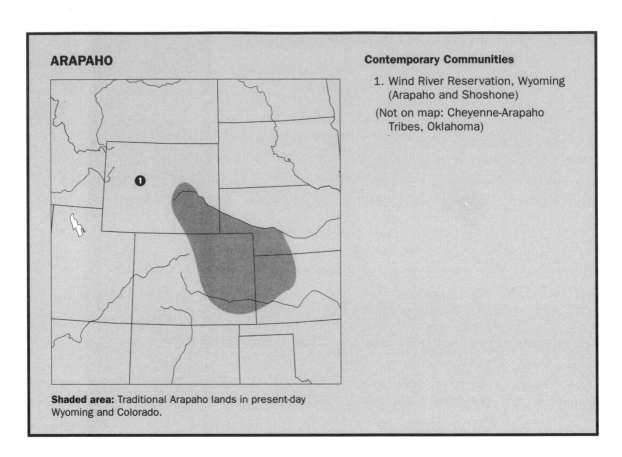

ARAPAHO

Contemporary Communities

1. Wind River Reservation, Wyoming
   (Arapaho and Shoshone)

   (Not on map: Cheyenne-Arapaho
   Tribes, Oklahoma)

Shaded area: Traditional Arapaho lands in present-day Wyoming and Colorado.

The Arapaho were a spiritual, peace-loving people who moved to the Great Plains in the mid-1600s. They gave up their farming lifestyle and roamed the plains, hunting buffalo on horseback. When gold seekers and settlers overran the West, the Arapaho offered them safe passage, then lost most of their lands—and their livelihood—to them. In the 1800s, after splitting into two groups to search for increasingly elusive herds of buffalo, the Arapaho were permanently divided and moved onto reservations.

HISTORY

From Great Lakes to Great Plains

Around the year 1000 B.C.E., most Algonquian speakers lived in the Great Lakes region. The Arapaho migrated in a southwesterly direction to the Great Plains and transformed themselves from farmers to wandering hunters.

By the 1700s the Arapaho had adopted a typical Great Plains lifestyle, living in hide-covered tepees and following the migrations of the great buffalo herds. Spanish explorers introduced horses to the New World, and the Arapaho acquired their own in the 1730s. They quickly became skilled horsemen and could hunt far more efficiently than they ever did on foot.

Relations with neighbors

The Arapaho established trading relationships with neighboring tribes who relied on farming. They gave surplus meat and hides to the Hidatsa and Mandan peoples in exchange for beans, corn, and squash. At the same time, they conducted raids and made war against other tribes, often for the purpose of accumulating more horses.

In the mid-1800s, a major wave of Americans streamed into Arapaho territory. Some were planning to stay; others were on their way to find gold in California. The vast wagon trains disrupted the migrations of the buffalo herds, sending the buffalo in different directions and making them harder to find. Plains tribes were forced into competition for game and land. The Arapaho began trading with whites in order to obtain guns, ammunition, and knives to fight their enemies. As hunting by non-Natives made game even more scarce, the tribe began to depend on whites for food and clothing. Sometimes they acquired these items in payment for escorting wagon trains through the territories of neighboring tribes who were hostile to the invading whites.

Division in the tribe

Around 1835, under increasing pressure from non-Native settlers, the tribe separated. The Northern Arapaho settled at the edge of the Rocky Mountains in present-day Wyoming. The Southern Arapaho settled along the Arkansas River in present-day Colorado. They remained in close contact with one another, a pattern that continues to this day.

Eventually, the Arapaho made peace with several of their former enemies, including the Dakota, Lakota, Nakota, and Cheyenne (see entries). The Arapaho were one of eleven tribes to sign the Fort Laramie Treaty of 1851, which set aside large tracts of land for the

IMPORTANT DATES

1600s to mid-1700s: The Arapaho migrate from the Great Lakes region onto the Great Plains and adopt a wandering, hunting lifestyle.

1835: The Arapaho divide into two groups: the Northern Arapaho settle near the North Platte River in Wyoming; the Southern Arapaho settle near the Arkansas River in Colorado.

1864: At least 130 Southern Arapaho and Cheyenne—many of them women and children—are killed by U.S. Army troops during the Sand Creek Massacre.

1867: The Southern Arapaho are placed on a reservation in Oklahoma, which they share with the Cheyenne.

1878: The Northern Arapaho move onto the Wind River Reservation in Wyoming, which they share with the Shoshon

Little Raven, head chief of the Southern Arapaho, 1868–1874.

Indians. Before long, however, white settlers wanted those tracts of land. Though the Arapaho were generally more peaceful than their neighbors, they did take part in several battles over domination of the Great Plains.

Sand Creek Massacre

Continuing conflicts between Plains Indians and whites who tried to take their lands reached a climax in November 1864. Cheyenne Chief Black Kettle told the U.S. government he wanted peace, and he asked to be directed to a safe place. They sent him with his people and members of the Arapaho tribe to Sand Creek in Colorado. There the Indians lived peacefully for a few weeks. Then, early one morning they were ambushed by American troops as they lay sleeping. At least 130 people were brutally killed in the Sand Creek Massacre, including the Southern Arapaho leader Left Hand, and many women and children. In retaliation, the Southern Arapaho, led by Little Raven, joined the Cheyenne in an all-out war against the whites. It lasted for six months.

After the war

By 1867 the Southern Arapaho population had been greatly reduced by war, disease, and starvation. Tribal leaders reluctantly agreed to accept placement on a reservation. In exchange for their former lands, the Southern Arapaho agreed to share land in western Oklahoma with the Southern Cheyenne.

The Northern Arapaho resisted the pressure to settle on a reservation. Urged to share the Pine Ridge Reservation in South Dakota with the Sioux, they insisted on receiving their own lands. In 1878 they finally agreed to accept lands on the Wind River Reservation in Wyoming. They had to share the reservation with their former enemies, the Shoshone, and for a time relations were tense. Finally the two groups reached an understanding. They live together but maintain their own identities, culture, and government.

Once on reservations, the Arapaho faced a great deal of pressure to abandon their traditional lifestyle and assimilate, or become like European Americans. The Northern Arapaho have been more successful in resisting the pressure, in part because Wyoming remains the

center of Arapaho religious life. The Southern Arapaho travel to Wind River Reservation each year for powwows (festivals of singing and dancing), rituals, and dances. The most important ceremony today is called the Offerings Lodge. It is held in the summer and allows participants to express their commitment to the Arapaho community.

RELIGION

The Arapaho were an intensely religious people. All aspects of their lives had spiritual significance, and they looked for signs and wonders everywhere. They believed in a Creator who made the world and the Arapaho people. They believed that they would be granted health and happiness if they prayed and offered gifts to the Creator. Their most sacred object was the flat pipe; it represented the power of the Creator on Earth.

The main Arapaho religious ceremony was the annual Sun Dance. The ceremony involved a number of sacred rituals centering on the sacred wheel (see box) or a sacred tree with a rawhide doll tied to the top. Although Arapaho who were to join in the Sun Dance fasted and went without sleep for several days in preparation, they

The Arapaho Ghost Dance, artwork by Mary Irvin Wright, c. 1900, based on photographs by James Mooney. The Ghost Dance provided new songs and religious dancing to hasten the elimination of U.S. settlers and the return of the old Indian world.

did not include self-torture in their Sun Dance like some other Plains tribes did, which involved piercing and tearing the flesh.

Missionaries tried to convert the Arapaho to Christianity in the late 1800s. Some converted, but others embraced the Ghost Dance religion when it spread among western tribes during the 1880s. Founded by Wovoka, a Paiute, the religion predicted a new age without white men, when plentiful game and dead ancestors would return to the Earth. Today, the Northern Arapaho continue to practice the Sun Dance, and many Southern Arapaho make an annual pilgrimage to the Wind River Reservation to participate.

The Native American Church (see box in Makah entry) and the Sweat Lodge ceremony also have found followers among the Arapaho. The Native American Church combines Christian and Native beliefs and practices, and features an all-night ceremony composed of chanting, prayer, and meditation. The Sweat Lodge ceremony is a purification ritual that involves a sweat bath.

LANGUAGE

The Arapaho spoke a dialect (variety) of the Algonquian language family, unusual among tribes of the Great Plains but common among those in the Great Lakes region. Few Native speakers remain among the Arapaho. The loss of their Native language has been a major problem for the Arapaho, and in recent times the Northern Arapaho have established a language program in reservation schools to encourage its use.

GOVERNMENT

Arapaho men acquired power within their group by capturing horses in raids. If a man had many horses and also displayed qualities such as generosity and competence, he might be chosen the leader of his group. However, leaders had limited powers. Important matters had to be discussed at length by every adult man and some older women in the group before decisions were made. The most weight was given to the opinions of leaders and elders.

Today, two separate general councils, made up of members of the Arapaho and Shoshone tribes who are ages eighteen and over, hold infrequent meetings at the Wind River Reservation. Both tribes are governed by business councils; six members are elected to serve two-year terms, and they elect chairpeople.

A joint tribal government operates at the Cheyenne-Arapaho Reservation in Oklahoma. Four members from each tribe are elected to serve four-year terms.

ECONOMY

The Arapaho divided labor according to gender, but the work of men and women was considered equally important. Long ago the economy was based on farming. When they moved to the Great Plains, they depended on buffalo for food, clothing, and shelter. Since horses were needed to hunt buffalo, a man's wealth was measured in the number of horses he owned. By the mid-1800s, though, the buffalo had become nearly extinct. Weakened by diseases and food shortages, tribe members often were forced to steal livestock from settlers. When the federal government finally authorized the distribution of food to poverty-stricken Arapaho, the Indians were often cheated by agents who were in charge of providing the food.

The Arapaho gradually began to support themselves by farming, cattle ranching, and selling or leasing reservation lands to whites. Both Northern and Southern Arapaho earn income from oil and gas revenues and from small businesses including smoke shops, casinos, bingo parlors, and convenience stores. The Northern Arapaho raise prize cattle and horses. Most Southern Arapaho own little land and live in poverty.

DAILY LIFE

Buildings

The Arapaho lived in portable tepees that were quick to assemble and take apart and were owned by the women of the tribe. Each family built its own tepee, which consisted of wooden poles set into the ground and arranged into a cone shape, with a cover of fifteen to twenty buffalo hides stretched over the top. After the buffalo became extinct, tepees were made of canvas obtained from the U.S. government.

In the winter, the tribe usually scattered into the foothills of the Rocky Mountains, where they were more sheltered from the elements. There they camped in groups of twenty to eighty families. Earth was piled in mounds around the outside of their tepees for warmth. The inside had a sleeping platform and a fire fueled with buffalo dung. The walls were sometimes painted with pictures of a man's successes in war. In the summer, when the whole tribe came together to hunt on the prairies, all the tepees were arranged in a large circle.

An Arapaho camp in Kansas, 1870, with buffalo meat drying.

Food

Before it became almost extinct in the late 1800s, the buffalo was a primary food source. Men also hunted deer, elk, and small game, but they would not eat bear because they considered bears their ancestors.

Arapaho women gathered roots and berries to eat fresh or make into a soup. The most common meal was a type of stew consisting of meat and wild roots like potatoes and turnips. The Arapaho also enjoyed a tea made with wild herbs.

Clothing and adornment

Most clothing was made of deer or elk hides. Women fashioned the skins into long dresses and moccasins attached to leggings that extended to the knee. Arapaho men wore shirts, breechcloths (garments with front and back flaps that hung from the waist), leggings, and moccasins. In the winter, they added buffalo-skin robes and snowshoes consisting of strips of rawhide attached to a wooden frame. Much of the clothing was decorated with painted or embroidered designs with religious themes.

The Arapaho adorned themselves with tattoos made by pricking the skin with cactus needles and rubbing charcoal into the wound. Men usually had three small circles across their chests, while women had a small circle on their foreheads.

Healing practices

The Arapaho believed that people could become ill merely by thinking or speaking about disease and death or by failing to show proper respect to the Creator. When a person became sick, his or her relatives would open the person's medicine bundle (a pouch with objects held sacred by the owner) and pray. Sometimes they offered gifts of food, property, or even flesh to make their loved ones well again. In extreme cases, they would call upon a medicine person called a shaman (pronounced *SHAY-mun*) for help.

The Arapaho have a special healing ceremony that is performed in extreme cases. It has been held only two times in the twentieth century: during a flu epidemic in 1918 and in 1985 after a rash of suicides of young people on the reservation. Called the paint ceremony, it was described in a magazine article by Ted Delaney: "One by one, people entered the tepee where the elders sat. The ceremony involved steps of cleansing, by prayer, by smoke, then by paint on the face. . . . When people emerged from the tepee, they left the grounds, silent. Most of the 5,000 people of the Wind River Reservation took part."

Education

Arapaho children regarded all adults as their mothers and fathers, and they learned by watching and imitating adults. Respected elders were often invited to dine and tell stories of their life experiences and successes.

Toys were miniature versions of adult items and helped teach children their expected adult roles. Girls played with tiny tepees and with dolls. Dolls were not treated as babies because the Arapaho believed that even to mention a baby could cause pregnancy. Boys played war and hunting games.

After the Arapaho moved to reservations, their children were sent away to boarding schools. Some boarding schools were located on the reservations, but others were often great distances from home. Children were cut off from their parents and forbidden to use their native language. Children who had never before experienced punishment were often treated harshly.

Today, on the Wind River Reservation, the custom of elders teaching children survives. Children have little contact with people outside the reservation until they graduate from reservation schools. Arapaho children in Oklahoma mainly attend local public schools, colleges, and vocational-technical centers. The tribe operates a number of Head Start centers.

ARTS

Inspiration for the decorative arts came to the Arapaho in dreams. Highly skilled women artists painted and embroidered these

THE SUN DANCE WHEEL

A Sun Dance was primarily intended as a religious ceremony, and it brought separate Arapaho groups together for a joyous reunion each summer. Its centerpiece was the Sacred Wheel, which was displayed on an altar and included decorations representing the Sun, Earth, sky, water, and wind. The following story explains the creation of the Sacred Wheel and the meaning of its various parts. The disk in the center of the wheel represented the Sun; the band of wood encircling it was painted like a harmless snake and represented the water; the markings on four sides symbolized the Four Old Men who controlled the winds; and the beads and feathers represented the sky and rain. The exact meaning of the constellations mentioned in the story is no longer known.

At one time, water covered all the Earth. No land could be seen in any direction. It was then that a man walked across the water for four days and four nights, thinking. In his arms he carried Flat Pipe, his only companion and good counselor. The man wanted to treat his pipe well and give it a good home. For six days he fasted while he thought how to do this. Finally on the evening of the sixth day he reached a firm conclusion. "To give Flat Pipe a good home there should be land, and creatures of all kinds to inhabit it."

On the morning of the seventh day he resolved to find land. Calling in all directions, he asked the animals to help. And from the four directions came all manner of animals willing to offer their aid. It took a long time, but finally, with their help, he made the Earth a home for Flat Pipe and placed the Four Old Men in the four directions to control the winds. The Earth was also to be the place of the Sun Dance Lodge, where every year the people would gather to worship together, praying for bounty and health for the tribe.

The man saw a tiny snake and said, "Come and sit near me, Garter Snake. You will be a great comfort to the people in the future and will have an important place in the Sun Dance Lodge. You will be the Sacred Wheel." Then, looking around to the many helpers that had gathered nearby, he said, "We will need material for a wheel."

Many offered, but Long Stick, a bush with flexible limbs and dark red bark, was most suitable. He said, "For the good of all, I offer my body for the wheel. I am anxious to do good. Please accept my offer so my name will live through the ages." All murmured approval, and they made Long Stick into the ring for the Sacred Wheel.

Then the eagle spoke up, saying, "My great strength and power carry me high above the Earth. My holy body and broad wings soar on the winds of the four directions. I offer my feathers as symbols of the Four Old Men. From here on, if anyone should give you eagle feathers to honor and respect, please remember this day and my request. Help them to use my feathers well."

The man then said, "Eagle, the good and faithful one, has asked that his feathers be used to represent the Four Old Men. We will honor his desire and tie four bunches of eagle feathers to the wheel."

After he had shaped the Sacred Wheel, the man painted it in the image of Garter Snake and arranged the eagle feathers in positions of the Four Old Men—northwest, northeast, southeast, and southwest—and tied them carefully. Then on the wheel the man placed Morning Star, the Pleiades, and Lone Star. Next he placed other groups of stars, such as Chain of Stars, Seven Buffalo Bulls, the Hand, the Lance, and the Old Camp. Finally he painted on the Sacred Wheel the symbols of the Sun, the Moon, and the Milky Way. The man thanked Garter Snake, who was pleased to serve the people in this way.

SOURCE: Jean Guard Monroe and Ray A. Williamson. "The Sun Dance Wheel." *They Dance in the Sky: Native American Star Myths.* Boston: Houghton Mifflin, 1987.

visions onto beautiful containers, medicine bundles, jewelry, and personal belongings.

CUSTOMS

Childhood

The Arapaho believed that the four stages of life corresponded with the four directions of the winds. These stages were childhood, youth, adulthood, and old age; each had special rituals. Immediately after a baby was born, for example, older relatives prayed for it to be strong and healthy and marked its face with red paint. Between the ages of two and five, Arapaho children had their ears pierced in a special ritual that helped the child learn to deal with future pain and hardship. As they approached puberty, boys and girls were separated from one another and began to prepare for adult life. Boys entered special societies, while girls spent considerable time with the older women of the tribe, dressing modestly and learning women's duties.

Societies

Arapaho males progressed through eight military societies, beginning as young boys. As boys became young men, they entered the Kit Fox Lodge. After they reached a certain level of skill and bravery, they progressed into the Star society. Other societies included the Tomahawk, Spear, Crazy, and Dog lodges. "Graduation" to each society brought added prestige and new responsibilities.

The seven tribal elders known as the Water-Pouring Old Men were the most respected members of the tribe. Their duties were to direct ceremonies, take care of the sacred flat pipe, and pray for the well-being of the Arapaho people.

In the days of buffalo-hunting, Arapaho women had their own society, the Buffalo Lodge. Members performed ceremonial dances to ensure a successful hunt. They wore costumes and painted their faces white to look like buffalo. They blew on special whistles to attract buffalo.

Hunting rituals

In the buffalo hunt, Arapaho men on horseback worked together, chasing down individual animals and cutting them off from the rest of the herd. At first they used bows and arrows made of cedar and sinew; later they used guns. They butchered the buffalo with flint or bone knives and then brought it back to camp, where women smoked or dried the meat and prepared the skins to make clothing, tepee covers, or containers for water and food.

Marriage

Most Arapaho marriages were arranged by a woman's male relatives. Women had the right to refuse marriage, but few did so. The wedding day began with an exchange of gifts between the bride's and groom's families. Then the bride's family hosted a feast, and the couple was allowed to sit together for the first time. Following the marriage, both the bride and the groom avoided contact with the other's parents.

Medicine bundles

Each member of the Arapaho tribe possessed a medicine bundle containing sacred objects that represented their personal relationship with the Creator. A vision revealed to a person what should go into the medicine bundle. During times of illness or war, the person could use their medicine bundle to make a special appeal to the Creator.

CURRENT TRIBAL ISSUES

The Arapaho have been involved in a number of issues concerning land and water rights. In 1989 the tribe successfully protested against a U.S. Forest Service plan to turn a sacred site in Big Horn National Forest into a tourist attraction. Other issues facing the Arapaho in the 1990s included regaining their native language and some cultural traditions, and finding stable sources of income and employment.

NOTABLE PEOPLE

Black Spot (born c. 1824) was a daring warrior and Arapaho chief who learned American ways as a boy. Accidentally left behind when his family moved camp in 1831, he was found by a white trapper and trader, who adopted him and renamed him Friday. He was educated in St. Louis. On a trip west in 1838, Black Spot was recognized by relatives and brought back into the Arapaho tribe. Thanks to his familiarity with white culture, Black Spot acted as a negotiator and interpreter during treaty negotiations, and was part of the group that secured the Wind River Reservation for his people.

Assisting Black Spot in negotiations with white men were a number of other famous Arapaho leaders. Among them were Black Bear, who was murdered by a group of white settlers in 1871; Medicine

Man, a revered healer who died about the same time; his successor, Black Coal; and Sharp Nose, who continued efforts that allowed the Northern Arapaho to remain in Wyoming.

FURTHER READING

"Arapaho Literature." [Online] www.indians.org/welker/arapaho.htm

Delaney, Ted. "Confronting Hopelessness at Wind River Reservation," *Utne Reader,* Jan/Feb 1990, pp. 61–3. Excerpted from *Northern Lights,* October 1988.

Eskin, Leah. "Teens Take Charge. (Suicide epidemic at Wind River Reservation)." *Scholastic Update,* May 26, 1989, p. 26.

Fowler, Loretta. *The Arapaho.* New York: Chelsea House, 1989.

Greymorning, Stephen. "Arapaho." *Native America in the Twentieth Century: An Encyclopedia.* Ed. Mary B. Davis. New York: Garland Publishing, 1994.

"The Story of the Origin of the Arapaho People." Stories told by Pius Moss, an Elder of the Arapaho Tribe on the Wind River Reservation. [Online] www.wyomingcompanion.com/wcwrr.html #arapaho.

Blackfeet

Name

Blackfeet (sometimes called Blackfoot). The people used a Crow name for themselves *Siksika*, which means "blackfeet people" and refers to their moccasin soles, which were darkened either by paint or by walking on charred prairie grasses. To avoid confusion, the word "Blackfeet" will be used here as opposed to "Blackfoot" (as the Canadians often refer to them).

Location

The three tribes in the Blackfeet Confederacy, the Blackfeet proper, the Piegan (pronounced *PEE-gun*), and the Blood, occupied the northwestern part of the Plains from the northern reaches of the Saskatchewan River in Alberta, Canada, to the southernmost headwaters of the Missouri River in Montana. Today, there are Blackfeet people scattered throughout the United States. Many live in northwestern Montana on the Blackfeet Reservation and large numbers live in the states of Washington and California. The Blackfeet people of Canada live in southeastern Alberta.

Population

In the early 1800s, there were an estimated 5,200 Blackfeet. Today about 15,000 Blackfeet live on reserves in Canada, while about 10,000 live on the Blackfeet Reservation in Montana. In a census (count of the population) done in 1990 by the U.S. Bureau of the Census, 37,992 people identified themselves as Blackfeet, making the tribe the eleventh-largest in the United States.

Language family

Algonquian.

Origins and group affiliations

The Blackfeet Confederacy is an alliance of three tribes who speak the same language and practice the same culture. Their ancestors probably came to North America thousands of years ago from Asia, crossing a land bridge that no longer exists between Siberia and Alaska.

The three tribes of the Blackfeet Confederation are the Piegan, meaning "the poorly dressed ones"; the Blood, or Kainah, meaning "many chiefs"; and the Siksika, or Blackfeet proper (also known as the Northern Blackfeet).

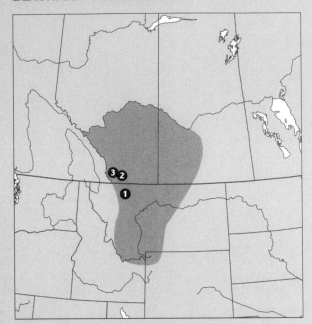

BLACKFEET CONFEDERACY

Contemporary Communities

1. Blackfeet Nation, Montana
2. Blood Nation, Alberta
3. Piegan Nation, Alberta

Shaded area: Traditional lands of the Blackfeet Confederacy in present-day Montana and Alberta, Canada.

For centuries, the Blackfeet wandered the rolling plains that rise westward to the forests of the Rocky Mountains. They hunted buffalo and gathered wild plants. As white settlers moved westward, Blackfeet life was greatly disrupted by the extinction of the buffalo and the disease epidemics the settlers carried with them. In modern times the tribe has battled poverty and assimilation (the acceptance of white ways) through efforts to develop their own businesses and pass their traditions down to succeeding generations.

HISTORY

A powerful tribe of Northern Plains

The Blackfeet migrated onto North America's Great Plains from the eastern woodlands before the coming of Europeans. Once there, the Blackfeet followed the enormous herds of buffalo, using tame dogs to carry their belongings. This period before they began using horses and firearms is known as the "Dog Days."

The Blackfeet used arrows and lances in wars with the Shoshone, Plains Cree (see entries), Flathead, and Assiniboin (pronounced *uh-SIN-uh-boin*). Most often their allies were their friendly neighbors, the Gros Ventre (pronounced *grow VAHNT*) and Sarsi. After acquiring horses and firearms around the middle of the eighteenth century, the Blackfeet became one of the most powerful tribes of the Northern Plains. By the middle of the nineteenth century, they had pushed their enemies, particularly the Shoshone, westward across the Rocky Mountains.

Impact of whites on the tribe

The first known whites to visit the region of the Blackfeet were fur trappers who came in the middle of the eighteenth century. They were exploring the West in the hope of establishing trading relationships with the Indians. Among them was British agent and fur-trapper David Thompson, who traveled into Blackfeet territory in 1787 and wrote in detail about the tribe. From this date until the disappearance of the buffalo in the early 1880s, the relationship between the trading companies and the Blackfeet became vital to the Natives' economic and social lives.

From their contact with whites at the trading post, the tribe was introduced to new technologies, such as the gun. The white diseases they encountered, which led to the smallpox epidemics of 1781, 1837, and 1869, killed off a great many of their population.

Blackfeet keep whites out of their territory

In the early 1800s explorer Meriwether Lewis (1774–1809; American explorer who headed the Lewis & Clark Expedition of 1803–06, opening territories from St. Louis, Missouri, to the Pacific Coast) encountered the Blackfeet on one of his journeys. As Lewis discovered, the people he referred to as "strong and honest" could also be very aggressive. The party of eight men he led was attacked by Blackfeet horse raiders. Lewis and his men managed to outwit their attackers and fled the area.

Shortly after 1810, the tribes in the area where the Blackfeet lived took sides in the struggle that was going on for territory in North America between the Americans and the British. The Blackfeet did

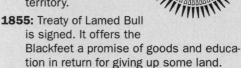

IMPORTANT DATES

1851: The Treaty of Fort Laramie sets and limits boundaries of Blackfeet territory.

1855: Treaty of Lamed Bull is signed. It offers the Blackfeet a promise of goods and education in return for giving up some land.

1870: About 200 Piegan Indians are massacred on the Marias River by U.S. soldiers led by Major Eugene M. Baker.

1883–84: Buffalo have almost disappeared from the Plains. A severe famine strikes, and one-quarter of the Piegan tribe starves.

1934: Indian Recognition Act is passed and the modern economic and political development of the Blackfeet begins.

everything possible to keep any whites out of their territory. But during the 1820s there was a new push by white trappers who wanted the Blackfeet area for themselves. The Blackfeet responded by traveling quickly to wherever whites were and trying to stop their progress. In 1823 alone, they killed more than 25 trappers and stole the guns and supplies of countless more. By the end of the 1830s, however, overtrapping and the loss of the beaver supply that resulted caused most white trappers to pull out of Blackfeet lands. Then in the 1840s American settlers on their way West began to travel in substantial numbers through the southern part of the Blackfeet territory. In the mid-nineteenth century, with the discovery of gold nearby, huge numbers of gold seekers flooded the whole Blackfeet region.

Treaties limit the Blackfeet

Over the years, the Blackfeet were particularly hostile to the Americans they encountered, in part due to problems and misunderstandings from earlier days. Settlers moving west heard about the reputation of the Blackfeet as fierce warriors and were terrified of them. The settlers applied to the U.S. government for protection. Settlers were so determined to obtain Blackfeet land that the federal government decided to make treaties with the tribe. In time, the tribe lost much of its territory to the United States in these treaties.

In 1851 the boundaries of the Blackfeet territory in the United States were set and limited by the Treaty of Fort Laramie, even though no Blackfeet were present at the negotiations. In 1855, the Blackfeet signed their first treaty, known as the Treaty of Lamed Bull for the powerful Piegan chief who signed it. This treaty stated that the U.S. government would pay the tribe $20,000 annually in goods and spend $15,000 each year toward educating and converting the Blackfeet to Christianity. In return, the Blackfeet were to give up one-half of their hunting area and live peacefully with their white neighbors. They also were supposed to allow white settlers to build railroads and telephone and telegraph lines.

For a while, relations between the Blackfeet and the settlers improved. The Blackfeet helped the settlers hunt buffalo and traded their own buffalo hides for such supplies as beads, guns, wool, wagons, and food. But within a short time, whites began to abuse the treaty. They gave the Indians spoiled food, damaged wagons, rusty guns, blankets with moth holes, and the alcohol that was to have a long-term negative effect on the Indians. Feeling disrespected and duped, the Blackfeet responded with anger.

The Baker Massacre

In the 1860s, hostilities with American settlers became so frequent that the Blood division of the Blackfeet, who usually split their time between Montana and the plains of what is now Alberta, Canada, decided to stay in Canada permanently. They joined the ranks of the northern Piegan who had already made that decision. Most of the Blackfeet who remained in the United States were southern Piegan.

In early 1870 a group of U.S. soldiers attacked the Piegan in an action that is called either the Piegan War or the Baker Massacre for the U.S. leader who led the attack. The Piegan who were attacked had never been involved in raids against the whites and had recently undergone a severe smallpox epidemic. At the time of the attack, most of the Piegan men were away on a hunting trip. But U.S. troops went ahead with their surprise attack and 200 Piegan, mostly women, children, and old people, were killed. The Americans suffered only one death, probably the result of an accident. The incident drew much criticism from political and media groups.

Later in 1870 the area of Alberta where the northern Piegan lived was given by the Hudson's Bay Company, a trading operation, to the Canadian government, who opened it up to settlers. To guard the area, the Canadian government established the Northwest Mounted Police ("Mounties"). The Mounties won the respect of the Blackfeet for their fairness and courtesy.

Blackfeet treaties in the United States and Canada

Treaties were signed in 1865 and 1868 that decreased the territory of the Blackfeet in the United States. Although the U.S. Congress never officially confirmed those treaties, an 1874 treaty officially established the Blackfeet Reservation in Montana. The Indians gave up additional land from the reservation in treaties signed in 1887 and 1896. When it was discovered that there was little gold there, the land was made part of Glacier National Park. The conditions of the treaties are still being disputed today.

In 1877, with Treaty No. 7, the Canadian government established reserves in the province of Alberta for the Blood, North Piegan, and Siksika (Blackfeet) people. Compared with the removal of Natives to reservations in the United States, the process in Canada went much more smoothly. The Canadians, wishing to avoid Indian wars like those of their American counterparts, generally treated the Natives more fairly and tried to honor their treaties.

Loss of the buffalo

By the 1880s, the buffalo on the Great Plains had become nearly extinct. Historians blame their disappearance on mass slaughter by white hunters, who killed the beasts for their tongues (which had become a taste treat in Europe) and for their hides that were made into fashionable clothing. Some men shot the animals out of the windows of passing trains for sport, leaving the carcasses to rot on the Plains. In 1860 when manufacturing firms began using buffalo cowhide to make machine belts for industry, the price of hides skyrocketed and the massacre of the buffalo went into high gear.

Blackfeet in the twentieth century

In the period following the disappearance of the buffalo, the Blackfeet people in Montana constantly faced starvation. From the late 1870s until 1935 the Blackfeet were dependent on the reservation agent for food and other essential supplies. In addition, they had to learn to adjust to the massive cultural change required by a new agricultural lifestyle.

After 1887 a new U.S. government policy called allotment went into effect. Reservation lands in Montana were divided into parcels called allotments, and Indians were given small allotments on which to farm or raise cattle. A drought that took place in 1919, and falling prices for beef, forced many Blackfeet to give up their lands for nonpayment of taxes.

New laws were passed beginning in the 1930s that lessened Blackfeet dependence on government handouts. The loss of their lands was halted by placing it in trust, an arrangement in which the federal government oversees land use. Beginning in 1935 and extending into the 1960s, the Blackfeet became self-sufficient. Today the Blackfeet Reservation in Montana remains vital and many of its people support themselves through jobs in ranching, industry, and oil and natural gas. Today, it is home not only to Blackfeet people but to non-Blackfeet Indians and whites as well.

RELIGION

The Blackfeet believed that the physical and supernatural worlds were closely bound together. Animals and natural elements had powers that could be acquired by humans. This transfer of power usually took place in a dream. An animal in human form appeared to the dreamer and provided him or her with a list of objects, songs, and rituals that would be needed to make use of the animal's power. The dreamer gathered the objects and placed them in a rawhide pouch called a medicine bundle. The person then used the medicine bundle and the songs and rituals during social and religious ceremonies. Sometimes tribe members held elaborate ceremonies at which they traded medicine bundles.

The most powerful bundle was the beaver medicine bundle. This was the one used by the Beaver Men to charm the buffalo and to assist in the planting of the sacred tobacco. The beaver medicine bundle was also used during medicine pipe rituals, which took place during thunderstorms.

LANGUAGE

The Blackfeet dialect (variety) of the Algonquian language is related to the languages of several Plains, Eastern Woodlands, and Great Lakes tribes. The Blackfeet dialect was influenced by their isolation from other tribes who spoke the same language. It was also influenced by interactions with speakers of other languages that took place during their westward move. The Blackfeet did not have written symbols that could be used to write the language. But they did record their traditional stories and important events, such as wars, in pictographs on the internal and external surfaces of tepees, and on their buffalo robes. Pictographs are pictures that represent ideas.

GOVERNMENT

The Blackfeet tribes were broken up into a number of hunting bands, which were led by both war chiefs and civil chiefs. The war

chief was chosen because of his reputation as a warrior, and the civil chief was chosen for his public speaking skills.

In 1934 the U.S. Congress passed the Indian Reorganization Act (IRA) in order to stop the damage that the allotment policies of the General Allotment Act or Dawes Act of 1887 had done to Indian reservations all over the country. The IRA restored some land to tribes and encouraged a form of self-government on the reservations. One result of the act for the Blackfeet was it stemmed the tribe's land losses by placing most Indian land into trust status, an arrangement whereby the federal government oversees land and what becomes of it. Today, the affairs of the tribe are run by the Tribal Business Council of the Blackfeet Reservation in Browning, Montana, which has nine members who serve two-year terms.

The Blackfeet reserves in Canada are run by a single governing body with one chairperson.

ECONOMY

In the early days, the Blackfeet were a wandering people who raised no food, but depended mostly on hunting for their food. The buffalo supplied not only most of their nutritional needs, but provided the raw materials used to make their clothing and shelter. In time, they engaged in fur trading, particularly with the English.

Around 1915, the U.S. government stopped urging the Indians on the Blackfeet Reservation to engage in farming, as they had for several decades, and suggested they begin raising livestock. But a 1919 drought and a big drop in beef prices forced many Blackfeet to give up their land because they were unable to pay their taxes. In the 1920s a tribal leader encouraged the people to begin small, manageable farms growing grains and vegetables.

Today, many people grow grains and raise livestock. Others make their living in construction and the timber industry. About one-third of the people on the reservation are employed by the tribal government. Nearly forty percent of jobs are linked to federal government programs such as the building of government-funded housing. Small businesses manufacture pens and pencils, tepees, and canvas carrying bags. Coal, oil, and natural gas are present on the reservation, but the mining of these resources has not been developed. On the Canadian reserves, manufactured items include houses, clothing, moccasins, and Native crafts.

DAILY LIFE

Families

The typical Blackfeet family was made up of two men, three women, and three children. Perhaps because many Blackfeet men were killed in battle and there were excess numbers of women, men often had more than one wife. Second and third wives were usually sisters of the first wife. The wives worked together on the daily chores.

Buildings

Because of their hunting lifestyle, the Blackfeet built single-family tepees that were easy to construct and move. The frame consisted of about nineteen pine poles, each averaging eighteen feet in length. The poles were covered with six to twenty buffalo skins, often decorated with pictures of animals and geometric designs. Furnishings included buffalo robes for beds and willow backrests.

After the buffalo disappeared and the reservations were created, the Blackfeet replaced the tepee with the log cabin. It was the symbol of a new, settled way of life, in which ranching and agriculture became the primary means of survival.

Clothing and adornment

The Blackfeet used buffalo, deer, elk, and antelope skins to make their clothing. Women fashioned ankle-length sleeveless dresses held

up by straps. They were decorated with porcupine quills, cut fringe, and simple geometric designs colored with earth pigments. In the winter, separate skin sleeves were added to the dresses, and buffalo robes also provided warmth. After contact with white traders, clothing changed. Women began using wool and cloth to make many of their garments. However, the buffalo robe remained an important piece of clothing during the nineteenth century.

The men wore leggings made of antelope, and moccasins, shirts, and breechcloths (flaps of material that hung from the waist and covered the front and back). In winter they wore long buffalo robes, often decorated with earth pigments or plant dyes and elaborate porcupine quill embroidery. Most Blackfeet men wore this type of dress until the last decade of the nineteenth century. Faced with pressure from Christian missionaries and the disappearance of the buffalo, they began to wear what was called "citizen's dress." This outfit consisted of a coat and pants, but the Blackfeet rejected the stiff shoes of the white man in favor of moccasins.

Blackfeet men usually wore their hair long and loose, while women parted theirs and wore it in long braids. Both men and women frequently washed and brushed their hair and applied buffalo fat to make it shine. They wore necklaces of braided sweet grass. Men also wore necklaces made from the claws and teeth of bears, while women wore bracelets of elk or deer teeth.

Food

Buffalo was boiled, roasted, or dried. Pieces of fresh meat were cooked with wild roots and vegetables to make a stew, and intestines were cleaned and stuffed with a meat mixture to make a type of sausage. Dried meat was stored in rawhide pouches or was made into *pemmican* (see box), an important food source during the winter and other times when buffalo were scarce. Men also hunted other larger game, such as deer, moose, mountain sheep, antelope, and elk, but fish, reptiles, and grizzly bears were considered by most Blackfeet as unfit for human consumption.

Blackfeet women gathered roots, prairie turnips, bitterroot, and camas bulbs to supplement buffalo meat. They also picked wild berries, chokecherries, and buffalo or bull berries, and gathered the bark of the cottonwood trees to make use of the sweet inside portions.

Education

Blackfeet boys were taught how to hunt, track game, endure physical pain, and to recognize signals from both the physical and spiritual worlds. Girls were trained how to prepare food and clothing, how to sew and do bead work, and how to dress game and tan hides.

As early as 1859, Roman Catholic missionaries had introduced Catholic religious practices and educational systems to the Blackfeet people. Catholic priests started schools that taught the Indians how to farm and raise cattle. The priests served as go-betweens for the Blackfeet and whites. They also learned the Blackfeet language and helped to preserve it by translating Christian texts into the language.

But the Catholic influence lessened in the early 1900s when the federal government established a boarding school and day schools for the Indians. One of the purposes of the government schools was to prevent the children from speaking their native language or following their traditional ways or religion. Children were punished for singing Indian songs or doing tribal dances. Such schools were often overcrowded and unsanitary. Canadian officials established similar schools sponsored by the Church of England.

During the 1960s and 1970s the Montana Blackfeet began encouraging tribal elders to teach their native language and old customs to the younger people. The Algonquian language and Blackfeet cultural values are taught through Head Start programs on the reservation. Similar programs have also been created for adults at neighboring colleges, such as the Blackfoot Community College in Browning, Montana. A Blackfeet dictionary was published in 1989 and a Blackfeet grammar book two years later in Alberta.

The Blackfeet in Montana have established a program to try and rid the reservation of the problem of alcoholism. Programs teach children how to make good choices. Instruction in outdoor skills and crafts involves the children in worthwhile activities and encourages a sense of pride in their traditions.

Healing practices

The Blackfeet believed that spirits were an active and very real part of everyday life. Illness was understood as the visible presence of an evil spirit in a person's body. Illnesses could only be cured by a professional medicine person who had acquired in a vision the ability to heal the sick. Many of the most popular Blackfeet physicians were women.

During healing ceremonies, a medicine person might remove some object from the sick person (an object the doctors may have brought with them). The object was presented as proof that the ceremony had been successful. Healers learned to use natural herbs in treating lesser injuries, such as cuts. Horses were often offered as payment for a medicine person's services.

ARTS

The Blackfeet were known for their fine craftwork, and their tepees, weapons, and riding equipment were beautifully designed. On the reservation, the people began to use the supplies available from whites to create elaborate beaded headdresses, clothing, and accessories that made use of such new items as brass tacks and brass bells.

Today, the Museum of the Plains Indian in Browning, Montana, features Blackfeet pottery, clothing, art, decorative items, moccasins, shields, and jewelry.

CUSTOMS

Gender roles

Unlike many other tribes, the Blackfeet were somewhat flexible about what was considered male or female work. Men sometimes sewed their own clothing, and married women could become healers. Before the 1880s, it was common for a young, married woman with no children to go along with the men into battle, during the hunt, or on raids. While these women joined in the duty of preparing food, they also engaged in waging war and herding stolen horses back to their tribe. Some nineteenth-century women, such as Elk Hollering in the Water, became well known for being skillful horse raiders. Perhaps the most famous woman warrior, Running Eagle, led hunting, raiding, and warring parties, and could outride and outshoot most of her male companions.

Festivals and ceremonies

The major community religious ceremony, the Sun Dance, was held each year in late summer. Proper preparations by the medicine woman in charge and the dancers determined the success or failure of the Sun Dance. First, a Sun Dance lodge was erected around a central cottonwood pole in the village. Dancers prepared by making sacred vows and fasting from both food and water. Then began the dance, which lasted for four days.

Dancers sang sacred songs and chants and called on the Sun to grant them power, luck, or success. Some dancers pierced their breasts with sticks, which were then attached to the center pole by rawhide ropes. Summoning their courage, the dancers pulled away from the pole until the skewers tore free. Sometimes men and women would cut off fingers or pieces of the flesh from their arms and legs. Government officials forbade the Sun Dance in the late-nineteenth and early-twentieth centuries, but it never totally disappeared. It is still performed by some Blackfeet today.

In modern times, Canadian Blackfeet in Alberta sponsor the Blackfoot Indians Art Show at Fort MacLeod. The show is called "Heritage Through my Hands" and features Native paintings, beadwork, quillwork, and sculpture. Visitors are offered a selection of Native fare including frybread, buffalo and venison pemmican, griddlecakes, and fine jams and jellies from berries found on Blackfeet land.

Every year the Blackfeet Powwow is held in Browning, Montana. The four-day celebration, open to Natives and non-Natives alike, features singing and dancing, storytelling, drumming, and various games. On the

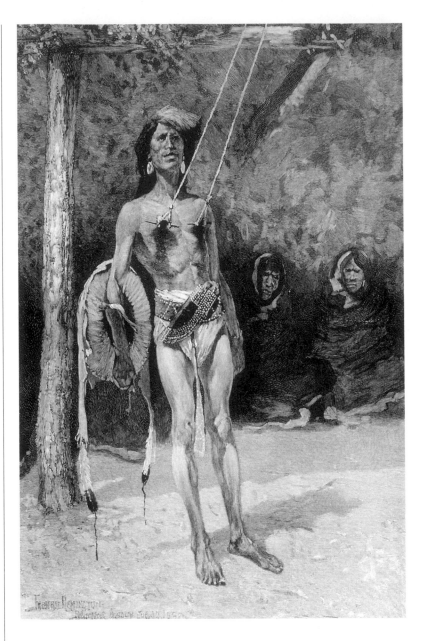

"The Ordeal in the Sun Dance among the Blackfeet Indians," drawn by Frederic Remington.

menu are Native foods such as boiled beef and deer meat, boiled potatoes, sarvisberry soup, baking powder bread, and fry bread. The powwow also serves to help educate whites about the ways of the Indians.

Buffalo hunting

The buffalo was the primary source of food, clothing, shelter, household supplies, and military equipment. The Blackfeet had more than sixty different uses for parts of the buffalo. Until the near disappearance of the buffalo in the late 1870s, the animals roamed the Plains in huge herds. In the old times, people chased the buffalo on foot, surrounded the herd, and drove the animals off a cliff. Once they had horses, they preferred to charge the buffalo on fast, well-trained horses called buffalo runners. This method of hunting required courage and skill.

Societies

Blackfeet warrior societies had the duty of protecting the people, keeping order, punishing offenders, and organizing raids and hunts. There were societies for each age group. For example, young boys might belong to the Doves, while men who were waiting to become warriors were part of the Mosquitoes, and warriors might belong to the Braves. The most respected societies were the Bulls and the Brave Dogs, made up of men who had proven themselves in battle. There were other Blackfeet societies for the practice of medicine, magic, and dance. An arts society was largely made up of women.

Courtship and marriage

Blackfeet marriages were arranged by the bride's parents when she was still a child or later by close friends or relatives of the couple. Before a wedding could take place, the groom had to convince the bride's father, relatives, or friends that he was worthy. This meant that he had to prove that he was a powerful warrior, a competent hunter, and able to offer financial security. Because of these requirements, very few men married before the age of twenty-one.

Gift exchanging was central to the marriage ceremony. Horses were among the most valuable gifts, and the families of the young couple also gave them household goods and robes. After the wedding, the bride and groom lived in either their own hut or in the home of the husband's family.

Funerals

Dying people made known their wishes for the distribution of possessions. When no such arrangement was made, members of the tribe simply took whatever they could gather after the person died.

The face of the dead person was painted, and the body was dressed in fancy clothes and wrapped in buffalo robes. The corpse was either buried atop a hill or in a ravine, or was placed between the forks of a tree. Both men and women mourned the death of loved ones by cutting their hair, wearing old clothes, and smearing their faces with white clay.

When a prominent chief of the Canadian Blackfeet died, his possessions were left within his lodge, and his horses were shot. It was believed that the spirit of the deceased did not leave this world, but traveled to the Sand Hills, an area south of the Saskatchewan River. Invisible spirits of the dead lived there much as they had in life, and often communicated with the living who passed through the region.

CURRENT TRIBAL ISSUES

The Blackfeet have always been concerned with their land, which is both sacred and important to their survival. Today the tribe is making claims for water rights on the reservation, and rights to certain natural resources within the boundaries of Glacier National Park. They are also working to ensure the appropriate use of reservation lands by both members and non-members.

The Blackfeet people are concerned about the preservation of their culture. Programs have been established to strengthen the sense of community, which may help the Blackfeet overcome such social problems as alcoholism, poverty, and crime. The tribe is also making efforts to further develop industry, the use of oil and natural gas resources, and the maintenance of ranches on the reservation.

Blackfeet in Montana are trying to draw more tourists to the St. Mary's entrance to Glacier National Park, which borders the reservation on the west. Visitors are encouraged to go to the reservation's shopping sites and attend Native festivals. Some travel agencies offer tours of reservation lands.

NOTABLE PEOPLE

At the age of seven Earl Old Person (1929–) began presenting Blackfeet culture in songs and dances at statewide events. For many years he has served as chairperson of the Blackfeet Tribal Business Council. Under his guidance, recreational, industrial, and housing projects have been completed on the reservation. Old Person has also served as head of a number of nationally recognized Native organizations. In 1978, Old Person was given the honorary lifetime appointment as chief of the Blackfeet Nation. His efforts have made for better relations between Indian communities and the larger U.S. society.

Other notable Blackfeet include: architect Douglas Cardinal (1934–); Blood tribal leader Crowfoot (1830–1890); Blood politician

James Gladstone (1887–1971); painter Gerald Tailfeathers (1925–1975); and Blackfeet/Gros Ventre novelist James Welch (1940–).

FURTHER READING

Dempsey, Hugh A. *Crowfoot: Chief of the Blackfeet.* Norman: University of Oklahoma Press, 1972.

Ewers, John C. *The Blackfeet: Raiders on the Northwestern Plains.* Norman: University of Oklahoma Press, 1958.

Ewers, John C. *Indian Life on the Upper Missouri.* Norman: University of Oklahoma Press, 1968.

Lacey, Theresa Jensen. *The Blackfeet.* New York: Chelsea House Publishers, 1995.

Web site: Society-Blackfoot at http://lucy.ukc.ac.uk/EthnoAtlas/ Hmar/Cult_dur/Culture.7833

Cheyenne

Name

The Cheyenne (pronounced *shy-ANN*) called themselves *Tsistsistas,* meaning "beautiful people" or "our people." The name Cheyenne is derived from the Sioux word shyela, meaning "red talkers" or "people of different speech."

Location

Most Cheyenne people live on the Great Plains, mainly in Montana and South Dakota, and in Oklahoma.

Population

Although early estimates of the Cheyenne population varied widely, one estimate says that 3,500 Cheyenne lived on the Plains in 1800. In a census (count of the population) done in 1990 by the U.S. Bureau of the Census, 7,104 people identified themselves as members of the Cheyenne tribe.

Language family

Algonquian.

Origins and group affiliations

The Cheyenne people, who once lived near the Great Lakes, were forced to move west by other eastern tribes who used guns obtained from the Europeans who were coming into their lands. In the Great Plains, the tribe united with another tribe, the Sutaio, who had also been forced out of their Great Lakes home. The Sioux referred to the union of the two groups as *ha hiye na,* meaning "people of alien speech." In the 1990s, the two main groups of Cheyenne lived on the Northern Cheyenne Reservation in Montana and the Cheyenne-Arapaho Reservation in Oklahoma (also see Arapaho entry).

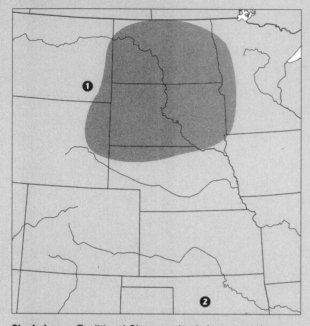

CHEYENNE

Contemporary Communities

1. Northern Cheyenne Tribe, Montana
2. Cheyenne-Arapaho Tribes, Oklahoma

Shaded area: Traditional Cheyenne lands in present-day North Dakota and South Dakota (see also migrations map).

The story of the Cheyenne people is one of relocation. They were forced to move westward by their constant search for stable food sources and by pressure from other tribes who were being pushed into the West by the gradual expansion of the European-American population. The Cheyenne were known for having one of the most highly organized governments among Native American groups. They were also renowned for their mighty warriors, their ethics, and their spiritual ways.

HISTORY

The Cheyenne move West

The Cheyenne probably had their origins in the western Great Lakes region of present-day Minnesota. In the early 1600s they began to have occasional contact with French and English fur traders. The first Europeans to encounter them were probably French explorers, who were building Fort Crevecoeur at a site on the Illinois River in

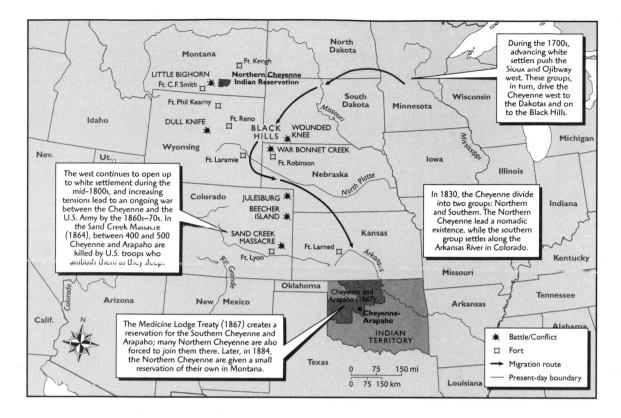

During the 1700s, advancing white settlers push the Sioux and Ojibway west. These groups, in turn, drive the Cheyenne west to the Dakotas and on to the Black Hills.

The west continues to open up to white settlement during the mid-1800s, and increasing tensions lead to an ongoing war between the Cheyenne and the U.S. Army by the 1860s-70s. In the Sand Creek Massacre (1864), between 400 and 500 Cheyenne and Arapaho are killed by U.S. troops who ambush them as they sleep.

In 1830, the Cheyenne divide into two groups: Northern and Southern. The Northern Cheyenne lead a nomadic existence, while the southern group settles along the Arkansas River in Colorado.

The Medicine Lodge Treaty (1867) creates a reservation for the Southern Cheyenne and Arapaho; many Northern Cheyenne are also forced to join them there. Later, in 1884, the Northern Cheyenne are given a small reservation of their own in Montana.

Battle/Conflict
Fort
Migration route
Present-day boundary

A map of the migrations of the Cheyenne, 1700–1884.

present-day Minnesota. The Cheyenne lived nearby in farming communities. During the late 1600s the Cheyenne moved into what is now North and South Dakota where they built villages of earthen dwellings and farmed the land.

In time, pressure from the Sioux tribes and the Ojibway (see entry) drove the Cheyenne even farther west into the area of the Black Hills. By the 1800s the Cheyenne were able to hunt for food on horseback (horses were introduced to the Americas by the Spanish). Many left their villages to follow the buffalo herds across the Great Plains. In the first quarter of the nineteenth century, the tribe split up into two groups. The Northern Cheyenne preferred to roam the northern country in search of horses and buffalo. The Southern Cheyenne chose to take up permanent residence along the Arkansas River in Colorado.

Conflict

During the mid-nineteenth century, the fortunes of the Cheyenne underwent great change. The United States took for itself much of the land in the West and white settlers began to stream westward. They traveled on trails that led through the land of many Great Plains tribes, including the Cheyenne. The increasing white population caused a rapid decline in the number of buffalo. As a result, armed conflicts between the Indians and settlers (and U.S. soldiers who came to protect them) grew more and more common. The U.S. government began efforts to protect white settlers and to give money to the tribes to help pay back their losses of buffalo and land.

The Sand Creek Massacre

In 1851 the U.S. government and eleven tribes, including the Cheyenne, signed the Treaty of Fort Laramie, which provided that the U.S. government give annual payments to the Indians of the Great Plains. It also clearly defined the boundaries of the territory belonging to each tribe. In return, the Indians agreed that the United States could build roads and military posts in their territories. They also agreed to end warfare among themselves and stop their attacks on white settlers. However, by 1856 tensions began again as the numbers of whites crossing Indian Territory (part of present-day Oklahoma) continued to grow. From 1857 to 1879, a war broke out between the Cheyenne and the U.S. Army. The bloodiest encounter of that war was the Sand Creek Massacre.

In 1861 the Southern Cheyenne chief Black Kettle, who had tried to secure a peace with honor for his people with the U.S. government, signed a treaty giving up all their lands to the United States, except the small Sand Creek Reservation in southern Colorado. The barren land could not support the Indian people and in time many young Cheyenne men decided it was necessary to prey upon the livestock and goods of nearby white settlers in order to survive. One of their raids so angered white Coloradans that they sent an armed force that opened fire on the first group of Cheyenne they met.

Black Kettle spoke with the local military commander and was told he and his people would be safe if they stayed at the Sand Creek Reservation. But Black Kettle suffered a terrible betrayal. On November 29, 1884, a large group of Cheyenne and Arapaho people lay sleeping at their camp at Sand Creek. In short order, 105 women and children and twenty-eight men were slaughtered by Colonel John M. Chivington and his Colorado Volunteers. Women were mercilessly attacked, children beheaded, and old people dismembered. Chief Black Kettle rode into the gunfire waving his American flag to show he was under the protection of the American government, but it was no use. Then the Indians' horses were scattered across the Plains and their settlement was destroyed by fire. In the conflict, only nine soldiers were killed and thirty-eight were wounded. Soon after, the soldiers paraded through the streets of Denver with body parts of the victims displayed on the ends of their daggers.

Following the massacre, a series of hearings was held by the U.S. Congress, who then formally condemned the event and the men who were in charge of it.

Native Americans defeat Custer

The Medicine Lodge Treaty of 1867 created a reservation for the Southern Cheyenne and Arapaho in northern Oklahoma. The Northern Cheyenne continued fighting the Americans. The conflict peaked with the 1876 Battle of Little Bighorn, when the tribe helped the Sioux (see Lakota entry) defeat General George Armstrong Custer (1839–1876). In retaliation, U.S. troops rounded up the Northern Cheyenne who had participated in the battle and forced them to move onto the Cheyenne reservation in Oklahoma. The people missed their northern homeland and found conditions on the reservation unbearable. In 1878 they escaped and fled north. U.S. troops captured them in Nebraska, and many perished from gunfire and ill treatment by the soldiers. The survivors were sent to Montana, and six years later, in 1884, were given a small reservation of their own there.

Tribe fragmented

By the 1880s the buffalo had been hunted to near extinction. As a result, the Cheyenne grew dependent on the government for food, shelter, and clothing. Efforts were made by state officials in both Oklahoma and Montana to introduce cattle raising and to encourage the Cheyenne to become ranchers. However, U.S. officials opposed this. They preferred to make the Cheyenne into farmers, but their plans did not prove successful.

In 1887 the Dawes General Allotment Act was passed. By this act, the reservations were divided into small plots of land, called allotments, that were to be owned and farmed by individual Indians; the remaining land on the reservations was opened to white settlement.

IMPORTANT DATES

1825: The Cheyenne divide into Northern and Southern groups.

1851: The Cheyenne are one of eleven tribes to sign the Treaty of Fort Laramie, which promises annual payments to the tribes for their land.

1864: More than 100 sleeping Cheyenne and Arapaho are killed by U.S. soldiers in the Sand Creek Massacre.

1876: The Northern Cheyenne join with the Sioux in defeating General George Custer at the Battle of Little Bighorn.

1884: The Northern Cheyenne Reservation is established in eastern Montana.

1989–90: Passage of the National Museum of the American Indian Act and the Native American Grave Protection and Reparations Act brings about the return of their burial remains to Native tribes.

Cheyenne traveling to their reservation, 1870s.

Cheyenne traveling to their reservation, 1870s.

The breakup of their reservations divided the people and led to the breakdown of the Cheyenne culture. Today, though, the Cheyenne people are working hard to maintain their cultural heritage.

RELIGION

The Cheyenne people believed that plants, animals, and people all had spirits, and that they were direct descendants of the creator-god, Heammawihio, who taught them how to hunt, when to plant and harvest corn, and how to use fire. The Cheyenne prayed to the spirit of the Earth, asking the spirit to keep the crops growing, provide herbs, and heal the sick. The people also prayed to the North, South, East, and West. The West, where the Sun set and rain and storms originated, was the most important of the four directions.

The Sun Dance, a ceremony common among many Plains Indians, was the central religious ceremony of the Cheyenne. It celebrated the power of the Sun and sought the renewal of the Earth's resources. The Sun Dance lasted eight days. During the first four days the dance lodge was built and secret rites were performed in the Lone Tepee. During the last four days a public dance was held in the Sun Dance Lodge.

In the late 1800s, the U.S. government banned the Sun Dance. The Cheyenne continued to perform the ceremony but renamed it the Willow Dance. In 1911 the Willow Dance was forbidden, and repeated efforts by the Cheyenne to reinstate it were rejected.

LANGUAGE

The Cheyenne spoke a language of the Algonquian family. (Other Algonquian languages include Cree, Menominee, Fox, Delaware, and Micmac.) The language had fourteen letters that were combined together to create very long words. While the Cheyenne nation was strong, its language was widely spoken. However, as the tribe became influenced by the Sioux, the Cheyenne language began to change and became a mix of the two languages. Because there were so many variations of the language, it has been difficult for historians to track the names of groups and determine how many groups of Cheyenne there were. The Cheyenne language is spoken today in southeastern Montana, in central Oklahoma, and on the Northern Cheyenne Indian Reservation. Some Cheyenne words are: mahpe (pronounced *MA-pee*) meaning water and vee'e (pronounced *VEE-uh*) meaning tepee.

GOVERNMENT

From early times, the Cheyenne have had a highly organized government. The governing body of the Cheyenne, the Council of Forty-Four, met annually during the summer. It was comprised of forty-four men who were elected from ten Cheyenne groups to serve ten-year terms. Chiefs discussed problems within the tribe, and planned how to deal with other tribes. The head of the Council, the Sweet Medicine Chief, performed religious and political duties. He kept the Chief's Medicine, a sacred bundle of grass, and devised a code establishing how tribal members were to behave. The chiefs shared power; there was no one absolute authority.

Today Montana's Northern Cheyenne tribe is governed by a tribal council made up of the president and twenty-four council members.

Young Cheyenne woman, photograph by Edward S. Curtis.

Council members from five separate districts are elected to two-year terms. The president serves a four-year term.

ECONOMY

Cheyenne women contributed to the tribe by picking berries and digging up edible roots. They cooked and dried meat brought home by hunters. They tanned hides, made tepees, and sewed leather clothing and moccasins. Men hunted antelope, buffalo, deer, elk, and wild sheep. They trapped foxes and wolves for their fur.

Today Northern Cheyenne are employed in many fields. Some work on ranches or for coal companies. Some are trained firefighters who help control fires throughout the West. There are also professionals in fields such as law and teaching. More than forty small businesses operate on the reservation, among them laundromats, gas stations, grocery stores, and restaurants. The tribe manages a buffalo herd, and employs about 300 of its members as social workers, health care workers, and in forestry and casino operations. Their bingo hall generates about $11,000 a week.

The Cheyenne-Arapaho people in Oklahoma earn money from leasing farming and grazing lands, from oil and gas royalties, and from two gaming facilities. Nevertheless, the reduction of federal funds for Indian tribes has become a serious problem for all Cheyenne, who are striving to become financially self-sufficient.

DAILY LIFE

Families

The chief duties of the women of the tribe were to care for their homes, raise their children, and gather food. They made furnishings for their tepees using grass, earth, and buffalo hides. They were also expected to pack up belongings when the tribe changed camps. Men hunted and protected their territory from enemies.

Buildings

The Cheyenne lived as farmers in Minnesota and the eastern Dakotas from the 1600s to the early 1800s. They lived in earthen

lodges made of wooden frames covered with sod. As they moved onto the Plains and began to hunt buffalo, they adopted the tepee. This was a dwelling made of wooden poles and buffalo hides that could be moved easily with the aid of horses. A fire was built in the center of the tepee and beds of buffalo robes lined the walls. Men would sometimes paint their tepees with designs they had seen in a vision. Dome-shaped sweat lodges were used for bathing and purification rituals.

Clothing and adornment

Cheyenne clothing was designed to permit freedom of movement. In warm weather, most men wore only moccasins and breechcloths (material that goes between the legs and is fastened at the waist). In colder weather they also wore leggings and shirts. Women wore dresses and moccasins, adding leggings in winter. In the sixteenth and seventeenth centuries, these items were made of animal skins, usually deer or elk.

Everyday clothing was usually very plain, but clothing for ceremonial occasions could be very elaborate. It might be decorated with beads, quillwork, bells, and fringes. Designs for men's clothing were determined by their status as warriors. Often the designs told a story about the wearer. The most spectacular were the knee-length shirts of warriors, which were adorned with beads and quillwork.

The Northern Cheyenne favored heavily beaded shirts, while the Southern Cheyenne shirts had dark-green fringes and relied more on color for effect. Medicine bags, eagle feathers, and berry beads also

CHEYENNE BREAD

The Cheyenne once lived as an agricultural people in fixed villages. Later they became wandering buffalo hunters. Their rituals still reflect the period when they lived in permanent villages and grew corn before moving to the Great Plains. Their use of cornmeal to make various breads is related to a time when young women were taught home economics at boarding schools near the reservation.

1 quart milk or water

2 cups yellow or white cornmeal

3 eggs, separated

4 tablespoons melted butter

1/2 teaspoon pepper

Preheat oven to 375°F.

Bring milk to a boil in a large saucepan over medium heat. Gradually stir in cornmeal and cook, stirring, for a few minutes until thickened.

Beat in egg yokes, butter, and seasonings.

In a separate bowl, beat egg whites until they stand in stiff peaks. Fold whites into corn mixture and pour into a 2-quart baking dish.

Bake for 20 to 30 minutes, until puffed and golden brown on top.

Serves 6.

From Beverly Cox and Martin Jacobs, *Spirit of the Harvest.* New York: Stewart, Tabori & Chang, 1991, p. 109.

provided decoration. Men wore handsome robes when the weather was very cold or to impress visitors.

Food

When the Cheyenne lived in Minnesota and the Dakotas, they raised corn, beans, and squash, supplementing the crops with deer and bear meat. When they moved to the Great Plains, Cheyenne men hunted buffalo. Women used all parts of the buffalo for food, tepee coverings, and other necessities. Later the Cheyenne traded with Americans for new food items, including coffee, sugar, and flour, plus needles and other metal items, and beads.

Women planted and prepared vegetables from their gardens, such as turnips, which were sliced, boiled, and dried in the sun. They collected fruit from the prickly pear cactus, an especially difficult task because the fruit had prickly spines. The dried fruit was used as a thickener for stews and soups. Women made pemmican balls from dried ground animal meat, dried berries, and animal fat. They made similar balls substituting ground corn for the meat.

Education

Cheyenne girls learned the daily tasks of women by watching their mothers and other women work, and played with deerskin dolls in imitation of the way their mothers took care of their babies. Boys learned to use small bows and arrows, and were taught to practice shooting arrows until they never missed a target. They also learned to hunt rabbits, turkey, and fowl. Boys and girls were shown how to ride horses, and older boys were taught to tend the tribe's horses. When a boy reached the age of twelve, his grandfather instructed him in men's duties, including buffalo hunting and horse raiding. Today, Dull Knife Memorial College, a modern facility on the Northern Cheyenne Indian Reservation in southeastern Montana, serves 300 students. It offers associate degrees in arts and in applied science. Programs are available in office skills and becoming an entrepreneur (learning how to create a new business enterprise).

Healing practices

Cheyenne medicine men called shamans (pronounced *SHAY-muns*) performed healing rituals. They sucked the evil that was causing the illness out of the patient and spit it out onto the ground. Shamans also said prayers, blew whistles, beat on drums, and used rattles made of gourds, animal bladders, or eagles' heads as part of their healing rituals. Priests were called in if the shamans were unsuccessful. Priests wore more elaborate costumes and conducted more involved rituals than did shamans. They also practiced minor surgery.

Drums were an important part of the healing process. The round shape of the drum represented the entire universe, and its steady beat represented the pulsing heart. Drums soothed tortured minds and healed bodily suffering.

ARTS

Cheyenne women were known for their creativity in decorating objects with horsehair, feathers, and the bones and skin of animals. By the 1800s, they had introduced the trinkets, beads, commercial paints, and metal brought by the white traders into their clothing and craft designs.

Oral literature

The oral literature of the Cheyenne was made up of war stories, sacred stories, and hero myths. An important figure was Wihio, a

POPULATION OF CHEYENNE TRIBES: 1990

There are four groups of people in the United States who identify themselves as Cheyenne. Their two major reservations are the Northern Cheyenne Reservation in Montana and the Cheyenne-Arapaho Reservation in Oklahoma. The Northern Cheyenne reservations spans nearly 450,000 acres in southeastern Montana. The Cheyenne-Arapaho Tribal Jurisdiction Area spreads across an eight-county area in northwest and north central Oklahoma. In the 1990 census, members of the various Cheyenne groups identified themselves this way:

Tribe	Population
Cheyenne	7,104
Northern Cheyenne	4,398
Southern Cheyenne	307
Cheyenne-Arapaho	2,629

SOURCE: "1990 census of population and housing. Subject summary tape file (SSTF) 13 (computer file): characteristics of American Indians by tribe and language." Washington, DC: U.S. Department of Commerce, Bureau of the Census, Data User Services division, 1995).

trickster who resembled the Coyote trickster of the stories of many other tribes.

CUSTOMS

Festivals

The most sacred of the Cheyenne ceremonies was the annual renewal of the Sacred Arrows, which took place during the summer solstice (June 21, when the Sun is at its highest point at the tropic of Cancer). The Sacred Arrows were found in the Black Hills of South Dakota by the prophet Sweet Medicine, who then brought them to the Cheyenne. The arrows' special powers helped the Cheyenne hunt buffalo and defeat their enemies in battle.

Only men were allowed to attend the four-day Sacred Arrow ceremony. On the first day, offerings were brought to the Great Spirit and men were chosen to erect the Sacred Arrow Lodge. On the second day, a man, painted red and dressed only in a buffalo robe, presented a bundle of sacred arrows to the high priest. The unity of each Cheyenne family within the tribe was celebrated on the third day. Sticks representing each family were burned in an incense fire. On the fourth day, the sacred arrows were placed on public view in the sunlight. All the men and boys of the tribe walked past the arrows to obtain their sacred powers. A large tepee called the Sweet Medicine Lodge was then erected over the arrows. That evening, the medicine men went inside the tepee and sang sacred songs. Just before daybreak on the fifth day, all participants went into the sweat lodge for a cleansing.

Today several powwows and celebrations take place each year on the Northern Cheyenne Reservation in Montana. A powwow is a celebration at which the main activity is traditional singing and dancing. In modern times, the singers and dancers at powwows come from many different tribes. In Oklahoma, the Cheyenne-Arapaho people hold three annual powwows: Jackie Beard Pow Wow in May; the Cheyenne-Arapaho Summer Fest and Pow Wow in August; and the Veterans' Day Pow Wow in November.

War rituals

The Cheyenne were organized into five military societies: Bowstring, Dog, Elk, Fox, and Shield. Four leaders were in charge of each society. Two were the war chiefs and decision-makers, and two were peace leaders and ambassadors to other societies. Each group had unique war costumes, rituals, and chants. During the 1800s, the society called the Dog Soldiers, which fought with U.S. government troops, was the most famous and most feared on the Great Plains.

Courtship and marriage

A Cheyenne woman often waited years before accepting a marriage proposal. Those who remained pure were held in high esteem. A man never proposed to a woman directly. Instead, he asked an older female relative to take gifts to the woman's family and make his case for him. If the woman accepted the proposal, the bride was brought to her husband's family. She was placed on a ceremonial blanket, carried into the tepee, and adorned with new clothes and paint. Then a feast was held. A man who was very prosperous sometimes had several wives; he was expected to supply a tepee for each one.

Death

A close relative usually prepared the body for a Cheyenne burial. The body was dressed in fine clothing and wrapped in blankets. It was then bound up with ropes and carried to the burial site. Mourners sang and prayed. The deceased person's dearest possessions were placed next to the body. For example, a man might be buried with his gun or knife; sometimes his best horse was shot. His remaining goods were distributed among non-relatives, but his widow was allowed to keep a blanket.

Two young Cheyenne men in traditional battle dress.

CURRENT TRIBAL ISSUES

Exploiting natural resources

Exploiting the rich natural resources on their land in a responsible way is an important issue for many tribes, including the Cheyenne. The discovery of coal in the late 1960s on the reservation in Montana promised an opportunity for economic independence. Supporters of coal mining pointed out that money obtained in this way could be used to start educational and health programs to improve living conditions on the reservation. Others feared environmental destruction. They believed coal companies would benefit, while the tribe was left in poverty. Those who opposed won out and the land was preserved.

Human remains and sacred sites

In 1986 the Northern Cheyenne discovered that the American history museum, the Smithsonian Institution in Washington, D.C., possessed remains of thousands of Native humans beings and funeral objects (items that had been placed with the dead to accompany them into the next world) as well. Natives started a movement that resulted in passage of the National Museum of the American Indian Act (1989) and the Native American Grave Protection and Reparations Act (1990).

The first act required that the Smithsonian list all the remains and objects in its possession and then return them to the appropriate tribes. The act also authorized the creation of a Native American Museum. The second act required that all remains held by local, state, or federal agencies had to be returned to their native tribes.

NOTABLE PEOPLE

Women's rights activist Suzan Shown Harjo (1945–), a member of the Cheyenne and Arapaho tribes, is a journalist and poet. She has been a major activist in Washington, D.C. for reshaping federal Indian policy.

In 1992 Ben Nighthorse Campbell (1933–), a member of the Northern Cheyenne tribe, became the first Native American to be elected to the U.S. Senate in more than sixty years. He is also the first Native American to chair the Senate Committee on Indian Affairs. Of Apache/Pueblo/Cheyenne and Portuguese heritage, he is an Air Force veteran, a college graduate, and holds a sixth-degree black belt in judo. He has been a teacher, a horse breeder and trainer, and an award-winning jewelry designer and maker.

FURTHER READING

Brown, Dee. "War Comes to the Cheyennes," in *Bury My Heart at Wounded Knee*. New York: Holt, 1970, pp. 67-102.

Hoig, Stan. *The Cheyenne*. New York: Chelsea House, 1989.

Lodge, Sally. *The Cheyenne*. Vero Beach, Florida: Rourke Publications, Inc., 1990.

Sneve, Virginia Driving Hawk. *The Cheyennes*. New York: Holiday House, 1996.

Sonneborn, Liz. *The Cheyenne Indians*. New York: Chelsea House Publishers, 1991.

Comanche

Name

The Comanche (pronounced *cuh-MAN-chee*) called themselves *Nerm* (the word has various spellings), meaning "people." "Comanche" probably came from the Ute word for the tribe, *Koh-Mahts,* which means "anyone who wants to fight me all the time." The Spanish altered the spelling to "Komantcia," and the Americans changed it to Comanche.

Location

The Comanche roamed the southern Great Plains, including parts of Texas, New Mexico, Oklahoma, Kansas, Colorado, and Mexico. Today, descendants of the Comanche share reservation lands with the Kiowa and Apache tribes (see entries). The reservation is located eighty-seven miles southwest of Oklahoma City, Oklahoma.

Population

There were about 20,000 Comanche at the height of their power in the early 1800s. The population declined to 1,500 in 1900 as a result of wars and diseases. In a census (count of the population) done in 1990 by the U.S. Bureau of the Census, 11,267 people identified themselves as Comanche (170 identified themselves more specifically as Oklahoma Comanche), making the tribe the twenty-first most populous in the United States (the most populous is the Cherokee, with about 350,000).

Language family

Uto-Aztecan.

Origins and group affiliations

The Comanche were a branch of the Shoshone tribe (see entry) until the 1600s. The Comanche then separated from the Shoshone and migrated south from Wyoming and Montana along the eastern slopes of the Rocky Mountains.

COMANCHE

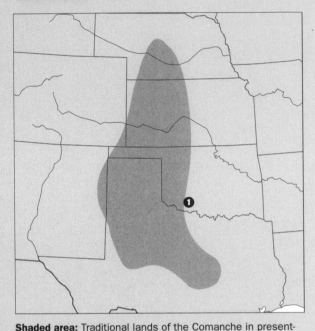

Shaded area: Traditional lands of the Comanche in present-day Nebraska, Texas, New Mexico, and Oklahoma.

Often referred to as the "Lords of the Southern Plains," the powerful Comanche tribe once controlled a vast expanse of territory known by the Spanish term *Comanchería*, land of the Comanche. Loosely organized into wandering groups of highly skilled horsemen and warriors, the Comanche lived lives of danger and discomfort beyond our imagining. At one time or another they fought with nearly every Plains tribe, and they also took on the Spanish, American settlers, the Texas Rangers, and the U.S. military in a fierce defense of their lands. Comanche resistance is largely responsible for slowing the settlement of the American West during the nineteenth century. They were a cunning people, who learned how their enemies thought—and added to their population base—by adopting captured prisoners into the tribe.

HISTORY

Horses transform lifestyle

The Comanche separated from their relatives, the Shoshone tribe, in the late 1600s. They migrated south from the mountains of Wyoming and Montana onto the Great Plains. Sometime before 1705 they acquired horses from their Ute (see entry) neighbors, who had gotten the animals from the Spanish in Mexico. The lifestyle of these wanderers, who had always hunted on foot, was transformed. The Comanche became the first Plains people to make extensive use of horses, and by 1750 their men, women, and children were excellent riders. Hunting became easier, and over the next century the tribe amassed a larger herd of horses than any other Native American group.

Comanche warriors sometimes owned as many as 250 horses, and the most prominent members of the tribe might have as many as 1,000. Some horses were taken by conducting raids on neighboring tribes or on white settlements, but the Comanche were also one of the few groups who knew how to breed and train horses. Their mounts responded to verbal commands, and Comanche warriors could lean over their horses' necks and fire arrows from beneath the animals' chins while at a full gallop.

Having horses allowed the Comanche to control a large expanse of territory. Between 1750 and 1875, Comanche groups spread across central and western Texas, eastern New Mexico, southeastern Colorado, southwestern Kansas, and western Oklahoma. This 24,000-square-mile area became known as the Comanchería.

Occupied by trade, raids, and war

The Comanchería was situated between territory claimed by Spain in the Southwest and by France in Louisiana. The Comanche developed trading relationships with both the Spanish and the French, but they had better relations with the French. The Comanche traded prisoners of war to be used by the Spanish as slaves; they traded buffalo hides with the French. In return they got horses from the Spanish and guns from the French, and acquired even more power. They jealously guarded their territory against Spanish expansion and trespassing by other tribes.

In the early 1800s, events happening in faraway places had a far-reaching effect on the Comanche. In the Louisiana Purchase of 1803, France sold a huge tract of land to the United States, extending from the

An engraving of Comanche buffalo hunting.

Mississippi River in the east to the Rocky Mountains in the west, and from the Gulf of Mexico in the south to what is now Canada in the north. The lands the United States gained in this agreement doubled its size. But these lands were already inhabited by Native people.

With this vast new area now in its control, the U.S. government decided to make room for American expansion by forcing eastern Indian tribes to move into these new lands west of the Mississippi River. There the relocated tribes competed with the Comanche on the Great Plains for a share of the buffalo herds. Next, American settlers began pressing toward the borders of the Comanchería. In 1821, Mexico gained control of present-day Texas from Spain, and Mexican settlers began moving into Texas and taking over more Comanche lands.

The Comanche resented any intrusion into their territory and fought the newcomers bitterly, sometimes killing white hunters and traders and taking white captives. After 1830, U.S. government officials tried to meet with the Comanche to discuss the possibility of moving eastern tribes onto parts of the Comanchería. But the Comanche were a loosely organized people, and at first no spokesmen could be found. When representatives of the tribe finally met with U.S. delegates in 1834, little was accomplished.

Problems in Texas

In 1835 the Texas Revolution freed Texas from Mexican rule. American settlers moved onto isolated ranches and farms in Texas with their cattle and their new breeds of larger horses. They were easy targets for Comanche raids, and the Texas Rangers (a police group) had frequent skirmishes with the Comanche. The conflicts came to a head in San Antonio in 1838, when Texas Rangers tried to capture Comanche leaders who had come to conduct a peaceful negotiation. Thirty-five Comanche were killed and many others were wounded.

Over the next three decades, Texas became part of the United States, and gold was discovered in California. More settlers poured into Texas, and gold miners galloped across the Comanchería, spreading diseases and disrupting the migrations of the buffalo herds. Weakened now by diseases and hunger, the Comanche fought on. They had a brief period of relief when the United States was distracted by the Civil War (1861–65). After that war, the U.S. government could devote its attention to ending the violence on the Great Plains once and for all.

The Buffalo War

After the Civil War the Comanche had to contend with the Texas Rangers and the full force of the U.S. military, sometimes under the command of famous Wild West hero Christopher "Kit" Carson. Then, in the 1870s, professional hunters armed with high-powered rifles began to kill off the remaining buffalo herds for use in eastern industries. One such hunter could kill hundreds of buffalo in a day.

Finally, in 1874, a band of Comanche under the leadership of the Chief Quanah Parker (c. 1852–1911) tried to stop this tragic slaughter by attacking a group of buffalo hunters. Though the hunters used their rifles to turn back the Comanche and their allies, this event marked the start of the Red River War (also known as the Buffalo War). After U.S. troops killed hundreds of horses and burned their food and tepees, most Comanche were forced to surrender.

Quanah Parker and his followers held out until June 1875. When he and his people were placed on a reservation in Oklahoma, nearly two centuries of Comanche domination of the Southern Plains ended.

On the reservation

The U.S. government tried to turn the Comanche into farmers, and tried to force the people to accept American ways and values. The Comanche were forced to depend on the Bureau of Indian Affairs for food, clothing, and shelter. Since the move to the reservation, the Comanche have endured hunger, poverty, and legal and illegal takeovers of their land. Though poverty and discrimination remain alive, the Comanche proudly struggle to retain their traditions.

RELIGION

The Comanche did not believe in a creator god but thought they had originated from animals, perhaps wolves. Religion for them was a matter of learning how to please the supernatural powers who lived in rocks and animals. By pleasing them they sought to get favors they needed to survive. They believed that when a person found out what the powers wanted and provided it, he or she could face the future without fear.

The practice of religion was considered a private matter, and men established a personal relationship with the supernatural through a vision quest (see "Customs"). The Comanche were one of the few tribes of the Great Plains that did not practice the Sun Dance. In fact, there were few group ceremonies of any kind, and there was no special class of religious leaders.

The Comanche believed that the spirits of the dead lived through eternity in a land where everyone was young and there was plentiful game and fast horses. Almost everyone who died gained an afterlife. The exceptions included warriors who were scalped in battle. The Comanche scalped their enemies to prevent them from enjoying life after death, and they fought fiercely over a fallen comrade to prevent his scalp from being taken.

Unable to adjust to reservation life, many Comanche took solace in the Peyote (pronounced *pay-OH-tee*) Religion, which brought people together for singing, praying, and taking peyote, a drug derived from cactus that causes mild hallucinations. In 1918, the popularity of the Peyote Religion led to the founding of the Native American Church, which combined Native with Christian practices. Today, some members of the Comanche tribe still belong to the Native American Church, while others have converted to Christianity.

LANGUAGE

The Comanche spoke a Shoshonean dialect (variety) of the Uto-Aztecan language family. The language was frequently used during trade because many people on the Plains understood it. On the other hand, because the Japanese could not understand it, the language was used in World War II (1939–45) by seventeen young Comanche men, who served the U.S. Army as Code Talkers, relaying secret messages in their native language (see box, "Code Talkers," in Navajo entry).

By 1993 only about 250 elderly members of the tribe could speak the language. Comanche elders are reluctant to teach the language to outsiders. They believe that to know it is to have power over the tribe.

GOVERNMENT

The Comanche lived in many separate groups and were loosely organized. There were no real leaders except those chosen to lead during wartime; after a war was over, the war leader's authority ended. Decisions were reached after everyone who wished to speak had his say. Every adult male in the group had to agree with the decision; those who could not agree with the majority left and joined another group.

Women had no say in decision-making and could not be present at meetings unless invited.

The Comanche adopted a tribal constitution in 1967, after concluding that the reservation's joint business council (which included representatives of the Kiowa and Apache tribes) was not working in their interests. Today, the tribe is governed by a seven-member elected business committee, which handles financial matters. Members, who can be either male or female, serve three-year terms. The Comanche tribe is headquartered in Medicine Park, Oklahoma.

ECONOMY

The Comanche economy changed in the eighteenth century. Before that, it was based on gathering and hunting buffalo on foot, a difficult and dangerous undertaking. After 1700 the economy expanded to include horses, mules, and slaves. They were traded along with buffalo robes to the Spanish for more horses and to the French for guns and luxury items. What they could not get through trading, the Comanche got through raiding (stealing from neighboring communities).

After moving to the reservation, the Comanche struggled to support themselves by farming (although most of the land was not suitable for farming), raising cattle, and by working for white farmers and ranchers. Today they continue these activities and they also earn money by leasing mineral rights and rights to raise cattle on their lands. Small businesses such as a bingo hall, a snack bar, and a smoke shop operate on the reservation.

Comanche wishing to remain on or near the reservation face conditions of extreme poverty. The unemployment rate on the reservation hovers around 30 percent, which means that nearly one-third of those who wish to work cannot find a job.

Some Comanche have upheld the tribe's warrior traditions by serving in the American armed forces during wartime, and military service remains a popular career option for young Comanche men and women. Many Comanche work off the reservation in the oil fields of Oklahoma and Texas or in skilled occupations in urban areas.

DAILY LIFE

Families

Families consisted of a husband, wife, children, and close relatives. Because Comanche life was so hard and many children died young, all

A daughter of a Comanche chief, 1872.

children were cherished, even children taken in raids, who were often adopted into the tribe.

Adults were always hard at work. The primary tasks of men were to hunt, make war, and fashion their own war shields. When they were too old for this work (many were worn out or dead by the age of thirty), they made bows and arrows out of wood. Women did every other job; they were usually worn out by the age of twenty-five from hunger, hard work, and the difficulty of bearing many children at a young age.

Education

Since Comanche parents were often busy, grandparents played an important role in child-rearing. Children learned by observing and imitating adults, and they learned at a young age their most important task: making sure there was enough food to eat.

After the Comanche moved to the reservation, Christian missionaries and government agents opened schools, hoping to convince Comanche children to reject their traditional culture. Comanche parents objected, and few children attended the schools. According to author Willard Rollings, Comanche children who currently attend Oklahoma's public schools still face problems. He wrote: "Local school boards show little respect for Indians and their culture and continue to try to convert their children to the culture of white Americans."

Buildings

The Comanche were a wandering tribe that moved when the buffalo did or when they needed new patches of grass for their horses. They required a home that could be quickly put up and taken down. Their tepees consisted of four base poles (most Plains tribes used three poles) stuck into the ground and tied together at the top to form a cone shape. Eighteen to twenty smaller poles gave support. A covering of up to seventeen buffalo hides was stretched tightly around this frame.

Sometimes the tepee covers were painted with abstract designs and geometric figures. In the summer, the hide covers were rolled up to let in fresh air. In extremely hot weather, the Comanche slept

outdoors in brush shelters. Inside the tepee was a fire and a low sleeping platform covered with buffalo robes along the rear wall.

Food

The search for food was constant. Buffalo was the primary food source, but the Comanche also hunted elk, bear, antelope, and deer. When game was scarce, they ate horses. However, because they considered dogs and coyotes to be relatives of their ancestors, the wolves, they would not eat them, nor would they eat fish. They ate turtles steamed over the fire, but they would not eat fowl unless they were starving, because they considered it food for cowards. When non-Native American ranchers began raising cattle on the Comanchería, the tribe often raided the herds and ate beef.

The Comanche did not practice agriculture but obtained plant foods in other ways. They traded with other tribes for corn and tobacco, and they gathered wild plants such as grapes, currants, plums, mulberries, persimmons, roots, and tubers. A favorite high-energy food was pemmican, a cake-like substance made of dried buffalo meat, melted fat, and various nuts and berries.

Clothing and adornment

MEN'S EVERYDAY CLOTHING Everyday clothing was plain and practical, but the clothing the Comanche wore to make war was col-

*Asa Havi (Bird Chief), a
Penateka Comanche.*

orful and elegant (see "War and hunting rituals"). Comanche men usually wore a buckskin breechcloth (a piece of material that wrapped between the legs and tucked into a belt); fringed buckskin leggings extending from the belt to the ankles; and buckskin moccasins with tough, buffalo-hide soles. Men did not usually wear shirts. Young boys commonly went naked until they reached the age of nine or ten when they donned adult attire. Men's clothing was sometimes decorated with fringes made of deerskin, fur, or human hair, but it lacked the elaborate beadwork found among some other Plains tribes.

Comanche men grew their hair long and parted it in the middle. They often painted their scalps where the hair was parted, and wore braids (sometimes wrapped with fur or cloth) on each side of their faces. A tiny braid known as a scalplock hung over the forehead and was often decorated with cloth, beads, and a single feather. Comanche men plucked their facial and body hair, including their eyebrows. They adorned themselves with bracelets of leather and metal and earrings made of shell, brass, or silver.

WOMEN'S CLOTHING Comanche women wore moccasins and long, one-piece buckskin dresses with wide sleeves, flared skirts, and fringes. Young girls wore clothing from the time they could walk. Women's special occasion clothing was ornamented with beads, fringes, and bits of metal that made sounds. The women usually cut their hair short and painted their faces and bodies in bright colors. In the winter, all members of the Comanche tribe wore heavy buffalo robes and knee-high boots for warmth.

Healing practices

Comanche people suffered from hunger, exposure to the elements, and diseases. The people learned at an early age to endure extreme pain and discomfort without self-pity. Their doctors were hunter-warriors who had a little extra "pull" with the spirit world and demonstrated practical skills. They knew how to apply tourniquets and perform minor surgery, and they used a wide variety of herbal remedies to treat wounds and cure illnesses. They knew how to suck out the poison from snake bites and even how to fill cavities in teeth. Sometimes older women were allowed to practice medicine.

ARTS

The Comanche were wanderers, always searching for food, and they had little time to devote to the development of the arts. They had few songs or dances, rituals or ceremonies. Comanche men did devote particular attention to the creation and decoration of their war shields, which are described under "War and hunting rituals."

CUSTOMS

War and hunting rituals

In preparation for a buffalo hunt, the Comanche prayed to the buffalo spirit for a good catch. They usually hunted by encircling a group of buffalo with their horses and then killing as many animals as possible using lances or bows and arrows. Sometimes they stampeded a herd of buffalo over the edge of a cliff. When individuals hunted alone, they disguised themselves in buffalo robes to sneak up on the herd.

When preparing to make war, Comanche men performed a war dance and prayed to spirits such as the eagle for strength. They painted their faces and bodies with symbols of their personal power. Warriors wore headdresses with buffalo horns and carried shields that were painted and decorated with feathers, bear teeth, horse tails, and human hair.

Comanche warriors traveled long distances and attacked their enemies without warning. Male enemies were usually tortured and killed because it was not practical to take them prisoner. A prisoner who displayed exceptional courage under torture was sometimes released. Warriors often returned to camp bearing women and children prisoners and dressed in items of European clothing taken from their enemies.

Vision quest

A young man about to embark on a vision quest (a search for spiritual guidance) climbed to the top of a hill, stopping four times along the way to smoke a tobacco pipe and pray. He remained alone on the hill for four days and nights without food or water. In the morning he prayed to the rising Sun for a vision.

A vision might be as simple as hearing the sound of a wolf call. When he received his vision, the young man returned to the tribe to ask the medicine man to explain it. From the explanation he knew what materials he needed for his medicine bundle, which represented his personal power and his relationship with the supernatural.

Courtship and marriage

A young man became eligible to marry after he completed his vision quest and participated in his first war party. However, most both Scissor-tail and Hawk at the same time, and the bones went to the night side, and the day people began to guess.

Time and again the luck went back and forth, each team seeming to be about to beat the other. Time and again the luck changed, and the winning team became the losing one.

The game went on and on. Finally the Sun, waiting on the other side of the world to find out what was going to happen to him, got tired of it all.

The game was so long that Bear got tired, too. He was playing on the night side. He got cramped sitting on the log, and his legs began to ache. Bear took off his moccasins to rest his feet, and still the game went on and on.

At last the Sun was so bored that he decided to go and see for himself what was happening. He yawned and stretched and crawled out of his bed on the underneath side of the world. He started to climb up his notched log ladder to the top side, to find out what was happening.

As the Sun climbed the light grew stronger, and the night people began to be afraid. The game was still even; nobody had won. But the Sun was coming and coming, and the night animals had to run away. Bear jumped up in such a hurry that he put his right foot in his left moccasin, and his left foot in his right moccasin.

The Sun was full up now, and all the other night animals were gone. Bear went after them as fast as he could in his wrong moccasins, rocking and waddling from side to side, and shouting, "Wait for me! Wait for me!"

But nobody stopped or waited, and Bear had to go waddling along, just the way he has done ever since.

And because nobody won the game, the day and night took turns from that time on. Everybody had the same time to come out and live his life the way he wanted to as everybody else.

SOURCE: Alice Marriott and Carol K. Rachlin. "Why the Bear Waddles When He Walks." *American Indian Mythology.* New York: Crowell, 1968.

Comanche men waited to marry until they had proven themselves to be skilled hunters, able to provide for a wife and children. It was common for men to marry within their group; no group wanted to lose a hunter-warrior.

The man sent his relatives to meet with the chosen woman's family and secure their permission for the match; the woman had no say in the matter. Once these informal arrangements had been made, the man formally proposed marriage by giving the woman's male relatives a gift of horses. If they agreed to the union, there was no formal marriage ceremony; the couple simply went together to the man's tepee. In keeping with the Comanche belief that no woman should be left unattached, a man sometimes married his wife's sister too. If a wife was unfaithful, her husband was allowed to mutilate or kill her.

Children

Children were named by a prominent member of the tribe, who usually chose a name with religious significance. If the child became ill or appeared to suffer from bad luck, the family might go through the naming ceremony again and select a different name.

Games and festivities

The Comanche still enjoy the hand game that has provided entertainment for many generations (see "Why the Bear Waddles When He Walks" box). They also hold an annual Homecoming Powwow during the month of July near Walters, Oklahoma. Powwows are celebrations at which the main activity is traditional singing and dancing. In modern times, the singers and dancers at powwows come from many different tribes. In 1972, a group of Comanche established the Little Ponies, an organization that holds powwows and sponsors other events to help keep tribal traditions alive.

CURRENT TRIBAL ISSUES

Some internal issues divide the Comanche tribe. For example, conflicts have developed on the reservation between Christians and members of the Native American Church and between full-blood and mixed-blood Comanche.

NOTABLE PEOPLE

Quanah Parker (c. 1852–1911) was a Comanche leader, the son of a white woman, Cynthia Parker, who had been kidnaped as a child and incorporated into the Comanche tribe. She eventually came to prefer the Comanche way of life and was married to a powerful member of the tribe, Peta Nocona. On the death of his father in 1867, Quanah Parker led the Comanche and their allies in many successful battles against U.S. troops until he was finally forced to surrender in 1875. Parker adapted quickly to reservation life, learning the ways of whites and making deals to benefit his people. He was an important symbol of Comanche courage and pride.

LaDonna Harris (1931–) is a Comanche woman who has promoted equal opportunity for Indian people on a national level. She is also an advocate for world peace.

FURTHER READING

Hagan, William T. *Quanah Parker, Comanche Chief*. Norman: University of Oklahoma Press, 1993.

Rollings, Willard H. *The Comanche*. New York: Chelsea House, 1989.

Sultzman, Lee. "Comanche History." http://www.dickshovel.com/coman.html

Wallace, Ernest, and E. Adamson Hoebel. *The Comanches: Lords of the Southern Plains*. Norman: University of Oklahoma Press, 1952.

Crow

Name

The name Crow comes from a translation of the tribe's name for themselves, *Absaroka* or *Apsaalooke,* which means "children of the long-beaked bird."

Location

The Crow formerly lived along the Yellowstone River and its branches in Montana. Today, many live on the Crow Indian Reservation in Bighorn County in south central Montana, or in the nearby towns of Billings and Hardin.

Population

Before 1740, there were about 8,000 Crow. In 1944, there were about 2,500. In a census (count of the population) done in 1990 by the U.S. Bureau of the Census, 9,394 people identified themselves as Crow, making the tribe the twenty-ninth largest in the United States.

Language family

Siouan.

Origins and group affiliations

Crow tales say that the tribe originated from a land of many lakes—probably Manitoba, in Canada's Lake Winnipeg area. Historians agree that the origins of the Crow date back prior to 1300, to the headwaters of the Mississippi River and as far north as Lake Winnipeg, where they formed a part of the Hidatsa tribe. The Crow parted ways with the Hidatsa people, wandering westward and first entering Montana in the 1600s. Their enemies were the Blackfeet, the Sioux (Dakota, Lakota, Nakota), and the Cheyenne (see entries). They sometimes traded with their allies, the Shoshone (see entry) and the Flathead.

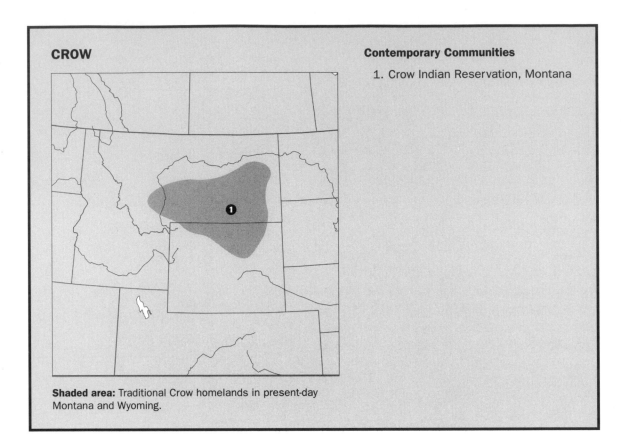

CROW

Contemporary Communities

1. Crow Indian Reservation, Montana

Shaded area: Traditional Crow homelands in present-day Montana and Wyoming.

T he Crow people were western hunters. The men were known as fierce warriors, but the people were hospitable to strangers. Despite their early cooperation with whites, they were forced to give up their claims to all but a small part of their traditional homeland. In modern times, the Crow people have managed to preserve much of their cultural and language traditions.

HISTORY

Change from farmers to hunters

Early in their history, the Crow were part of the Hidatsa tribe. They stayed in one place and lived as farmers. In the early 1600s, a powerful tribal leader called No Vitals had a vision that told him to take his people west into the Rocky Mountains to search for a sacred tobacco plant. He believed that the seeds of the plant would give his people a special identity and make them strong.

Some time during the mid-1600s or early 1700s, about 500 people separated from the Hidatsa to fulfill No Vitals' vision. They migrated to an area near the Yellowstone River in present-day southern Montana and northern Wyoming. They soon abandoned their former lifestyle in favor of a typical Great Plains existence, living in hide-covered tepees, following the movements of the great buffalo herds, and hunting for the plentiful game in their new homelands. The new tribe became known as the Crow.

In the mid-1700s the tribe came into the possession of horses, which greatly aided them in traveling, hunting, and warfare. By the early 1800s, they had more horses than any other tribe east of the Rocky Mountains, averaging between 20 and 60 animals per household.

Crow people split into two groups

When American explorers Meriwether Lewis and William Clark encountered them in 1806, the Crow were part of a large group of Indians and whites who had gathered to trade near Bismarck, North Dakota. Soon after the Lewis and Clark Expedition, even more fur traders arrived in Crow territory and began constructing forts and trading posts.

In 1825, following a disagreement between two powerful chiefs, the Crow divided into two main groups. Chief Long Hair led the Mountain Crow into the high country south of the Yellowstone River, while Chief Arapooish and the River Crow remained north of the Yellowstone River, along the Musselshell and Judith rivers that flowed into the larger Missouri River. As white settlers pushed westward, the Crow got involved in conflicts with other tribes, including the Sioux and the Blackfeet, who moved into their territory. Because they were usually outnumbered, the Crow rarely started wars on their own, but they did steal horses from their neighbors.

Peaceful relations with whites

By the 1850s, more and more white settlers streamed into Crow country. At times the Crow conducted raids on the newcomers, but most often their relationships with whites were peaceful.

Wars and smallpox epidemics depleted the Crow population, and experts predicted that the tribe would soon perish. Instead, the

IMPORTANT DATES

1600s: The tribe splits off from the Hidatsa and begins its westward move.

1825: After a disagreement between two powerful chiefs, the Crow divide into two main groups, the Mountain Crow and River Crow.

1868: The Second Fort Laramie Treaty establishes a reservation for the Crow in Montana, south of the Yellowstone River.

1876: Crow warriors act as scouts for General Custer before his defeat in the Battle of Little Bighorn.

1934: The Crow refuse to accept the provisions of the Indian Reorganization Act.

1948: The Crow write their own constitution and establish a tribal government.

Hunting buffalo in the Missouri River. The huge, migrating herds that had long provided Great Plains Indians with food, shelter, and clothing were nearly gone by the 1880s. The Plains culture as it had been could not survive without the buffalo.

Crow established a cooperative relationship with the U.S. Army and settled peacefully on a reservation in Montana. The Crow signed the Fort Laramie Treaty of 1851, which gave them 38.5 million acres in southern Montana, northern Wyoming, and western South Dakota. The Second Fort Laramie Treaty, signed in 1868, established the Crow Reservation south of the Yellowstone River.

In the late 1800s the Crow leader Plenty Coups (pronounced *Coo*; see "Notable people") learned in a vision that his people needed to continue cooperating with the whites in order to survive. As a result, he had Crow warriors become allies of U.S. Army troops in several battles against enemy tribes. For example, they fought alongside American soldiers against the Nez Perce and Sioux tribes in the 1870s, and they acted as scouts for General George Armstrong Custer (1836–1876) before his defeat in 1876 at the Battle of Little Bighorn (see Lakota entry). Crow cooperation with whites did not earn them any better treatment than the tribes that resisted whites in battle. Still, the protection of the U.S. Army may have saved them from perishing at the hands of the Sioux.

Traditional way of life shattered

During the 1880s, many miners, trappers, and settlers moved into Crow country, establishing forts and railroads. Because the whites had slaughtered buffalo on a large scale, by 1883 the buffalo herds had disappeared. The traditional way of life of the Crow also then came to an end.

The Crow people, suddenly without their main source of food and clothing, were forced to depend on government Indian agents for survival. Over the next few decades, the Crow reservation was reduced in size several times, declining to 2.3 million acres by 1905. At the same time, the Crow culture was in the process of disintegrating as Christian schools were established on the reservation and federal laws were enacted that prohibited traditional Native ceremonies and practices.

The Allotment Act of 1887 divided reservations into individual plots and opened what was left over to white settlement. The purpose of the act was to force the Indians to become more like whites, with each one farming a small plot rather than a plot owned by the whole tribe. Many Crow were not interested in farming and ended up selling their land allotments on the reservation to whites. In time, Crow territory became a checkerboard of Native and non-Native parcels.

Regaining Crow culture

In the late 1800s, Chief Plenty Coups spent much time in Washington, D.C., where he developed good contacts with important people and became shrewd in the workings of the white government.

For example, if a government official refused to listen to his demands for aid for his people, Plenty Coups would pay a visit to the official's rivals. They were happy to pay attention. He also learned that when the Crow spoke out about being cheated by government officials or local merchants, Christian church leaders often came to the Indians' defense.

In 1911 the Crow formed a business committee to represent the tribe in all its official business (see "Government"). It was headed by a young Crow man who had been educated in white-run schools, Robert Yellowtail (d. 1988). During the 1920s, a general council replaced the business committee. Over time the Crow attending the council meetings became active participants in the process, along with their elected leaders.

The year 1934 marked the beginning of the revival of Crow culture. That was when the tribe refused to adopt provisions of the Indian Reorganization Act. The Act would have allowed the Crow to write a constitution, but only under the supervision of the federal government. The Crow decided to remain independent. In 1948, under the leadership of Chief Robert Yellowtail, the Crow developed their own constitution. The Crow, now more in control of their affairs, began to practice the Native religion freely and to follow their traditional ways without fear of the criticism of non-Indians.

The Crow in modern times

During the 1950s the Crow were forced to sell their land rights in Bighorn Canyon to the U.S. government, which planned to build a dam there. In a strange turn, the completed project was named Yellowtail Dam and Reservoir after Chief Robert Yellowtail, who had strongly opposed it.

Today, the Crow reservation is home not only to the Crow people, but also to several thousand non-Indian residents who have leased or purchased land from the Crow. The tribal government employs many of the Native people, and money from the federal government has helped to establish health, education, and housing programs.

RELIGION

The religion of the Crow was based on the relationship between each tribal member and the guardian spirit who guided him or her throughout life. The guardian spirit was the source of an individual's power, wealth, and success. Guardian spirits, in the form of animals or features of the natural environment, usually revealed themselves during a vision quest (see "Festivals and ceremonies").

The Crow believed that tobacco had supernatural power and played an important role in their survival. The people who cared for the tobacco plants, the only crop the tribe cultivated, were members of the Tobacco Society. They had the ability to influence events in the natural world. Only men were allowed to smoke tobacco, and strict rules surrounded the practice.

Tobacco still plays a role in Crow religious life today, and the people continue to make use of sweat lodges (buildings in which water is poured over hot rocks to produce steam) for purification. While some belong to Christian churches, others practice the Peyote (pronounced *pay-OH-tee*) religion in special tepees where ritual smoking takes place. Peyote, which comes from a cactus plant, can cause visions and is used as part of certain Native religious ceremonies, especially those of the Native American Church.

LANGUAGE

The Crow speak a dialect (variety) of the Siouan language. Although the language is spoken by several Great Plains tribes, the Crow version is most closely related to that spoken by the Hidatsa, since the two tribes descended from the same people. The Crow language was still spoken by the majority of Crow adults and children on the reservation in the 1990s, and it is used in reservation schools through the eighth grade.

GOVERNMENT

Each band of the Crow was led by a chief who had earned his position by accomplishing four feats: leading a successful raid against an enemy tribe; capturing an enemy's horses; taking a weapon from a live enemy; and being the first member of a war party to touch an enemy with a coup stick—a practice that was called counting coup. Most bands had more than one chief. The one who was selected as the band's political leader usually demonstrated additional abilities in leadership, influence over the spirits, and public speaking, as well as generosity. When the band experienced a period of bad luck, they simply agreed upon a new chief.

Today, the Crow are led by the general council—a group that consists of all adult members of the tribe. Along with four elected officials and various tribal committees, any person of voting age can

A Crow chief.

provide input at council meetings. A tribal court settles disagreements among tribal members.

ECONOMY

The Crow economy in traditional times was based mostly on hunting, which required a great deal of moving about. Before horses were introduced to the Crow in the 1730s, the people used tame dogs to carry or pull their belongings as they traveled. Horses provided more mobility and allowed for greater success in hunting. Before the European Americans came, Crow territory was full of large game animals—from huge herds of buffalo to deer, elk, bighorn sheep, and grizzly bears. Hunting supplied most of the tribe's food, clothing, and shelter.

Women took care of preparing the animal carcasses. They also gathered plant foods, collected firewood and water, cooked meals, prepared hides, and made clothing and tepee covers. They set up and disassembled tepees when the tribe moved, and cared for the children and the family's horses. The Crow did not generally practice crafts such as basketry or pottery.

Today, the tribe gets most of its income from leasing its land to coal, gas, and oil companies, and from federal government grants. Additional money comes from timber, fisheries, and hunting. While some tribal members have tried to make a success of farming and ranching, they often lacked the funds needed to buy the necessary cattle, tools, and seeds. Now many people lease out their land to outsiders. The U.S. government is the largest employer of individuals on the reservation. Others have found work elsewhere as teachers, social workers, policemen, cowboys, and in the restaurant and coal mining businesses. Still, finding employment is a challenge for the people on the reservation, and at one period in the late twentieth century unemployment stood at forty-four percent (more than four out of ten Crow looking to find work were unable to do so).

The Crow reservation is the site of the Custer Battleground National Monument, which commemorates the lives lost during the 1876 Battle of Little Bighorn. Every year, around 300,000 tourists travel there to attend reenactments of the battle. The Crow earn profits from the motel and heritage center they have built near the site.

DAILY LIFE

Families

The Crow lived in bands of various sizes, depending upon the availability of food. The major social unit was the extended family or clan. Clans are a group of Crow families who trace their families back to a common ancestor. In their society, descent followed the mother's clan. Tribal members could depend on their clan members to protect, defend, and help them in times of trouble. In fact, being told "You are without relatives" was the worst possible insult to a Crow.

The Crow had a strict code of behavior for how people interacted with one another. Boys were expected to pay special respect to their elder male relatives and to their father's kin. Some relatives were to be avoided. For example, married men and women were not supposed to talk with their father-in-law or mother-in-law. Members of the same clan could not marry one another. The complicated and wide-ranging Crow system of relationships ensured that even as they wandered from their immediate homes, the Indians were sure to encounter people with whom they had special ties and with whom they could band together against common enemies.

Buildings

After separating from the Hidatsa, the Crow adopted the hide-covered tepees used by most tribes of the Great Plains. Each tepee had a cone-shaped wooden frame—made up of 20 poles, each about 25 feet long—and was covered with buffalo skins. Tepees usually had a fireplace in the center and a hole at the top to allow smoke to escape. Crow families slept on hide mattresses laid along the sides of the tepee. They built small, dome-shaped sweat lodges, in which men poured water over hot rocks and purified themselves in the steam.

Clothing and adornment

The Crow were known for their striking appearance. Crow men, in particular, were very careful about how they dressed, and wore finely made clothes. Their everyday apparel was made up of a shirt, hair-trimmed leggings held up by a belt, moccasins, and a buffalo robe. For special occasions, they wore fancy costumes decorated with dyed porcupine quills or beads. The bridles, saddles, and blankets used on their horses were also ornate. Crow men usually wore their hair long, and they sometimes extended it by gluing human or horse-hair to the ends. They often hung strings of ornaments in their hair and wore earrings and necklaces made of bone, bear claws, or abalone

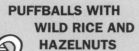

PUFFBALLS WITH WILD RICE AND HAZELNUTS

A puffball is a fungus that resembles a mushroom. Single specimens or clusters of round or pear-shaped white puffballs spring up in August or September in the moist soil of forests or on rotting wood. According to author E. Barrie Kavasch, the Crow believed that puffballs were fallen stars that landed to provide food for the people. Kavasch offered this recipe, which incorporates puffballs and two other Native American staples: wild rice and hazelnuts. Unless you are an expert at identifying wild foods, you should substitute cultivated mushrooms for the puffballs.

4 Tablespoons hazelnut or sunflower seed oil

1/2 cup scallions or green [spring] onions, chopped fine

1 cup fresh puffballs [or cultivated mushrooms], cut in bite-size pieces

3 cups water or stock

1/2 teaspoon salt (optional)

1 cup wild rice, rinsed [see note]

1 cup maple syrup

1 cup chopped, roasted hazelnuts

Heat the oil in a medium pan over moderate heat. Add the scallions and sauté for 2 minutes; then add the fresh cut puffball [or mushroom] pieces, stirring well, and sauté for another 5 minutes. Set aside.

Bring water or stock to a rolling boil in a large pot over medium-high heat. Lightly salt the water and carefully sprinkle the wild rice over the boiling water; add the maple syrup, stirring well. Cover pot and reduce the heat to a simmer. Continue cooking for about 45 minutes, until almost done. Uncover and stir in the puffball [mushroom] mixture. Simmer for another 5 minutes, then stir well and turn out into a big serving bowl. Top with roasted hazelnuts.

This may be served hot or cool as a side dish or salad over summer greens and herbs.

Serves 6 to 8.

[Note: Wild rice should be carefully rinsed before use. It is also best to soak or pre-cook it before it is used. Before starting the recipe, put the rice in twice its volume of water (2 cups of water to 1 cup of rice) and either soak it for one hour or simmer it for 10 to 15 minutes.]

From E. Barrie Kavasch, *Enduring Harvests: Native American Foods and Festivals for Every Season.* Old Saybrook, Connecticut: Globe Pequot Press, 1995, p. 300.

shells. They painted red designs on their faces and applied yellow paint on their eyelids.

Crow women, who spent long hours doing difficult tasks around the camp, tended to be less neat and less elaborately dressed than were the men. Women usually wore calf-length dresses made of deer or mountain sheep skins that were often decorated with rows of elk teeth both front and back. They also wore leggings and moccasins. Crow women often had short hair. They either pulled it out or cut it short when they were mourning the death of a relative.

Food

As they moved about the countryside on their hunts, the Crow kept alert for available foods. In spring, they searched for wild turnips, rhubarb, and strawberries. Summer, along with the search for buffalo, brought the hunt for chokecherries, plums, and other fruits. Throughout the year, the Crow diet depended on rabbit, deer, elk, grizzly bears, bighorn sheep, and other game.

Education

Although the early Crow had no formal schools, children learned by imitating adults in the tribe. To prepare their sons to become successful hunters and warriors, fathers taught them survival skills, such as hunting and trapping. Mothers taught their daughters how to prepare food, make clothing, and take care of a home.

Beginning in 1884, Crow children older than six had to attend a day school near the reservation. Some students were sent away to boarding schools in nearby states, and even as far away as Pennsylvania. Most children in these schools were required to dress like whites and speak only English. Conditions at the boarding schools were harsh and some were so unsanitary that the children there became ill. But despite pressures for children to assimilate (adopt the ways of the whites) the Crow made great efforts to keep their families intact and retain their Native beliefs.

Today the Crow Reservation has three high schools. Because they are financed by the income from coal mining on the reservation, two of their schools are among the wealthiest in Montana. The town of Crow Agency is the home of the Little Bighorn Community College, a two-year college with a student body that is 90 percent Crow. It offers associate arts degrees in areas that will contribute to the developing economies of the Crow Indian Reservation community.

Healing practices

The Crow had two types of healers. One treated minor illnesses and injuries using worldly knowledge, such as by rubbing plant products on sores or lancing swollen areas. The other type, shamans (pronounced *SHAY-muns*), treated major problems like snakebites or diseases by consulting with the spirits. Every Crow person also had his or her own medicine bundle, a small pouch containing sacred objects that symbolized the power of the person's guardian spirit. The medicine bundle was thought to be the source of health, luck, and power. In modern times, health care for people living on the reservation is provided at a hospital in the town of Crow Agency.

ARTS

Shields

Crow people took special care in decorating the rawhide shields they carried into battle. The images that appeared on them often came from visions experienced by the artist and related to his connection with the supernatural. Shields sometimes had sacred objects such as feathers attached to them. They were thought to arm the user with a type of personal protection, and often were passed down through the generations. Decorated buckskin covers protected the shields.

Oral literature

Many Crow stories center on Old Man Coyote, who is often portrayed as a trickster. Old Man Coyote is also recognized as the creator of the world and of the Crow people.

CUSTOMS

Sodalities

After reaching adulthood, most Crow men were recruited into a *sodality,* or voluntary men's organization. The members of these groups enjoyed a special, family-like bond with one another. Intense rivalries often existed between different sodalities, such as the Lumpwoods and Foxes, the two most popular.

Festivals and ceremonies

Of all the traditional Crow ceremonies, the Sun Dance was the most sacred. Sun Dances were held in order for a man to receive a special vision, usually to help him cure a sick child or exact revenge on an enemy for the death of a relative. The man who held the Sun Dance was called the whistler. He enlisted the help of a shaman who possessed a sacred doll. The dolls were considered gifts from the gods and were passed down from one generation to another.

Other men seeking visions could participate in the Sun Dance by fasting and inflicting wounds on themselves. For many years the U.S. government prohibited traditional Crow ceremonies. The Sun Dance was reintroduced to the tribe in 1941 by William Big Day. Today, the tradition continues, and the Crow hold two or three Sun Dances each summer, drawing up to 100 participants.

Every year, during the third week in August, Crow Agency, the capital of the Crow Nation, becomes the "Tepee Capital of the World."

At that time the Crow hold a giant homecoming featuring powwows (celebrations of Native singing and dancing), arts and crafts displays, a rodeo, and a road race. This celebration at the Crow Fairgrounds has been held for more than ninety years. Food booths offer frybread, Indian tacos, and the traditional *menudo*, a mixture of chili and tripe (part of an ox's stomach). Among other popular treats are puffball mushrooms and blueberry pudding.

Vision quest

When a young man undertook a vision quest to connect with his guardian spirit, he first purified himself in a sweat lodge, then traveled to a sacred site on a mountaintop. There he fasted from food and water for three days and slept uncovered in the cold for three nights. Some visionaries cut off the first joint of one finger and offered it to the rising Sun. On the fourth day, after he had proved his courage and willingness to deprive himself, the young man's guardian spirit would appear to him in a vision.

The spirit would provide the man with a sacred song or a symbol that he could use to appeal to the spirit for help in the future. Another way for a young man to seek a vision was to cut two slits in the skin of his chest and insert a wooden skewer. He then tied each end of the skewer to a tall pole, and ran around the pole or leaned back until the skewer was ripped from his flesh. Often in the midst of his pain, the man would receive a vision.

Courtship and marriage

In the Crow culture, girls usually married before their first menstruation. Young men, who could not join the hunt until after they were married, spent most of their time grooming themselves to show off before eligible young women. To propose marriage, the man offered horses to the woman's brothers and meat to her mother. Some Crow men had more than one wife. Cheating on one's spouse was common among both men and women.

Berdaches

Another element of Crow society were *berdaches*—men who enjoyed dressing as women. The Crow considered berdaches to be a third gender and believed that they possessed special powers.

CURRENT TRIBAL ISSUES

Like many other tribes, the Crow have been involved in a number of land claims and land use disputes over the years. They remain concerned about how their lands are being used and feel that too often non-Indians are profiting from their land. The parcels of land that tribal members received in the early 1900s were not enough land to support the population growth. If a father divided his land among his children at his death and they divided their portion among their children, after a while some parcels of land were divided so many times individual plots were less than an acre. This arrangement has made farming or ranching impractical, and much of the reservation land has been sold or leased to large agricultural or mining interests.

The Crow have experienced difficulties in obtaining what they believe to be a fair proportion of the income from the use of their natural resources. However, they did receive a $9.2 million land claim settlement from the U.S. government in 1961, plus another $2 million in 1963 for the Yellowtail Dam and Reservoir property. The Crow used the funds to purchase land, for industrial development programs, and to make loans to tribal members. In recent times, the tribe had plans to invest in a trout farm, a hog-raising operation, and a power plant.

NOTABLE PEOPLE

Plenty Coups (c. 1848–1932), or Alaxchíiaahush ("Bull That Goes Against the Wind"), was the last traditional chief of the Crow. As a boy, Plenty Coups had a vision that convinced him that the only way to save the Crow people was to cautiously cooperate with non-Native settlers and the U.S. government. Plenty Coups effectively represented the interests of the Crow people before the federal government. In 1921, the chief was chosen to represent all Native Americans at the dedication of the Tomb of the Unknown Soldier at Arlington National Cemetery near Washington, D.C.

Other notable Crow include: scout Curly (c. 1859–c. 1935); educator and administrator Barney Old Coyote (1923–); and president of Little Big Horn College Jeanine Pease-Windy Boy (1949–).

FURTHER READING

Frey, Rodney. *The World of the Crow Indians: As Driftwood Lodges.* Norman: University of Oklahoma Press, 1987.

Lowie, Robert H. *The Crow Indians.* Lincoln: University of Nebraska Press, 1983.

Wood, Leigh Hope. *The Crow Indians.* New York: Chelsea House Publishers, 1993.

Kiowa

Name

The name Kiowa (pronounced *KIE-uh-wuh*) comes from the Comanche word "Kaigwa," meaning "two halves differ," describing Kiowa warriors who cut their hair on only one side and left the other side long. It later evolved into the name "Kiowa," which means "the Principal People" to the tribe. Their name for themselves was *kwuda*, which means "coming [or going] out," a reference to their origin story.

Location

The Kiowa's earliest known homeland was in western Montana. In 1700 they were living near the Black Hills of South Dakota but moved to the southern Great Plains in 1785. In the 1990s, nearly 6,500 lived in several small cities in southwest Oklahoma near their former reservation, which no longer exists. (See map on page 806.)

Population

In the early nineteenth century, there were about 1,800 Kiowa. In a census (count of the population) done in 1990 by the U.S. Bureau of the Census, 9,460 people identified themselves as Kiowa (8,936 Kiowa and 524 Oklahoma Kiowa).

Language family

Tanoan-Kiowan.

Origins and group affiliations

Tribal stories say the Kiowa originated near the sources of the Missouri and Yellowstone rivers in western Montana. They say their ancestors came into this world from an underworld by passing through a hollow log. On the way out, a pregnant woman became stuck, barring the way so those behind her could not exit; this explains why there were so few Kiowa. Some then married Sarci Indians and produced a tribe called the Kiowa Apache. After 1700 the Kiowa were alternately friends and enemies with the Apache, Crow, and Cheyenne (see entries).

Although they were few in number, the Kiowa were respected across the Great Plains as proud and fierce warriors. Their ferocious resistance to the American settlement of their homeland made them legends. They may have lost their reservation, but they have not lost their traditions.

HISTORY

Early days on the Great Plains

The ancient Kiowa were wandering hunters who traveled the northwestern Great Plains, following the vast herds of buffalo that were their primary food source. Seventeenth-century French explorer René-Robert Cavelier, Sieur de La Salle, was the first European to record information about the Kiowa. Although he did not meet them on his expedition in 1682, he wrote that they possessed many horses that were probably acquired from Spanish settlers in Mexico. Horses made life easier, allowing the Kiowa and other Plains tribes to hunt and kill buffalo more efficiently than they could ever do on foot.

By the 1700s the Kiowa had roamed as far east as the Black Hills of South Dakota, where the tiny tribe formed a close alliance with the large and powerful Crow nation. Plains Indians gained honor within their tribes by raiding, horse thieving, and warring. The Crow and Kiowa prospered in that way, but they often had to deal with other tribes whose lifeways were the same. They fought constantly with the Comanche and Shoshone in the West, the Cheyenne and Arapaho in the north, and the Sioux in the East.

Move to southern Plains

The unending fighting, combined with a disastrous smallpox epidemic in 1781 that killed nearly 2,000 Kiowa, led to a decision to leave the Black Hills region in 1785 and migrate to the southern Plains. Soon afterwards, the weakened Kiowa made peace with the much larger Comanche tribe. The two tribes agreed to share hunting grounds and often joined forces in raids against other tribes. Together they took control of the southern Plains from the Apache and Wichita (see entries). They gained a reputation as the fiercest of Plains warriors, especially in Texas and New Mexico, where they met the Spanish, established a trading relationship, and began to terrorize white settlements—something they continued to do for many years.

American explorers Meriwether Lewis and William Clark saw the Kiowa in 1804. By then the Plains culture was in full flower. The Kiowa had just begun to trade with the French, who were more willing to give them guns than the Spanish were. Lewis and Clark observed the Kiowa among several Indian groups attending a large trade fair at one of the French trading posts that had been springing up along the Missouri River. The explorers noted there was much singing, dancing, and general merriment going on.

Disasters strike

Smallpox epidemics struck in 1801 and 1816, killing many Plains Indians. Though weak, the Kiowa continued their pattern of fighting and raiding. When vast numbers of white settlers began to move across the Great Plains, most of the tribes put aside their differences and joined forces to attack wagon trains. This alliance did not include the Osage tribe (see entry), however. In 1833 a group of Kiowa who were gathering food were attacked by warriors from the Osage tribe. Many Kiowa were killed and beheaded in what came to be called the Cut-Throat Massacre; some women and children were taken captive.

In 1834 U.S. soldiers returned to the Kiowa one captive girl taken in the massacre. This generous act marked the first contact between the U.S. government and the Kiowa. When the government suggested a peace conference to put an end to warfare on the Plains and open the area for white settlement, the Kiowa were willing to listen.

In 1837 the Kiowa signed their first treaty with the United States. The Treaty of Fort Gibson gave U. S. citizens the right to travel unhindered through Indian lands. The Kiowa were guaranteed hunting rights in the southern Plains, including the territory that would become the state of Texas. Two years later another smallpox epidemic swept through the Plains. In 1849, half the tribe perished in a cholera epidemic; some committed suicide to avoid being overtaken by the terrible disease.

More treaties

The remaining Kiowa strongly objected to the movement of settlers into Texas and continued raiding there. When Texas became a state in 1845, the U.S. government stepped in to put an end to trouble in the region. When the U.S. Army could not put the Kiowa down, a government agent was sent to try and talk peace. In 1853 he

IMPORTANT DATES

1837: The Kiowa sign the Treaty of Fort Gibson, promising peace with fellow Indian tribes and the United States.

1853: The Kiowa sign the Treaty of Fort Atkinson, promising peace with Mexico and a renewal of peace with the United States.

1865: The Kiowa are assigned to a reservation in Oklahoma.

1901–06: Kiowa-Comanche reservation is broken into individual allotments and is opened for white settlement.

1968: Kiowa Tribal Council is formed.

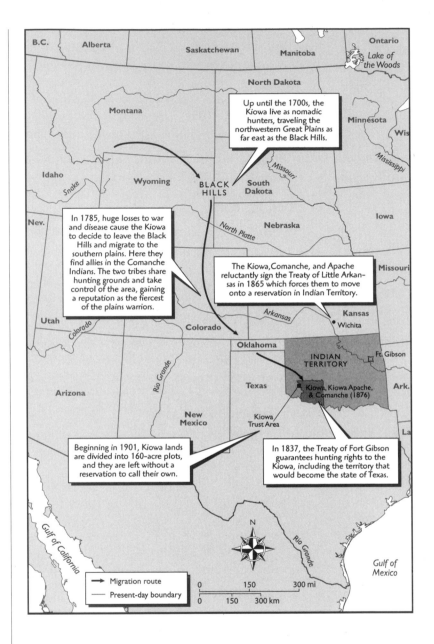

A map showing the migrations of the Kiowa to the end of the nineteenth century.

Up until the 1700s, the Kiowa live as nomadic hunters, traveling the northwestern Great Plains as far east as the Black Hills.

In 1785, huge losses to war and disease cause the Kiowa to decide to leave the Black Hills and migrate to the southern plains. Here they find allies in the Comanche Indians. The two tribes share hunting grounds and take control of the area, gaining a reputation as the fiercest of the plains warriors.

The Kiowa, Comanche, and Apache reluctantly sign the Treaty of Little Arkansas in 1865 which forces them to move onto a reservation in Indian Territory.

Beginning in 1901, Kiowa lands are divided into 160-acre plots, and they are left without a reservation to call their own.

In 1837, the Treaty of Fort Gibson guarantees hunting rights to the Kiowa, including the territory that would become the state of Texas.

→ Migration route
— Present-day boundary

0   150   300 mi
0   150   300 km

convinced the Kiowa, along with their Kiowa Apache and Comanche allies, to sign the Treaty of Fort Atkinson. The treaty—which was never accepted by all the Kiowa chiefs—called for peace in the region and granted the U.S. government the privilege of building roads and forts in return for annual payments for the next ten years.

Kiowa and Comanche warriors continued their raiding against Indians and whites alike. Finally, the U.S. government called for a new peace council, which was held in 1865 at the mouth of the Little Arkansas River (near present-day Wichita, Kansas). It resulted in the Treaty of Little Arkansas, a bitter pill for the Kiowa to swallow. By its terms, they, the Apache, and the Comanche were to move to a reservation in what was then called Indian Territory (now Oklahoma). They were also required to renounce their claims to any other lands. When it appeared the Indians were not going to sign the treaty, the government agreed to allow them to hunt in western Kansas and Texas, but they still had to make the reservation their home.

Another treaty in 1867 required that the Kiowa and other signers agree to learn to farm, and they were promised cattle, farming equipment, and clothing.

Resistance to farming

Government officials hoped to transform a warlike, wandering people into peaceful farmers who lived like European Americans, a process called assimilation. The Kiowa resisted this transformation, and continued with the Comanche to raid other tribes and Texans. This resistance was finally quashed after a punishing campaign by the U.S. military over the winter of 1868-69. General George Armstrong Custer (1839–1876) told the Kiowa bluntly that they must surrender or be destroyed.

Kiowa Chief Lone Wolf, 1869.

For the next sixty years, the government pressured the reservation Kiowa to give up their ways. Meanwhile, nearby ranchers and farmers wanted Kiowa land and pressed the government to permit settlement on it. Some simply sent their cattle to graze illegally. Bolder men built a railroad on reservation land, and towns grew up along the tracks.

Under pressure, Congress passed the General Allotment Act in 1887. The act called for the division of reservation lands into individual plots called allotments; any land left over would be sold to whites.

Reservation lost

The Kiowa objected to the whole idea of allotment and filed lawsuits that delayed the process. They lost, and the parceling out of their land into small plots began in 1901. By 1906, individual Kiowa had

160-acre parcels of land and no reservation to call their own. They endured years of poverty and suffering; some left for good. Today some of the Kiowa people live on land in Oklahoma that was once part of the vast reservation. Although they are surrounded by white communities, many members of the tribe have worked to preserve their cultural heritage.

RELIGION

The Kiowa believed in supernatural forces that could give power to human beings. One of the most important of these spirit forces in the Kiowa religion was the Sun. They worshiped the Sun and obtained power from it in the ceremony called the Sun Dance (see "Customs").

By 1890 many Kiowa and other Indians were fed up with reservation life. They adopted the Ghost Dance religion developed by Wovoka, a Paiute Indian. Wovoka urged Native Americans to perform the dance until the white man was gone and the buffalo was restored to the numbers that had existed in the past. The Ghost Dance was banned by the U.S. government, and the last one performed by the Kiowa took place in 1887.

The late nineteenth century also saw the rise of the Peyote (pronounced *pay-OH-tee*) religion among the Kiowa. Practiced by many Native American tribes, the religion involves consuming part of a small, spineless cactus that grows in the southwestern United States and Mexico. The person then enters a trance state and sees visions. The Kiowa practiced a version known as the Little Moon peyote ceremony, which lasted for one full day. Over the years, peyote use has become part of a religion, the Native American Church, which was founded in Oklahoma in 1918. Many Kiowa men are members of this church, which is credited with contributing to a revival of traditional ceremonies. Women and other members of the tribe are more likely to belong to Christian churches, usually Methodist or Baptist.

LANGUAGE

The language spoken by the Kiowa belongs to the Tanoan-Kiowan language family, but it is quite different from most Tanoan languages (spoken by many Pueblo tribes) and resembles the Uto-Aztecan languages (spoken by the Hopi). The language includes no *r* and is full of nasal and choking sounds.

In the modern world, members of the Kiowa tribe are more and more likely to abandon their Native language in favor of English. Still, some of the older generation speak the language, and young people receive schooling in their native language.

GOVERNMENT

Each Kiowa band was ruled by a chief, chosen for his religious powers or for his outstanding skills in war or healing. Occasionally all these band chiefs came together to discuss matters of importance to the whole tribe, such as whether to make war or peace or when to hold ceremonies.

On the reservations, the Kiowa were no longer hunters or warriors, and Kiowa men had no opportunity to distinguish themselves as leaders. The people were expected to obey government policies. One such policy was the creation of the Inter-tribal Business Committee, whose members were chosen by government agents from each of the three tribes on the reservation. These committee members did not have the loyalty of the Kiowa people, and the Kiowa saw them as puppets (under the control) of the U.S. government.

Federal government policies toward Indians changed in the 1930s, and new laws were passed that would allow tribes to have more say in their own affairs. But many Kiowa opposed government requirements that they re-establish a reservation, giving up their individual plots of land and allowing the land to be controlled by the tribe as a whole, and they declined to do so.

In 1968 the Kiowa Nation created a governing body called the Kiowa Tribal Council. The council serves to represent both individual Kiowa and the tribe as a whole in negotiations with the federal government. Areas of concern are health, education, and economic development.

ECONOMY

Before contact with white traders, the Kiowa economy was based on hunting and trading with other tribes. The Kiowa exchanged horses, mules, and pemmican (dried buffalo meat mixed with fat and berries) for garden goods produced by farming tribes on the Missouri River. Later they traded buffalo hides for European goods, and what they could not acquire by trading, they got by raiding. Favorite targets were horses, food, and captives.

A buffalo yard in Dodge City, Kansas. By the 1880s, there were only about a thousand buffalo left. Without buffalo, Plains Indians were faced with starvation and had little choice but to move to the reservations.

On the reservation, government agents tried to turn them into farmers, but Kiowa hunter-warriors looked down on farming as "women's work." They hated the government's proposal to divide their land into individual farms (allotments) and strongly opposed it. They continued to refuse to farm and, with the buffalo gone by the 1870s, poverty and starvation were common. Within a short time the Kiowa came to depend on government handouts.

Those Kiowa who turned to farming found that their farms did not prosper. They were affected by drought and soil erosion that led to the Dust Bowl of the 1930s, where large parts of the Great Plains suffered from drought and tremendous dust storms. Some Kiowa men left to serve in the military in World Wars I (1914–18) and II (1939–45); some did not return.

Then, new government policies in the 1950s and 1960s offered money and other incentives to young Indians in rural communities if they would agree to relocate to urban areas and learn new skills. Many Kiowa took advantage of the offer and set out for Texas and California, where they took jobs as carpenters and laborers. Some who stayed behind chose to lease their land to whites, but even with that income, the majority of the Kiowa live in a state of relative poverty. Many supplement their family income through arts and crafts products.

DAILY LIFE

Education

Early efforts to force an American-style education on their children left the Kiowa mistrustful of white authorities, and this led to a condition of under-education that still exists. Over the years, the lack of education has contributed to a gradual loss of the Kiowa language and culture. Some trends of the last half century have been promising, though. Today, young people are taught the Kiowan language at the Kiowa Tribal Complex in Carnegie, Oklahoma, as part of continuing effort to preserve and renew the tribe's traditional culture. Likewise many attempts have been made to promote Kiowa art, dance, song, and literature in various publications and on Kiowa land at the Kiowa Nation Culture Museum.

An increasing number of Kiowa students take advantage of federal grants to attend college.

Buildings

TEPEES Like other wandering Plains tribes, the Kiowa lived in the tepee, a cone-shaped tent assembled from a group of sturdy wooden poles tied at the top and enclosed with sewn-together buffalo hides. The entrance was small, perhaps three or four feet high, and always faced east. Although tepees varied in size according to the number of inhabitants, a large one might measure twenty feet in diameter and stand at least as high. Outside, Kiowa tepees were decorated with the same symbol that appeared on a warrior's shield or with a special design that identified the family who lived within. Each tepee housed a family of four or five individuals.

The interior was kept quite simple. In the center was a fire hole for cooking and warmth, while beds—made from a small frame of willow rods and covered with buffalo skin—were placed along the perimeter of the tent. The task of erecting the tepee was women's work. The process was fairly simple, allowing the Kiowa to move easily in order to follow roaming buffalo herds.

MEDICINE LODGES When all of the Kiowa gathered together in the spring for the annual Sun Dance, a special building called a medicine lodge was built. This lodge consisted of seventeen poles arranged in a large circle and standing in the ground vertically. A roof frame made of similar poles was then extended above. At the central point of this frame hung the sacred Sun Dance fetish, a small human figure carved from green stone called the *tai-me*. Outside, the medicine lodge was covered by cottonwood branches that formed the walls of the structure, while the roof was left open to the sky.

Food

Like most Plains-dwellers, the Kiowa relied mostly on buffalo for food, clothing, and shelter. Kiowa men also killed other large hoofed creatures, such as antelope, deer, and elk. Women gathered foods such as fruits, nuts, and roots, to round out the Kiowa diet.

Clothing and adornment

Nearly all clothing and household materials came from the animals of the Plains, primarily buffalo, deer, and other smaller creatures. Men usually wore only leggings and buckskin moccasins in the summer months, with the addition of a deerskin shirt or a buffalo hide robe during the winter season. Women wore dresses of the same materials, along with leggings and moccasins.

The Kiowa adorned themselves with shells, animal bones or teeth, or porcupine quills. Robes were often painted or decorated with embroidery. Animal furs were occasionally worn for warmth. Often, these hides would be thrown over the body with the head still attached, and allowed to rest over the left shoulder. Warriors used decorative shields adorned with paintings of figures they saw in the dream visions that told them they were destined to be warriors. Geometric patterns—such as boxes, hourglass shapes, feathered circles, and striped or symmetrical designs—were also displayed on shields or other items.

Healing practices

The Kiowa believed that natural objects and creatures contained spiritual powers, including the power to heal, bring rain, or see the future. These objects—teeth, animal skins, stones, food, or other items—could be gathered together in bundles called personal "medicine." Such medicine was the property of the shaman (pronounced *SHAY-mun*) who specialized in healing the sick.

Kiowa shamans belonged to the religious society of Buffalo Doctors. Greatly respected by the other members of the tribe, Buffalo

Doctors usually received their curing powers in the form of a dream vision—a sign to the dreamer that he was to become a healer. If he were successful in restoring health to the patient, the Buffalo Doctor was handsomely rewarded.

The personal medicine of an especially successful healer became important to the whole tribe. That was the case with ten sacred Kiowa medicine bundles, known as the Ten Grandmothers. No one but a specially chosen priest was allowed to open these bundles, so their actual contents were unknown to the Kiowa. Before the last priest died in the 1890s, the bundles were opened annually at a special purification ceremony. The bundles are regarded with deep reverence, and they symbolize the well-being and continuance of the old Kiowa ways. Today, each bundle is guarded by one man and one woman who inherit this honor and continue the tradition. Only nine bundles remain; the tenth was destroyed in a fire in the 1930s.

ARTS

Kiowa men and women were renowned for centuries for their painting. They used colors obtained from earth and rocks to paint geometric designs on clothing and containers, and men covered their tepees with scenes from their personal history and from their battles.

Americans recognized the talent of Kiowa artists when some members of the tribe were imprisoned in Florida by the U.S. military in the 1890s. They were given drawing materials to pass the time and used the opportunity to record their histories. In 1891 Kiowa artists were asked to paint works for display at international art shows. In the 1930s five young Kiowa artists were invited to attend the University of Oklahoma School of Art. The group, which consisted of Jack Hokeah, Spencer Asah, James Auchiah, Stephen Mopope, and Monroe Tsatoke, is famous around the world as the "Five Kiowa Artists."

In a society where most of the honor and glory went to warriors and horse raiders, it was difficult for a woman to shine. Certain Kiowa women belonged to artist societies, whose members knew all the secrets of quillwork and beadwork and would pass the secrets on for a fee. Quilled robes made by these women artists were highly prized; one such robe might be traded for a horse.

Today Kiowa men and women are known for their work with buckskin, beads, featherwork, and German (nickel) silver. Their work can be seen at the Oklahoma Indian Arts and Crafts Cooperative.

A Plains custom in warfare, counting coup, or touching the enemy during battle.

CUSTOMS

Sun Dance

The Sun Dance was an annual ceremony held in the spring or early summer. The Sun was worshiped and prayers were offered for the renewal of the buffalo. The Kiowa did not include self-torture in their Sun Dances, as many versions of this popular Great Plains celebration did. Violence was a part of the ten-day ceremony, though, because it ended in raiding and warfare. The last Kiowa Sun Dance took place in 1887; it disappeared along with the buffalo herds on the Great Plains.

War rituals

The Kiowa were hunters and warriors, and many of their activities featured demonstrations of bravery and strength. Status was achieved by warriors through individual acts of courage, such as success in the hunt or "counting coup," coming close enough in battle to touch but not kill an enemy. Warrior societies were formed based on age and experience. Young boys would be members of the *Polanyup*, or Rabbit Society. Other groups included *Adaltoyuo*, Young Sheep; *Tsentanmo*, Horse Headdresses; *Tonkonko,* Black Leggings; *Taupeko,* Skunkberry People or Crazy Horse; *Ka-itsenko,* Dog Warriors.

The highest military honor a man could attain was to be named one of the *Koitsenko*; these were the greatest and bravest of the Kiowa warriors, and could never number more than ten.

Rank in society

Social rank was clearly marked out in Kiowa society. At the top were the *onde,* which included the finest warriors, leaders, and priests. The *ondegup'a,* made up of those warriors of lesser wealth and stature, were directly beneath them, while the *kaan* and *dapone,* poor people, made up most of the tribe.

Not surprisingly in this military culture, women were esteemed far less than men and were obliged to undertake most of the domestic tasks in Kiowa society, including building tepees, preparing food, tanning hides, and making and repairing clothing. A small group of older women, however, did belong to the secret and highly respected Bear Women Society.

Social organizations

In addition to warrior societies, there were religious societies, healing societies like the Buffalo Doctors or the Owl Doctor Society (whose members could see into the future), and the Sun Dance Shield Society and Eagle Shield Society (whose members guarded the tribe's magical and sacred objects).

By the middle of the twentieth century, all the old societies seemed to have disappeared along with much of the traditional Kiowa way of life. Then the Black Leggings warrior society was revived by soldiers who served in the two World Wars. Two other societies, the Gourd Dance Society and the O-Ho-Mah Society, are also being revived. People meet in various cities in Oklahoma to perform modern versions of old rituals. Each year, the Kiowa travel to Andarko, Oklahoma, where the Apache tribe is headquartered, to participate in the American Indian Exposition.

Sweat baths

Among the most important Kiowa customs was an emphasis on ritual cleansing, both as the first step in the proper performance of a religious ceremony and as a way of overcoming disease by getting rid of harmful spirits in the body. Those undergoing the cleansing entered a sweat lodge—a wooden structure containing a fire that heated rocks and produced steam vapor from a nearby water vessel.

The Kiowa calendar

The Kiowa believed in the importance of a calendar history. Two times each year, the happenings of the past season were recorded in the form of painted illustrations on buffalo hide. The oldest calendar now in existence dates from the year 1833 and is a valuable chronicle of more than a half century of Kiowa history.

CURRENT TRIBAL ISSUES

Many of the tribe's current difficulties are related to their placement on the Oklahoma reservation. Living in isolated rural areas, they face overwhelming problems of unemployment in American society. Health care is inadequate, in part because the people do not trust government medical facilities. Schooling, which is generally geared toward white rather than Indian children, has often failed to interest Kiowa children or provide them with opportunities for future employment.

NOTABLE PEOPLE

N. Scott Momaday (1934–), of Kiowa, white, and Cherokee ancestry, is one of the most widely recognized Native American writers. He is the Pulitzer Prize-winning author of *House Made of Dawn* (1968), the tragic story of a Kiowa man whose life falls apart when he tries to adjust to life in a city. Native issues figure prominently in his novels and poetry. He is also a well-respected professor of literature. His book *The Way to Rainy Mountain* (1969) details several centuries of Kiowa history and legend, including the tribe's origins, migrations through the Plains, and contact with white settlers.

Satanta (1830–1878) was born on the northern Plains, but later migrated to the southern Plains with his people. Much of Satanta's adult life was spent fighting U.S. settlers and their military forces. In 1866, when he became the leader of the Kiowa, he favored military resistance against U.S. settlers. In 1867, he spoke at the Kiowa Medicine Lodge Council, an annual ceremonial gathering, where, because of his eloquent speech, U.S. observers gave him his nickname, "The Orator of the Plains." At the council, Satanta signed a peace treaty that obligated the Kiowa to resettle on a reservation in present-day Oklahoma. Shortly thereafter, however, he was taken hostage by U.S.

officials who used his imprisonment to coerce more Kiowa into resettling on their assigned reservation. After his release, Satanta carried out raids against whites in Texas, including an ambush of a train carrying General William Tecumseh Sherman, commander of the U.S. Army. When he attended a peace council a short time later, Satanta was arrested and sentenced to death, but at the protest of humanitarian groups and Indian leaders, he received parole on the condition that he remain on the Kiowa Reservation. Hostilities on the Plains continued, and in 1874, Satanta presented himself to U.S. officials to prove that he was not taking part in them. They rewarded this gesture with imprisonment. Four years later, an ill Satanta jumped to his death from the second story of a prison hospital after being informed that he would never be released.

Other notable Kiowa include; Kiowa/Delaware playwright, editor, and choreographer Hanay Geiogamah (1945–); tribal leader Kicking Bird (c. 1835–1875); attorney and educator Kirke Kickingbird (1944–); and physician and educator Everett Ronald Rhoades (1931–).

·FURTHER READING

Brown, Dee. "The War to Save the Buffalo." in *Bury My Heart at Wounded Knee*. New York: Henry Holt, 1970.

Haseloff, Cynthia. *The Kiowa Verdict*. Unity, Maine: Five Star, 1996.

Wunder, John R. *The Kiowa*. New York: Chelsea House, 1989.

Osage

Name

The name Osage (pronounced *OH-sa-je*) comes from a French misunderstanding of one Osage clan's name, the *Wah-sha-she*. They called themselves the "Little Ones" (a name that shows their modesty) and *Ni-u-ko'n-ska*, the "Children of the Middle Waters," referring to the way they saw their place in the universe.

Location

For hundreds of years the Osage controlled a vast territory in parts of what are now the states of Missouri, Kansas, and Arkansas. Today they live on or near the nearly 1.5-million-acre Osage Reservation in Pawhuska, Oklahoma. (The town's name, Pawhuska, comes from the name of an Osage chief).

Population

In the late 1600s, there were possibly 17,000 Osage. In 1815, there were 12,000. In 1871, there were about 3,679 full-blooded Osage and 280 mixed-bloods and intermarried citizens. In 1906 there were only 2,229 Osage, about half mixed-bloods and half full-bloods. In a census (count of the population) done in 1990 by the U.S. Bureau of the Census, 10,430 people identified themselves as Osage.

Language family

Dhegiha Siouan.

Origins and group affiliations

Long ago the Osage belonged to a large Siouan group called the Dhegiha. The Dhegiha were mostly farmers who lived in settled towns and cities along the lower Ohio River. Their culture was related to the mound-building communities of the Mississippian culture (see entry on Mound Builders) that flourished from 800 to 1500. The Dhegiha gradually moved west, broke into five groups, and settled at various spots along the Mississippi and Missouri rivers. The group who settled along the Little Osage River became the Osage people.

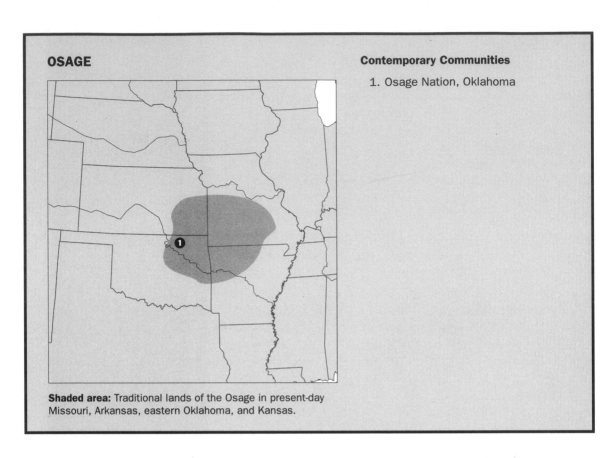

OSAGE

Contemporary Communities

1. Osage Nation, Oklahoma

Shaded area: Traditional lands of the Osage in present-day Missouri, Arkansas, eastern Oklahoma, and Kansas.

The Osage were a proud, shrewd, well-organized, adaptable, and often ferocious people who for decades were forced to give up land to the United States. They finally settled in northeastern Indian Territory (modern Oklahoma). When oil was discovered on their lands in 1906, they became some of the richest people in the world. Wealth brought tragedy and decades of infighting, but it has also allowed them to maintain their culture in a way few other tribes have been able to do.

HISTORY

Forced to move westward

The Osage are generally thought of as Plains people, a culture known for its powerful warriors, skilled horsemanship, and the buffalo hunt. Actually the Plains culture lasted only about 200 years. It emerged in the late 1700s as a result of tribes being pushed eastward by American pioneers. Osage ancestors had farmed for hundreds of years along the Ohio River before they, like so many other

Native groups, moved out to the Great Plains in the early 1600s. The Osage had settled on the Little Osage River by the mid-1600s.

The French were then exploring the region. They first appeared in Osage territory in 1673 and remained there until the 1760s. The French found a tribe that famous American writer Washington Irving ("The Legend of Sleepy Hollow") later described as "the finest looking Indians I have ever seen."

Osage men were of gigantic proportion, often reaching from six feet five inches to seven feet in height. The Osage (who shaved their eyebrows) called the French "the Heavy Eyebrows." According-ing to author John Joseph Mathews: "The Heavy Eyebrows with their dried sweat and armpit odors made some of the Little Ones sick. . . . Until recently they have wondered why . . . white men in general . . . kept their body odors imprisoned by collars and trousers." The Osage found the Europeans undignified and, therefore, unthreatening.

Plains culture in full flower

The Osage and French got along well together, because each group had something the other wanted. The area was rich in fur-bearing animals. The French wanted luxury furs, deerskins, and bearskins to satisfy the growing demand for these products in Europe. Osage skins and furs were especially desirable because the Indians had an excellent way of preparing the skins. The Osage liked the items they got in trade from the French: fine fabrics, plus the European guns, ammunition, clubs, and axes they could use for hunting and against unwanted Europeans and other Indian tribes.

Before the arrival of the Europeans, Osage warriors had occa-sionally raided the villages of other tribes to steal horses. Now, with their appetites tempted by French trade goods, the Osage ranged into land claimed by other tribes to expand their fur trade.

The Osage were known far and wide as fierce warriors and clever traders. Until the end of the 1700s, everyone—other tribes, the French, the Spanish who arrived in the 1760s, and other Europe-ans—recognized that the Osage were in control of Missouri, Arkansas, eastern Oklahoma, and Kansas. Anyone not aware of Osage control soon learned they were in Osage territory when they saw the severed human heads on stakes that served as territorial markers.

In 1802, just before the Louisiana Purchase (in which the United States purchased a vast area of land from the French) brought the Osage under the control of the United States, nearly half the Osage people decided to leave their villages for a new home farther south. This resulted in the tribe being split into two factions that no longer lived close together. The division into two parts affected their ability to protect their territory against enemies. It made them less able to withstand the pressure of American settlers heading West.

Under U.S. control

After the Louisiana Purchase of 1803, the American government and its citizens forced the Osage to move even farther westward. Between 1808 and 1825 alone, the Osage were forced to hand over to the U.S. government nearly 100 million acres of their land in exchange for $166,300, primarily in the form of livestock, horses, farming equipment, and other goods. They were bluntly informed that if they wished to be friends and trading partners with the United States, they had to cooperate.

The Civil War (1861–65) interrupted Americans' westward push, but when the war was over the migration started up again with renewed vigor. That same year the Osage gave up two more large tracts of land—nearly four million acres—to the U.S. government. They were given six months to relocate to a 12-million-acre reservation in southeastern Kansas, far from their traditional homeland. Three years later, the Osage were forced to agree to sell their remaining eight million acres to the government, who in turn would offer it for sale to settlers.

Even before the land could be sold, American settlers began moving onto it illegally, claiming squatter's rights (squatters occupy a piece of public land in order to gain ownership of it). Between 1865 and 1869, more than two thousand settlers had crossed the boundaries of the Osage reservation and were squatting on some of the best farmlands there.

Unhappy times in Kansas

According to Dennis McAuliffe, the family of writer Laura Ingalls Wilder (*Little House on the Prairie*) squatted on Osage land. In one of her books Wilder is said to have described the Osage as "beggars and thieves." McAuliffe noted that the Osage she described "were hungry because white men such as her father were burning their fields, forcing them at gunpoint from their homes and threatening them with death if they returned, stealing their food and horses, even robbing their graves—all to force them to abandon their land."

Settlers demanded that the U.S. government remove the Osage people. Finally, President Ulysses S. Grant sent a Quaker by the name of Isaac Gibson to attempt to resolve the Indian problem fairly. Gibson confirmed Osage claims that Americans were stealing horses and ignoring Indians' rights. Gibson reported to the U.S. government: "The question will suggest itself, which of these peoples are the savages?"

Meanwhile, the Osage were also being attacked by other tribes. The situation reached the point that they could no longer hunt buffalo on the western Plains. Abandoning their reservation seemed their only choice. Osage leaders asked for the assistance of Indian agent Gibson, and with his help laws were passed in 1870 that provided for Osage removal to yet another reservation. Land was available for purchase from the Cherokee. The U.S. government offered to buy the Osage reservation in Kansas for $1.25 an acre (Washington's previous offer—two years earlier—had been 19 cents an acre). The Osage agreed to sell. While other Oklahoma tribes lost a great deal of land during the allotment period, the nearly $9 million settlement for their land made the Osage the richest Indians in America. As one Osage chief commented: "All them other Indians got [was] their ass and a hat; the Osage got money."

With their money, they bought a new reservation in northeastern Indian Territory (now Oklahoma), and they moved there in 1871. Although they were unhappy about leaving the graves of their children behind in Kansas, the Osage were content with their new reservation. There they had abundant game and buffalo, and no one bothered them.

Osage refuse allotment

In 1887 Congress decided that Native Americans were not assimilating (becoming like white Americans) fast enough, and the General Allotment Act was passed to speed up the process. The law allowed the president to divide reservations into parcels called allotments. Each Indian would receive an allotment from the land formerly owned by the whole tribe. Leftover lands would be sold to non-Indians.

The Osage could not agree among themselves whether to accept allotment. Many mixed-blood members of the tribe were pushing for it, but in 1896, before a decision was made, oil was discovered on Osage land. In 1906, the Osage negotiated their own allotment act

Osage representatives on the steps of the U.S. Capitol building, 1920.

with Congress. They agreed to accept the policy of individual 160-acre allotments. However, because they had bought and paid for their land, they refused to agree to make surplus land available to American settlers. Any excess land on the reservation after allotment would then be divided equally, and given to each member of the tribe, which then numbered 2,229.

Land divided into "headrights"

Each of the 2,229 Osage received an allotment of 657 acres of land; the allotment was called a "headright." But individual ownership applied only to the surface land. It did not extend to mineral (oil) rights. Any underground riches would be held in common by all members of the tribe. Each headright was worth 657 acres of land in what is now Osage County, Oklahoma, and one annuity share, or one two-thousandth of the total of all income derived from the production of oil and natural gas beneath the reservation, regardless of who owned the land above. According to the terms of the agreement, the number of headrights would forever remain 2,229. Headrights could be passed on to an owner's heirs, even if they were not Osage, and could be divided among the heirs. Some Osage might even own more than one headright.

As it turned out, the Osage were living on top of one of the biggest oil fields in the United States. When the fields were tapped, the Osage became some of the richest people in the world. At once, greedy people began to close in, hoping to cash in on some of the Osage wealth. Some even married Osage headright holders solely to enjoy their newfound riches.

824 | *Great Plains*

By the 1920s the Osage were flaunting their wealth. They bought expensive cars and other trappings of rich American society. Dennis McAuliffe vividly described the new lifestyle they embraced. He spoke of opulently dressed, free-spending men and women who excited the envy and mockery of newspaper readers all around the world. He described their "mansions, filled with the finest in furniture, paintings, sculpture, china, and other luxury items—but often no occupants. Many Osage preferred sleeping outside, on their lawns, or continued their nomadic traditions of frequent and seasonal traveling—but this time in style."

But hard times were not over for the Osage. In the "Osage Reign of Terror" of the 1920s, which claimed writer McAuliffe's grandmother as a victim, murder after murder on the reservation finally brought in the Federal Bureau of Investigation (FBI). Between one and two dozen Osage were murdered or "disappeared" from their oil-rich lands. The FBI eventually succeeded in securing sentences of life in prison for the offenders in what became one of the FBI's most celebrated cases.

Osage in the twentieth century

During the twentieth century, oil wealth has come and gone again from Osage lands. During the Great Depression, an economic slowdown during the 1930s, oil income decreased considerably. The international energy crisis of the 1970s renewed interest in Osage oil and brought the tribe new wealth. The boom continued into the 1980s and fell off again in the 1990s. The overspending of the 1920s has given way to a wiser use of oil wealth so it is available during hard times.

The Osage have maintained more of their culture than some tribes in Oklahoma have been able to do, partly because of the poverty other tribes have experienced, and because, with their oil income and ownership of their land, the Osage people have been able to remain apart from others.

RELIGION

Traditional beliefs

The Osage creation story speaks of four original groups of people who at some point in the distant past united on Earth into one tribe. They were the Land People, the Sky People, the Water People, and the Isolated Earth People. During a time when there were no enemies to fight and plenty of food had been gathered, certain old men had the leisure to contemplate the meaning of life. These wise men, elderly warriors, devised a religion for the Osage. From then on, Osage wise men were referred to as the Little Old Men.

The Osage believed the Earth was sacred. It is possible that their warlike and ferocious nature, which was often noted by European settlers, was due to their belief in their role as Earth's caretakers.

The ancient Osage discovered the Great Mysteries, which, according to Osage author John Joseph Mathews, "send the wind howling like wolves, and . . . send down balls of ice to pound their heads, and breathe snow across the land." The Osage wasted no time in trying to understand these mysteries and the struggles they had endured adjusting to life on Earth (where everything was chaos). Mathews suggested the Osage felt uncomfortable exploring such "disagreeable things." They accepted that they were simply here, as were the Sun, the Moon, and the stars.

After contact with Europeans

After contact and intermarriage with Europeans, many Osage religious ceremonies had to be abandoned because they required the participation of members of clans that were being affected by mixed marriages. Spiritual confusion resulted, leaving the Osage more open to the teachings of Christian missionaries. Many converted to Christianity, both Catholicism and Protestantism. Some Osage followed the teachings of a Paiute called Wovoka (also John Wilson), who brought the Ghost Dance religion to the Osage in the 1890s. The Ghost Dance instilled hopes that, if it were practiced well, the world would become as it had been before the Europeans came to the Americas—buffalo and other game would return in plenty, dead ancestors would come back, there would be a return to traditional Indian values and lifeways, and the white man would be gone forever. The Osage were introduced by Wovoka to peyote (pronounced *pay-OH-tee*), a substance that comes from cactus; when it is consumed, it can create visions, which are taken to be spiritual paths by many Native participants. Some Osage took up the new religion with enthusiasm, and peyote meetings are still held on the reservation.

LANGUAGE

The Osage spoke a branch of the Siouan language called Dhegiha Sioux. The Sioux were the largest group of tribes on the Plains, and the term Dhegiha Sioux was used for eastern tribes who had been forced by more aggressive tribes to migrate to the Plains. There were four dialects (varieties) in the Siouan language family. The Osage

Plains Indians of different tribes using sign language to communicate, an illustration by Frederic Remington.

spoke the same dialect as the Iowa, Kansa, Missouri, Omaha, Oto, Ponca, Quapaw, and Winnebago tribes. According to Terry Wilson, there were an estimated 300 speakers of fluent Osage in 1993. Classes in the language are held on the reservation.

Because the Plains tribes lived in a widespread area and had come from all over the East, it was rare for groups like the Osage to understand the languages of other groups from the Siouan language family. However, because trade among tribes was common, it became necessary for the Plains tribes to develop a sign language, which proved effective in allowing them to communicate with other groups.

GOVERNMENT

In the early times, Osage groups were governed by a war chief and a peace chief, who guided tribal affairs with the advice of the Little Old Men, the wise, elderly warriors who contemplated Osage life and spirit.

In 1881 the Osage people established a tribal government loosely patterned after that of the U.S. government. Conflicts arose when mixed-bloods (the offspring of intermarriages with the French and others) became numerous in the tribe. Their views often clashed with those of full-blood Osages.

In 1900 the U.S. government declared that the Osage tribal government no longer existed; its members ignored the government's order. In 1906 the U.S. Congress returned governing authority to the tribal council. It was also decided that only the 2,229 Osage who had headrights (and afterwards, their heirs) could vote in tribal elections,

President Calvin Coolidge and his Indian Commissioner with an Osage delegation at the White House, 1920s.

hold tribal office, and receive money from oil proceeds. This system created many headaches for the tribe, and divisions among members of the tribe grew wider. Tribal membership continued to grow, leaving more and more people ineligible to vote. As headright holders died, they passed shares in their headright to their children. Thus, a mother might leave her headright to her three children, and the three children then would have one-third of a vote in tribal elections. Naturally, control of oil wealth was a major issue.

This resulted in a situation where nonvoting Osage, who were often the children of officeholders (and headright holders), were attempting to gain some voice in tribal affairs. At the same time tribal elders and officeholders feared that nonvoters were trying to wrest their headrights from them.

By 1994 only 56 people were on the voting list, yet the tribal council considered them the entire tribal membership. The 1996 membership roll showed an Osage population of 14,000. In 1991 a lawsuit was filed to challenge the tribal voting restrictions. A lower court ruled in 1993 that the Osage had to form a new government and open up voting to include more people. An appeal was filed in a higher court, and in 1997 it was decided that only the U.S. Congress can order a change in tribal government. The right to vote in tribal elections was still restricted to headright owners.

The Osage Tribal Council announced plans to look into the matter of allowing more people to have a say in who represents them on the council. However, the council stated: "we are equally committed to a protection of the mineral [oil] estate, and will adamantly defend the right of shareholders to have the exclusive control over their mineral assets." In other words, although more people may be allowed to vote, they will have no say in how oil money is distributed.

In modern times, the Osage Tribe has been governed by an elected president and vice-president and the eight-member Osage National Council.

ECONOMY

Once the Osage acquired guns and horses from the Spanish and French in the seventeenth century, they no longer depended on farming for their survival. They gained the ability to travel distances and to hunt buffalo. They eagerly took up fur trading with the French, which changed their way of life. Throughout the year Osage villages were open for trade with the French and English. Early summer, before the hunt began, was a favorite time for trading. The Osage provided animal skins and dried meat in exchange for brass cooking utensils, whiskey, weapons and ammunition, English cloth, and fine French ribbons and lace.

Today, in addition to the money from oil, the reservation economy is based on ranching, farming, and the service industry. Many people are employed by the tribal government and in the bingo business.

DAILY LIFE

Education

In traditional times, the education of Osage children was the responsibility of the entire village. Boys were instructed in hunting and warfare, girls in the domestic arts, gardening, and the gathering and preservation of food. Grandmothers were responsible for moral instruction. Discipline for unacceptable behavior began with ridicule and progressed to exclusion from the group—the most severe punishment.

Catholic priests and nuns established a mission school for Osage Indians in Kansas in 1847. Boys were instructed in manual labor, while girls were taught domestic skills. After the move to Oklahoma, many Osage children attended government-run boarding schools both on and off the reservation. There they endured an almost military-style education. They wore uniforms and marched from class to class. Their day began at 5:45 a.m. and ended at 8:30 p.m. with the playing of "taps," the bugle call or drum signal that army camps use to signal "lights out." Osage parents were vocal in objecting to this way of educating their children. They especially resented their children being forced to perform chores. The boarding schools were finally phased out in favor of public schools.

Buildings

The Osage built two styles of dwellings according to the environment and their activities. On the prairies where they farmed, they built lodges or longhouses—circular or rectangular structures ranging from 30 to 100 feet long, 20 feet wide, and 10 to 20 feet high. These were built with a frame made of hickory poles and covered with mats (and later with buffalo skins). The mats were overlapped like shingles to help shed water. Osage women were responsible for the gathering of rushes to weave into mats, a task that took up a great deal of their time. The mats were also used to make furniture and beds.

In the center of the lodge was a fireplace, which vented through a hole in the roof. The fire's central location in the lodge was symbolic of the center of the universe, and the fire served not only for warmth and cooking but also as a communal gathering place. Dried roots, mats, and ears of corn, as well as cooking utensils, hunting supplies, and medicine bags were strung about the room. Sacred pipes hung from the walls and were taken down and smoked as a welcome to visitors. Lodges faced the rising Sun so that those exiting in the morning could begin their prayers to Grandfather Sun. From 10 to 15 people occupied the lodge or longhouse.

During the hunting season, semipermanent structures (that could be taken down and moved) were built. Sometimes some of the building elements from the permanent lodges were carried along and used. Hickory poles were laid out in a circle and the ends were gathered at the top with flexible branches. Bark and rushes, leaves and moss were used to cover the outside. Later, when horses made buffalo hunting possible, lodges were covered with buffalo skins.

In some villages there was a Lodge of Mystery, to which the Little Old Men retired for discussions. This building was built in the same way as the residential lodges, but only the finest animal skins were used to cover it.

Food

The Osage hunted, gathered, and planted gardens. For hundreds of years, whether living in the East or near the Plains, Osage women had been planting squash, corn, beans, and pumpkins. Once a garden was planted in spring and the young plants had established themselves, the Osage moved to another environment to take advantage of whatever plants and animals were available. Every healthy man and woman set off on this expedition, leaving behind the old and feeble to watch over the food preserves from last year's hunt and harvest. They gathered wild nuts and berries, persimmons, pawpaws (fruit from the pawpaw tree, which is common in the eastern and southeast United States), plums, grapes, roots, and potatoes, which they preserved for winter use. They hunted deer, bear, elk, wild turkey, and small game. When they knew their gardens were ready, the Osage returned to their villages to harvest.

Clothing and adornment

Many of the early traders and travelers who encountered the Osage wrote of their striking appearance. The men were extremely tall and very fond of personal adornment. Osage men wore their hair "roached," a style in which the sides and back of the head are shaved, leaving a lock about two inches high at the top. This strip of hair might be further ornamented with the long hairs from a deer's tail. One or two strands were left long to be decorated with feathers and beads. The Osage also plucked or shaved their eyebrows. Some were tattooed around the eyes and mouth, and their shoulders, arms, and chest were painted. Most men pierced their ears; some inserted large bones in their ears to make an even larger opening for earrings to be inserted. Necklaces of wapiti teeth (a wapiti is a large deer) and moccasins trimmed with squirrel tails were also worn.

Warm-weather wear for men usually consisted of a simple loincloth secured by a belt. In cold weather they wore buffalo-skin capes or trade blankets. The fringes on their deerskin leggings were intended to resemble eagle feathers, since the Osage believed they

had originally landed on Earth like an alighting eagle. Warriors trimmed their leggings with scalplocks, pieces of scalp with hairs attached, which they removed from an enemy's head during battle.

Osage women favored tattooed breasts and some wore a long shirt that covered one shoulder. Women and girls might also have worn an apron-like garment made of deerskin. Beads were strung into necklaces and several long strands were worn. Single women wore their long hair in decorated braids, while married women merely pulled it back and tied it with a leather thong. Sometimes the part in a woman's hair was painted red to symbolize the Sun moving over the Earth.

Healing practices

Medicine men or women occasionally served as religious leaders, but they were most highly regarded for their knowledge of how to extract drugs from plants and herbs. Medicine men were paid for their services to the sick. When their herbal remedies failed and the patient got no better, a medicine man called upon mysterious forces. To get their attention, he wore special clothing made of bear or snake skins and sometimes decorated with deer hooves. The medicine man generally performed a ritual song and dance over the patient, accompanied by the music of rattles.

One of the medicine man's most important responsibilities was to put together medicine bundles for warriors. These contained herbs and other items designed to ward off evil spirits and curry favor with good spirits. A different mixture was required for each warrior. Medicine bags were made from the skins of birds, animals, or reptiles. Renowned painter of American Indians George Catlin (1796–1872) remarked that "the value of the medicine-bag to the Indian is beyond all price . . . for he considers it the gift of the Great Spirit."

ARTS

Osage women are known for their beautiful finger weaving and for their ribbonwork. In ribbonworking, the women cut intricate designs into ribbons and then sew them in several layers onto clothing and ceremonial objects such as dance blankets.

CUSTOMS

Clans

Osage society was organized into a complicated system of clans, or family groups. Originally there were fourteen clans, but they were later expanded to twenty-four. Clans were further divided into Sky People and Land People. The Osage believed all members of a clan were descended from a common ancestor and were related. The common ancestor could have been a plant, animal, or a natural phenomenon. Clan leaders, who inherited their positions through their fathers, shared a limited rule over the entire Osage Nation. Each clan controlled the part of the village in which it lived and the clan functioned as a military unit during wartime.

Courtship and marriage

When Osage boys and girls reached puberty, they were considered ready for marriage. Osage women usually married immediately, but men usually waited until they were at least in their late teens. A mate was chosen by the man's parents from another clan. Four "good men" were asked by the groom's parents to determine that the bride was indeed from a different clan and to set up the exchange of gifts that was the main event of a simple wedding ceremony. Divorced and widowed women were considered outcasts, suitable only as mates for white men.

In the earliest times, it was the custom for Osage newlyweds to move in with the groom's parents. When the Osage took up hunting and raiding, the custom was reversed and the couple moved in with the bride's parents. A household that included men from several different clans had an advantage: when some clans left on hunting and raiding expeditions, others could stay behind and contribute in other ways to the household.

Babies and children

Osage infants were tied to boards, which their mothers carried on their backs. An infant was bound so tightly to the board that the back of its head was flattened; this was considered an attractive feature.

Naming ceremonies were held; after the ceremony a young child was considered a "real" person and member of a clan. This was the occasion when a child acquired a special clan hairstyle that he or she wore until puberty.

Festivals and ceremonies

Other than child-naming, important occasions that required elaborate ceremonies included a weeks-long preparation for war, the celebration of a warrior's success in battle, the celebration of peace, and the mourning of those who died in battle.

The Osage have held their most important dance every spring since 1884. It is called *I'N-Lon-Scha,* the Playground of the First Son. Each year, a boy is chosen to be drum keeper, which is considered a great honor. His family keeps the drum for a year and is in charge of hosting the last dances in the four-day spring event. At those last dances, lavish gifts are bestowed by the host family upon their guests.

The Osage were among the first Native Americans to send their men and women off to fight in World War II (1939–45). Before they departed, a ceremony was held, and warrior names were bestowed upon them.

CURRENT TRIBAL ISSUES

Oil wealth has affected the lives of Osage in ways never experienced by other Native Americans. Terry Wilson reported in *Native America in the Twentieth Century* that "Osage politics is still almost completely shaped by the overriding concerns of oil leasing and headright payments."

At issue for the Osage in the late 1990s was the placement of the centuries-old remains of deceased Native Americans that were being held by the anthropology department at Missouri University at Columbia. The Osage Nation was pressing for the return of the remains, if it could be determined that they were indeed Osage remains. The university contended that the remains would give students an opportunity to learn more about Native American history.

NOTABLE PEOPLE

Maria Tallchief (1925–) was born in Fairfax, Oklahoma, and began dance and music lessons at age four. Following high school, she joined the Ballet Russe, a world-famous Russian ballet troupe, and worked under the renowned choreographer (composer and arranger of dance steps) George Balanchine. In 1946, she married Balanchine and moved to Paris with him. Tallchief was initially treated with disdain in Paris. Her debut at the Paris Opera was the first ever for any American ballerina, but Tallchief's talent quickly won French audiences over. She later became the first American to dance with the

Paris Opera Ballet at the Bolshoi Theatre in Moscow. In 1949 she became the first Native American to become prima ballerina at the New York City Ballet, and that year she danced what was perhaps her greatest role in the Balanchine-choreographed version of the *Firebird*. In 1965, Tallchief gracefully retired from performance in order to teach ballet. Ten years later she headed the Chicago Lyric Opera Ballet, and in 1987 she founded the Chicago City Ballet.

Other notable Osage people were: Charles Brent Curtis (1860–1936) of Kansas, the first Native American to be elected vice president of the United States (under Herbert Hoover); Corine and Leona Girard, mixed-blood sisters, active during the 1920s in the fight to obtain voting rights in tribal affairs for Osage women; John Joseph Mathews (1894–1979), the author of the first university-published book to be sold by the Book-of-the-Month Club and a major figure in Osage tribal politics; and Andrew "Buddy" Redcorn, the most-decorated Native American in the Vietnam War.

FURTHER READING

Liebert, Robert. *Osage Life and Legends: Earth People/Sky People.* Happy Camp, California: Naturegraph Publishers, 1987.

Mathews, John Joseph. *The Osages: Children of the Middle Waters.* Norman: University of Oklahoma Press, 1961.

McAuliffe, Dennis, Jr. *The Deaths of Sybil Bolton: An American History.* New York: Random House, 1994.

Wilson, Terry P. *The Osage.* New York: Chelsea House, 1988.

Wilson, Terry P. "Osage." *Native America in the Twentieth Century: An Encyclopedia.* Ed. Mary B. Davis. New York: Garland Publishing, 1994.

Pawnee

Name

The name Pawnee (pronounced *PAW-nee* or *paw-NEE*) probably comes from the Sioux term *pa-rik-i,* meaning a horn. The word refers to the distinctive hair style of the Pawnee warriors, who coated their hair with thick grease and paint so that it stood up like a horn. Some groups of the Pawnee called themselves *Ckirihki Kuruuriki,* meaning "looks like wolves," or *Chahiksichahiks,* meaning "men of men."

Location

The Pawnee once lived on the Plains in what is now Nebraska, concentrating in the valleys of the Loup, Platte, and Republican rivers. Today, the Pawnee reservation is located on 20,000 acres of land in north central Oklahoma, about 50 miles west of Tulsa.

Population

At their height, the Pawnee probably numbered about 35,000. In 1790, there were about 10,000 Pawnee. In 1900, there were about 650. In a census (count of the population) done in 1990 by the U.S. Bureau of the Census, 3,387 people identified themselves as Pawnee.

Language family

Caddoan.

Origins and group affiliations

The Pawnee and other Caddoan-speakers may be descendants of the prehistoric hunter-gatherers who roamed the Great Plains region of North America as many as 7,500 years ago. Some historians believe they came from Mexico but moved northward, and by 1600 they were in control of large parts of the western Plains. Many Pawnee have different, more spiritual, beliefs about their origins.

The Pawnee nation consisted of four related bands: the *Chaui,* or Grand Pawnee; the *Kitkehahki*; the *Pitahauerat,* or *Tappage* Pawnee; and the *Skidi,* or Wolf Pawnee. The Arikara were once considered part of the Pawnee, but they split from the main group many years ago and are now considered a separate group. The major enemies of the Pawnee were the Cheyenne and the Sioux tribes (see Cheyenne, Dakota, Lakota, and Nakota entries).

PAWNEE

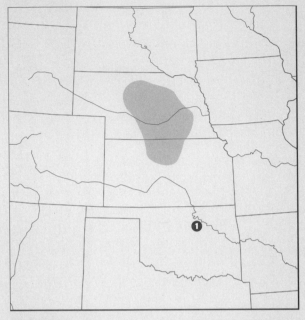

Contemporary Communities

1. Pawnee Indian Tribe of Oklahoma

Shaded area: Traditional lands of the Pawnee in present-day Nebraska.

The Pawnee were a peaceful farming people who could be fierce when pushed to defend themselves. Because they stayed in one area, they made easy targets for other wandering Plains tribes who could catch them off their guard. Still, other tribes regarded them as mysterious, and were awed by their poetic stories and rituals concerning the heavens and the Earth.

HISTORY

Pawnee in ancient times

For centuries the Pawnee way of life revolved around pursuing the Plains buffalo on foot, stampeding them over cliffs, trapping them in corrals, and killing and butchering them with chipped-stone tools. The Pawnee also farmed part-time, raising corn, squash, and beans in the fertile river valleys of the Great Plains.

Sometime around the early thirteenth century, the Pawnee left the Great Plains, perhaps because of a change in the climate. While some scholars believe they settled in the Southwest, others believe they moved into the Southeast near the Mississippi River delta. But by the year 1300, the ancestors of today's Pawnee returned to the Great Plains. They settled in the river valleys of modern Kansas and Nebraska between the Apache people to the west (see entry) and the Sioux people to the east. From the fourteenth through the sixteenth century, Pawnee civilization flourished on the Great Plains.

Horses arrive on the Plains

In 1541, about 250 years after the tribe returned to the Great Plains, Spanish explorer Francisco de Coronado encountered people he called *Harahei* north of the Arkansas River in what is now Kansas. These people were probably the Pawnee. Coronado, then in search of the riches, did not stay long among them.

Sometime before 1680, horses (originally brought from Spain) became a common sight on the Great Plains and the Pawnee began to use them. Horses allowed the Pawnee to travel farther in search of buffalo. However, while tribes such as the Sioux and the Cheyenne used the horse to take up the wandering way of life year-round, the Pawnee remained primarily an agricultural people.

Tribe faces changes

Many changes occurred among the Pawnee in the nineteenth century. Their lands were overrun, first by eastern whites who had heard stories of free, fertile land in the West, then by gold seekers on the way to California after gold was discovered in 1848. The waves of migrant people, intent on crossing the Great Plains to find riches, frightened the buffalo on which the Pawnee relied for their survival. Sometimes starving Pawnee were forced to attack white wagon trains and settlements.

The whites brought with them European diseases to which the Pawnee had no immunity. A smallpox epidemic in 1831 cut their numbers in half. In 1849 cholera, a deadly disease that spreads rapidly, reduced the tribe by half again. By 1857, widespread measles and tuberculosis had made the Pawnee dependent on aid from the U.S. government. That year, the U.S. government placed what few

IMPORTANT DATES

1300 : The Pawnee begin their migration to Nebraska.

1541: Francisco de Coronado meets the Pawnee on the Great Plains while looking for treasure.

1817 : The Pawnee chief Petalésharo puts an end to the tradition of the Morning Star maiden sacrifice.

1876: The U.S. government forces the Pawnee to abandon their land in Nebraska for a reservation in Oklahoma.

1960s–1970s: The federal government returns Pawnee reservation lands in Oklahoma to the tribe.

members of the tribe were left on a reservation on the Loup River near what is now Genoa, Nebraska. But on the reservation the Pawnee were vulnerable to raids by other Plains tribes, particularly the Sioux tribes. In 1864, the U.S. government began a campaign to subdue the hostile Sioux, and Pawnee warriors volunteered to assist. Pawnee warriors fought bravely alongside the U.S. Army regulars.

On the reservation

On the reservation the Pawnee tried to live as before, hunting and farming in their communal style, whereby all the people shared in the work and divided equally the crops they produced. The federal agents wanted them to farm as individuals. They were also asked to live in wooden houses and send their children to schools where they were forbidden to speak their native language.

Then more disasters struck, both natural and manmade. A drought resulted in the dehydration and death of most of the buffalo and harmed the crops, and a plague of grasshoppers destroyed the crops that had survived. By this time, after all the disease and disorientation, the Pawnee were very weak. On August 5, 1873, a day when their men were away hunting, Pawnee women and children were attacked by a large party of Sioux. Between 75 and 115 of these innocent people were killed at what came to be called the Battle of Massacre Canyon.

In the face of continuing demands by white settlers for more Pawnee lands, in 1876 the U.S. government convinced the tribe to move from Nebraska to a reservation in Oklahoma. The federal government pushed the Pawnee off their Nebraska lands so quickly they did not even have time to harvest their crops, and the people spent a terrible winter with little food to eat.

Pawnee Chief Alex Mathews holding the flag at a meeting of President Bill Clinton and a group of Indian leaders.

Rebirth of a Nation

Government acts in 1887 and 1898 further reduced the land holdings of the remaining Pawnee, whose lives by now were full of sickness and misery. In 1893, as the federal government was once again pressured to provide more land for white settlers, most of the Pawnee Reservation was allowed to be purchased and settled by non-Indians.

By the early twentieth century, the Pawnee seemed to all but disappear. Then in the early 1930s, the U.S. government decided to try to right some past wrongs and help the ailing Pawnee become a functioning tribe. The Indian Reorganization Act of 1934 restored some rights, but it was not until the mid-1960s that the federal government finally returned Pawnee reservation lands in Oklahoma to the tribe. In 1966, the tribe was awarded $7 million from the Indian Claims Commission for their original lands in Kansas and Nebraska that had been taken by the United States in the nineteenth century. During the 1970s the Pawnee regained more tribal lands.

Today, most of the Pawnee live in Pawnee, Oklahoma, the site of their tribal government. Although many have adapted to mainstream American life, they still hold celebrations of their Pawnee heritage throughout the year.

RELIGION

The religion of the Pawnee is inspired by the Sun and stars of the Great Plains sky, which they once used to guide them on their travels. Many of the stars and planets were worshiped as gods (see box). The Pawnee believed that after death, human souls followed the Milky Way to heaven and lived out eternity with Tirawa, their Creator.

Pawnee priests served as messengers between the invisible spirit world and the everyday world. They watched the skies during planting and growing season, and if storms or other dangers threatened the crops, they performed rites to drive them away. They used stuffed birds and animals in religious ceremonies.

LANGUAGE

The Pawnee spoke a language that was distantly related to the languages of the Wichita, the Caddo (see entries), and the Arikara, three other tribes whose language were in the Caddoan family of languages. Caddo was related to the languages of the Sioux and the Iroquois. Caddoan speakers all made use of Great Plains sign language for communicating outside their tribal group.

GOVERNMENT

In traditional times, a Pawnee chief inherited his position from his father. Still, he had to prove he had the necessary knowledge and power to deserve the position. Pawnee leaders were respected for speaking in a quiet tone of voice, and for leading in a wise, patient, and understanding manner.

In modern times, the tribe is governed by two eight-member governing bodies: the business council and the chiefs of the Nasharo Council. The chiefs are chosen by their bands, while the president, vice-president, and secretary/treasurer of the business council are elected by the entire tribe.

ECONOMY

The Pawnee relied on two different economies: the farming economy and the hunting economy based on the Plains buffalo. To produce the best crops, it was important to know when the spring planting should take place; this was the focus of the Ground-breaking Ceremony (see box on page 849).

The Pawnee way of life changed in the early 1700s with the introduction of guns and horses. The people came to rely on hunting to supply things that their crops could not give them, including meat and hides made into clothing and shelter. All parts of the buffalo were used. Buffalo hair was braided into rope, horns were made into spoons and tools, and the animals' shoulder blades were used as hoes.

Today, the tribe gets most of its money from government grants and contracts, as well as from the leasing of tribal land for agricultural use and for oil and gas exploration. In the mid-1990s the tribe was planning to build a chemical plant and to renovate the tribal bingo hall. Individual Pawnee people make their living as farmers, housepainters, silversmiths, bead makers, and as members of the military, among other ways.

THE MAJOR GODS OF THE PAWNEE

The most important Pawnee god is *Tirawa,* who represents the open sky. Tirawa created the universe to relieve his loneliness. He first created the four primary stars: the Evening Star in the West, with the Moon as her helper; the Morning Star in the East with the Sun as his helper; and the North and South Stars marking the other two directions. Tirawa also created stars for the skies of Northeast, Northwest, Southeast, and Southwest, and gave them the task of holding up the Earth.

The Evening Star and the Morning Star were responsible for the creation of the Earth and the ancestors of the Pawnee. The Evening Star created the Earth from a clap of thunder and a flash of lightning. Then the Morning Star persuaded Evening Star to marry him and they produced the first of the Pawnee. Their first-born child, a girl, was lowered to Earth on a whirlwind. Their second-born child, First Man, became Chief of Center Village and of all the Pawnee. First Man had to assemble and bring the important sacred bundles to the various Pawnee villages. Aided by Evening Star and Morning Star, the people developed their ceremonies, symbols, and songs. Bound by their shared gifts, the people then banded together to form a nation.

DAILY LIFE

Families

The oldest woman was the most important person in a family or in a household. Women raised the children, did the farming and the cooking, and made bowls and spoons and other utensils. The men hunted, made war, fashioned weapons such as bows and arrows, went on twice-yearly buffalo hunts, and served as the chiefs or healers. Since a Pawnee man could have more than one wife, he did not always live with his children, but it was his job to provide them with food and other necessities. A woman might have more than one husband, but all her children considered themselves brothers and sisters.

Buildings

The Pawnee built two types of structures: earth lodges and tepees. They lived in earth lodges during the spring and fall while they were planting and harvesting their crops. They carried tepees with them on the buffalo hunt.

Earth lodges were made of dirt piled over a wooden framework of cottonwood and willow. They were well suited to the changing climate of the Great Plains, but they only lasted three to six years and were hard to build and maintain. It took the timber from four large trees and up to one hundred smaller trees or bushes to build one lodge. Tepees required less labor but were not as sturdy. They were made from buffalo hide and were meant to be easily carried from place to place.

Ten to twelve lodges made up a village and each could shelter as many as ten related families. A lodge usually had a covered entryway, measuring about twelve feet high, seven feet across, and eight feet long. The entryway led to the main part of the circular dwelling, which was about forty feet in diameter and about fifteen feet high at the smoke hole in its center.

SACRED ARCHITECTURE Both the earth lodge and the tepee were built according to Pawnee ideas of sacred architecture. They were intended to be miniature models of the universe, with the roof representing the sky overhead, and the floor representing the earth underfoot. Each lodge or tepee had a sacred spot called the *wi-haru,* "the place of wonderful things." The *wi-haru* represented Pawnee Paradise, where the corn was always ripe and the buffalo were always plentiful. It was always located along the western wall of the dwelling and included an altar with a buffalo skull and the family's sacred bundle. Sacred bundles were sacks that contained items such as pipes, tobacco, paints, corn, and parts of birds; they were thought to be gifts from the gods.

Clothing and adornment

The Pawnee made most of their clothing from buckskin. Women wore a leather dress or wrap skirt, adding leggings and an overblouse in winter. Men wore leather breechcloths (garments with front and back flaps that hung from the waist), a loose shirt, and

PAWNEE GROUND ROAST POUND MEAT WITH PECANS

Author E. Barrie Kavasch, an authority on Native American culture and cookery, spent time with the Pawnee of north-central Oklahoma. He noted that the Pawnee are known for their generosity and for the skill of their drummers and dancers. Their celebrations, accompanied by traditional Pawnee foods, draw large crowds. One Pawnee specialty, ground roast pound meat with pecans, is a favorite festival food. At one time the dish was prepared with buffalo. Today, beef replaces buffalo.

1 (5-pound) lean rump roast

salt and pepper to taste

1 cup warm water

2 pounds shelled pecan halves

1/2 cup sugar

Preheat oven to 350°F. Place the roast, lightly seasoned with salt and pepper, in a well-greased roasting pan and roast for 50 to 60 minutes until moderately well done. Remove roast and allow to stand and cool for 30 minutes.

Lower the oven to 325°F. Cut cooked roast into large chunks, and feed, one by one, through a hand grinder. Coarsely grind the beef and spread it in another broad roasting pan. Place the first roasting pan [on a stove burner] over low heat and [add] the 1 cup of warm water, stirring and scraping all the meat residue from the pan sides and bottom to make a broth [a procedure called deglazing]. Simmer for about 10 minutes while stirring. Pour the broth over the ground meat in the second roasting pan, then sprinkle the meat mixture with the pecan halves. Season overall with sugar, salt, and pepper.

Place this pan in the 325° oven and roast for 20 to 25 minutes, stirring once to blend thoroughly. Serve hot and enjoy with other festival foods. This is especially delicious with hot corn and squash.

Serves 10

From E. Barrie Kavasch, *Enduring Harvests: Native American Foods and Festivals for Every Season.* Old Saybrook, Connecticut: Globe Pequot Press, 1995, p. 76-7.

leather leggings. They wore two belts. One held up their clothes and the other held necessities, such as the tomahawk, knife, pipe, and tobacco. Men carried buffalo robes to impress visitors with their power and status. A man's status was also shown by the quality of his skin shirt, with its decorations of quillwork, scalps, or skins.

Shirts and robes were decorated with moons, suns, or stars to represent the tribe's special relationship with the heavens. Hide moccasins were usually left plain, although they might be decorated for special ceremonies, such as burials or warfare. Men sometimes wore turbans of hide or cloth. On special occasions, they wore war bonnets adorned with suns, moons, and stars.

Food

On their farmland in the fertile river valleys of Kansas and Nebraska, the Pawnee raised ten to fifteen different kinds of corn, eight kinds of beans, and seven kinds of pumpkins and squash, as well as watermelons, sunflowers, and tobacco. They also harvested a grain similar to modern wild rice. The village chief assigned plots of land to various families. When they caught buffalo, the Pawnee, who in later times were often near starvation, would gorge on hunks of the roasted or baked meat.

Education

Grandparents were the primary teachers of Pawnee children, instructing them in the tasks of tribal life. Grandmothers also took care of their daily needs and gave them toys and treats. Grandfathers joked with their grandchildren and sometimes took the boys outside on a winter morning, sometimes dumping them into the snow or into a stream in order to "toughen them up." Uncles taught the boys how to hunt, fight, and make tools. Girls learned from women how to take care of the lodge and work in the fields.

From childhood, tribal members were treated as independent, respected persons who were expected to be self-reliant. Children were taught to share their goods with others, a lesson that produced adults without the strong sense of personal possessions that is found in many modern societies. Today, most Pawnee students attend area public schools.

Healing practices

The Pawnee had two separate types of "medicine men": the holy men who maintained the tribal relationship with Tirawa, the Creator, and the other gods; and the shamans (pronounced SHAY-muns) who maintained the tribal relationship with animals and the natural world. The shamans were organized into eight "doctor groups," and each had its own unique healing ceremonies. Each group conducted at least two healing ceremonies each year and took part in "mesmerizing contests," where they demonstrated their skills in hypnotizing people.

Only members of the doctor groups could practice the healing arts. Others who did so were considered witches and were treated with contempt. Today, tribal members receive health care services through the U.S. Public Health Service Clinic.

ARTS

Pawnee people enjoyed decorating their homes, tools, and clothing with colorful feathers, beads, and paint. Porcupine quills were a favorite material. The quills were dyed various colors and were woven or sewn into designs on clothing, hunting shields, and other objects. In later years the crafters also used European glass beads. Paintings were done on a variety of surfaces, ranging from buffalo hides to the painter's body. They often depicted important events or battles, as well as images of the land, sky, and stars.

CUSTOMS

Much has been written about Pawnee practices, because four Pawnee men (James Murie, Roaming Scout, He Arrives in the Lead, and Mark Evarts) cooperated with American anthropologists (people who study the cultures of various peoples) to record and preserve many Pawnee traditions.

Festivals and ceremonies

Without a doubt, the most famous Pawnee rite was the Morning Star ceremony, in which the Pawnee sacrificed a young girl to the Morning Star god to thank him for creating the tribe. The ceremony began when a warrior had a special dream about Morning Star. He then went before the priests of the tribe, who gave him permission to kidnap a young girl of about thirteen from another tribe—usually a Sioux band, according to tradition.

The warrior carried the girl back to his village, where she was tenderly cared for until the time for the ceremony came. The warrior placed her on a platform. As the sun rose, a priest shot her through the heart with an arrow. Then every male in the tribe, even the youngest, shot the girl's body with arrows. This practice was brought to an end by the Pawnee chief Petalésharo in 1817. He interrupted a ceremony and freed the young woman before she could be sacrificed, giving her food and a horse so that she could return to her own people.

Another popular ceremony was the Harvest Festival. It lasted for twenty nights and featured chanting, music, and performances by magicians and clowns. White people who witnessed the performance reported seeing fantastic sights like the sudden appearance of people dressed as bears and other animals who chased and mangled people to death. The "dead" people were then cured by shamans and arose unharmed.

Every year since 1946 the Pawnee nation has hosted the Pawnee Indian Homecoming around the Fourth of July, where all members of

Pawnee and Sioux get together at a Nebraska powwow in 1925 after many years of hostility between the two groups.

the tribe are welcome to return to their traditional homelands. Dressed in Native clothing, they play Pawnee games and do tribal dances.

War and hunting rituals

The main objective of most Pawnee attacks was to steal horses. When they did raid enemy villages, they approached quietly in the night and swept off herds of horses. Sometimes they cut off the scalps of the enemy as war trophies.

The Buffalo Dance was held to ensure that a hunt would result in a large kill. Painted dancers, carrying spears and wearing large buffalo masks, reenacted a hunt. Moving to the beat of a drum that represented the beating heart of the Pawnee hunter, a dancer circled the fire until a blunt arrow shot by another dancer hit him. Then the buffalo dancer collapsed and was dragged out of the circle. Non-dancing participants pretended to skin and butcher the dead "buffalo," but in the end released him.

All Pawnee buffalo hunts were supervised by a society called the Hunt Police, who kept the people in order so the animals would not be frightened and stampede. Anyone caught disturbing the silence was seized and beaten by the Hunt Police.

Courtship and marriage

Girls who had learned how to care for a home and family were considered ready to marry at about age fifteen. Boys often married when they were about eighteen.

CURRENT TRIBAL ISSUES

Like other Native peoples, after years of poverty and the shattering of traditions by government policy, the Pawnee face such problems as alcoholism, drug abuse, poverty, child neglect, and hunger. The Pawnee have developed some effective ways to deal with these social problems. These include health, substance abuse, and community services programs; and programs that deal with child welfare and the feeding of the elderly.

How to deal with the remains of deceased tribal members that are being displayed at museums and private collections is also an issue. The Pawnee Tribal Business Council has developed a process for bringing the remains of their ancestors back to the reservation. They see that the remains are given appropriate burials.

THE GROUND-BREAKING CEREMONY

Each year, the time to plant was determined through a Pawnee ritual known as the Ground-Breaking Ceremony. This was the only Pawnee ritual in which women played a major role.

A woman who had a wintertime dream about planting reported it to the priests of the tribe. If they decided the dream was inspired by Tirawa, they pronounced the woman and her family the sponsors of the Ground-Breaking Ceremony.

Shortly after the first budding of the willows in spring, the woman performed a special dance to launch the annual planting. The following day was devoted to ceremonies and rituals describing the process of planting and caring for the crops, especially corn. For the next six days the entire tribe worked to weed and plant the crops.

NOTABLE PEOPLE

The self-taught Pawnee artist Charles W. Chapman (1944–) began attracting attention during the mid-1980s for his dramatic portraits of Native Americans. For many years before, Chapman had been employed primarily as a horse breeder, rodeo rider, and construction worker. His artwork draws on his Pawnee heritage, usually depicting shamans, warriors, scouts, and hunters in their Native dress. He has won many awards for his art.

Other notable Pawnee include: attorney and Indian rights activist John E. Echohawk (1945–); attorney Walter R. Echo-Hawk (1948–); and chief Petalésharo (c. 1797–c. 1832), who was honored as a great warrior who tried make conditions better for all human beings, Native or white.

FURTHER READING

Fradin, Dennis B. *The Pawnee*. Chicago: Childrens Press, 1988.

Hahn, Elizabeth. *The Pawnee.* Vero Beach, FL: Rourke Publications, Inc., 1992.

Myers, Arthur. *The Pawnee.* New York: Franklin Watts, 1993.

Pawnee Images: Excerpts from an Exhibit. [Online] http://www.indiana.edu/ ~mathers/pawnee.html

Sioux Nations: Dakota

Name

Dakota (pronounced *Dah-KO-tah*) is the Dakota's name for themselves and means "friend" or "ally." The Dakota are also known as the Santee Sioux. The Sioux tribes (Dakota, Lakota, and Nakota) were once given a name that means "little snakes" by their enemies, the Ojibway. The French shortened the Ojibway word to "Sioux," the name by which the tribes are collectively known.

Location

The Dakota formerly occupied lands east of the Mississippi River along the Minnesota-Wisconsin border. Today they live on nine reservations in North and South Dakota, Minnesota, Montana, and Nebraska, and on seven small reserves in Canada. The largest reservation is Lake Traverse in South Dakota.

Population

In 1839, about 3,989 Dakota lived in the Minnesota territory. In a census (count of the population) done in 1990 by the U.S. Bureau of the Census, 107,321 people identified themselves as Sioux, and 10,999 people as Dakota or by reservation (see box on page 859).

Language family

Siouan.

Origins and group affiliations

The Dakota belong to the Great Sioux Nation, which also includes the Lakota and Nakota peoples (see entries). Some Sioux creation stories trace their origins back to the Black Hills of South Dakota, but in other stories the origination point was in the Minnesota woodlands, where they were living at the time of first contact with Europeans. Seven Sioux bands made up the *Oceti Sakowin,* or Seven Council Fires. At some point, quarrels developed, and the Nakota and Lakota broke off from the Dakota and moved west. There are four Dakota groups: *Wahpeton, Mdewakantonwon, Wahpekute,* and *Sisseton.*

Dakota enemies were the Ojibway (see entry) to the north, and the Mandan, Potawatomi (see entry), Winnebago, and Sac (see entry).

DAKOTA

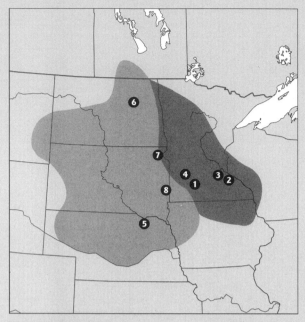

Contemporary Communities

Minnesota
1. Minnesota Mdewakanton Sioux
2. Prairie Island Dakota Community
3. Shakopee Mdewakanton Sioux
4. Upper Sioux Community of Minnesota

Nebraska
5. Santee Sioux Tribe

North Dakota
6. Devil's Lake Sioux Tribe

South Dakota
7. Lake Traverse Reservation, Sisseton-Wahpeton Sioux Tribe (extends to North Dakota)
8. Flandreau Santee Sioux Tribe

Darker shaded area: Traditional Sioux lands in present-day Minnesota and Wi4sconsin.

Lighter shaded area: Homelands of the Sioux tribes from the mid-1700s, after the Ojibway pushed them south and west into the Great Plains.

The Dakota tribe is considered the parent of the Great Sioux Nation, which also includes the Lakota and Nakota tribes. The Dakota enjoyed a comfortable life among the great natural abundance of Minnesota until their lands were overrun with settlers in the mid-nineteenth century. They tried to accommodate the newcomers but were finally forced into the bloody Santee War of 1862. After that they endured much misery but have kept their colorful culture alive.

HISTORY

Tribal divisions

Before contact with Europeans, the Sioux people lived as far north as Mille Lacs in present-day Minnesota. They say they once hunted, fished, and planted on nearly 100 million acres of land in the region. At some distant time in the past, the tribe split into three groups. The Nakota moved to the prairies of South Dakota, and the Lakota moved to a place west of the Missouri River. The Dakota, the largest of the three groups, stayed in Minnesota. All three groups maintained close ties.

In the mid-1700s, the Dakota were pushed south out of Mille Lacs by the Ojibway, who used weapons they had acquired in trade with the French. (The Dakota also traded with the French, who arrived in the region in about 1640, but it appears the Ojibway received more ammunition and guns.) The Dakota moved into the southern half of Minnesota and built villages along the Mississippi and Minnesota rivers. In the new territory their culture changed. Where once they had lived in villages year-round and planted gardens, they now adopted a partial Plains lifestyle in which they gathered wild rice and moved around for part of the year to hunt buffalo.

IMPORTANT DATES

1805: The Mdewakantonwon band of Dakota signs a treaty with Zebulon Pike.

1837–51: More treaties are signed. The Dakota lose most of their land and move to a reservation in Minnesota.

1858: The Dakota reservation is cut in half.

1862: Santee War is fought; afterwards, thirty-eight Dakota warriors are executed.

1863: The Forfeiture Act is passed; it takes away all Dakota treaty rights.

1870s: The Dakota move to reservations in North and South Dakota, Nebraska, and Canada; some Dakota attempt to return to Minnesota.

From British to American hands

When England gained control from the French of all land east of the Mississippi River in 1763, the Dakota traded with the British. When the American colonies declared war against the British in 1775, the Dakota sided with their trading partners because they believed American dreams of expansion posed a greater threat to their way of life than the British did. The British lost the war, and within a few decades American settlement of the land of the Dakota people began in earnest.

In 1805 the American soldier Zebulon Pike (1779–1813) was sent to explore the region and to obtain land from the Indians for a fort. Pike signed a treaty with the Dakota that exchanged 100,000 acres of land for $2,000 and some presents. In 1819 the American government built Fort St. Anthony (later renamed Fort Snelling) at the mouth of the Minnesota River. The fort served as a meeting place for Dakota and American soldiers and government officials throughout its existence.

Meanwhile white settlers began to pour into Dakota lands in Minnesota. More treaties were signed, until finally the Dakota had given up most of their land and were crowded into a small reservation along the Minnesota River. Altogether, the Dakota yielded control of more

Dakota chief Big Soldier,
painting by Karl Bodmer, 1833.

than 24 million acres in return for about 12.5 cents per acre, to be paid in cash, food, and other supplies. The treaties stated that much of the money for their land would be given directly to traders, who deducted large amounts from it before giving the rest to the Dakota people. The traders claimed the money was owed them for supplies.

Events leading up to Santee War

On the reservation, the Dakota were unable to hunt or move about as they once did; when they ventured off the reservation to hunt, there was trouble with whites. Missionaries came and criticized Dakota culture and spiritual beliefs. Their resentment grew.

In 1862, the crops failed, and the cash owed the Dakota by the U.S. government did not arrive when due. In July, thousands of Dakota gathered outside the headquarters of the Indian agent who was supposed to distribute the money. A rumor spread that the money was not coming because it was being spent on the U.S. Civil War (1861–65). When the agent refused to release food from the full warehouse until the money came, the Dakota, by then starving, were furious. The situation grew worse and worse. At one point a white trader said: "So far as I am concerned, if they are hungry let them eat grass or their own dung."

Author Dee Brown described the reaction of Dakota leader Little Crow to these crude words: "For years he had tried to keep the treaties, to follow the advice of the white men and lead his people on their road. It seemed now that he had lost everything. His own people were losing faith in him, blaming him for their misfortunes, and now the agents and traders had turned against him. Earlier that summer [his people] had accused Little Crow of betraying them when he signed away their lands by treaties. . . . In the old days he could have regained leadership by going to war, but the treaties pledged him not to engage in hostilities with either the white men or other tribes."

Soon after, a starving group of young Dakota men shot five white settlers in a dispute over a hen's nest and a few eggs, and the tensions finally escalated into a full-blown battle called the Santee War.

Aftermath of Little Crow's war

Before the Santee War was over, Little Crow and his Dakota warriors had killed between 450 and 800 settlers and soldiers. On September 26, 1862, they surrendered at their own camp, renamed Camp Release.

Hundreds of Dakota were rounded up, imprisoned, and tried in a military court. Because they had no legal rights, no lawyer was appointed to defend them. More than 300 men were found guilty and scheduled to be executed, but President Abraham Lincoln intervened. After studying the case, he reduced the number to thirty-eight men. The thirty-eight were hanged at Mankato, Minnesota, but not before many of them denied participating in the fighting.

The men who escaped hanging were imprisoned, and 1,700 Dakota women and children were sent to Fort Snelling, facing assaults and taunts by angry white settlers on the way. Little Crow was not hanged at Mankato. He fled from Minnesota into Canada, but later returned to Minnesota. On July 3, 1863, he was shot and killed while picking berries with his son Wowinapa. Little Crow was scalped, and his bones were taken and displayed at the Minnesota Historical Society. In 1971, his bones were finally returned to his family and reburied near Flandreau, South Dakota.

Minnesota cries for removal

Even after the thirty-eight men were hanged and Little Crow was killed, settlers still called for the removal of all Dakota from Minnesota. The Minnesota governor, echoing this sentiment, declared that "the Sioux Indians of Minnesota must be exterminated or driven forever beyond the borders of the state." In 1863, the Minnesota legislature passed the Forfeiture Act, which took away all Dakota treaty rights and their reservation, and ordered them to leave Minnesota.

Following their banishment from Minnesota, many Dakota were transferred to the Crow Creek reservation in present-day South Dakota. The soil was no good for farming, and there was scant rainfall as well as little drinkable water or wild game to hunt. They suffered from terrible living conditions, starvation, and disease. Some communities fled to the Devil's Lake reservation in North Dakota and the Sisseton reservation in South Dakota. Still others hoped to find a better existence in Canada and moved north in search of safety and land. After three terrible years at Crow Creek, the Dakota living on the desolate reservation moved to the Santee reservation in northern Nebraska.

Over the years, a few families slowly moved back into Minnesota from scattered locations and formed communities at Prairie Island and Prior Lake. The Dakota who ventured back into Minnesota were required to carry papers from the government, declaring them "peaceful Indians."

Modern problems and challenges

The Dakota faced many of the same problems on their reservations as had other tribes. They lost much of their land following the Dawes Allotment Act of 1887, which divided reservations into individual plots and opened what was left over to white settlement. (The purpose of the Allotment Act was to force the Indians to become more like whites, each one farming a small plot rather than a plot owned by the whole tribe.)

Today the largest Dakota reservation is Lake Traverse Reservation on the border of North and South Dakota. Lake Traverse, officially called the Sisseton-Wahpeton Sioux Reservation, was originally 12 million acres. It was gradually reduced and divided, so that today the tribe owns only 26,976 acres of it; 107,245 acres are allotted lands, owned by individual members of the tribe.

Missionaries and government officials tried to force the Dakota to give up their religious beliefs and cultural practices. Despite the losses of their land and repeated attacks on their cultural and spiritual beliefs, many Dakota have maintained strong ties to their communities, the Great Sioux Nation, and their traditional beliefs. Efforts continue today to reclaim lands and traditions taken from them over the years.

RELIGION

The Dakota believed that every aspect of the physical world, including the Sun, Earth, stars, thunder, rocks, trees, and animals, contained spirits that had to be honored and worshiped. All of the spirits were made and controlled by *Wakan Tanka* (the Great Spirit), who also created the universe. Because *Wakan Tanka* placed spirits everywhere, the Dakota say that they do not have a religion, but a way of life. Spiritual beliefs influenced their everyday activities, from harvesting corn to hunting for elk.

The Dakota performed the Sun Dance, a religious ceremony conducted by many buffalo-hunting tribes (see "Festivals and ceremonies"). Christian missionaries in the United States and Canada were appalled by the ceremony, and it was banned in both countries. The tribes performed the ceremony in secret until attitudes towards Indian religious freedom changed in the twentieth century.

Today, many Dakota mix traditional practices with those learned from the Christian missionaries who began to arrive in the 1830s. Others belong to the Native American Church, a mixture of traditional and some Christian elements that features an all-night ceremony composed of chanting, prayer, and meditation.

LANGUAGE

Originally, the Dakota, Lakota, and Nakota spoke the same language. But as the Lakota and Nakota moved away from the Dakota, the three began to speak their own form of the language. All three could still understand each other because the languages remained similar. For example, the word for friend is "koda" in Dakota, "kona" in Nakota, and "kola" in Lakota. Today, all three dialects (varieties) of the language still survive, although the Nakota branch is less common than the other two.

A Congregationalist missionary named Stephen Return Riggs (1812–1883) began to work among the Dakota in the 1830s. He and his wife, Mary Ann, began studying the Sioux language and preparing translations of the Christian Bible into Sioux. The first Bible entirely in Sioux was printed in 1879. Today, efforts are being made to revitalize the Dakota language through community and school programs.

GOVERNMENT

Each of the four Dakota bands was an independent unit, and the band council was the governing body. The council was made up of a chief and representatives from each clan. Important matters were discussed and a vote was taken; then messengers went about the villages announcing the council's decisions.

The council appointed *akicita,* outstanding warriors who served as hunt policemen. When there was a buffalo hunt, four men were in charge, and they had absolute power as long as the hunt lasted. They were assisted by the policemen, who were in charge of making sure that no one disrupted the hunt.

Long ago, the chief was chosen for his wisdom, but at some point the position became hereditary (it was passed down from father to son). Today, the various reservations are governed by elected tribal councils. Although the people are scattered over a wide area, they still consider themselves one people, the Great Sioux Nation.

ECONOMY

Dakota men and women contributed equally to the survival of their villages. Women made maple sugar, farmed, gathered food, and helped collect wild rice. Dakota men hunted, helped break up the soil for planting, collected wild rice, and fished. White observers often commented on the hard lot of Dakota women, and even called them "slaves" to their husbands. Both men and women played important, though different, roles in the economic survival of their communities.

The Dakota traded surplus items with other tribes. Even before they began trading with Europeans, the Dakota had an extensive trade network. They journeyed to the James River in South Dakota each year to meet and trade with their Lakota and Nakota kinsmen at a gathering known as the Dakota Rendezvous (pronounced *RON-day-voo*).

On the reservations, the Dakota struggled for years to make ends meet. Many were forced to sell off their land to survive. Today the Dakota people have learned to adapt to life in cities or on reservations. Many are involved in the South Dakota tourism industry; others are farmers. Many reservations still have high unemployment rates, but casinos and bingo halls have helped to create jobs and provide funds for cultural revitalization programs.

DAILY LIFE

Families

A Dakota household was usually made up of a maximum of four related families, consisting of grandparents, their daughters and their daughters' husbands, and grandchildren. They had a complicated system in which certain aunts and uncles were considered like an individual's parents, and the children of these aunts and uncles became additional brothers and sisters. With so many mothers and fathers, few children could become orphans. If they did lose their parents, children were absorbed into the larger family.

The Dakota had strict rules for how different people were supposed to interact with one another. For example, daughters-in-law were not supposed to talk directly to their fathers-in-law.

Education

Dakota boys learned from their parents to hunt, make war, or become medicine men, while girls learned to build homes and gather food. Grandparents taught proper behavior and tribal customs and beliefs.

For many years, the Dakota endured a mix of government, church-run, and public schools, where little sensitivity was shown to their culture. Finally, in 1975 the Lake Traverse Reservation Tribal Council drew up plans for two schools that would emphasize tribal values. They are Tiospa Zina Tribal School and Sisseton-Wahpeton Community College. The college is recognized as a leader in "distance education," offering interactive Dakota language courses and a course in Dakota history and culture on an Internet home page. Education is also important to the Dakota people in Minnesota. Two reservations there have their own charter schools, even though the populations are very small.

Buildings

Women built Dakota homes and were considered the homeowners. The Dakota lived in two different types of dwellings depending on the season. During the warm summer months, families resided in villages so the women could cultivate crops. The summer communities consisted of roomy wood and bark homes that families returned

DAKOTA POPULATION: 1990

In the 1990 census, a total of 107,321 people identified themselves as Sioux. Some further classified themselves as members of specific bands or reservations. But 44,354 failed to do so. They simply called themselves Sioux, without indicating whether they are Dakota, Lakota, or Nakota. Those who are members of Dakota Sioux bands or reservations are shown below. To further complicate a count of the people, some Nakota live on the Devils Lake and Fort Peck reservations.

Dakota group	Population
Dakota Sioux	538
Devil's Lake Sioux	2,227
Flandreau Santee	191
Fort Peck Sioux	847
Lake Traverse Sioux	52
Lower Sioux	81
Mdewakanton Sioux	294
Prior Lake Sioux	59
Santee Sioux	2,284
Sisseton Sioux	884
Sisseton-Wahpeton Sioux	3,491
Wahpeton	51
Total	**10,999**

SOURCE: Selected from "American Indian Population by Selected Tribes: 1990," U.S. Department of Commerce, Economics and Statistics Administration, Bureau of the Census, 1990 Census of Population, *Characteristics of American Indians by Tribe and Language*, Table 1, 1990 CP-3-7.

to several years in a row. The women built these sturdy homes by setting wooden posts in the ground to create a frame. The posts were covered with elm bark to create walls and a roof. Inside were benches covered with buffalo robes, which served as beds, tables, and chairs.

During the fall and winter months, the Dakota needed portable homes so the people could follow wild game. They relied on the cone-shaped tepee. The walls and floors were covered with buffalo or deer hides, and a space was left in the center of the floor for a fire. Tepees were warm and comfortable during the cold, wet months of fall and winter.

Food

The Dakota homeland in Minnesota was filled with abundant resources, and each community enjoyed a healthy, varied diet. The Dakota, who were once primarily farmers, became hunters and gatherers after they moved to the Plains.

Beginning in the spring (the Dakota new year), the men and women scattered from their winter villages and went their separate ways. The women, young children, and elders camped near maple tree groves, where they collected sap for maple sugar. At the same time, the men divided into small hunting parties and left in search of muskrats and buffalo, which were either used for food and furs or traded for other provisions.

In the late spring, Dakota families and friends reunited in their summer planting villages. The women plowed and planted small gardens of corn, pumpkins, and squash. Then the village broke up again, although members still used the village as a base. The men left to go on short hunts for deer, ducks, turtles, and geese or to fish in the lakes and streams. The women went off to pick ripe fruits and vegetables, including cherries, plums, and berries, the psincha and psinchicha (roots found at the bottom of shallow lakes), the mdo (potato), and wild turnips. Some women and children remained behind to scare away crows from their corn fields.

In the fall, the women and some of the men collected wild rice from nearby lakes. They stood in canoes and beat the heads of the rice plants with a stick to release the grain. They also harvested corn and dried what they did not need right away. Some men left for the deer hunt. As winter set in, the communities broke up into small groups of one to three families to hunt for deer, buffalo, or other sources of meat, or to ice fish. When spring arrived, the cycle started again.

Clothing and adornment

Long ago, Dakota women relied on buckskin and buffalo hides to make clothing. When trade began with Europeans, they turned to cloth. Skirts were made from a single piece of cloth, sewn together at the side, and looped over a belt. Cloth leggings reached from their knees to their ankles, where they were tucked into their moccasins. Most of their clothing was decorated with bead and quill work. They wore bead necklaces and earrings. They rarely painted their faces but did paint a strip of vivid red in the part of their hair. They wore their hair in two or more long braids, sometimes wrapping the braids with otter fur.

In the summer men wore cotton shirts, leggings, and breechcloths (garments with front and back flaps that hung from the waist). In the winter, they wore long coats that reached past their knees. Their clothes and moccasins were decorated with bead and quill work. They cut their hair in the front, but wore the rest long in two or more braids fastened with silver ornaments or wrapped with otter fur. Headwear ranged from headdresses made of eagle feathers, to war bonnets, sashes worn as turbans, or hoods to keep out cold or mosquitoes.

Healing practices

The Dakota believed that diseases were caused by spirits, so their *wakan*—medicine men and women—appealed to the spirit world when trying to cure a sickness. They used chants, rattles, and dances, and sucked on the infected area to bring the person back into harmony with the spirit world. They also used various roots, vegetables, berries, and bark to treat ailments.

Medicine men and women were initiated into a medicine lodge, a secret order that could only be joined by those who had earned the honor. Membership was by invitation only. A medicine dance was held, and a period of probation followed, until the men and women proved themselves worthy and learned the secret methods of curing diseases.

CUSTOMS

Festivals and ceremonies

The Dakota made sure that food-gathering areas were not overused. In order to honor the spirits, they offered feasts and sacrifices before harvesting wild rice or hunting for animals. For example, a dance was held before an elk hunt, and an offering was made to the

THE EAGLE AND THE BEAVER: A DAKOTA TALE

Out of the quiet blue sky there shot like an arrow the great War-Eagle. Beside the clear brown stream an old Beaver-woman was busily chopping wood. Yet she was not too busy to catch the whir of descending wings, and the Eagle reached too late the spot where she had vanished in the midst of the shining pool.

He perched sullenly upon a dead tree near by and kept his eyes steadily upon the smooth sheet of water above the dam.

After a time the water was gently stirred and a sleek, brown head cautiously appeared above it.

"What right have you," reproached the Beaver-woman, "to disturb thus the mother of a peaceful and hard-working people?"

"Ugh, I am hungry," the Eagle replied shortly.

"Then why not do as we do—let other folks alone and work for a living?"

"That is all very well for you," the Eagle retorted, "not everybody can cut down trees with his teeth, or live upon bark and weeds in a mud-plastered wigwam. I am a warrior, not an old woman!"

"It is true that some people are born trouble-makers," returned the Beaver, quietly. "Yet I see no good reason why you, as well as we, should not be content with plain fare and willing to toil for what you want. My work, moreover, is of use to others besides myself and family, for with my dam-building I deepen the stream for the use of all the dwellers therein, while you are a terror to all living creatures that are weaker than yourself. You would do well to profit by my example."

So saying, she dove down again to the bottom of the pool.

The Eagle waited patiently for a long time, but he saw nothing more of her; and so, in spite of his contempt for the harmless industry of an old Beaver-woman, it was he, not she, who was obliged to go hungry that morning.

SOURCE: Charles A. Eastman and Elaine Goodale Eastman. "The Eagle and the Beaver." *Wigwam Evenings: Sioux Folk Tales Retold*. Lincoln: University of Nebraska Press, 1990: 28–30.

---

spirits after an elk was killed. During wild rice gathering, men and women staged feasts and offerings to the "water god" to assure they would not drown during the harvest. Later, after more ceremonial offerings, the rice was harvested and prepared for more feasting and eventual storage.

In addition to these everyday practices, the Dakota conducted important ceremonies throughout the year, such as pipe ceremonies, medicine dances, *Wakan* (spiritual) feasts, and *inipis,* or sweat lodge ceremonies that purified people.

SUN DANCES In the summer, the Dakota often gathered with their scattered Lakota or Nakota relatives to perform the sacred Sun Dance. According to the Sun Dance tradition, warriors or others who found themselves facing certain death, might offer a prayer to the Sun for their survival. If they came through the ordeal, they would participate in the Sun Dance the next summer to offer thanks and to atone for their weakness in the face of death. Before the dance, a sturdy pole was set up in a clearing. After the opening ceremonies, the participants danced without stopping for a day and night, gazing at the Sun, and blowing on an eagle bone whistle. Late in the dance, incisions were made in the participants' chests, and wooden skewers were placed through the cuts and attached with thongs to the pole. The men would then pull until the skewers broke free from their chest. The dancers' sacrifice fulfilled their vow to the Sun.

The Dakota still hold Sun Dances and sweating and pipe ceremonies throughout the year. On the anniversary of the hanging of the thirty-eight men at Mankato, the Dakota hold a ceremonial powwow to commemorate their deaths. According to the participants, thirty-eight eagles always appear overhead during the ceremony.

War and hunting rituals

Warfare was an important way for a Dakota man to prove his manhood. They earned honor and prestige for their bravery and skill in war. Men organized and carried out frequent war parties against their enemies and remained ever on guard against attacks on their summer planting villages.

A man—and sometimes a woman—usually organized a war party after a dream or vision. The call went forth to form an expedition, and volunteers joined the leader to fulfill the vision. Early observers called Dakota men "savage," but Dakota warriors respected their enemies and tried to show their strength and bravery by selecting and attacking key enemy warriors, not by destroying everyone in a village. A warrior who faced certain death sang a special death song; the thirty-eight warriors at Mankato sang the song just before they were hanged.

Men made their own weapons for hunting and war, and women were forbidden to touch them. Women made war bonnets to be awarded to successful warriors, but once the bonnets were finished, the makers could never touch them again.

Naming practices

Dakota people received several different names in a lifetime. When babies were born, they received a name based on their place in the family. For instance, the first male child was always called Caske and the first female child was always named Winona. When the child reached five or six years old and had developed a personality, a nickname was given. At the age of twelve, children participated in a naming ceremony, where they accepted a name they had earned.

Courtship, marriage, and babies

A young man had to earn his adult name before he could court a young woman. He courted her by playing sweet music on an instrument made of a bird's wing or wood, or by offering to help with her chores. Once he gained her affection, he might give gifts to her parents to show what a good provider he would be. Or he might move in with her family for a while, and during that time the young woman would prove she was able to keep house. If all went well, the young woman and her female relatives built a tepee, a feast was held, and the groom took his bride to their new home.

When a child was expected, the husband sometimes left the village to hunt or visit his family until the baby was born. The expectant mother was assisted in the birth by the older women of the village, who tied the newborn onto a wooden board called a cradle board. Young children slept with their parents or grandparents until they were about four years old.

Death and burial

Old people were respected in Dakota society. When an elderly person sensed that death was near, he or she sometimes left the village to die alone. If the group was moving to a new location, a sick or dying person might stay behind so as not to be a burden.

When a person died, family members wailed over the death, cut their skin or hair, and gave away possessions to show grief. Sometimes a lock of hair was removed from the deceased to make a "spirit bundle." The bundle was hung in the family's lodge and a dish of food placed under it. After a year, a feast was held, and the spirit bundle was buried.

The deceased was dressed in his or her best clothes and new moccasins for the journey to the Land of Ghosts. The body was then wrapped with blankets or buffalo robes, and prized weapons or items were bound up in the wraps or placed nearby. The body was positioned on a scaffold (a raised platform) so that the remains could fall back to Mother Earth.

CURRENT TRIBAL ISSUES

Despite their separation among various reservations throughout the United States and Canada, Dakota people have shared many similar experiences. They have filed claims against the federal and Canadian governments for land losses, and some of these claims have been successful. For example, residents of the Sisseton-Wahpeton Reservation (or Lake Traverse Reservation) received money for some of the land that was taken from them during allotment. Some land claims are still pending.

Throughout the Dakota nation, efforts have been made to bring home the bones of deceased members that are housed in museums and historical societies. Minnesota Dakota have worked with the Park Service to remove a campground from a known Dakota burial site.

The Dakota and the other members of the Seven Council Fires (Sioux) continue to stress the importance of presenting a united front on land and water rights, gambling, and other issues. For example, in November 1996 the Santee reservation in Nebraska seemed ready to accept money for land lost to the federal government. The other Sioux tribes strongly opposed this move and urged the Santee not to take actions the other nations might have to follow.

NOTABLE PEOPLE

Charles A. Eastman (1858–1939) was born in Minnesota and raised in a traditional Santee setting. He had little contact with American society until he went to school in Flandreau, South Dakota. He received a degree in medicine in 1890, then became a physician at the Pine Ridge Indian Reservation in South Dakota (Oglala Sioux; see Lakota entry), the first Native American in a position of authority there. Eastman wrote about Indian culture and the differences between Native beliefs and those of U.S. society in his autobiographical works *Indian Boyhood* (1902) and *From the Deep Woods to Civilization* (1916). He was active in the Young Men's Christian Association and was one of the founders of the Boy Scouts of America. His other works include *Red Hunters and the Animal People* (1904), *Old Indian Days* (1907), *Wigwam Evenings: Sioux Folktales Retold* (1909), *The Soul of the Indian* (1911), *The Indian Today,* (1916), and *Indian Heroes and Great Chieftains* (1918).

Other notable Dakota are: Gabriel Renville, chief of the Sisseton-Wahpeton tribe from 1862 to 1892. He helped to establish the Lake Traverse Reservation, where he was a successful farmer and helped maintain traditional Santee customs. William G. Demmert, Jr. (1934–) was a Tlingit/Dakota university professor and writer of many works on Indian education. Hank Adams (1943–) was an Assiniboin/Dakota activist from Montana who joined the struggle over Indian fishing rights in the Northwest. Santee activist, actor, and musician John Trudell (1947–) was a member of the American Indian Movement (AIM) who joined the group occupying Alcatraz Island (see Yana entry). Sisseton-Wahpeton songwriter and performer Floyd Westerman (1936–) played the role of Ten Bears in the film *Dances with Wolves*. Paul War Cloud (1930–1973) was a Sisseton-Wahpeton painter who depicted Dakota culture and tradition in his works.

FURTHER READING

Brown, Dee. "Little Crow's War." in *Bury My Heart at Wounded Knee,* Holt, Rinehart And Winston, 1970.

"A Guide to the Great Sioux Nation," http://www.state.sd.us/state/executive/tourism/sioux/sioux.htm

Sisseton Wahpeton Sioux Tribe Home Page, http://www.swcc.cc.sd.us/homepage.htm

"Timeline of events relevant to the Northern Plains tribes." [Online] http://www.hanksville.phast.umass.edu/june95/lakota/timeline2.html

Sioux Nations: Lakota

Name

Lakota (pronounced *lah-KOH-tah*) is the Lakota's name for themselves and means "allies." They are also known as Teton Sioux; Teton comes from their word *Titunwan,* meaning "prairie dwellers." The Sioux tribes (Dakota, Lakota, and Nakota) were once given a name that means "little snakes" by their enemies, the Ojibway. The French shortened the Ojibway word to "Sioux," the name by which the tribes are collectively known.

Location

The Lakota moved in the mid-1700s from Minnesota to the Black Hills region of western South Dakota, eastern Wyoming, and eastern Montana. They currently live on the Cheyenne River, Lower Brule, Pine Ridge, Rosebud, Crow Creek, and Standing Rock reservations in North and South Dakota, and at Fort Peck Reservation in Montana.

Population

In a census (count of the population) done in 1990 by the U.S. Bureau of the Census, 46,943 people identified themselves as Blackfoot, Brule, Cheyenne River, Crow Creek, Lower Brule, Oglala, Pine Ridge, and Standing Rock Sioux. An additional 44,354 people simply identified themselves as Sioux.

Language family

Siouan.

Origins and group affiliations

Some Sioux creation stories trace their origins back to the Black Hills of South Dakota, but other stories say they originated in the Minnesota woodlands, where they and the Nakota (see entry) were all part of the Dakota tribe (see entry). In the mid-1700s, the tribe broke into three groups after wars with the neighboring Ojibway (see entry). The Dakota remained in Minnesota, and the other two groups, calling themselves Lakota and Nakota, moved westward.

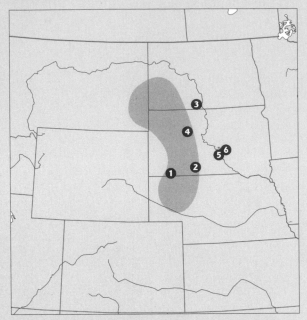

LAKOTA

Shaded area: Traditional lands of the Lakota in the northern Plains of present-day North Dakota, South Dakota, Nebraska, Montana, and Wyoming.

The Lakota were once the most powerful tribe in North America, controlling a large area of the northern Great Plains. Lakota leaders—including Sitting Bull, Crazy Horse, and Red Cloud—were among the best-known Native Americans of the nineteenth century, and the tribe was involved in two of the most famous incidents in American history, the Battle of the Little Bighorn in 1876 and the Massacre at Wounded Knee in 1890. In recent times, the Lakota have been at the forefront of the Indian rights movement.

HISTORY

Golden Age of the Lakota people

Before their move to the Great Plains in the mid-1700s, the Lakota were part of the Dakota tribe and lived as woodland farmers in present-day Minnesota. Warfare with the Ojibway (see entry) forced the Dakota to break up into three separate groups. The adventurous group that moved westward onto the Great Plains came to be called the Lakota.

The Lakota acquired horses from neighboring tribes and adopted the wandering ways common among tribes of the Great Plains. They soon came to depend on the buffalo for food, clothing, shelter, weapons, and household objects, and began following the great herds on their annual migrations. Though their lifeways differed from their relatives, the Nakota and Dakota, who were more settled, the Lakota considered these groups allies and did not fight against them.

During the late eighteenth century the Lakota divided into seven bands (see box on page 872) and scattered throughout the region. After forming alliances with the Northern Cheyenne and Northern Arapaho (see entries), the Lakota became a powerful force on the Northern Plains. The years from 1775 to 1868 are sometimes called the tribe's "Golden Age."

A bad start with Americans

Their first encounter with white Americans happened in 1804, when Meriwether Lewis and William Clark's expedition reached the area of present-day Pierre (pronounced *PEER*), South Dakota. Lewis and Clark had been sent by President Thomas Jefferson to find a waterway to the Pacific Ocean. Lewis had orders from the president to seek out the Sioux, to make a good impression on them, and to secure them as friends of the United States.

The meeting went badly, with misunderstandings on both sides. At the explorers' second meeting with the Lakota people, matters at first seemed to be going better. The Brule band was celebrating a victory over the Omaha tribe, and treated Lewis and Clark to a performance of the first scalp dance ever seen by Americans. But when the Lakota expressed their displeasure at the gifts Lewis and Clark gave them, relations soured. Lewis wrote that he found the Sioux to be "the vilest miscreants [evildoers] of the savage race."

The Sioux did not realize it then, but Lewis and Clark's visit was an announcement that the United States was claiming ownership of Sioux territory. Fur traders followed Lewis and Clark, and word

IMPORTANT DATES

c. 1770s: The Lakota move to the Black Hills, divide into seven bands, and disperse throughout the region.

1804: The Lakota meet Lewis and Clark expedition. Trading posts are established in their territory.

1851: Fort Laramie treaties are signed, defining boundaries of Lakota territories and marking the beginning of westward movement by miners and wagon trains on the Oregon Trail.

1866–68: Red Cloud leads a successful fight to close Bozeman Trail, which leads through Lakota hunting grounds to the gold mines of Montana.

1868: The U.S. government gives up its claim to Lakota lands—including the Black Hills—in the Fort Laramie Treaty.

1874: Gold is discovered in the Black Hills. Goldseekers pour in.

1876: Lakota warriors defeat General George Armstrong Custer in the Battle of the Little Bighorn.

1890: Sitting Bull is murdered. U.S. troops kill more than 300 Lakota men, women, and children in the Massacre at Wounded Knee.

1973: American Indian Movement (AIM) activists occupy Wounded Knee and engage in a 71-day standoff with government agents.

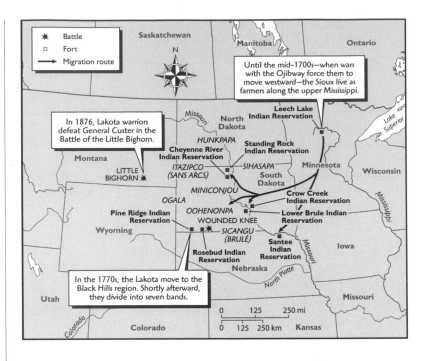

A map showing the migrations of the Lakota.

Battle
Fort
Migration route

Saskatchewan
Manitoba
Ontario

Until the mid-1700s—when wars with the Ojibway force them to move westward—the Sioux live as farmers along the upper Mississippi.

In 1876, Lakota warriors defeat General Custer in the Battle of the Little Bighorn.

Leech Lake Indian Reservation
Missouri
North Dakota
Lake Superior

HUNKPAPA
Standing Rock Indian Reservation
Cheyenne River Indian Reservation
Montana
ITAZIPCO (SANS ARCS)
SIHASAPA
Minnesota
Wisconsin

LITTLE BIGHORN
MINICONJOU
South Dakota

OGALA
Crow Creek Indian Reservation
OOHENONPA
Pine Ridge Indian Reservation
WOUNDED KNEE
Lower Brule Indian Reservation
Wyoming
SICANGU (BRULÉ)
Santee Indian Reservation
Iowa
Rosebud Indian Reservation
Missouri
Nebraska
North Platte

In the 1770s, the Lakota move to the Black Hills region. Shortly afterward, they divide into seven bands.

Utah
Missouri
Colorado
0   125   250 mi
0   125   250 km
Colorado
Kansas

spread in the East about the vast new lands. In 1825 the government sent soldiers to awe the Indians with American military might and to sign treaties with them.

Treaty era begins

In 1825 treaties were signed with three Lakota bands. The United States claimed the right to control trade in the region, and agreed to protect the Lakota and their property against trespassing by whites. The United States also agreed "to receive [the Indians] into their friendship" and to grant them "such benefits and acts of kindness as may be convenient" in the eyes of the president. Chief Wabasha expressed his wish that "this peace will last a long time."

The Lakota enjoyed trading with American companies for goods that made their lives much more comfortable—goods like guns and cooking utensils. Unfortunately, the newcomers brought with them diseases and alcohol, or "the water that makes men foolish," as the Lakota called it. They grew increasingly dependent on American goods, and experienced disease epidemics.

Wagon trains head West

Until the 1840s relations between whites and Indians on the Great Plains remained fairly peaceful. But then the wagon trains started to head West. More and more white settlers crossed Lakota territory and disrupted their lifestyle, driving away the buffalo and forcing the Lakota to travel farther in search of them. These travels took them closer to the lands of their enemies, the Kiowa and the Crow (see entries), and made them easier targets for attacks. The tribe tried various ways of discouraging the pioneers. They threatened, they robbed, they attacked the wagon trains, but nothing could stop the westward flow.

In 1850 the U.S. Congress decided to act by making treaties with "the wild tribes of the prairies." Word was passed among the western tribes that representatives of "the Great White Father" (the American president) wished to talk peace at Fort Laramie, Wyoming. Thousands of Indians gathered at the fort, many of them starving because the buffalo were nearly gone.

Fort Laramie treaty made and broken

The Lakota signed the Fort Laramie Treaty of 1851, which recognized their rights to more than 60 million acres of land, including the Black Hills. In return, the Lakota agreed to guarantee safe passage of settlers on the Oregon Trail, an agreement that would put an end to their way of life. As author Edward Lazarus put it: "The treaty outlawed many essential aspects of plains life, the raiding, horse thieving, and warring that brought honor and authority to both a man and his tribe."

Such a treaty was bound to be broken, and so it was. Violence erupted as tribes continued to battle with each other over trade disputes and access to hunting grounds. Meanwhile, back in the nation's capital, the U.S. Senate was changing the terms of the treaty. Instead of annual payments for fifty years in the form of cattle, farming implements, seeds, and grains, the Senate decided to make annual payments for only ten years.

To war over a lame ox

For a few years the pioneers were allowed to pass through Lakota lands unmolested. Then one day in 1854, a party passing through on its way to Utah met a group of Lakota warriors. One of them, a Lakota man named High Forehead, spotted a lame ox at the end of the wagon train and shot it for food. All the parties rushed off to Fort Laramie to argue about the case, but they could not reach a satisfactory agreement. A few days later, the fort's commander led a party of volunteers to arrest High Forehead, who refused to surrender. In the bloody battle

that followed, the commander, his troops, and a Lakota chief named Conquering Bear were killed.

The U.S. government decided to teach the Lakota a lesson. Thirteen hundred armed U.S. troops attacked a Brulé camp and murdered eighty-six men, women, and children; none of the dead had played any part in the matter of the lame ox. According to Lazarus, the Lakota considered the loss of eight or ten people a terrible disaster. They had never experienced a loss of such magnitude. Confused and upset, they headed for the Black Hills to think and grieve.

In 1857 thousands of Sioux gathered in the Black Hills and vowed to allow no further takeovers of their lands by whites. But gold was discovered in Colorado in 1859, and by 1861 rumors had spread that there was gold to be found in Montana too. Traffic increased on the Oregon Trail and on the Bozeman Trail into Montana. As settlers passed through, many decided to stay and explore the Great Plains and prairies of the Lakota hunting grounds. It seemed that war was unavoidable.

Red Cloud's War

The Sioux wars began with the Dakota in Minnesota in 1862 (see Dakota entry). Some survivors fled to Lakota country, where they and their kinsmen now joined in battles against U.S. soldiers. All over the West, Indians fought white soldiers, whose orders were to "attack and kill every male Indian over twelve years of age." Women and children were not spared in the bloodbath either.

In 1865, with the American Civil War over, Congress turned its attention to the Indian situation in the West. A decision was made to build roads into the Montana gold district where the Lakota hunted, and also to make peace with the Indians. Some Lakota groups who were starving signed treaties. But many thousands of Lakota warriors camped in the Black Hills and Powder River country were still hostile toward the American government. Their leader was the powerful and respected warrior, Red Cloud (1822–1909). When Red Cloud learned the Americans were talking about peace and presents for the Indians while at the same time building forts and preparing to build roads along the Bozeman Trail, the famous warrior declared: "I am for war."

Red Cloud's War or the War for the Bozeman Trail lasted from 1866 to 1868. Crazy Horse and other Lakota warriors led attacks against soldiers in American forts, outsmarting them at every turn. The U.S. government finally admitted defeat in 1868. In the Fort Laramie Treaty of 1868, the Lakota received title to the Great Sioux Reservation, which occupied half of present-day South Dakota (west of the Missouri River and including the sacred Black Hills) as well as the Bighorn Mountain region of Wyoming and Nebraska. The Lakota were also given tools, cattle, and other materials designed to convert them into farmers and ranchers.

Gold discovery at Black Hills

Gold was discovered in the Black Hills in 1874, and miners and settlers again began trespassing on Lakota lands. Responding to citizen pressures to obtain more land from the Indians, the U.S. government tried to buy the Black Hills from the Lakota. Lakota leaders refused to give up the land they held sacred. Crazy Horse said: "One does not sell the Earth upon which the people walk." Hunkpapa Sioux Chief Sitting Bull (c. 1831–1890) stated: "We want no white men here. The Black Hills belong to me. If the whites try to take them, I will fight."

The U.S. Army was sent in 1876 to force the Lakota to give up their traditional lifestyle and become farmers on a reservation—or, more realistically, to give up land. Intense fighting followed in the war for the Black Hills (also called Sitting Bull and Crazy Horse's War; Crazy Horse [c. 1842–1877] was an Oglala Brulé warrior). Some of the most famous battles in American history were fought during this war.

Sitting Bull and Crazy Horse's War

In 1876, the Lakota scored victories at Powder River in Montana, at Rosebud Creek in South Dakota, and in the valley of the Little Bighorn River in Montana. In the battle at Little Bighorn, which came to be known as "Custer's Last Stand," General Custer and 250 men attacked a camp of 2,500 Lakota and Cheyenne warriors. Sitting Bull, Crazy Horse, and Gall (1840–1894; a Hunkpapa Sioux leader) led the counterattack, in which Custer and all his men were killed. This was the last great Indian victory on the Great Plains.

The defeat of Custer led to renewed American calls for the "extermination" of the Indians. Over the course of the next six months, the Lakota suffered defeats at War Bonnet Creek in Nebraska, Slim Buttes

Bordey   *warren*   *meyer*

Sitting Bull   *Swift Bear*   *Spotted Tail*   *Red Cloud*

Chiefs Sitting Bull, Swift Bear, Spotted Tail, and Red Cloud pose during negotiations, 1880s.

in South Dakota, and Wolf Mountain in Montana. They also lost the Battle of Dull Knife in Wyoming. By mid-1877, many Lakota chiefs surrendered and were placed on reservations.

Lakota resistance broken

Crazy Horse went to Fort Robinson, Nebraska, in September 1877, promising that he would forge a peaceful settlement to the conflict.

Nevertheless, the U.S. Army tried to put the great chief in prison and he was killed when he resisted arrest. In the meantime, Sitting Bull and his followers fled to safety in Canada.

The power of the Lakota and their allies over the Northern Plains was broken. On January 31, 1876, the U.S. Congress declared that the Black Hills belonged to the United States. The Lakota were ordered to move away from the region. South Dakota became a state in 1889, and the federal government again faced pressure to make more land available to white settlers. The Sioux Act of 1889 was passed, which broke the Great Sioux Reservation into four smaller reservations. Heads of Sioux families and each family member were given individual plots of land, under the policy called allotment. Land left over was then made available to white settlers.

Massacre at Wounded Knee

In 1890, Sitting Bull was living at the Standing Rock Reservation. Although he was fifty-six years old, the U.S. government feared that he might lead a new Indian resistance movement. The government became more uneasy when the Lakota took up the Ghost Dance (see "Religion") in 1890 as a way of coping with life on the reservation. Government agents who oversaw Indian lands did not understand the Ghost Dance and found it threatening. Sitting Bull made no effort to stop the dancing. A law was passed forbidding the performance of the dance, but by November 1890, nearly all other activities on the reservation stopped as the people performed the dance anyway. The Indian agent sent a message to Washington, D.C.: "Indians are dancing in the snow and are wild and crazy. . . . We need protection and we need it now."

In December 1890, U.S. troops under General Nelson Miles were sent to arrest Sitting Bull. A fight broke out, and the great chief and seven of his warriors were killed. The grief-stricken people of the reservation fled, seeking refuge at Pine Ridge Reservation, where Red Cloud was in charge, and at the camp of Lakota leader Big Foot. A U.S. government order went out for the arrest of Big Foot, who, like Sitting Bull, was considered a troublemaker. Planning to arrange for peace, Big Foot made his way to join Red Cloud at Pine Ridge. He and his followers were intercepted by American troops. He was ordered to set up camp near Wounded Knee Creek. When the soldiers tried to disarm Big Foot's men, a rifle went off. In the battle that followed, more than 300 people were killed, most of them women and children. This incident came to be called the Massacre at Wounded Knee. It marked the end of the Ghost Dance era and Indian wars.

AMERICAN INDIAN MOVEMENT

During the civil rights struggle of the 1960s, a new movement emerged called the Red Power movement. It sought a return to American Indian traditional values and practices. The Lakota became deeply involved in the Indian rights movement.

In 1968 a Yankton-Oglala Sioux named Russell Means, together with Dennis Banks (Ojibway) and Clyde Bellecourt (Ojibway) and others, founded the American Indian Movement (AIM). Its membership included many Lakota and Native Americans from all tribes. AIM's methods sometimes included aggressive confrontation with government authorities to promote its cause. In 1972, AIM sponsored the Trail of Broken Treaties. A large group of Native Americans walked across the United States from Seattle, Washington, to Washington, D.C., to protest the treatment of Indians by the government. Once in the capital, AIM activists barricaded themselves inside the Bureau of Indian Affairs (BIA) for six days, from time to time releasing documents to the press that they felt demonstrated the agency's ineffectiveness.

AIM was especially active on the Oglala Pine Ridge Reservation in South Dakota, where they revived the Ghost Dance. Tribal Council President Richard ("Dicky") Wilson tried to ban AIM from the reservation and formed a tribal police force supported by the Federal Bureau of Investigation (FBI), to stop the group's activities. In 1973, AIM activists arranged a protest against Wilson and his violent tactics at the town of Wounded Knee, near the site of the Wounded Knee Massacre. Surrounded by federal agents, the armed group occupied the site for seventy-one days. During this time, two AIM members were killed. Though thirty activists were arrested at the end of the standoff, all were set free because of illegal actions by the government.

In 1975, during a very tense time on the Pine Ridge Reservation, two FBI agents were killed during a shootout with a number of AIM activists. AIM activist Leonard Peltier and two other Lakota men were charged with murder; the other men were tried together and were found not guilty. Peltier was tried later, found guilty, and sentenced to life in prison. Since then, information has surfaced that suggests that the government engaged in underhanded tricks to make sure Peltier was found guilty. Many celebrities, members of Congress, religious leaders around the world, and the human-rights organization Amnesty International have appealed for a new trial for Peltier, but this has not come to pass. The case became the subject of a 1983 book, *In the Spirit of Crazy Horse* by Peter Matthiessen, and a 1992 documentary film, *Incident at Oglala*.

Reservation years

Many Lakota resisted the government's allotment policy, but the U.S. government continued to pressure them. Through land allotment the U.S. government hoped to turn the Lakota into farmers. People who refused to farm were not given the government money and goods they were entitled to by treaties. They went hungry, and many died.

The tribe continued to lose land through the early 1900s as the reservations were broken into individual allotments. During the allotment period, the Lakota lost not only land but also many aspects of their culture. Their children were sent away to boarding schools, and missionaries arrived on the reservations to convert the Lakota to

Christianity. Traditional ceremonies and practices were forbidden until laws passed in the 1930s restored religious freedom.

Lakota in the twentieth century

The Lakota faced many problems and challenges in the twentieth century. Their struggle to regain lost land is primary and ongoing. They have never accepted the 1877 order that granted ownership of the Black Hills to the United States. Instead, they believe that these sacred lands belong to the tribe as given them by the Creator and promised them by the U.S. government in the Fort Laramie Treaty of 1868.

In 1980, the U.S. Supreme Court awarded the Lakota $105 million for the wrongful taking of their territory a century earlier. But despite their dire need for money, the Lakota refused to accept the monetary settlement and continued to insist that their traditional lands be returned to tribal control. As the century drew to a close, they continued to refuse the money.

RELIGION

The Lakota believe that all life is interrelated. Their god, known as *Wakan Tanka*, or the Great Mystery Power or Creator, includes all elements of nature, so the Lakota have deep respect for their environment. The spirits of the Sun, sky, Earth, buffalo, bear, and four directions of the winds are particularly important to them.

According to Lakota sacred lore, a holy woman named White Buffalo Calf Woman gave the people their religious teachings, including the knowledge of the sacred pipe and how to use it in seven ceremonies that made the celebrants one with the universe.

In the 1850s Catholic priest Father Pierre Jean ("Black Robe") De Smet began to live, preach, and teach among the Lakota. Though many Lakota became members of the Roman Catholic Church, and later the Episcopal Church, traditional religion under the guidance of Lakota spiritual leaders remains the primary form of worship.

In 1890 the Lakota reacted to their loss of freedom and life on the reservations by practicing the Ghost Dance Religion. A Paiute holy man named John Wovoka started the movement, teaching that if they performed the Ghost Dance, Indians could return the Earth to a natural state, with huge herds of buffalo and all the dead ancestors returned. No whites would inhabit this world. Many unhappy tribes conducted Ghost Dance ceremonies as a form of peaceful resistance. But two Lakota medicine men, Kicking Bear and Short Bull, claimed that dancing the Ghost Dance and wearing protective Ghost Dance shirts could shield the people from white men's bullets. The tribe had lost its most basic ways of life and faced terrible conditions and starvation. The Ghost Dance offered hope. The U.S. government outlawed the ceremony on all reservations, but the Lakota continued to sponsor large gatherings.

LANGUAGE

The Lakota speak one of three dialects (varieties) of the Siouan language family. The other two dialects are spoken by the Dakota and Nakota. Although there are some differences (see Dakota entry), all three groups can understand one another. The Lakota language is still spoken today by many people on the reservations. It is taught throughout the grade levels at reservation schools, and it is used in traditional ceremonies. In 1987 it was estimated that about 6,000 Lakota living in the United States and Canada spoke their Native language.

GOVERNMENT

In the early days on the Great Plains, the Lakota lived in small settlements that were organized without powerful leaders. Older people with outstanding personal qualities were respected and their opinions might be asked, but they had no great authority. This way of organizing themselves changed in the 1800s when the Lakota way of life was threatened by whites. They began to come together in larger groups and pledged their allegiance to strong leaders.

Once the Lakota were on reservations, government agents discouraged the system of having head chiefs. It was not long before more and more people claimed to be chiefs. With so many chiefs came conflicts, as people divided their loyalties among them and quarreled with each other.

The Indian Reorganization Act of 1934 called for a new form of tribal government. The Lakota set up elected tribal councils at several reservations. However, the Bureau of Indian Affairs has often been thought to have hand-picked the leaders. There has been conflict between the tribal council leaders and some of the Lakota traditional leaders, who have at times felt that the tribal council has been corrupt or in the control of the federal government and does not fairly represent the Lakota people.

ECONOMY

Before they moved to the Great Plains, the Sioux tribes' economy depended on hunting, fishing, gathering, and a little farming. After moving and acquiring horses, the economy came to depend on trade in buffalo hides. They raided other tribes for horses, and drove many of the tribes away, finally reaching the point where they dominated much of the Great Plains trade.

After the earliest treaties were signed with the U.S. government, with most of the buffalo gone, many Lakota people became dependent on government handouts. Some began to hang around American forts, and were despised by their fellow tribe members and by whites at the fort. On the other hand, many became successful farmers and ranchers on the reservations until the Great Depression struck in the 1930s. The Great Depression was a downturn in the economy that threw millions of people out of work. Afterwards, many Lakota were unable to recover economically and instead had to sustain themselves by leasing their lands to white farmers; some still earn money in this way.

Lakota reservations were among the poorest communities in the United States in the 1990s, with up to 80 percent unemployment (this means that four out of five people who wanted to work could not find work). Many must seek work off the reservations. Some farming and ranching are done, and tribal government is a major employer. Casinos, bingo halls, and small businesses are opening to expand the economy. The remote locations of the reservations make the business prospects more bleak.

Education

Because the Lakota moved around so much, boys and girls learned about geography and plant life. Boys learned from a young age how to be successful competitors. At three they learned how to race ponies and took part in games that tested their skill and strength; top spinning and javelin throwing were popular. Later their survival skills were tested by undertaking long, difficult trips into the wilderness.

Teenage boys had several career options open to them. They could become warriors or buffalo hunters or join one of several societies (the Kit Foxes, the Crow Owners, or the Brave Hearts, for example), whose members organized buffalo hunts or were in charge of moving the camp.

In the 1880s, Chief Red Cloud petitioned the federal government to allow Jesuit priests to come to Sioux reservations to start schools. Generations of Sioux children were educated in the Catholic schools begun by the Jesuits.

Today, reservation schools emphasize the teaching of the Lakota language and culture, beginning with Head Start programs for preschoolers and continuing through college. Sitting Bull College on the Standing Rock Reservation has an Indian studies program. There are more than a dozen private and public schools at Pine Ridge Reservation, including Oglala Lakota College.

Buildings

Like many tribes of the Great Plains, the Lakota lived in tepees, which were easy to assemble and carry. A framework of wooden poles was arranged into a cone shape and was covered with eight to twelve buffalo skins, carefully prepared and stitched together. During the winter, stones held the tepees in place. In the summer, the covers were rolled up to let in fresh air. Sometimes Lakota men would decorate the outsides of their tepees with paintings that recorded special events in their lives.

The Lakota also built sweat lodges that were used for ceremonial purposes. The Lakota believed that sweating rid the body and mind of impurities and made one ready to deal with the spirits.

After about 1900, traditional Lakota tepees were replaced by tents and then by log cabins supplied by the U.S. government.

SIOUX PLUM RAISIN CAKES

Author E. Barrie Kavasch, an authority on Native American culture and cookery, observed that Native Americans living in the north-central part of the United States often mark midwinter with a celebration. Naturally, these celebrations prominently feature food. Kavasch's recipe for Sioux Plum Raisin Cakes, which resembles a Christmas fruitcake, was inspired by a visit to the Cheyenne River Sioux Reservation in Eagle Butte, South Dakota, where wild plums are plentiful. Berries also work well in this recipe.

1 cup dark raisins, cherries, or currants

1 cup boiling water

1 (16-ounce) can purple plums, drained and pitted

1 cup toasted hazelnuts, chopped

1/2 cup butter, melted, or corn oil

4 cups sifted all-purpose flour

3 teaspoons baking soda

1½ teaspoons salt

1½ teaspoons ground allspice

1 teaspoon ground cloves

1 cup honey

1/2 cup maple syrup

Preheat oven to 350° F.

Place the raisins, cherries, or currants in a small glass bowl. Cover them with 1 cup boiling water; soak them until plump, for about 30 minutes. Lightly oil 24 or more muffin cups.

Mash the plums in a large mixing bowl. Add all the remaining ingredients to the plums and mix well.

Add the soaked raisins (or other fruit) and their liquid. Blend all together well. Carefully measure by tablespoonfuls, filling each muffin cup halfway.

Bake 25 to 30 minutes, until a toothpick inserted in the center of a muffin comes out clean. Cool for 10 minutes on a wire rack, then loosen the sides and turn out cakes. Serve warm with flavored honey.

Makes 24 cakes (muffins).

From L. Barrie Kavasch, *Enduring Harvests: Native American Foods and Festivals for Every Season.* Old Saybrook, Connecticut: Globe Pequot Press, 1995, p. 147-48.

Food

The great buffalo herds provided the primary means of food and other necessities for the Lakota. Their diet relied almost entirely on buffalo and chokecherries.

Lakota men handled most of the hunting duties, while women butchered the animals, prepared the hides, and cooked or preserved the meat. The Lakota also hunted other animals, such as deer, elk, and small game. They collected roots and berries, and traded for food with farming tribes of the region.

Clothing and adornment

The Lakota were famous for their colorful clothing, mostly made of deer or elk hides. The men wore fringed buckskin shirts and leggings, often decorated with brightly colored porcupine quills or locks of hair. They also wore buckskin moccasins with tough, buffalo-hide soles. They adorned themselves with earrings, armbands, and bear-claw necklaces. Younger men often shaved the sides of their heads and let the hair in the middle grow long. Lakota warriors painted both themselves and their horses with fierce symbols and patterns, and they wore eagle feathers in their hair as a sign of their acts of bravery.

Lakota women wore buckskin dresses that reached to the ankle over leggings that extended to the knee. Their clothing, too, was elaborately decorated with fringes, porcupine quills, or beads. The women usually let their hair grow long and wore it in two braids woven with pieces of cloth or beads. Lakota children of both genders had their ears pierced when they reached the age of five or six, and from that time on they wore strings of colored beads as earrings.

Healing practices

Many Lakota spiritual leaders and healers had learned of their future role when they were children, when a buffalo spoke to them in a dream. Such children were called Buffalo Dreamers. The Lakota people consulted with them about a variety of problems, including illnesses and injuries. Healers made medicine out of herbs, tree bark, wild fruits, and ground buffalo hooves. They also appealed to the spirits for help in diagnosing and curing illnesses by singing, dancing, and praying in special ways.

Today, health conditions on the reservations are below the national average. Due to high incidences of alcoholism and suicide, a Lakota male can expect to live to the age of fifty; white males can expect to live to about age seventy-three.

ARTS

Oral literature

Historians say the Black Hills became the Lakota spiritual center after their move there in the 1700s. However, some Sioux origin stories say that the Sioux Nation (Dakota, Lakota, and Nakota peoples) originated on Earth in the Black Hills and were chosen by the Creator to be protectors of the area, which they call *He Sapa*. According to their oral traditions, the Sioux lived peacefully beneath the surface of the Black Hills, but they were tempted to leave their safe dwelling and rise above the surface. They say they emerged through Wind Cave in the Black Hills, leaving their leader behind. Their leader then came above the Earth's surface as a buffalo, offering his body as everything the people needed to survive.

When I pray really hard I see my long ago ancestors.
In 1919 we stand on the threshold of a new and different time. We live in a wooden house.
I dreamed my long ago ancestors over for a visit to see my grand-children and our new house. They said my grand-children were good. Some of them sat in that automobile. They liked it.

"The Visit," a painting by Lakota artist Arthur Amiotee, 1995.

CUSTOMS

War and hunting rituals

Like the Dakota tribe, the Lakota had war chiefs who could be anyone able to convince a group of volunteers to follow him into battle. Upon returning from a successful battle, they held scalp dances to celebrate. William Clark of the Lewis and Clark Expedition described a Lakota scalp dance he witnessed in 1804 (the spelling is his):

> A large fire made in the Center, about 10 musitions playing on tamberins made of hoops & skin stretched. long sticks with Deer & Goats Hoofs tied So as to make a [jingling] noise and many others of a Similer kind, those men began to Sing & Beet on the Temboren, the women Came forward highly Deckerated in theire way, with the Scalps an Trofies of war of ther father

Driving buffalo over a bluff.

DRIVING BUFFALO OVER A BLUFF.

Husbands Brothers or near Connection & proceeded to dance the war Dance. Women only dance—jump up & down. . . . Every now and then one of the men come out & repeat some exploit in a sort of song—this taken by the young men and the women dance to it.

During the annual *wani-sapa,* or "fall hunt," hundreds of Lakota worked in large groups to hunt enough game to supply the tribe with food for the winter. Their group hunting methods included surrounding a herd of buffalo with a circle of fire lit on the grass, and stampeding a herd over the edge of a cliff or into a corral made of stones and brush. Women and children participated in the stampeding method, shouting from the sidelines to frighten the buffalo over the cliff.

Keeping of the Soul

One of the seven sacred rites brought to the people by White Buffalo Calf Woman is called Keeping of the Soul. In the old times, it marked the end of a one-year period of mourning following a death. After a year, many gifts were distributed by the relatives of the dead person. Today, such giveaways are held to celebrate various important occasions, including births, marriages, graduations, and a young person's acceptance into the U.S. Armed Forces.

Sun Dance

Versions of the Sun Dance are performed by many American Indian groups. The dance is one of the seven sacred rites given to the

Lakota by White Buffalo Calf Woman, and its name refers to the fact that the dancers gaze into the Sun. The Sun Dance was prohibited by U.S. authorities from the late 1800s to 1935, and some tribes gave it up completely, but the practice has been revived by the Lakota. It lasts three to four days, and features fasting, dancing, singing, and drumming. The dancers have skewers inserted through the skin of their breast or back (arm for women) and are tied to a center pole. As they dance, they tear themselves away from the skewers. This sacrifice pleases the Creator, who accepts thanks for past blessings and grants future blessings.

Vision quests

Around the time they reached puberty, all Lakota men (and some women) traditionally participated in a vision quest in order to forge a personal connection with the supernatural being who would guide the person through life. The first step for young people undertaking vision quests was to purify themselves in a sweat lodge. Then they traveled to a sacred place, accompanied by two helpers who constructed a platform, then left the vision seekers alone. The person seeking a vision paced around on the platform, praying, smoking a sacred pipe, and fasting from food and water. The vision seeker kept careful track of everything he or she saw and heard during this time.

After four days had passed, the helpers returned and brought the seeker back to camp. There the spiritual leaders explained his or her vision, providing special songs, prayers, and objects that from that time on represented the seeker's connection with the supernatural. Upon successfully completing a vision quest, a Lakota gained power and was considered an adult in the eyes of the tribe.

Rites of passage

An important Lakota ceremony honored a young woman at the time of her first menstrual period. She was sent away to stay in a special hut outside the camp, where older women visited her to explain her adult responsibilities. A few weeks later, her father hosted a ceremony that celebrated her passage into womanhood. During the ceremony, the right side of the young woman's face and the part in her hair were painted red, a sacred color, and a feather was placed in her hair for good luck in producing children.

When a young Lakota man participated in his first successful hunt or joined his first war party, his family celebrated his passage to manhood with a special ceremony and a feast.

Courtship and marriage

Marriages were usually arranged by a young couple's parents. Sometimes, however, couples simply fell in love and decided to elope. The couple was formally recognized as husband and wife when gifts were exchanged between the two families and the couple moved into a tepee together.

Death and burial

When a member of the Lakota tribe died, his or her body was placed on a scaffold (a raised platform) or in the branches of a tree along with selected possessions and food for the journey to the next world. Though the Lakota were expected to face their own death with dignity, they deeply mourned the loss of relatives.

CURRENT TRIBAL ISSUES

Some of the ongoing issues facing the Lakota today include the poor economic conditions on reservations and land disputes over the Black Hills. Although they could use the money, the Lakota continue to fight for the return of their traditional lands rather than accept a cash settlement. The people are also divided between traditionals who wish to retain the old Lakota ways and those who prefer to accept the mainstream American culture, government, and economy.

In 1998 the Standing Rock Sioux sought ways to cope with a rash of teen suicides. Between August 1997 and March 1998, six young people killed themselves, and at least forty others attempted suicide. The federal Centers for Disease Control and Prevention agreed to send a team of suicide experts to the reservation to look for causes and help with prevention.

NOTABLE PEOPLE

Sitting Bull (c. 1834–1890) was a great chief of the Hunkpapa band of Lakota. Born Tatanka Iyotake, he gained a reputation as a fearless warrior from an early age. As a young man he adopted an orphan boy, Gall, who eventually became his best friend and partner in battle. In 1863 Sitting Bull visited the Santee Reservation and saw the deplorable conditions there. From that time on, he believed that only force could prevent white settlers from taking over Lakota territory. A medicine man, he inspired the Lakota warriors who defeated General George Armstrong Custer in the Battle of the Little Bighorn in 1876, but the following year he was forced to retreat to Canada. After the Canadians refused to assist him, Sitting Bull surrendered to the United States in 1881 and took up residence at the Standing Rock Reservation. Following a tour of Europe with Buffalo Bill's Wild West Show and after many speaking engagements in the white world, he returned to Standing Rock, where he continued to resist the U.S. government's effort to Americanize his people. Reservation police killed him on December 15, 1890, two weeks before the massacre at Wounded Knee.

Billy Mills (1938–) set a world record in track at the 1964 Olympic Games. He then returned to Pine Ridge Reservation to become a role model to Lakota young people there. Well respected throughout the United States, his story was told in the movie, *Running Brave*. Today Billy Mills is an active spokesperson for Indian causes and serves as director of the highly successful charitable organization, Running Strong for Native American Youth.

Among the many other notable Lakota are: tribal leader and warrior Red Cloud (1822–1909), who was known for his powerful resistance to the occupation of the Dakota territory by American settlers, and later for his attempts to secure peaceful relations between his people and the U.S. government; spiritual leader Black Elk (c. 1863–1950), subject of a 1932 book *Black Elk Speaks*; military and tribal leader Crazy Horse (c. 1840–1877), called "Our Strange One" by his people because he kept to himself, wore no war paint, took no scalps, and would not boast of his brave deeds; Mary Brave Bird (also known as Mary Crow Dog; 1953–), who dictated two books about how the American Indian Movement gave meaning to her life—*Lakota Woman* and *Ohitika Woman*; Indian rights activist Russell Means (1939–); imprisoned activist Leonard Peltier (1944–); and political figure Ben Reifel (1906–1990), the first member of the Sioux Nation to serve in the U.S. Congress.

FURTHER READING

Ambrose, Stephen. "Encounter with the Sioux," in *Undaunted Courage: Meriwether Lewis, Thomas Jefferson, and the Opening of the American West*. New York: Simon & Schuster, 1996.

"The Battle of Little Bighorn. An eyewitness account by the Lakota Chief Red Horse recorded in pictographs and text at the Cheyenne River Reservation, 1881. [Online] www.pbs.org/weta/hewest/ wpages/wpgs660/bighorn.htm

Bonvillain, Nancy. *The Teton Sioux*. New York: Chelsea House, 1994.

Brown, Dee. *Bury My Heart at Wounded Knee: An Indian History of the American West*. New York: Holt, Rinehart, and Winston, 1970.

Cheyenne River Tribe web site. [Online], http://www.siux.org

Dolan, Terrance. *The Teton Sioux Indians.* New York: Chelsea House, 1995.

Freedman, Russell. *The Life and Death of Crazy Horse.* New York: Holiday House, 1996.

"A Guide to the Great Sioux Nation." [Online] http://www.state.sd.us/state/ executive/tourism/sioux/sioux.htm

Larson, Robert W. *Red Cloud: Warrior-Statesman of the Lakota Sioux.* Norman: University of Oklahoma Press, 1997.

Lazarus, Edward. *Black Hills White Justice: The Sioux Nation versus the United States 1775 to the Present.* New York: Harper Collins, 1991.

Rosebud Reservation home page. [Online] http://www.littlesioux.org/

"Timeline of events relevant to the Northern Plains tribes." [Online] http://www.hanksville.phast.umass.edu/june95/lakota/timeline2.html

Sioux Nations: Nakota

Name

Nakota (pronounced *nah-KO-tah*) is the Nakota name for themselves and means "allies." The two Nakota bands are also known as the Yankton and the Yanktonai. *Ihanktunwan* (Yankton) means "end village," and *Ihanktunwanna* (Yanktonai) means "little end village." The Sioux tribes (Dakota, Lakota, and Nakota) were once given a name that means "little snakes" by their enemies, the Ojibway. The French shortened the Ojibway word to "Sioux," the name by which the tribes are collectively known.

Location

Both the Yankton and Yanktonai bands of Nakota inhabited the region near what is today Mille Lacs, Minnesota, in the seventeenth century. They traveled westward into parts of modern North and South Dakota and Iowa over the course of the eighteenth century. Today many live for at least part of the year on the Yankton Reservation in South Dakota; returning to live in urban areas in South Dakota and Iowa. Some live with the Lakota people on the Standing Rock and Crow Creek reservations in South Dakota, at the Devil's Lake Reservation in North Dakota; and at the Fort Peck Reservation in Montana.

Population

In the early 1800s, there were about 4,000 Nakota. Today, Nakota-speakers are no longer counted separately from the Sioux; there are probably at least 10,000 Nakota.

Language family

Siouan.

Origins and group affiliations

The Nakota and the Lakota peoples were originally part of the Dakota tribe; the Nakota were the smallest of the three divisions. The Yankton, Yanktonai, and a third group, the Assiniboin (*uh-SIN-uh-boin*), called themselves Nakoda or Nakota. The Assiniboin left in the sixteenth century and moved north into Canada and west into Montana. The Nakota fought mostly with the Cree in Minnesota but were on good terms with neighboring tribes after their move to the prairies.

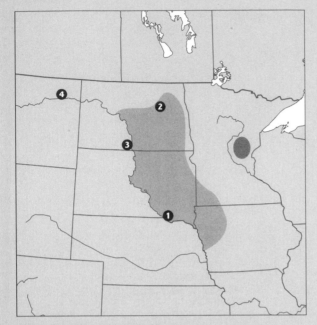

NAKOTA

Darker shaded area: Traditional lands occupied by the Nakota near Mille Lacs, Minnesota, before the eighteenth century.

Lighter shaded area: Lands occupied by the Nakota from the eighteenth century in present-day North and South Dakota and Iowa.

Contemporary Communities

South Dakota
  1. Yankton Sioux Tribe

North Dakota
  2. Devil's Lake Sioux Tribe
  3. Standing Rock Reservation

Montana
  4. Fort Peck Assiniboine and Sioux Tribes

The Nakota were the only one of the three Sioux tribes who never officially took up arms against the United States. In spite of the friendly relations between them, the Nakota gave up more than 13 million acres to Americans. On the reservations, they have managed to retain many of their traditions.

HISTORY

Driven from their homeland

During the 1600s, the Nakota, as part of the larger Dakota (Sioux) tribe that also included the Dakota and Lakota) occupied the area near Mille Lacs in what is now Minnesota. Explorers in north-central Minnesota noted their location on a map in 1683, and in 1700, the French trader-explorer Pierre Charles LeSueur encountered the Sioux near a quarry in Minnesota, where they may have been collecting stone to make their sacred pipes.

In response to hostility from nearby Cree and Ojibway (see entries), the three Sioux groups (Dakota, Lakota, Nakota) began to move south and west in the 1700s. The Nakota finally settled in a region east of the Missouri River in South Dakota. They built their villages along the Missouri, and controlled the areas around the Big Sioux, Des Moines, and James rivers.

Choose friendship with Americans

Because of their control of the rivers, the Nakota were ideally situated for trading furs with the French. They quickly became familiar with white ways, and enjoyed the European goods they acquired in trade.

Their relationship with the French ended with the Louisiana Purchase of 1803, when the United States acquired a vast parcel of land from France, including Nakota territory. The next year President Thomas Jefferson sent Meriwether Lewis and William Clark to explore the region. Their orders were to make friends with the Sioux and enlist them as partners in a new American trading system. The Nakota people were the first Sioux encountered by the Lewis and Clark expedition.

Lewis and Clark found the Nakota to be very friendly. They admired their orderly camps and their handsome cone-shaped tepees. They passed out some cheap presents and designated one Indian man to become "first chief" in charge of relations with the American government. In spite of this arrogant treatment and their displeasure with the presents, the Nakota decided to accept the Americans' offer of friendship.

Land giveaways begin

Although the Nakota were friendly toward the Americans, other tribes were not, and the Nakota joined American soldiers in fighting the other tribes. In 1830, in an effort to make peace in the area and keep the warring tribes apart, the Yankton band agreed to give up a large piece of their land—about 2.2 million acres—to the U.S. government.

IMPORTANT DATES

1700: Pierre Charles LeSueur encounters the Yankton and Yanktonai.

1804: Lewis and Clark visit both Nakota tribes in the upper Missouri River region and find them friendly.

1858: Yankton give all lands, except for a reservation on the Missouri River, to the United States.

1865: Yanktonai sign peace treaty with the U.S. government and give up lands.

1887–90: Reservation lands divided into individual allotments.

1932: A tribal constitution is adopted.

1961: Tribal constitution is amended; the Yankton Sioux Tribal Business and Claims Committee becomes the governing body at Yankton Reservation.

A Nakota encampment.

Trading posts sprang up throughout Nakota territory. Visitors came from the East to travel in steamboats up and down the Missouri River. When they returned home, they spread the word about the wonderful farming land there. Settlers flocked in, and pressure grew for the government to move the Nakota out of the way and place them on a reservation. The Nakota had to decide whether to go peacefully or join the other Sioux tribes (Dakota and Lakota) in resisting. The Nakota chose peace.

In 1858 more than 11 million acres of Yankton land were given to the United States, in exchange for $1.6 million in money and services, to be paid out in installments over fifty years. The tribe retained 430,000 acres of reservation land between the Missouri River and Chouteau Creek in southern South Dakota.

On the reservations

Other Sioux tribes were furious at the giveaway of the Yankton land. The Yanktonai said the land given away belonged to them and they had merely loaned it to the Yankton when that tribe had given up its land to the United States in 1830. But the Yankton were determined to keep the peace. They again displayed their loyalty to the United States in 1862 when they refused to join with their kinsmen in the Sioux wars against whites in Minnesota (see Dakota entry).

The Yanktonai fought until 1865, when they signed a peace treaty and gave up their lands to the United States. The people were split between the Crow Creek, Devils Lake, and Standing Rock reservations in the Dakotas and the Fort Peck Reservation in Montana (see Lakota entry).

The Yankton settled on their reservation in 1859, and government agents were sent to teach them farming and ranching methods.

Allotment period

In 1887 Congress passed the Dawes Act, or the General Allotment Act. The purpose of this act was to make Indians on reservations assimilate (become like whites) faster. It also very clearly made vast areas of Native lands available to settlers. The act divided reservation lands into individual farms ranging from 40 to 160 acres in size. The land left over was sold to whites. This division of land meant that people who were used to owning their land communally (as a group) would now work on their own separate farms, responsible for themselves, not the group. This was a complete reversal of traditional ways.

For the Nakota, the process was completed over the next three years, and by the time it was over, the 435,000-acre Yankton Reservation in South Dakota was reduced to 40,000 acres under tribal ownership. For the several decades that followed, the U.S. government encouraged Indians to abandon their traditional culture. The government hoped that the Yankton and Yanktonai would become productive farmers and ranchers, but the policy did not work. Unable to support themselves, many Nakota left the reservation and moved to urban centers in the Plains and the West.

Nakota in the twentieth century

By the 1930s the American government realized that its policies toward reservation Indians were ineffective. The Indian Reorganization Act (IRA) of 1934 was passed, which encouraged American Indian tribes to adopt written constitutions and set up their own governments, but the new tribal governments were under federal government supervision. The Yankton refused to accept the terms of the IRA, and ever since they have been overlooked when government funds are being distributed to Indian tribes. In their search for ways to make a living, the Nakota finally achieved considerable success when they opened the Fort Randall Casino in 1991.

RELIGION

The Nakota shared many religious customs with the Dakota and Lakota (see entries). They worshipped the Great Spirit, Wakan Tanka,

THE YANKTON SIOUX AND THE GREAT RED PIPESTONE QUARRY

The famous writer and painter George Catlin was one of the visitors who travelled through Yankton Sioux country in the early 1800s. He heard tales of a quarry where a fantastic kind of red clay stone (called pipestone) could be found, and decided to see it for himself. As he came upon the area, he and his party found "great difficulty in approaching, being stopped by several hundred Indians who ordered us back and threatened us very hard, saying 'that no white man had ever been to it, and that none should ever go.'" Catlin painted the Indians at the quarry, wrote about his findings, and sent a sample of the red stone to the nation's capitol to be analyzed. The new stone was called catlinite in his honor.

Poet Henry Wadsworth Longfellow heard about the pipestone and mentioned it in his 1855 poem, *The Song of Hiawatha*. What Catlin and Longfellow described was the Red Pipestone Quarry in Minnesota, the place, according to Sioux oral tradition, where the Great Spirit sent a flood that cleansed the Earth and left behind only the blood of the Sioux ancestors—in the form of red pipestone.

The Sioux believed the quarry was sacred. Historians say that many different tribes came to it in the summer to quarry stone for use in making their sacred pipes. The pipestone quarry was given up by the Dakota Sioux in a treaty signed with the U.S. government in 1851. The Yankton Sioux objected to the giveaway. When they signed over their lands to the United States in 1865, they insisted that 648 acres in Minnesota be handed over to them as the Pipestone Reservation. Pipestone Reservation was sold by the tribe in 1929 on condition they could have access to the stone quarry there. In 1937 the land was designated a national monument. The Upper Midwest Indian Cultural Center now located on the site preserves the ancient craft of pipemaking.

and performed the Sun Dance. All three Sioux groups conducted the ceremony of the sacred pipe, which was originally taught to the Sioux by a holy woman they called White Buffalo Calf Woman. The ceremony was performed in a sweat lodge. It began with a period of fasting and consisted of prayers to the Great Spirit for cleansing and guidance. Successful participants of the ritual were rewarded with a dream vision.

The Sacred Pipe ceremony was frowned upon by white missionaries who began to arrive in the late 1830s, but it was performed secretly by Yanktons who practiced the old religious ways. In recent years the ceremony has been held openly on the Yankton Reservation, where some residents also practice the Peyote (pronounced *pay-OH-tee*) Ceremony. In this ceremony, people consume peyote, a substance obtained from cactus; in the trance state peyote induces, they hope to experience visions with spiritual meaning.

LANGUAGE

Originally, the Dakota, Lakota, and Nakota spoke the same language. But as the Lakota and Nakota moved away from the Dakota, each tribe began to speak its own form of the language. People from all three tribes could still understand one another because the languages remained similar. Today, people who live on the Crow Creek Sioux Reservation speak Nakota.

GOVERNMENT

Nakota bands were governed by a council, which consisted of a hereditary chief (the position passed from father to son or another related heir) and other important leaders and warriors from the clans (groups of related families who traced their heritage back to the same ancestors). Once the Nakota people were on reservations, federal agents appointed chiefs to be in charge of distributing goods and money. Agents also set up a tribal police force, formed a new Nakota band whose members were people of mixed Indian and white blood, and generally oversaw all aspects of Indian life. Meanwhile, the Nakota's old chief, Struck-by-the-Ree, encouraged his people to accept this government interference and adapt to white ways.

In the 1930s the government did an about-face and decided to return control of their own affairs to Indian tribes. Congress passed the Indian Reorganization Act (IRA) in 1934. The act allowed members of the tribe to vote to write a new constitution under the supervision of the federal government. If they voted in favor of it, the tribe would also become eligible to receive money from the federal government for development. The tribe at the Yankton Reservation had already adopted their own constitution in 1932 and decided to remain independent.

Today the Yankton Reservation is governed by the Yankton Sioux Tribal Business and Claims Committee, whose members are elected to two-year terms. The committee looks for ways to make the reservation an attractive place for members of the tribe to live and work.

ECONOMY

To the early hunting-gathering economy, the Nakota added fur trading with the French and then the Americans in the 1700s and 1800s. They received blankets, cloth, clothing, cooking utensils, tools, beads, and guns in exchange.

In the early days on the reservations, they continued many of their old hunting-gathering ways. When there was not enough food to be had there, they were allowed to go off the reservation to hunt buffalo. Slowly they adopted white ways of farming, but they faced obstacles such as frequent floods, drought, plagues of grasshoppers, and blizzards. Their economy gradually came to rely heavily on farming, but in the 1920s prices for farm goods fell, and many Yankton could no longer afford to farm. More economic and natural disasters followed. People began to sell off their plots of land and moved away to work in the non-Native economy. The traditional Nakota way of life seemed to have disappeared.

In the 1960s the federal government began to expand federal funding for Indian programs, and some money found its way to the Yankton Reservation. Efforts to modernize the reservation economy using those funds included an electronics industry in the 1960s and the construction of a pork-processing plant in the 1970s. These ventures worked for a time but then failed. More people fled the reservations in the 1960s to find jobs in cities and towns. The economy improved when gambling was introduced on the Yankton Reservation in 1991. The casino was an immediate success in terms of jobs and money, and some people returned to live on the Yankton Reservation. Today, the major employers there are the casino, the Indian Health Service, the Bureau of Indian Affairs, the Marty Indian School (Marty is the city in South Dakota where tribal headquarters is located), and the tribal government.

DAILY LIFE

Education

The first missionary arrived on the Yankton Reservation in 1839, and soon the first of many religious schools sprang up. Their goal was to discourage traditional practices and coax the people into accepting white ways. The federal government got into the act in 1882 when it opened a boarding school in nearby Greenwood, South Dakota; it operated for nearly forty years. School officials removed children from their homes. Indian children were taught reading, writing, and arithmetic for half the school day. For the other half day, girls learned homemaking skills, and boys were taught how to farm and raise livestock.

Today, the Yankton operate their own boarding high school and a junior college and teach Nakota culture in buildings originally established by missionaries to teach white ways.

Food

The Yankton and Yanktonai adjusted their diet according to the different environments they found as the moved about. While living

Boys at the government school at the Yankton Agency.

in Minnesota, the Nakota-speakers built dugout tree-trunk canoes and practiced spear-fishing in the nearby lakes and rivers. They also hunted large game, such as moose and deer, and grew grains and vegetables, including corn, squash, and pumpkins.

After they moved to the Great Plains and later acquired horses, the Nakota adopted a Plains lifestyle. They hunted the buffalo that became the major source of food and other raw materials they used to make their clothing and shelter. They continued to grow some crops, especially corn and squash, and rounded out their diets by gathering wild plums, cherries, and edible roots.

Buildings

In Minnesota the Nakota lived in houses covered with bark or small earth-covered lodges. When they moved to the Great Plains and had to follow the buffalo herds, they built portable buffalo-skin tepees, painted various colors and sometimes decorated with drawings that recorded special events in their lives.

CUSTOMS

Festivals and ceremonies

The traditional Sioux religious ceremonies are still held (Sun Dance, Peyote rituals, ceremony of the Sacred Pipe; see "Religion"). They are accompanied by elaborate feasts requiring days of preparation. Large quantities of food and gifts are distributed for people to take home from these feasts. Now, instead of ponies and guns, the gifts might include the beautiful star quilts and handcrafted, beaded jewelry still made by Yankton women.

The Yanktons also host large powwows, celebrations at which the main activity is traditional singing and dancing. In modern times, the singers and dancers at powwows usually come from many different tribes.

CURRENT TRIBAL ISSUES

The Yankton Sioux Tribe was the subject of a Supreme Court decision in 1998 in a complicated case called *South Dakota* v. *Yankton Sioux Tribe et al* [and others]. The case arose after local officials announced in 1992 a plan to open a solid waste landfill on land that was originally part of the 1858 reservation but was later sold to a non-Indian. The tribe objected to the landfill, claiming that it would be authorized to accept asbestos, lime and waste water sludge, industrial waste, waste oil, lead-acid batteries, and other toxic waste. The tribe and many local residents believed that contaminants from such a dump would endanger their health and the health of their livestock. The tribe also believed it should have a say in whether such a landfill was built "within the territorial boundaries" of the Yankton Reservation.

The case that went to the Supreme Court did not involve the issue of the landfill. Rather, the issue that was argued was whether the 1858 reservation still existed. The state of South Dakota argued that the reservation ceased to exist when tribal members accepted the 1887 allotment act that divided up their 430,000 acres among themselves and sold what was left to settlers. The Supreme Court decided that the lands that were sold were indeed no longer part of a reservation, but the court refused to make a decision on whether a reservation now existed.

Meanwhile, construction on the site went forward, and the Yankton Sioux are continuing their fight against its location on the lands they consider their own.

NOTABLE PEOPLE

Gertrude Simmons Bonnin (1876–1938), also known as Zitkala-Sa or Red Bird, was a writer, educator, musician, activist, and feminist. She was born at the Yankton Sioux Agency in South Dakota and graduated from Earlham College in Richmond, Indiana. Her accomplishments were many. An accomplished musician and writer, Bonnin devoted her life to Indian reform issues, including speaking out for employment of Indians in the Indian Service, the preservation of accurate Indian history, and citizenship for all Indians. Her book *Old Indian Legends* was released in 1901. One of her last undertakings was the composition of an Indian opera with William F. Hanson entitled *Sun Dance*.

Other notable Nakota include: Yankton ethnologist, linguist, and novelist Ella Cara Deloria (1889–1971); Yankton writer Vine Deloria, Jr. (1933–); Yankton artist and professor Oscar Howe (1915–1983); and Yanktonai Sioux policeman Red Tomahawk, believed responsible for the 1890 slaying of Chief Sitting Bull.

FURTHER READING

Hoover, Herbert T. *The Yankton Sioux.* New York: Chelsea House, 1988.

"A Short History of Pipestone." A brief history of Pipestone, Minnesota, compiled by Lisa M. Ray, *Minnesota Calls*, March/April 1994. [Online] http://www.pipestone.mn.us/Museum/HISTORY.HTM

"Sioux." *Ready Reference: American Indians.* Ed. Harvey Markovwitz. Pasadena, CA: Salem Press, 1995.

Wichita

Name

The name Wichita (pronounced *WITCH-i-taw*) comes from a Choctaw word and means "big arbor" or "big platform," referring to the grass arbors the Wichita built. The Spanish called them *Jumano,* meaning "drummer" for the Wichita custom of summoning the tribe to council with a drum. The Siouan tribes called them the Black Pawnee because of their skin color and because they are related to the Pawnee.

Location

In 1541, the Wichita were living in western Oklahoma but were pushed south to the Red River area on the Oklahoma-Texas border. Today most live in Oklahoma, on or near the Wichita and Affiliated Tribes Reservation.

Population

In 1780, there were about 3,200 Wichita. In 1910, they numbered about 318. In a census (count of the population) done in 1990 by the U.S. Bureau of the Census, 1,241 people identified themselves as Wichita.

Language family

Caddoan.

Origins and group affiliations

The Wichita were part of the Caddo people who lived in the Oklahoma region for 3,500 years before being disturbed by Europeans in 1541. They broke off from the Caddo sometime before European contact and went looking for better farm land. They traveled north from Caddo territory to establish their tribe on the Arkansas River in present-day Kansas. The Pawnee, an offshoot of the Wichita, continued farther north to the North and South Platte rivers.

A group of Caddoan speakers formed a unit called a confederacy. Nine of the tribes who formed the confederacy have been identified, but the only ones that still exist are the Wichita and a few Waco people. The Wichita were most strongly allied with the Waco and Kichai (see box) and were enemies with the Apache and the Osage (see entries).

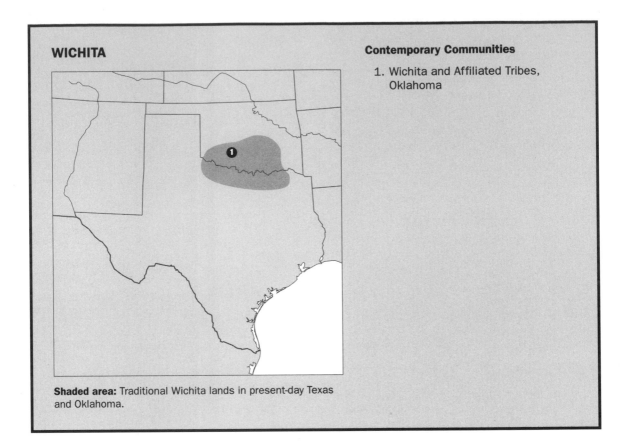

WICHITA

Contemporary Communities

1. Wichita and Affiliated Tribes, Oklahoma

Shaded area: Traditional Wichita lands in present-day Texas and Oklahoma.

The Wichita were a small and fairly peaceful tribe who farmed for centuries in the fertile river valleys of Kansas. Although they acquired horses in the 1700s, they continued to be known as farmers and did not fully adopt the Plains buffalo-hunting culture as other tribes did. They were famous for their unusual dwellings. The Wichita are probably best known today for lending their name to a city in Kansas and to several counties, some hills, and rivers in Texas and Oklahoma.

HISTORY

Discovered by Spanish gold seekers

It is said that one of the strangest expeditions ever undertaken for gold was the one led by Spanish explorer Francisco Vásquez de Coronado in 1541. Earlier explorers in the New World had returned to Spain with tales of the Seven Golden Cities of Cíbola. Coronado set off to explore the then-unknown wilderness north of Mexico, leading a group made up of hundreds of Spaniards, slaves, Indians, and cattle, sheep, and pigs. Instead of golden cities, he found the Indian pueblos of the Zuñi people (see entry). Coronado's hopes flared again when an Indian slave told him of rich lands to the north, in "The Kingdom of Quivira." This was the territory of the Wichita tribe. Instead of riches, Coronado found twenty-five poor Indian villages. He noted that the people ate raw meat, like their enemies, the Apaches. Coronado admired their grass houses, though, and considered them to be more advanced than their neighbors because they grew corn instead of living by raiding. (Coronado's slave confessed he had invented the story about Quivira gold; he was executed.)

IMPORTANT DATES

1541: Wichita encounter Spanish explorer Francisco Vásquez de Coronado.

1719: Wichita begin trading with French.

1758: Wichita repel Spanish attack.

1835: A peace treaty is signed by warring Native tribes. Wichita move to Indian Territory.

1858: U.S. troops kill many Wichita and destroy their property in the Battle of the Wichita Village.

1890: Wichita win a case for lands wrongfully taken by the United States.

1901: Wichita land is divided into parcels under the allotment policy.

Coronado left Wichita territory after failing to find the riches he sought, but his companion, the missionary Juan de Padilla, decided to remain with the tribe and convert them to Catholicism. Three years later, Padilla began to work with another tribe. The Wichita grew jealous and they killed him. No more Europeans bothered the Wichita for a long time afterwards.

Begin trading and warring

In 1719 the Wichita were living along the Canadian River in present-day Oklahoma, when French explorer Bernard de La Harpe began to trade with them. La Harpe estimated the population to be 6,000 people at his first meeting with them. La Harpe also noted that the Wichita had many prisoners of war from a recent conflict with another tribe, and they were preparing to eat them (some tribes believed that if you ate the body of a dead warrior, you ingested the warrior's strength). The French called the Wichita (and other Caddo) traders *Taovayas* or *coureurs de bois*, meaning "runners of the woods." Wichita Taovayas acted as go-betweens for the French, trading crops and French tools to the tribes of the West for buffalo robes and furs.

In the 1700s the French and Spanish were battling for control of the lands in the American Southeast. Their fighting placed the tribes of the region in a complicated position. The tribes were forced to keep changing sides as they tried to engage in trade with both the French and Spanish. Meanwhile, the Wichita were continually being forced to move farther south by hostile tribes.

In 1747 the French persuaded the Wichita to become allies with the Comanche in a war against the Apache and the Osage (see entries). Even with the help of the Comanche, however, the Wichita could not stand up against the Apache. They retreated farther south and settled at the present-day border of Oklahoma and Texas in the upper Red River Valley.

War continued, with the Apache, Osage, and the Spanish on one side, and the French, Wichita, Caddo, and Comanche on the other side. In 1758 the Wichita paid for their support of the French side—the Spanish attacked the main Wichita community. Supplied with weapons by the French and flying the French flag, the Wichita and their allies repelled the Spanish forces. In 1762 the defeated French gave up their lands in the Southeast to Spain. But the Wichita continued to fight the Spanish, carrying out raids against the Spanish settlement of San Antonio (Texas). In 1765, the Wichita captured a Spaniard and held him prisoner. Conflicts continued. In 1772 and again in 1778, the Spanish government attempted to formalize peace with the Wichita but were apparently not successful.

Battling continues

The Spanish took over trade in the region, and the Wichita *Taovayas* no longer held their position of power managing trade with the tribes of the West. In 1803 the United States acquired Wichita land in the Louisiana Purchase when they bought vast territories from France. Americans began to move there in droves. Like the Caddo, the Wichita were enthusiastic about the American presence at first, because the Americans paid more for furs.

Conflicts among the Native tribes continued. The Wichita joined forces with the Caddo and Choctaw in the continuing struggle against the Osage. But Native populations began to decline from the constant warfare and from white-introduced diseases such as smallpox.

In 1834, U.S. Army Colonel Henry Dodge intervened in the conflicts and arranged a peace among the Wichita, their allied tribes, and the Osage. The following year, the Wichita, the Comanche, the Caddo, and the Choctaw signed their first peace treaty with the U.S. government.

The peace between the Wichita and the United States ended in 1858 with the Battle of the Wichita Village. The Comanche had been carrying out raids against American settlers in Texas at the time. One day, when a peaceful group of Comanches had dropped in to visit the

Wichita, all were suddenly attacked by U.S. troops. Many were killed, including Wichita women, and the village was completely destroyed. The Wichita lost all their horses, crops, and homes. The Comanche thought they had been betrayed, and they later took their revenge by raiding and stealing Wichita horses.

The Wichita fled to Kansas during the Civil War (1861–65) to avoid getting caught up in the conflict. The site where they settled became the future city of Wichita, Kansas. The Wichita suffered greatly during the Civil War years, and many died from starvation and disease. In 1872 they agreed to move to a reservation with the Caddo and other tribes, north of the Washita River in Oklahoma. The U.S. Congress never officially accepted the agreement, though, and so the Wichita never received title to their land.

Peace was nearly shattered a year later, in 1873, after the killing of Wichita Chief Isadowa by the Osage during a buffalo hunt that almost erupted into war. Chief Ches-tedi-lessah succeeded Isadowa and Tawakoni Jim followed as the next chief.

In 1894, 152 chiefs of the Wichita and related tribes signed away their rights to any lands in Indian Territory. The Wichita felt as though they were being forced to sign the agreement, and they protested. Their case was brought before the U.S. Court of Claims, who found in favor of the Wichita. As a result, plots of land called allotments were given to 965 Wichita, and the remaining Wichita lands were opened to white settlers in 1901.

Today the tribe jointly owns about 2,400 acres with the Caddo and Delaware tribes. Because the tribe is so small, the people have had to struggle to maintain their culture.

RELIGION

Kinnikasus was the great creator of all or Spirit Over All among the Wichita. His name means "Man Never Known on Earth" or "Not Known To Man." The tribe worshiped many other spirits, including those contained in the Sun, called "Man Reflecting Light"; the Moon, called "Bright Shining Woman"; the Water, called "Woman Forever In The Water" and many gods, such as Morning Star and the Earth Mother. They also believed in spirits that inhabited objects.

The Wichita believed that animals and other guardian spirits could give tribal members power and knowledge. They believed in an afterlife, a spirit world located in the sky, where those who had died would lead a life of happiness free of the miseries of earthly life.

KICHAI AND WACO TRIBES

Several tribes were originally part of the Wichita confederacy and have since been folded into the group, which organized in 1961 as the Wichita and Affiliated Tribes. Among the several groups who shared language and many customs are the Kichai and Waco.

The Kichai called themselves Kitsash, meaning "going in wet sand." The name Kichai translates from the Wichita language as "red shield." The French called them the "roving nation" because of their wandering lifestyle.

In 1778 there were two Kichai settlements on the Trinity River in what is modern-day Texas, with a total population of about 500 people. By 1849 this number had dropped to about 300, and by 1950 it had slipped to only 150, 47 of whom were full-blooded.

The Kichai were expert hunters and guides who killed deer, buffalo, antelope, and other plains animals for raw materials used for tools and clothing, and for meat.

The name "Waco" may come from the Wichita word for Mexico, *wéhiko*. They once lived near the Arkansas River in what is now Oklahoma. Today they are probably best remembered for giving their name to a town in Texas. In 1824 the Waco were reported to number about 400. In the years after that, the total population of the tribe was hard to figure because of their close contact with several neighboring tribes. By 1894 there were 37 Waco, and about 60 in the 1950s.

Like the Wichita, the Waco mainly grew corn but also did some buffalo hunting. One of their major rituals was a rain bundle ceremony, which was designed to assure the strength of the buffalo herds. Several other rites were used to obtain magic from the natural world, such as the "Surround-Fire." Though many tribal customs are no longer practiced, the 1990s witnessed a resurgence of interest in the Waco tribal heritage. This new trend has resulted in a project to record songs and traditional stories so that they might be passed on to future generations.

Religious leaders called shamans (pronounced *SHAY-muns*) conducted ceremonies and also were healers. Like Caddo shamans, the Wichita shaman could perform rituals that brought him spiritual power to cure the sick or wounded.

Today, many Wichita are Baptists. Some are practicing members of the Native American Church, formed in Oklahoma in 1918 by John Wilson (c. 1840–1901). The religion combines elements of Christianity and traditional Native beliefs and practices.

LANGUAGE

Of the many languages in the Caddoan language family, three major languages have survived to the twentieth century: the Caddo language, the Pawnee language, and the Wichita language. All the tribes in the Wichita group except the Kichai (see box) spoke the same Caddoan language as the Wichita, which is similar to Pawnee. By the 1990s there were only about twenty speakers of the Wichita language left, but those speakers were assisting in a program to keep the language alive by recording it on audio tapes.

GOVERNMENT

The Wichita were part of a larger confederacy of people who spoke the same language and shared many customs and traditions. Each group had its own chief and subchief. Chiefs were elected by warriors, and their main job was to handle relations with other groups. The subchief was called "The One Who Locates"; his job was to scout out suitable sites for villages in case a move was necessary.

Chiefs were chosen who had distinguished themselves in some way, either by bravery, generosity, or some other outstanding trait. They could only make decisions after consulting with everyone in the village.

Once they were on a reservation, the Wichita were controlled by federal government agents. U.S. government policies changed in the twentieth century, and tribes were allowed to form new governments. The Wichita did so in 1961. Their elected executive council is made up of a president, vice president, secretary, treasurer, and three members. Tribal offices are near Anadarko, Oklahoma.

ECONOMY

The Wichita economy was based on agriculture, mostly corn, which they grew and traded to other tribes. The Wichita depended less on hunting buffalo and trading buffalo robes than other Great Plains tribes.

Today, most of the tribe's income comes from leasing farm lands and buildings to non-Indians through WCD Enterprises, a business the Wichita own with the Caddo and Delaware tribes. The tribe was contemplating a gambling enterprise in the mid-1990s. Some Wichita are employed in the tribal government, at the Riverside Indian School, and by the Anadarko Indian Health Center.

DAILY LIFE

Families

The Wichita had a complicated family organization in which some aunts and uncles were regarded as extra fathers and mothers, and some cousins were regarded as brothers and sisters. A woman's many sisters helped her with her household tasks, while a man's many brothers often accompanied him on hunting or warring expeditions.

Education

Children were taught through the example of their parents and relatives. Mothers had the primary responsibility for teaching both boys

and girls until they were about ten years old. Punishment was rare, but if a mother felt she could not handle her child's misbehavior, she might turn the job over to a relative, who was free to choose any type of punishment. Once she had asked for such assistance, the mother gave up any right to interfere. Usually only one such request for outside punishment was necessary, and the child behaved from then on.

When a boy reached the age of about ten, his father took over his education. The boy learned how to hunt and raid. Today, Wichita children mostly attend public schools in Oklahoma. Some attend a reservation boarding school.

Buildings

The Wichita were famous for their sturdy and unusual grass houses. They built them in villages overlooking rivers, and many villages contained as many as one thousand. The houses were fifteen to thirty feet in diameter, were shaped like cones, and were peaked at the top to symbolize the gods of the four quarters of the world. To make these complicated structures, forked cedar poles were covered with dry grass, and a ceremony was carried out during the building process.

Inside were eight to ten sleeping platforms surrounded by buffalo hide curtains, a central fire that vented through a hole in the roof, and a hollowed-out tree trunk for grinding corn.

Near the grass houses, the Wichita built arbors, which were open-sided grass structures set on raised platforms. These arbors were used for resting in the heat of the summer. Other arbors were built to store food; meat and corn were laid out on the roofs to dry.

Smaller thatched huts set on platforms held the village's unmarried girls, who were carefully guarded.

Food

The Wichita relied on farm products more than meat, even after horses made hunting more efficient. When they did hunt, they sought out buffalo, deer, antelope, bear, and other wild game. They mostly grew corn, beans, melons, tobacco, pumpkins, squash, gourds, and plums. They also gathered fruits and nuts. Surprisingly, even though they lived near rivers, the Wichita did not eat fish.

Clothing and adornment

French traders made up the name *Pani Pique* for the Wichita, which means "Tattooed Pawnee," or "punctured" or "pricked" because their faces and bodies were tattooed with sharp instruments. Both men and women wore intricate tattoos on their faces and bodies, consisting of dotted and solid lines and circles. Both men and women wore tattoos around their eyes, with either a horizontal line branching from the outside corner of each eye (men) or a line from the bridge of the nose to the upper lip and a chin line tattoo from ear to ear (women). Because of this style, they often referred to themselves as the "raccoon-eyed people."

Some decorated the backs of their hands with claw-like designs, which boys earned after killing their first birds. Other marks were earned as war honors. Men also hung ornaments from four piercings in their ears. Women wore tattoos on their necks, arms, and breasts.

George Catlin, a painter renowned for his paintings of Native Americans, noted that the Wichita were unlike other Plains Indians in that they were shorter, stockier, and their skin was darker. In summer, the Wichita wore scanty clothing, perhaps only loincloths (flaps of material that hung from the waist and covered the front and back) and moccasins. In colder weather, the men wore leggings, robes, and shirts in addition to their loincloths and moccasins. Women wore skirts of buckskin or buffalo hide, usually decorated with pretty ornaments.

CUSTOMS

Rituals observe life passages

The Wichita had a rich ceremonial life. They had secret societies for both men and women. Each society had its own special ceremonies and dances, such as the singing of songs before a war party set out and when it returned. They observed rituals for childbirth, puberty, marriage, death, and home building.

Marriage

Marriages were often arranged by relatives, though sometimes marriages were made by mutual consent of the couple. Married couples usually had only one spouse.

Social ceremonies

The Wichita were fond of dances, and held them to mark all sorts of occasions. For instance, the entire tribe observed the Deer Dance three times a year, to celebrate the coming of spring vegetation, the growth, and finally the harvest of corn. The dance included ritual vomiting and a ceremonial foot race. It was designed to purge the tribe of evil influences, and to encourage health, long life, and prosperity.

War rituals

War was the way a man gained importance in the tribe. Wichita warriors who wished to lead a war party had to convince others to follow them. Although war parties tended to be small, a warrior who was known for his ability—who had counted more coup (pronounced *COO*)—was likely to have more followers than one who was unproven. A coup was a feat of bravery, especially the touching of an enemy's body without causing injury. After warriors returned from a successful raid, there was much singing, dancing, and feasting. Back home, war leaders resumed their usual position of esteemed warrior; they were no longer in charge but were equal to all other warriors.

Burial

The Wichita buried their dead in shallow graves with the things they would need in the afterlife. Men were buried with weapons and tools; women were buried with domestic tools. When a loved one died, mourners cut their hair and gave away some of their possessions.

FURTHER READING

Carter, Cecile Elkins. *Caddo Indians*. Norman: University of Oklahoma Press, 1995.

Gregory, H. F., ed. *The Southern Caddo: An Anthology*. New York: Garland Publishing, 1986.

Miles, Ray. "Wichita." *Native America in the Twentieth Century, An Encyclopedia*. Ed. Mary B. Davis. New York: Garland Publishing, 1994.

The Plateau

The Plateau

A number of Native tribal communities of the Plateau region of the Northwest continue to live in their ancestral lands, which spread across the Columbia River Plateau of eastern Oregon and Washington State. Many years ago, ancestors of the area's tribes migrated south from northern territories in present-day British Columbia and eventually moved throughout the northwestern United States.

The various Native American nations on the Plateau shared their natural environment as well as an array of cultural traditions. Tribal elders of the Spokane (pronounced *spoh-KAN*), Flathead, Nez Perce (pronounced *NEZ-PURSE*), Cayuse (pronounced *KIE-yoos*), Okanagan (pronounced *OAK-uh-NAHG-uhn*), Wishram (pronounced *WISH-rum*), and neighboring tribes were united by the belief that their Creator had placed them on the Plateau. Their history began when the Earth was new. The tribes in the area possess remarkable oral traditions about their origins and their interactions with nature.

For generations the Plateau tribes adapted their lifestyle to the landscape, developing complex cultures around the rich natural environment of the region's salmon-filled rivers. Their land was lush with fertile soil, evergreen forests, and wide varieties of game and vegetation. Inevitably, such natural wealth attracted the attention of white explorers and settlers, especially as Americans began journeying westward at the turn of the nineteenth century.

Encountering outsiders

Many of the Plateau tribes played significant roles in the expedition American explorers Meriwether Lewis (1774–1809) and William Clark (1770–1838) led through the Plateau and out to the Pacific Ocean between 1804 and 1806. These pioneers surveyed the Plateau region and its peoples while outlining the potential development of the continent for U.S. president Thomas Jefferson.

Lewis and Clark—the first whites that many Plateau tribes had ever encountered—entered the land of the Nez Perce in October 1805. The tribe offered them food and canoes, enabling the expeditionary force to travel to the Pacific Coast. Other Plateau region tribes—the Wishram, the Walla Walla, and the Cayuse among them—sent diplomatic representatives to meet Lewis and Clark. Goods were exchanged. A special medal bearing the image of two hands shaking and engraved with the words "Peace and Friendship" was presented to tribal chiefs by the U.S. government, and more than 50 Native chiefs accepted an invitation to meet President Jefferson in Washington, D.C.

PLATEAU REGION TRIBES

The Plateau Region tribes include the Cayuse, Chelan, Columbia, Colville, Flathead, Kalispel, Klamath, Klickitat, Kootenai, Lake, Lillooet, Nez Perce, Okanagan, Palouse, Sanpoil, Shuswap, Spokane, Tenino, Thompson, Umatilla, Walla Walla, Wenatchee, Wishram, and Yakima.

Impact on Native culture

William Clark later returned to the Plateau to work with area tribes. When he became superintendent of Indian Affairs for much of the West in 1907, he was widely recognized as a fair and effective advocate of Native interests. Clark and others like him attempted to maintain peace and forge satisfactory relationships with the region's Indians, but they were not able to prevent the devastating consequences brought about by the development of the West. The transformation of the Plateau region into U.S. territory would alter nearly every aspect of life for the Native American tribes who resided there.

The United States eventually stated its claim to the entire Northwest, including the Plateau region, and began encouraging white settlement in the area. Because Lewis and Clark had observed and reported on the numerous furbearing animals of the region, traders and fur trading companies took an immediate interest in developing the fur industry on the Plateau. Within a matter of years, the animal population was decimated (reduced drastically) by trappers and traders, and the tribes had lost a valuable natural resource.

Decades before the American development of the West, certain cultural changes began taking place among the tribes of the Plateau. The Shoshone tribe acquired horses—probably through trade with Spaniards—and as a result travel by horse became popular throughout the Plateau region. Prior to that time, the Plateau tribes were engaged solely in hunting, fishing, and gathering activities. Contact with traders, explorers, and missionaries who moved through these tribal territories also brought exposure to non-Native diseases, especially smallpox, which struck the Indian peoples hard early in the nineteenth century.

In an attempt to "civilize" Native American tribes, U.S. policymakers overlooked the importance of maintaining traditional Native ways of

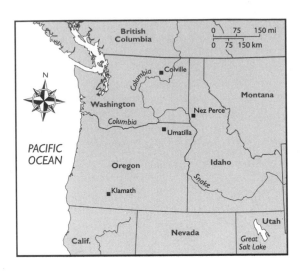

A map showing some of the contemporary Native American communities in the Plateau Region. (The Modoc live on the Klamath Reservation, shown, and on the Quapaw Agency in Oklahoma, not on the map.)

life. White American reformers had little or no knowledge of the region's Indian cultures, their traditional economic practices, or their heavy reliance on natural resources. The tribes ended up being forced onto reservations by the U.S. government. (Reservations are lands set aside for use by tribes.)

Allotment

In 1887 Congress passed the Allotment Act, which divided the reservations into small plots of land that were to be owned by individual tribal members. (Before government interference, almost all Native communities owned land communally, and this was a vital part of many Native traditions.) After tribal members received their allotments, remaining reservation land was sold to nontribal members who used it for timber, farming, and ranching. The American government began allotting tribal reservation land in the Plateau region in the 1890s and continued the process until 1914. Conservative Native Americans (those who favored the old ways and were opposed to change)—especially elders in the tribes—rejected the allotment process. Many were worshippers of the Washani religion, a belief system that emphasized the preservation of Native American land and traditions. Still, the government's policy continued.

On June 19, 1902, Congress passed a resolution directing the secretary of the Department of the Interior to allot Spokane tribal land holdings. Spokane tribal members could do nothing to prevent the division and destruction of their territory. Land that wasn't distributed among the Spokane people was sold to white-owned businesses, farmers, and ranchers.

On the Flathead Reservation the allotment process yielded similar results. In its original form, the Flathead Reservation consisted of about 1.25 million acres of land. From 1904 until 1908, U.S. policymakers allotted 80 acres each to Indians designated as "farmers" (not many Plateau Indians farmed) and 160 acres each to those designated as "ranchers." In all, less than 2,500 Native Americans were assigned allotments on the Flathead Reservation. The 400,000 acres that remained—a third of the original reservation—were sold, and the state of Montana retained about 60,000 acres for the construction of schools.

Aside from losing significant portions of their lands, the Plateau tribes became victims of treaty violations—violations that robbed

them of fishing rights and timber interests. For example, the Nez Perce filed petitions with the Indian Claims Commission in July 1951 for the theft of their original homelands in northeastern Oregon and western Idaho. The claim was not settled until 20 years later, when the victorious Nez Perce received $3.5 million to compensate for the loss.

Termination and beyond

During the 1950s the U.S. government began to "terminate," or put an end to, the reservation system and the treaty relationships it had established with tribes throughout the United States. The Confederated Tribes of the Colville Reservation in the state of Washington were particular targets of the termination policy. Colville tribal members who were not living on the reservation accepted termination in the hopes that it would bring them individual cash settlements. But those tribal members living on the reservation rejected termination, fearing it would lead to the loss of historically established treaties and the destruction of the Colville tribal culture.

The Colville fought termination for many years. Finally, in the late 1960s, the U.S. government ended the termination policy. The Colville Reservation remains intact and is stronger than ever. Workshops are offered to revitalize tribal culture, and the annual Powwow and Circle Celebration help unite tribal members and enhance community life. A sawmill, a mail-order log cabin sales business, and a trading post enhance economic development among the Colville Indians.

The Flathead Reservation has also undergone vital tribal economic and cultural revitalization over the past two decades. There, the Kootenai (pronounced *COO-ten-eye*), the Kalispel, and the Flathead tribes work hard to preserve tribal languages, oral histories and stories, and traditional ways of life. Financial support for this critical mission comes from business partnerships established between the tribe and the Montana Power Company. The operation of the Kerr Dam on the reservation land and the development of a tourist resort at Blue Bay on Flathead Lake provide key economic support for the reservation's cultural outreach programs, as well as jobs for many Flathead Reservation tribal members.

Freed from the destructive policy of termination, the tribes of the Plateau Region are now focusing their energies on other issues. For example, the Cayuse, Umatilla (pronounced *you-muh-TILL-uh*), and Walla Walla tribes of the Umatilla Reservation in Oregon are trying to cope with the devastating consequences of depression, especially among the younger generations of tribal members. The rates of alcoholism and suicide are statistically much higher among the Indians on the reservations than among the rest of the American population. Tribal leaders are determined to reverse these trends.

Fanning the fires of tradition

Throughout the nineteenth and twentieth centuries, the tribes of the Plateau region have sought to retain a measure of tribal identity, control, and uniqueness. U.S. government policy has no doubt had a devastating impact on Indian culture, land, and resources. But the Plateau tribes are working to preserve traditional Native American cultural experiences through education, language training, and social activities. Their respect for old ways, however, has not blinded them to the realities of life in modern America. They offer scholarship programs for college education, day care centers to allow more parents to work in tribal enterprises, and public health programs aimed at treating and preventing alcoholism, depression, and a host of other social ills. Education—both in tribal traditions and in standard college courses and job-training programs—has become the key survival tool of all the Plateau region tribes.

By the end of the twentieth century, the Plateau region tribes were actively engaged in sharing their own story of the Northwest expansion. Tribes have invested in extremely successful gaming resorts, arts and crafts, enterprises, business councils, wildlife and fisheries management, timber processing and protection, and legal claims to tribal land, fishing, and water rights. The conservation of salmon sources, as one example, has been the focus of intense effort on the part of the Nez Perce, Yakima (pronounced *yah-KEE-muh*), and Palouse (pronounced *puh-LOOS*) over the past decades. Fortunately, an increasing number of white Americans have come to respect the rights of America's Native peoples. Tribal fishing rights were a hot political issue in the 1992 campaign for governor of the state of Washington; the state elected a staunch supporter of Native American treaty rights.

Clearly, the tribes of the Plateau region have found the means to provide for themselves and control their own destiny. Whether they are seeking renewed rights to old salmon fishing territories, reclaiming ancestral lands, developing new industries, securing political support, or devising tribal educational and public health strategies, the tribal leaders of the Plateau are becoming—like Lewis and Clark—pathfinders in their own terrain. At the dawn of the twenty-first century, Native Americans were seeking to recapture the West for themselves.

Elizabeth I. Hanson
The College of Charleston
Charleston, South Carolina

FURTHER READING:

Champagne, Duane, ed. *Native Americans: Portrait of the People.* Detroit: Visible Ink, 1994.

Federal and State Indian Reservations. Washington, DC: U.S. Department of the Interior, 1974.

Ortega, Simon, ed. *Handbook of North American Indians.* Vol. 12: *The Plateau.* Washington, DC: Smithsonian Institution, 1978.

Taylor, Colin F., ed. *The Native Americans.* New York: Smithmark, 1991.

Waldman, Carl, ed. *Encyclopedia of Native American Tribes.* New York: Facts on File, 1988.

Colville

Name

The Colville (pronounced *COAL-vill*) were known by many names. In 1846 a white man coined the term "Basket People," referring to the tall woven baskets the Colville made to snare salmon. But the name by which they are most commonly known, Colville, was that of Governor Eden Colville of the Hudson's Bay Company.

Location

The Colville Reservation, about 100 miles northwest of Spokane, covers about 1.4 million acres of land in northeastern Washington state, from the Okanagon River in the west, south to the Spokane River, and as far east as the Columbia River. The reservation has four districts: Omak, Nespelem, Keller, and Inchelium.

Population

In 1806, there were an estimated 2,500 Colville. In 1904, there were only 321. In a census (count of the population) done in 1990 by the U.S. Bureau of the Census, 7,057 people identified themselves as Colville.

Language family

Salishan.

Origins and group affiliations

The Colville settled in the Northwest around 1500 B.C.E., migrating from farther north in present-day British Columbia, Canada. They were closely related to other Salishan-speaking groups, including the Okanagon, Lake, and Sanpoil tribes. During the eighteenth century, the Colville allied with the Okanagon in making war on the Nez Perce (see entry) and Yakima tribes farther to the south.

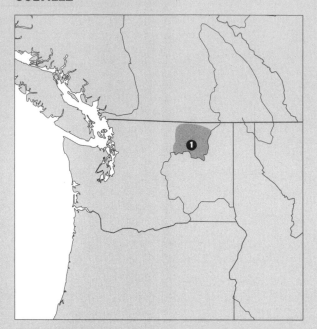

COLVILLE

Contemporary Communities

1. Confederated Tribes of the Colville Reservation, Washington

Shaded area: Traditional lands of the Colville in the present-day state of Washington.

The Colville were one of the largest tribes in the Pacific Northwest, inhabiting a land rich in natural resources. Once the Colville Reservation was established, at least ten different tribes lived there together, producing a rich new culture. Today, the land the tribes own together offers timber and mineral resources and potential for the development of hydroelectric plants (to make electricity from water power), as well as fish and wildlife preserves.

HISTORY

Early times as fur traders

The first contact between the Colville and Europeans probably occurred before 1800, but no records of the contact exist. Around 1782–83, a smallpox epidemic seems to have swept through the area, indicating that Europeans were nearby. Later epidemics would probably have killed off most of the tribe, but Roman Catholic priests gave vaccines to the people.

When the Colville people began riding horses in the eighteenth century, their territory expanded. In the early 1800s, the tribe began trading furs at the Northwest Company. In 1806 the Lewis and Clark expedition, which was exploring the western lands of the United States, visited the tribe.

The tribe avoids war

Kettle Falls became the center of Colville activities. There they fished, traded with Europeans, and met with Roman Catholic missionaries. Fort Colville was established in their territory in 1825. It came to be the second largest center for fur trading in the Northwest. The community was associated with the powerful English trading company, the Hudson's Bay Company.

In the mid-1800s the ever-growing groups of white settlers caused problems for the Natives, especially when they brought smallpox epidemics in 1853. The Colville way of life was further disrupted from 1858 to 1860 by white miners who crossed their territory on their way to search for gold near the Fraser River.

Members of the U.S. military were stationed at Kettle Falls in 1859 to man a new fort that had been established there. The fort was built when white people learned that the Indians in the area excelled at trapping and stalking game that would benefit the fur trade. Soon Father Pierre de Smet—a priest well known among other tribes of the Pacific Northwest—came among the Colville and established a mission near Kettle Falls. The Saint Francis Regis Mission soon became a favorite site where many American Indians of the region met to visit with one another.

The Colville had always been enemies of the Yakima tribe and sometimes engaged them in battle but they generally tended to be peaceful. They disliked the fact that large numbers of settlers, miners, and soldiers were crowding their territory, but Colville chiefs saw little sense in the wars waged against the settlers by other tribes. Facing superior firepower and superior numbers, the Colville saw that Indians had very slim chances of winning such battles.

The reservation and confederation

The 3-million-acre Colville Reservation east of the Columbia River was established in 1872 for the Colville and other area tribes, including the Okanagon, Sanpoil, Lake, Kalispel, Spokane, and Coeur d'A-

Yakima men from the Colville Reservation.

lene (*ker-duh-LEEN*). But American settlers wanted the fertile land of the river valley for themselves and urged the government to move the tribe again. Only three months after the reservation was established, the government gave in to these pressures and relocated the Colville and other tribes to a second reservation west of the Columbia River. The new reservation deprived them of a large and desirable piece of land.

The tribes on the new reservation formed the Confederated Tribes of the Colville Reservation. The newly united tribes struggled with white settlers and with each other over land rights, a struggle that continues today and has resulted in several lawsuits being filed. Today, the Confederation is made up of eleven bands of Indians, including the Wenatchee, Entiat, Chelan, Methow, Okanagon, Nespelem, Sanpoil, Lakes, Moses, Palouse, and Nez Perce. With a land so rich in resources, they have been able to thrive. They are very much a part of modern society, but they also strive to preserve their ancient customs.

INDIAN SHAKER RELIGION

The Indian Shaker Religion was founded in 1881 near Olympia, Washington, by John Slocum, a member of the Squaxin tribe. Slocum became ill and seemed to have died; he returned to life with a mission to found a new church. About a year later, as he was just starting his missionary work, Slocum fell ill again. As his wife, Mary, approached his sickbed, she began to tremble uncontrollably. Her shaking was seen as a divine sign and became a part of Slocum's religious services.

Slocum recovered, and word of his religion spread. It came to be known as the Indian Shaker Religion, and tribes from California to British Columbia took it up. Each tribe added its own variations.

The Indian Shaker Religion combined elements of Native and Christian belief and practices. Members used crucifixes, bells, candles, and pictures in their services. Christian missionaries and government Indian agents objected to their meetings, and the Indian Shakers called a defiant meeting on June 6, 1892, to assert their right to practice the religion. Finally, they were left in peace and the religion is still prac-

RELIGION

The Colville refer to their Supreme Being by various names; one is the Chief Above. The people believe that all things found in nature—animals, rocks, plants—contain spirits that can be called on for aid in healing, raising crops, and making war. Young men and women take part in a vision quest—a ceremony in which they undergo a secluded training period in the wilderness and seek out their guardian spirit. The guardian spirit protects the individual and guides him or her throughout life.

In the nineteenth century, some Colville adopted the Roman Catholic religion, while others became Protestants. The twentieth century has seen the Colville people become involved in the Seven Drum Religion (see Nez Perce entry), the Native American Church (see box in Makah entry), and the Indian Shaker religion (see box). Many Christian Colville take part in Native religious practices as well.

LANGUAGE

The Salishan language family includes twenty-three languages divided into three major branches: Coast Salish, Tsamosan Salish, and Interior Salish. The Interior branch spoken by the Colville is the most popular of the three branches. Today the language is spoken by more than 3,000 people.

GOVERNMENT

In the early days, each village was an independent unit headed by a chief. The chief was usually the oldest member of the group. He decided when it was time to move to a new area and was in charge of running ceremonies and keeping the peace within the village. Usually, the chief's younger brother took over the job when the chief died.

Today, a fourteen-member business council governs the Colville Reservation from its administrative/governmental seat in Nespelem. Members are elected to two-year terms. The administrative department of the reservation is overseen by an executive director and has four branches: Human Services, Management and Budget, Natural Resources, and Tribal Government.

ECONOMY

The Colville Reservation has extensive rangelands for grazing livestock (nearly 300,000 acres) and farmlands (about 135,000 acres). The tribe owns about 6,000 head of cattle and 1,000 horses. The tribe also runs a profitable meatpacking operation, and raises wheat, alfalfa, barley, and apple crops. Tribal officials are actively pursuing the expansion of irrigation to provide even more usable farmland. The tribal fish hatchery stocks many lakes and streams throughout north central Washington.

The tribal government has a construction company that generates money and offers employment. The tribe also owns valuable timberlands, and timber is processed at its sawmill and wood treatment plant. The Colville's treated posts and poles are marketed all over the world. The tribe's nursery grows and replants trees. A tribally owned log-house manufacturing facility was under consideration in the late 1990s.

Tourist attractions are provided by the Grand Coulee Dam on the reservation, and eighteen lakes including Lake Roosevelt, which backs up for 150 miles behind the dam. On the site of the dam is an art gallery and tribal museum, which features exhibits representing each of the eleven tribes of Indians that now live on the Colville Reservation. The nearby luxury houseboat rental operations was begun in 1988. The Kettle Falls Historical Center features Native American crafts, history, and a retail shop. The tribe also operates a marina-restaurant complex, as well as three casinos and three grocery stores.

DAILY LIFE

Buildings

Like many tribes who lived in cold climates, the Colville maintained both winter and summer homes. Their winter dwellings were about forty-five feet in diameter and were located almost completely

underground. These circular lodgings were entered through a hole in the roof. In summer, the Colville lived in cone-shaped homes with pole frames wrapped with mats made from rushes. They used portable tents made from animal skins when hunting buffalo further south. The Colville also constructed sweathouses, structures that were used by men and women for religious rites of purification. Visiting a sweathouse was part of the ritual in which they sought their guardian spirits.

Manufacturing

Living near so many rivers and lakes, the Colville often traveled in canoes they fashioned out of the bark of the birch or other trees. They also used trees to create many useful items, such as baskets from cedar bark, bows and arrow shafts of juniper, and snowshoes made from a variety of woods. They wove blankets from goat's wool or strips of rabbit's fur and sacks from bulrushes, bark, and hemp.

Clothing and adornment

In winter, Colville women wore tunics with leggings and moccasins. Men wore leggings, moccasins, and breechcloths (flaps of animal skin that covered the front and back and were suspended from the waist). Both sexes added fur robes for warmth. The Colville fringed, punctured, and embroidered their clothing using porcupine quills, and decorated them with various seeds, hoofs, shells, elk's teeth, and ermine skins.

Before stopping the practice in the nineteenth century, both men and women wore nose pins. Many people used face and body paint, but tattooing was uncommon. Sometime in the twentieth century, most men opted for very short hair over the traditional longhaired style.

Food

Their location near the Northwest Coast provided the Colville with a rich and varied menu. Their staple food was salmon, and they ate the entire fish, including the head. They often retrieved the salmon that died after spawning and ate those too. Traveling with nearby tribes, the men hunted deer, elk, bear, and beaver as well as buffalo. Following a hunt or large catch, a feast was held. Then the leftovers were dried or frozen for later consumption. The stored food supplied their nutritional needs during the winter.

As soon as spring arrived, the Colville got busy replenishing their food supplies. Food hunts were extremely well organized. Special camps were set up for fishing and collecting nuts, roots, and berries. Camas, an edible root, and other roots and huckleberries were particularly favored. In the early spring, before the salmon camps were established, the Colville sought out suckerfish and steelhead trout.

Education

Colville children learned how to conduct the duties of men and women by observing their elders. Mission schools operated during the nineteenth century, but today, most students attend public schools on the reservation or the nearby Paschel Sherman Indian School. A number of tribal members are seeking higher education in fields that will make them useful to the tribe, such as natural resource management, law, business, social work, and health policy.

Healing practices

Male and female healers called shamans (pronounced *SHAY-muns*) were responsible for curing the sick, with the assistance of guardian spirits. They underwent a difficult training period to learn how to remove evil spirits from the afflicted. They cured by singing sacred songs and chants to drive the evil from the body. They practiced preventive medicine by warding off evil spirits before they could enter the body. Being a shaman was a risky business; it was common for those who failed to be killed by a patient's family.

Today, the Indian Health Service provides health care services on the reservation, and the people make use of hospitals in nearby towns.

CUSTOMS

Festivals

In times past, the Colville scheduled festivals throughout the year. They performed puberty rites for girls, held a festival at the time when the trees bore their first fruits, and conducted various dances on the occasions of war, scalping, summoning guardian spirits, marriage, and to honor the Sun.

Today, the tribe holds a number of annual events, including the Powwow at the Omak Stampede in August, which features horse-related activities and Native food; the Trophy Powwow, a celebration of Native songs and dances; winter Chinook dances, and the annual spring thanksgiving Root Feast. The ten-day Fourth of July Powwow at Nespelem takes place in the tribe's "Circle," a traditional gathering place where Indians from several states come in Native dress to play stick games, and enjoy rodeo events. Memorial giveaways are held in honor of deceased tribal members.

Funerals

The Colville wrapped their dead in robes or mats and either buried them in the ground or placed them in canoes. The souls of the buried traveled to the land of the beyond, somewhere in the West or the South. After the death of a loved one, widows and widowers showed their grief by cutting off their hair and wearing old, tattered clothes.

CURRENT TRIBAL ISSUES

Since the middle of the twentieth century, the Colville tribal government has won a number of claims against the U.S. government for the illegal takeover of land or the purchase of land at unusually low prices. The tribe sued the government and won in a case that accused the federal government of mismanaging tribal resources. The case involved salmon runs that were destroyed by hydroelectric projects such as the Grand Coulee Dam. The money awarded as a result of these cases provides funds for a long-term program to repurchase former tribal lands.

In recent years the Colville people have begun to use a new method for making decisions called holistic management (see box). Holistic management brings into the decision-making process the feelings and values of the Colville people, and not merely the notions of experts. The Colville are determined to have their tribe managed wisely, to use its resources effectively, and to implement a plan for balanced economic and social development.

NOTABLE PEOPLE

Mourning Dove (c. 1885–1936; born Christine Quintasket) was a Colville/Okanagon writer and activist who fought for American Indian rights throughout her life. She helped found the Colville Indian Association, and was the first woman elected to the Colville Tribal Council. She is considered the first female Native American novelist. Her first novel, *Cogewea, the Half Blood: A Depiction of the Great Montana Cattle Range* was published in 1927. She then wrote traditional stories of her tribe, and her second book, *Coyote Stories,* was published in 1933. Her autobiography was published in 1990, long after her death.

FURTHER READING

Dawson, Dawn P., and Harvey Markowitz, eds. "Colville." *Ready Reference: American Indians.* Pasadena, CA: Salem Press, 1995.

Donovan, Peter. *The Colville Tribe Blazes the Trail.* [Online] http://www.orednet.org/~pdonovan/cct6.htm

Hodge, Frederick Webb. "Colville." *Handbook of American Indians North of Mexico.* New York: Pageant Books, 1959.

Leitch, Barbara A. "Colville." *A Concise Dictionary of Indian Tribes of North America.* Algonac, MI: Reference Publications, 1979.

Porter, Frank W. III. *The Coast Salish Peoples.* New York: Chelsea House Publishers, 1989.

Waldman, Carl. "Colville Reservation." *Encyclopedia of Native American Tribes.* New York: Facts on File, 1988.

Modoc

Name

The name Modoc (pronounced *MO-doc*) may mean "southerners." The Modoc called themselves *Ma Klaks* ("the people").

Location

The Modoc formerly occupied about 5,000 square miles on the California-Oregon border. Today they have no land base, but their tribal headquarters is located in Miami, Oklahoma. Most of the people live in California (200) and Oregon (178). The present separation of the tribe is a result of the Modoc War of 1872–73.

Population

Before contact with Europeans, there were about 2,000 Modoc. In a census (count of the population) done in 1990 by the U.S. Bureau of the Census, 521 people identified themselves as Modoc.

Language family

Penutian.

Origins and group affiliations

The modern Modoc are descendants of the Modoc group who were forcibly removed to Oklahoma in 1873. The tribe was divided into three groups: the Gumbatwas or "people of the west," the Kokiwas or "people of the far country," and the Paskanwas or "river people." Their major enemies were the Klamath and the Paiute (see entry), with whom they were forced to live for a while.

MODOC

Contemporary Communities

1. Klamath Reservation

(Not on map: Quapaw Agency and
    Modoc Headquarters, Oklahoma)

Shaded area: Traditional lands of the Modoc in the Cascade Mountain range in the present-day states of Oregon and California.

The Modoc were an optimistic people who saw the world as a friendly place. They first lived in the Lakes District of Oregon and California, where they hunted, fished, and gathered food. The Modoc believed that their land was fertile and if they worked hard it would provide them with the things they needed. But their history has been harsh, and only in recent years have they been able to reclaim a part of their heritage.

HISTORY

The coming of whites causes changes

For centuries before the coming of Europeans, the Modoc people roamed the land around Lost River, Tule Lake, Willow Creek, and Ness Lake, in what is now northern California and southern Oregon. They hunted and gathered food, and harvested reeds and grasses to weave clothing and baskets. They traded with some neighboring tribes and raided others. As a result of these interactions, they heard about white explorers, and they acquired European goods. They were quick to adopt any goods they considered superior to their own. Their use of steel knives, hatchets, iron pots, mirrors, and cloth soon began to change their way of life.

By the mid-1830s the Modoc had come into the possession of guns and horses, which brought further changes. They could now hunt deer, and began to wear buckskin clothing in place of grass or fur garments. Copying the Plains Indians, they applied war paint to their faces when they went on raids. In time, they even began to take non-Indian names.

Conflict with settlers

In 1843 American explorer John Charles Frémont (1813–1890) brought a team of white surveyors and explorers into Modoc territory. The party went about their business without incident, but when Frémont returned with another team three years later, they were attacked by nearby Klamath Indians and four men were killed. The white men burned a Klamath village in retaliation. Thereafter, both the Klamath and the Modoc were in awe of American ruthlessness.

By 1847 the Applegate Trail was heavily traveled by white settlers on their way to the Oregon Territory. The settlers frightened away the game on Modoc hunting grounds, making food scarce. Tragedy struck when disease epidemics brought by the settlers killed more than a third of the Modoc tribe. The Modoc blamed these troubles on the settlers. During the summer of 1847, Indians, possibly Modoc, attacked a group of wagon trains and stole the horses; several dozen whites were killed during the raid.

The discovery of gold in the West brought even more settlers, and conflicts with the Modoc became more frequent. Sometimes the Modoc were blamed for attacks carried out by neighboring tribes, and Americans retaliated against the Modoc, bringing more conflicts.

Sign Council Grove Treaty

During the fierce winter of 1861–62, heavy snows killed plants and drove away wild game, causing starvation among the Modoc. The

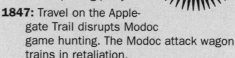

IMPORTANT DATES

1843: John Charles Frémont arrives in Modoc territory, and heads a survey and exploring party.

1847: Travel on the Applegate Trail disrupts Modoc game hunting. The Modoc attack wagon trains in retaliation.

1848: Modoc population falls to about 900 after epidemic diseases.

1864: In October, the Council Grove Treaty is concluded. Modoc, Klamath, and Paiute tribes are relocated to a single reservation in Oregon

1872: The Modoc War begins. Captain Jack (Kintpuash) refuses to return to the reservations, and leads a group of Modoc in revolt.

1978: Modoc tribe gains federal recognition.

1983: Completion of the Modoc Tribal Complex, the tribe's headquarters.

U.S. government offered to help the tribe out of its difficulties if they would agree to sign a treaty giving up their lands. Modoc tribal chief Old Schonchin urged his people to agree, but younger warriors, including Kintpuash, or Captain Jack, as the Americans called him, strongly resisted such a move. For a few more years the Modoc continued their struggle to survive, and some of the men had to take jobs in a nearby mining town.

After continued pressure from the U.S. government, Old Schonchin signed the Council Grove Treaty at Fort Klamath in 1864. The treaty provided that the Modoc tribe would give up most of its land to the federal government and move to the Klamath Reservation in southern Oregon to live with their enemies, the Paiute and the Klamath. In turn, the government was supposed to send them food and supplies every year.

Problems with the Klamath

Once the three enemy tribes were gathered on the reservation, problems arose. The reservation was located on former Klamath hunting grounds, and the Klamath felt this gave them special rights. They insisted that the Modoc turn over to them a certain amount of their cut timber. They put obstacles in the way of Modoc fishermen, and they bothered Modoc women who were gathering seeds at a lake. To add to these hardships, U.S. government agents failed to provide the food and supplies that they had promised. In a short time, the Modoc on the reservation suffered from almost constant hunger.

In an attempt to reconcile the tribes, an Indian agent suggested a "democratic" means of self government be adopted on the reservation. This would require electing leaders for a council similar to that of the U.S. Congress. This effort failed, and the Modoc requested a reservation of their own in California. The government turned them down.

Modoc leader Captain Jack.

The Modoc War begins

An unhappy group of Modoc, led by Captain Jack, decided to take matters into their own hands. They left the reservation in 1870 and returned to Lost River, only to find it had been overrun by white settlers. Nevertheless, they set up camp and began to hunt, fish, and visit in the nearby town of Eureka. Because they remained apart from white settlers, the Superintendent of Indian Affairs at first ignored their presence at Lost River. But before long, white settlers demanded that the "renegades" be removed, and U.S. army troops tried to force them to return to the reservation.

Just before the outbreak of hostilities with American soldiers, Captain Jack declared: "I am not a dog! I am a man, if I am an Indian. . . . I and my men shall not be slaves for a race of people that is not any better than my people. I shall not live here. If the government refuses to protect my people, who shall I look to for protection?"

Captain Jack refused to obey the order of federal troops to return to the reservation. Instead, he and his group fled south to the rugged lava beds of northeastern California, the place the Indians called "Land of Burnt Out Fires." For nearly a year, he and his small group avoided capture. In spite of being outnumbered, they won at least one battle and blocked all military attempts to flush them out.

The move to Oklahoma

Captain Jack finally agreed to a meeting to discuss peace. His followers were angry and called him a coward, and Captain Jack changed his plan. Convinced that if he killed the leaders of the army, U.S. troops would retreat, Captain Jack shot and killed several army officers.

Captain Jack's acts sealed the Modocs' fate. The army pursued them relentlessly, but in the end Captain Jack was betrayed by a comrade. He and three other leaders of the revolt were caught, tried, and executed. The remaining Modoc were sent to Oklahoma to live with the Wyandotte, Peoria, and Ottawa tribes.

The Modoc War was the single most costly Indian war in American history in terms of both money and the loss of human life. It was later estimated that the total cost to the U.S. government for the military campaign was about $1 million. If the government had simply bought land and established a reservation where Captain Jack suggested, the cost would have been about $20,000.

A new beginning

More than 4,000 acres of land were set aside in Oklahoma for the Modoc tribe. The people continued to suffer because of lack of food and clothing. Meanwhile the government adopted a new policy called allotment, and in 1891, reservation lands were allotted to the sixty-eight tribal members who remained. Allotment involved breaking up tribally-owned reservations and giving each member a plot for farming; any land left over was sold to whites. The government believed Indians would assimilate faster—become more like whites—if they owned individual plots of land.

During the half-century following allotment, many of the Modoc became successful farmers in northeastern Oklahoma, but over time they lost many of their Native ways. In 1967, the Oklahoma Modoc once again banded together to form a tribal government, and they are now called the Modoc Tribe of Oklahoma. The tribe was recognized by the federal government in 1978. Federally recognized tribes are those with which the U.S. government maintains official relations. Without federal recognition, the tribe does not exist as far as the government is concerned, and is not entitled to financial and other help.

The tribe owns no land but has headquarters in Miami, Oklahoma. The Modoc Tribal Complex, completed in 1983, houses the tribal office, library, and historical archives. In recent times, the

Modoc have been trying to reestablish a land base and preserve the ways of their culture.

RELIGION

According to Modoc beliefs, after the Creator made human beings and provided the food they needed, he and the other gods departed. In their place, the Creator left animals who were inhabited by spirits, including Frog, Mole, Fish, Rattlesnake, Coyote, and Hawk. With their help, human beings could influence events in their world.

The Modoc prayed to the spirits of the Moon, stars, and sky. Most religious ceremonies took place in the sweathouse, a tiny, airtight hut that contained heated rocks that produced steam when water was poured over them. The people thought that sweating purified the body and prepared a person to request good health, hunting, or fortune from the spirits.

During the 1870s, many of the Modoc people living in Indian Territory became members of the Society of Friends, also known as Quakers. Today, the religion of the Modoc combines elements of Christianity and traditional Native rituals.

LANGUAGE

The Modoc were closely related to the Klamath tribe, and together they formed the independent language family, Penutian. The Modoc spoke the Lituami dialect. Today, textbooks are being translated into Penutian to help keep the language vital and strengthen the community.

GOVERNMENT

The chief of each village, always a male, gained his position through his skills at public speaking, good judgment, friendliness, tact, and ability to handle himself in a crisis. The most important way to get people to follow was by effective argument and persuasion. Chiefs were not elected, but rather chosen by the agreement of the entire group in the village. A single village might have more than one leader who ruled with a council. The chief of the tribe was called *la gi* (leader).

In modern times, the tribe is governed by the Modoc Elected Council, which is made up of a chief, second chief, secretary/treasurer and two others, who serve four-year terms. Members of the council, the governing body for the tribe, serve four-year terms.

ECONOMY

For centuries, the Modoc were hunters, fishermen, and gatherers, who moved from place to place depending on the season. In spring they left their winter homes. The men fished. The women built drying racks to hold the day's catch and gathered parsley roots. Later in the spring the group moved so the women could harvest a vegetable root called epos. During the summer, the men traveled into the mountains to hunt deer and mountain sheep, leaving the women behind to harvest camas roots. Hunting trips continued until late summer, when full-time fishing resumed.

Men made canoes, built winter homes, and protected the tribe as needed. Women tended the children, gathered nuts and berries, dug for roots and bulbs, made baskets and clothing, and prepared and stored food.

Today, Modoc people work in ranching, teaching, small businesses, and other professions.

DAILY LIFE

Buildings

The framework of Modoc summer homes was made of willow poles stuck into the ground and tied together at the top. Mats of woven grass covered the poles.

In winter the Modoc lived in pit houses—earth-covered circular dwellings with an entrance ladder sticking out of the top. A round pit was dug, ranging from 15 to 40 feet in diameter and 3 to 4 feet deep. Then timbers were sunk into the pit to support the rafters and form a roof and walls. Woven mats of dried grass covered the roof and walls, which were topped with sheets of bark. Dirt from the pit was piled on top as a final layer. One entered by crawling across the roof and climbing down the ladder. The entrance also provided fresh air and light.

Two or three families shared each pit house, and a central fire provided warmth. The people slept on mats made of rushes and their fur blankets were stored at the outer edges of the house along the walls. A separate building made of grass mats was used for cooking.

Clothing and adornment

In winter, the Modoc wore moccasins, leggings, shirts, skirts, and robes made from animal hide. Fur or woven-grass robes were tied together and worn on top to provide added warmth. In summer, the people wore loincloths (flaps of material that covered the front and back and were suspended from the waist) and skirts made of tule or other plentiful grasses. Grass clothing did not last long, but it was easily woven and replaced.

Both men and women wore waterproof, basket-shaped hats woven from tule or rushes. The men's hats were usually plain, but the women's often had decorative designs. In winter, fur hats with earflaps were sometimes worn.

Food

During fishing season, the Modoc ate trout, perch, and sucker fish caught by the men. Women dried fish in the Sun and stored them in baskets of woven grasses for later use. The men hunted rabbit, squirrel, duck, geese, prairie chickens, deer, elk, antelope, and sheep for both food and clothing. Women prepared the meat and dried some for winter. The tribe camped near streams so the men could more easily fish or hunt. Then they moved on to another camp where the women could dig for camas bulbs and the root vegetable epos, as well as wild potatoes. They consumed some of these fresh, and dried others for winter use. They also ground the seeds of the pond lily with stones and ate them in a variety of ways.

Families who did not gather and store sufficient food during the rest of the year could end up starving in the winter. Those who did gather food buried it, covered the spot with grass mats and baskets, and kept its location secret.

Education

Children in Modoc families learned how to perform their adult duties by observing their elders. Girls learned to dig roots, get wood and water, cook, and care for babies. Boys learned to hunt, fish, and fight.

During the 1870s, Modoc children began attending a school run by a branch of the Society of Friends, also known as Quakers. They studied reading, writing, mathematics, and geography, and learned about the Bible and the importance of not drinking alcohol. Girls learned practical skills such as cooking, sewing, and caring for a house, and boys learned carpentry and farming. Today, Modoc children attend public schools.

Healing practices

Men or women who felt a calling to become shamans (pronounced *SHAY-muns*), or healers, went on a quest for spiritual guidance and spent five days fasting alone in the woods. In time spirits would appear and teach them special healing songs and dances and how to change the weather. Some learned how to inflict disease or death on a victim. Shamans were paid for their services and could become very wealthy. However, they were sometimes killed if their patients did not recover.

For minor ailments, shamans administered herbs. Puffball fungus was used on sores and skin swellings, rabbitbrush leaves and stems were steamed to produce a cough medicine, and sagebrush leaves relieved headaches and rheumatism.

CUSTOMS

Festivals

During the late 1800s, the Modoc embraced the Ghost Dance Religion. A Paiute named Wovoka started the religion after he had a vision. Wovoka predicted that one day whites would disappear and Indians would rise from the dead if everyone performed the Ghost Dance. Modoc dancers painted their faces red and drew two horizontal black lines on each cheek. They held hands and formed a circle around the fire, chanting and dancing.

Courtship and marriage

Marriages were arranged by the families. A boy's parents chose a mate for him, then visited her family together with relatives, bringing presents of food. The women from both families prepared the food and everyone feasted. If the girl's parents favored the match, they soon returned the visit. The boy's parents then assembled gifts such as baskets, beads, skins, furs, robes, weapons, and canoes. Relatives took the items to the girl's family, and if they liked the gifts, her family gave a favorable response. If they did not, the gifts were returned.

A wedding took place soon after the bride's family agreed to the match. More gifts were exchanged, and the bride was escorted by her family to the groom's house, marking the beginning of the marriage. For four days, the bride sat facing a wall, eating very little and speaking in whispers. For the four days, the groom appeared only in the late evening.

After four days, the bride began to take part in the activities of the household. Soon the couple moved in with the bride's family where they would stay until the birth of their first child. They could then choose whether to live with the bride's parents or the groom's parents.

War and hunting rituals

War chiefs, who were not the same as village chiefs, accompanied warriors into battle. Any man who could attract enough followers could become a war chief, but it was usually a man who had proven he was a successful raider. Raiding parties usually were made up of ten to twenty men. They raided for goods such as weapons or skins, and to capture people from other tribes to use as slaves. The usual targets of raids were the neighboring Pit River Indians (see entry), Paiutes, or Shasta.

Warriors sought the help of shamans if they wanted to kill an enemy through the use of magic or influence the outcome of a battle.

Gambling

A very popular pastime among the Modoc was gambling. Women enjoyed a game played with dice made of beaver teeth. Men played a complicated game in which they tried to guess how their opponents had arranged their playing pieces. They had to study the faces and body language of their opponents for clues. Players bet large amounts of goods during the game and a man might gamble away all of his possessions. Because of the risk of losing everything and starving, gambling did not take place in winter.

Funerals

The Modoc believed that after death, a person's soul went to the "land of the dead," somewhere in the West. They also believed that a person's soul could leave the body during sleep. For that reason, they slept with their heads facing East so their soul would not mistakenly go on to the land of the dead. Bodies were always cremated with their heads facing West. After the flames consumed the body of the corpse, the living tried to forget about the person.

CURRENT TRIBAL ISSUES

The Modoc are trying to establish a land base so they can work together to restore their culture. Meanwhile, members live elsewhere, mainly in Oregon and California. At their Oklahoma headquarters, some Modoc tribe members are involved in efforts to keep the language and oral histories alive. Elders are compiling family photographs and letters. Many Modoc travel to the Klamath Reservation to participate in ceremonies.

NOTABLE PEOPLE

Michael Dorris (1945–1997) was a novelist and anthropologist who taught Native American Studies at Dartmouth College. He published many scholarly works, including some on Native Americans. In his later years, Dorris was best known as a novelist. He wrote *Yellow Raft in Blue Water* in 1989, and a best-selling novel entitled *The Crown of Columbus* (1992) with his wife Louise Erdrich, a well-known fiction writer. Together, Dorris and Erdrich also wrote a prizewinning non-fiction book *The Broken Cord: A Family's On-Going Struggle with Fetal Alcohol Syndrome* (1989). The book described their adopted son, who had been damaged by his birth mother's drinking of alcohol while pregnant. Michael Dorris committed suicide in April 1997.

Kintpuash (1837–1873), the son of a Modoc chief, was called Captain Jack because he liked to wear a U.S. military jacket with brass buttons. Kintpuash is best known for protesting conditions on the Klamath reservation in Oregon and leading the Modocs in the Modoc War. He was hanged in 1873 for the shooting of American General Edward Canby.

Other notable Modoc include: last chief of the Modoc, Bogus Charley; Kintpuash's advisor Schonchin John; interpreter during the Modoc War, Winema Riddle; and shaman Curly-headed Doctor.

FURTHER READING

Faulk, Odie B. and Laura E. *The Modoc.* New York: Chelsea House Publishers, 1988.

McLeod, Christopher. "Mount Shasta: A Thousand Years of Ceremony." *Earth Island Journal,* 10 (January 1995).

Murray, Keith A. *The Modoc and Their War.* Norman: University of Oklahoma Press, 1959.

Owen, Roger C., James J.F. Deetz,, and Anthony D. Fisher, eds. *The North American Indians: A Sourcebook.* New York: Macmillan, 1967.

Nez Perce

Name

Nez Perce (pronounced *nez PURSE*; also spelled Nez Percé and pronounced *nay per-SAY*). The Nez Perce called themselves *Nee-Me-Poo* or *Nimipu*, which meant "our people." The name *Nez Perce* means "pierced nose" in French and was applied to the tribe by early fur traders, even though the tribe did not traditionally practice nose piercing.

Location

The Nez Perce lived on lands in present-day western Idaho, northeastern Oregon, and southeastern Washington. Today, most of the descendants of the tribe live on the Nez Perce Reservation near Lapwai, Idaho, or on the Colville Reservation in the state of Washington.

Population

There were approximately 6,000 Nez Perce in 1800; there were 1,500 in 1900. In a census (count of the population) done in 1990 by the U.S. Bureau of the Census, 4,003 people identified themselves as members of the Nez Perce tribe.

Language family

Penutian.

Origins and group affiliations

Before the coming of Europeans, the Nez Perce lived for centuries in small villages along the Clearwater, Salmon, and Snake rivers in the Pacific Northwest. They are linked culturally and by language to other tribes in that region, including the Yakima, Umatilla, Klickitat, and Walla Walla.

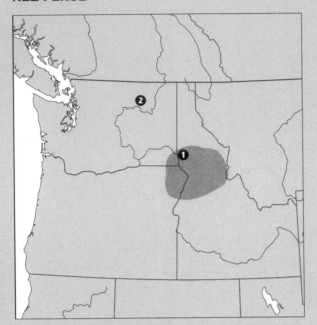

NEZ PERCE

Contemporary Communities

1. Nez Perce Reservation, Idaho
2. Confederated Tribes of the Colville Reservation, Washington

Shaded area: Traditional Nez Perce lands in present-day western Idaho, northeastern Oregon, and southeastern Washington.

Once, the Nez Perce were one of the largest and most powerful tribes of the Northwest, controlling a swath of territory along the Clearwater and Snake Rivers in present-day Idaho, and lands in Oregon and Washington. They lived there as semi-wandering fishermen, hunters, and gatherers. Chief Joseph is famous for his resistance to U.S. expansion into Nez Perce territory and his role in the tribe's final surrender. The dramatic "Flight of the Nez Perce" was front-page news in the United States when it occurred and is still studied by military historians.

HISTORY

Horses bring changes

Before the Nez Perce acquired horses in the early 1700s, they spent most of their time fishing, hunting on foot, or gathering wild plants for food. Within a generation of acquiring horses, however, their lifestyle changed. They started trading with neighboring tribes and began annual trips to the Great Plains to hunt buffalo. Their rich grasslands enabled the Nez Perce to raise some of the largest herds of horses of any Native group. They became skilled horse breeders and trainers, particularly of the sturdy, spotted horses now called Appaloosas.

The Nez Perce maintained friendly relations with most of their neighboring tribes, except those to the south, including the Shoshone, Northern Paiute, and Bannock. However, every summer the Nez Perce called a truce with their enemies in order to trade with them at a large gathering.

Whites move to tribal lands

The first contact between the Nez Perce and non-Native people took place in 1805 when the Lewis and Clark expedition wandered into the Wallowa Valley in western Idaho. At that time, the American explorers were cold, tired, and running out of food. The Nez Perce aided the members of the expedition and may have kept them from starving. Later, the Nez Perce helped them build boats and guided them to the Pacific Coast. Over the next few decades, the Nez Perce established friendly relations with French-Canadian and American fur traders, missionaries, and settlers.

Through the mid-1800s, the number of white settlers in the Northwest greatly increased. For the most part the Nez Perce were able to avoid the conflicts that plagued other tribes. They signed the Walla Walla Council of 1855, a treaty that handed over some of their ancestral territory to the government in exchange for money and a guarantee that the rest of their lands—13 million acres—would remain intact. But many of the Plateau tribes felt double-crossed when shortly thereafter, the Governor of Washington Territory, Isaac Ingalls Stevens, wrote a letter to an eastern newspaper proclaiming that the Northwest was open for settlement. Angry, several area tribes reacted with violence to his trickery, which resulted in a flood of settlers. However, the Nez Perce remained neutral and did not participate in any wars waged by neighboring tribes against the United States military.

In the early 1860s, gold was discovered on Nez Perce lands, and fortune seekers chose to ignore the 1855 treaty. In 1863, reacting to pressure from the new settlers, Nez Perce leaders tried but failed to

IMPORTANT DATES

1805: The Nez Perce assist American explorers Meriwether Lewis and William Clark during their expedition to the Pacific Coast.

1855: The Nez Perce enter into a treaty with the U.S. government.

1863: The 1855 treaty is amended by trickery and the document becomes known as the Thief Treaty.

1877: During the Nez Perce War, Chief Joseph and his people try fleeing to Canada but are pursued by U.S. Army troops and overcome.

1996: The Nez Perce are invited back to the Wallowa Valley.

A map showing the flight of the Nez Perce, 1863.

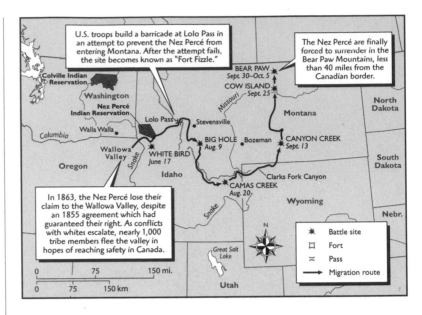

U.S. troops build a barricade at Lolo Pass in an attempt to prevent the Nez Percé from entering Montana. After the attempt fails, the site becomes known as "Fort Fizzle."

The Nez Percé are finally forced to surrender in the Bear Paw Mountains, less than 40 miles from the Canadian border.

In 1863, the Nez Percé lose their claim to the Wallowa Valley, despite an 1855 agreement which had guaranteed their right. As conflicts with whites escalate, nearly 1,000 tribe members flee the valley in hopes of reaching safety in Canada.

reach a new treaty agreement. Governor Stevens then collected the signatures of a few members of the tribe on a document that handed over another 7 million acres of Native land. This document, which came to be known as the Thief Treaty, cost the Nez Perce their claim to Wallowa Valley. Upon hearing the news, Old Chief Joseph, the peaceful leader of the Wallowa band and a Christian convert, tore up his Bible. Despite their anger and resentment, however, the Nez Perce remained peaceful in their relations with whites. They expressed their discontent by failing to go along with the treaty.

Nez Perce surrender

When Old Chief Joseph died in 1871, his son Young Chief Joseph took over leadership of the Wallowa group. In 1876 the young chief represented the Nez Perce in a meeting with U.S. government representatives. He informed them that he refused to honor the 1863 Thief Treaty and give up the tribe's ancestral valley. The government grew tired of waiting. The tribe was given thirty days to vacate Wallowa Valley and move to a reservation near Lapwai, Idaho. When it became clear that war was the only alternative to moving, Chief Joseph agreed to move. He said sadly: "I would give up everything rather than have the blood of my people on my hands."

Before the move began, young rebels from the tribe attacked a group of whites that had mistreated them, killing three men and wounding another. Chief Joseph, along with 250 warriors, 500 women, children, and elderly members of the tribe reluctantly joined

the rebels as they fled the valley, hoping to find safety in Canada. Nearly 2,000 U.S. Army troops set out in pursuit. So began the Nez Perce War of 1877.

Over the next four months, the Nez Perce traveled 1,600 miles. They crossed the rugged wilderness of Idaho, Wyoming, and Montana, trekking over mountains, through canyons, and across rivers. In all, they fought fourteen battles against a better-equipped enemy. Until the final battle, they consistently outsmarted and outfought the larger military forces.

In their final battle, which took place just thirty miles from the Canadian border and lasted for six days, the Nez Perce fought off one army unit but were finally surrounded by another. It was then that Chief Joseph gave his famous surrender speech. He said to his chiefs: "I am tired. My heart is sick and sad. From where the Sun now stands, I will fight no more forever."

Sent to reservations

After their surrender, the people were sent to reservations in Kansas and Oklahoma. They finally ended up on the Colville Reservation near Nespelem, Washington. Another part of the tribe was

Nez Perce Chief Joseph with U.S. Army General Oliver O. Howard, who gave the Nez Perce the order to move to a reservation within 30 days.

placed on the Nez Perce Reservation near Lapwai, Idaho. The Nez Perce rejected U.S. government attempts to reorganize them. Instead, in 1948, they established their own tribal constitution.

RELIGION

The Nez Perce felt a deep spiritual connection with the Earth and lived in harmony with nature. For the Nez Perce, all living things were closely related to each other and to people. Each member of the tribe had a guardian spirit, or *wyakin,* that protected him or her from harm and provided help when needed. For example, a person might pray to their wyakin to help conquer an enemy or for help in crossing a dangerous river. The Nez Perce often carried small medicine bundles containing materials that represented their wyakins.

Many modern Nez Perce have adopted Christianity but combine it with elements of the Dreamer religion. Followers of this traditional Nez Perce religion say that in past times, their prophets dreamed about and accurately predicted events like the arrival of Lewis and Clark and an earthquake near the present-day town of Whitebird.

LANGUAGE

The Nez Perce spoke a Sahaptin dialect (variety) of the Penutian language family, one of the oldest known language stocks in North America. The Nez Perce language is closely related to that of the Walla Walla and other tribes of the region. By the late 1990s, only some older members of the tribe could speak the language.

GOVERNMENT

Prior to meeting white missionaries in the 1840s, the seventy small communities that made up the Nez Perce people did not have a formal governing system. Each village had a council of three or four respected men, one of whom was called chief. The job generally went to the person who had the most relatives in the village. Upon the death of a chief, his son usually replaced him. The chief was expected to resolve disputes and to discipline unruly children. The Nez Perce had few laws and no system to enforce them. Order was maintained by social pressure. Meetings to discuss problems took place when people gathered to fish or harvest crops. Even then, no tribe member had to obey any group decision.

The Nez Perce lacked an overall tribal organization. Instead, each independent village or group had a headman who spoke for his own followers. When a major decision was needed, the headmen and other respected people would meet in a tribal council and attempt to reach an agreement.

In the 1990s, the Nez Perce Tribal Executive Committee was made up of elected officers who served three-year terms. The committee managed economic development, tribal social service programs, natural resources, and tribal investments.

ECONOMY

Before white people moved into their lands, the Nez Perce provided for their needs by digging roots, picking berries, and killing small animals for food. In May and June they caught salmon, which were preserved by drying and then eaten throughout the year. The people rarely wandered far from their homes. When the Nez Perce first acquired horses in the 1700s, they found them valuable for trade and for traveling long distances. Horses also enabled them to hunt buffalo for their own use. The Nez Perce traded dried berries and dried cakes made of sweet-tasting camas lily bulbs and corn-like roots called kouse, as well as salmon oil and dried salmon. They traded horns from mountain sheep, bowls and other objects made from the horns, cedar-root baskets, eagle feathers, and the hunting tools for which they were famous.

Some modern Nez Perce work at farming and lumbering, while others have jobs in the medical, legal, and engineering professions, among many others. The Nez Perce Reservation operates a tribal store, the Nez Perce Limestone Enterprise, and the Nez Perce Forest Products Enterprise. The tribe cultivates nearly 38,000 acres of reservation land. Wheat is the primary crop; other crops include barley, dry peas, lentils, canola, bluegrass seed, alfalfa, and hay. Cattle are also raised.

During the mid-1990s, the tribe's unemployment rate stood at 26.1 percent. That means that more than one out of four people who wanted a job were not able to find one. Per capita income was about $6,102, less than one-third of that of the average American. Per capita income is the average income one person makes in a year.

DAILY LIFE

Families

Large families were common among the Nez Perce. Although it was primarily the mother's job to raise the children, the job was shared by uncles, aunts, cousins, and older siblings. Most jobs in a family were assigned by gender. Women generally picked berries, dug

A Nez Perce man in ceremonial dress.

up camas bulbs, and made pottery. Men did the hunting and fishing.

Buildings

For centuries, the Nez Perce lived in houses covered with plant material. During the summer, when they moved in search of food, they lived in quickly-built lean-tos consisting of a pole framework covered with woven mats of plant fibers. Their winter shelters were pole-framed structures covered with layers of cedar bark, sagebrush, packed grass, and earth. Each winter dwelling, which usually housed several families, contained a small door and a smoke hole in the roof. Five or six houses made up a village.

As horses came more into use, the tribe could move around more and was exposed to other tribes. Nez Perce buildings then grew larger and more sophisticated. Their winter houses sometimes extended to 100 feet in length and housed many families. Hide-covered tepees were used during summer fishing and hunting trips.

Clothing and adornment

In early times, shredded cedar bark, deerskin, or rabbitskin were used to make clothing. In summer, men usually wore capes and breechcloths (flaps of material that cover the front and back and are suspended from the waist), adding fur robes and leggings when it turned cold. The women were known for the large basket hats they wove out of dried leaves and plant fibers. By the early 1800s, as the Nez Perce came into contact with tribes of the Pacific Coast and Great Plains, they began to imitate their tailored skin garments decorated with shells, elk teeth, and beads. Men wore their hair arranged in a high mound that stood straight up from the forehead. The remaining hair was braided and hung down the chest. Women began to wear long dresses of buckskin that had fringe at the hem and sleeves.

Food

Food gathering was a very time-consuming task for the Nez Perce, who lived in dry, rugged high country. The people mainly lived by fishing, hunting, and gathering fruit and vegetables from spring through fall, and storing surplus food for winter use. During the spring they fished for the large numbers of salmon that swam upstream to spawn. The Nez Perce fished using a variety of implements including spears, hand-held and weighted nets, small brush traps, and large enclosures. Though hunting was often difficult on the hot, open plateaus of their homeland, they managed with bows and arrows to hunt elk, deer, and mountain sheep. To approach their prey and kill them more easily, the Nez Perce sometimes disguised themselves in animal furs or worked together to surround an animal herd. After they started using horses, the Nez Perce sent a hunting party to the Great Plains to hunt buffaloes each year.

In the spring, Nez Perce women went out to the hillsides and used sharp digging sticks to turn up kouse. The kouse was ground up and boiled to make soup or was shaped into cakes and dried for later use. Other plants were gathered in summer, including wild onions and carrots, bitterroots, blackberries, strawberries, huckleberries, and nuts. In late summer, several Nez Perce bands came together to gather camas bulbs. These were steamed and then made into a dough or gruel (a thin, watery substance).

Education

Grandparents provided much of a child's education. From them girls learned food-gathering techniques and how to run a household. Boys learned from their grandfathers how to hunt and fish with small bows and arrows. Children also learned rules of conduct and tribal history from their grandparents.

The tradition continues in modern times as children at Nez Perce summer camps learn the importance of preserving their culture through the teaching of tribal elders.

Healing practices

Nez Perce doctors called shamans (pronounced *SHAY-muns*)—who could be male or female—had miraculous powers. They could change the weather, cause bad people to have misfortunes, and cure the sick by singing sacred songs and prescribing herbal remedies. Sometimes the shamans held cleansing ceremonies to purify spirits before special events, or to cure illness.

ARTS

Dances

Today, dances involving members of several tribes are held at the reservation. Both adults and children are encouraged to display their

"The Singers," a sculpture by Nez Perce Doug Hyde, 1973.

own personal interpretation of traditional Nez Perce dances to the beat of a drum. During men's traditional dances the dancers remain upright as they move to a drumbeat, looking down as though to examine the tracks of wild game or the enemy. In the Men's Fancy Dance they wear outfits adorned with feathers and ribbons and perform fast, spinning movements to a quick beat. During the Grass Dance they perform, graceful, swaying motions that resemble prairie grass bending before the wind.

In their traditional dance, women wear beautiful dresses decorated with beadwork, porcupine quills, elk's teeth, and ribbons. They gently bounce, dip and sway to the slow beat of the drum. During the Jingle Dance, they move in dresses adorned with cones made by rolling the lids from metal cans.

Oral literature

Nez Perce families often gathered to tell stories, especially during the winter months. Many of the stories they shared spoke of the interrelated nature of all things.

CUSTOMS

Festivals

The Nez Perce hold festivals several times a year in celebration of their heritage. These special events feature drumming, singing, and sharing traditional foods. Feasts are held to mark the arrival of edible plants and the major salmon runs. Older members tell stories that pass along the traditional dances, religion, and language.

Finding a guardian spirit

Traditionally, an important task for a Nez Perce youngster was finding his or her personal guardian spirit, known as the *wyakin*. Between the ages of nine and thirteen, boys and girls were instructed by an older tribe member who had a very strong wyakin. After being tutored for several years, the boy or girl went on a solitary journey to find this personal spirit-helper. The individual was not allowed to take food, water, or weapons on the journey. Sometimes the wyakin came to the young person through dreams that could be peaceful or agitated. Occasionally the adolescent returned home, frightened or homesick, without having acquired the wyakin. In winter, young people who had succeeded would dance and sing in ways designed to make them one with their guardian spirits. By watching and participating, other members of the tribe could often discover the identity of the young people's wyakins. The ceremony sometimes involved contests to see who had received the greatest powers from their wyakin.

Hunting and war rituals

When a young boy had his first successful hunt, or caught his first fish, a ceremony took place in which the meat or fish was served to the tribe's adult males. The people believed that this ceremony would make the young boy a good provider. A similar ceremony was held in which women of the tribe would consume the roots or berries that a girl had gathered for the first time.

As part of their war preparations, Nez Perce men stripped to breechcloths and moccasins. They applied brightly colored paint to their faces and bodies. Red paint was placed on the part in a warrior's hair and across his forehead. A variety of colors were applied to his body in special, individual patterns. The warriors also decorated themselves with animal feathers, fur, teeth, and claws representing their connection to their guardian spirits.

CURRENT TRIBAL ISSUES

Modern Nez Perce have been involved in several legal cases; in some instances, rights to hunt and fish on their ancestral lands have been restored.

The Nez Perce people have also taken steps to remember their unique and tragic tribal history. In 1996, descendants of the Wallowa band held their twentieth annual ceremony commemorating the members of the tribe who died in the Bear Paw Mountains during the Nez Perce War of 1877. They gathered to smoke pipes, sing, and pray. They also conducted an empty saddle ceremony—in which horses are led around without riders—in order to appease the spirits of the dead.

In the mid-1990s, declines in the timber and cattle markets brought hard economic times to non-Native residents of Wallowa Valley. Valley residents invited the Nez Perce to return to the area. A boom in tourism resulted. The Nee-Me-Poo Trail, the Nez Perce National Historical Park, and the burial site of Old Chief Joseph have become major tourist attractions. Valley residents raised money to build an interpretive center and purchase 160 acres of land for the tribe to use for cultural events. Many members of the tribe were pleased to recover some of their ancestral territory. "The whites may look at it as an economic plus, but we look at it as a homecoming," said tribal member Soy Redthunder.

NOTABLE PEOPLE

Chief Joseph (1840–1904), the son of Old Chief Joseph (died 1871), assumed leadership of the tribe after his father's death. When the U.S. Army attacked his people, who were fleeing the move to a reservation, Chief Joseph led his followers at the Battle of White Bird Canyon. His forces defeated the U.S. Army, killed 33 soldiers, and suffered no causalities. They fought valiantly and cleverly against U.S. forces until their final defeat four months later. Although his people were removed to sites in Washington and Idaho, Joseph was never allowed to return to his homelands in Oregon and Idaho. He died in 1904 before a Nez Perce reservation was established there.

FURTHER READING

Howard, Helen Addison. *Saga of Chief Joseph*. Lincoln: University of Nebraska Press, 1978.

Howes, Kathi. *The Nez Perce*. Vero Beach, FL: Rourke Publications, Inc., 1990.

Sneve, Virginia Driving Hawk. *The Nez Perce*. New York: Holiday House, 1994.

Trafzer, Clifford E. *The Nez Perce*. New York: Chelsea House, 1992.

Umatilla

Name

The name Umatilla (pronounced *you-muh-TILL-uh*) comes from the name for a village and means "many rocks." Another suggested meaning is "water rippling over sand."

Location

The Umatilla hunted, gathered, and fished the area ranging from the site of present-day Arlington, Oregon, east to the Walla Walla River. Today, 896 Umatilla live with members of the Cayuse, Walla Walla, Warm Springs, Nez Perce, and other tribes, on or near the Umatilla Reservation in northeastern Oregon.

Population

In 1780, there were about 1,500 Umatilla. In 1910, there were only 272. In a census (count of the population) done in 1990 by the U.S. Bureau of the Census, 1,285 people identified themselves as Umatilla.

Language family

Penutian-Sahaptian.

Origins and group affiliations

The Umatilla say they have lived in their homeland since the beginning of time. They reject scientists' theories that they migrated from Asia. Objects from their homeland that were dug up and studied indicate that the Umatilla culture may have begun there 10,000 years ago. The Umatilla intermarried with and were related to the Nez Perce, Yakima, Cayuse, Palouse, Modoc, and Walla Walla tribes of the Columbia Plateau region of Oregon and Washington states. In 1855 the Umatilla, the Cayuse, and the Walla Walla joined as the Confederated Tribes of the Umatilla Reservation.

CONFEDERATED TRIBES OF THE UMATILLA

Contemporary Communities

1. Confederated Tribes of the Umatilla Reservation, Oregon

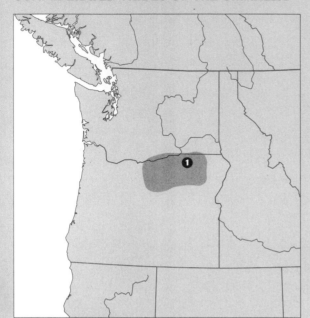

Shaded area: Traditional lands of the Cayuse, Umatilla, and Walla Walla in present-day northeastern Oregon and Washington.

The Umatilla prospered in a barren, dry landscape of sand and gravel in the Columbia Plateau, where the most attractive features were the warm winters and the abundant salmon to be found in the crystal-clear waters of the Columbia River. They moved from the river to the plains and mountains in a cycle that included hunting, fishing, celebrating, and trading. The tribe gave its name to a county, a town, and a river. The people have found prosperity through gaming (running gambling casinos) in the twentieth century, and they are using the profits to revitalize their ancient culture.

HISTORY

Lewis and Clark and the fur traders

Before explorers Meriwether Lewis and William Clark became the first European Americans to meet the Umatilla in 1805, smallpox had been introduced to the region. An epidemic swept through the tribe as early as 1775, brought by other tribes already in contact with white men. Smallpox greatly reduced the Umatilla population.

It appears that the first Umatilla to encounter Lewis and Clark had never seen guns before. After watching Clark shoot a crane, the people became very upset. "They said we came from the clouds and were not men," wrote Clark. But they calmed down when they saw Sacajawea (pronounced *sak-a-ja-WEE-a*), the young Shoshone woman (see Shoshone entry) who accompanied Lewis and Clark on their expedition.

Lewis and Clark found the people of the Columbia Plateau region to be rich in horses and dogs. Like their neighbors, the Nez Perce (see entry) and the Yakima, the Umatilla acquired horses through trade with other tribes in the early 1700s and became skilled horse breeders and trainers. Using the horse for transportation, the Umatilla could cover a larger territory in the search for food. They ventured all the way to the Great Plains east of the Rocky Mountains and hunted buffalo.

Soon after Lewis and Clark left, traders took their place. An American trading company set up a post in Oregon in 1812, and the Northwest Company (a huge fur-trading enterprise) set up shop on the Walla Walla River in 1818. Most of the tribes of the region found themselves caught up in trade, trading horses for European goods such as guns and ammunition, iron pots, blankets, cloth, beads, and cattle. Rivalry over trade added to the hostilities that already raged among the tribes in the region—hostilities that were fueled in part by the popular custom of raiding other tribes for horses and slaves. The Umatilla could not avoid becoming involved in the quarrels.

Fighting battles; losing land

In the 1840s, the Umatilla joined the Nez Perce in a fight against their Paiute enemies (see entry). To add to the already tense situation in the region, white settlers and missionaries began arriving in the 1840s. The missionaries were especially active among the Cayuse. When a measles epidemic struck the Cayuse in 1847, the Indians blamed the missionaries for it and killed several of them. Those killings (called the Whitman Massacre for the name of one of the missionaries), and concern over the flood of American settlers, led to the

IMPORTANT DATES

Early-1700s: Umatilla acquire horses.

1805: Lewis and Clark are the first whites to make contact with Umatilla.

1848–50: Cayuse War takes place.

1855: The Walla Walla Treaty is negotiated.

1855: Under the Walla Walla Treaty, the Umatilla, the Cayuse, and the Walla Walla join as the Confederated Tribes of the Umatilla Reservation.

1949: Confederated Tribes organize a tribal government.

1985: More than $2 million is awarded to Umatilla for land lost in 1855 treaty.

Cayuse Chief Umapine. The Cayuse and the Walla Walla joined the Umatilla as the Confederated Tribes of the Umatilla Indian Reservation in 1855.

Cayuse War (1847–50) between Indians and Americans. In 1848 a number of Umatilla warriors joined the Cayuse in that war. However, the tribes could not stand up to the superior manpower and fire-power of the Americans, and they finally gave up in 1850.

White settlers were land-hungry, and to keep them happy, the U.S. Congress passed the Donation Land Law of 1851. It granted white settlers permission to build homesteads on any Oregon lands, even those that belonged to Indians. The Indians were angered by this unjust new law and reacted with violence. To try and keep peace, in 1851 the U.S. government established the Umatilla Agency on the Umatilla River near present-day Echo, Oregon. The new agency provided area tribes with food and supplies and re-established the Saint Anne Mission that was abandoned after the Whitman Massacre.

First treaty is signed

Conflicts between the Americans and Indians continued to escalate, and on May 28, 1855, Washington Territory Governor Isaac Stevens called the Walla Walla Treaty Council. Stevens convinced some chiefs to sign a treaty in which they gave up their lands to the United States. The treaty formally combined the Umatilla, Walla Walla, and Cayuse in one group as the Confederated Tribes of the Umatilla Indian Reservation. The treaty reduced the tribes' 6.4 million acres of land to a 250,000-acre reservation along the banks of the Umatilla River near present-day Pendleton, Oregon.

Like all the tribes that signed treaties in 1855, the Umatilla were distrustful of the U.S. government and reacted violently to further trespassing by American settlers on lands they considered their own. It took more than four years for Congress to ratify (make legal) the Walla Walla Treaty. The fact that it was not legal did not stop Governor Stevens from announcing that American settlers were welcome to come and build homesteads.

Another war

Increasing numbers of immigrants trespassed on tribal lands and farms. When gold was discovered in the area, even more people—

miners and settlers—flooded the area. The Yakima tribe were the first to lose patience with the settlers, and they started the Yakima War of 1855–56. The Umatilla joined the Yakima in their war against the Americans while still defending themselves against Paiute raiders. The Umatilla were forced to flee several times during the Yakima War when they were attacked by the Paiute. The war went badly for the Indians, as the U.S. Army gradually took control of the territory, and the Umatilla surrendered along with many of the Yakima during the second Walla Walla peace council in 1856.

Though the Umatilla had agreed to peace, other tribes still made war with the Americans for several years. Meanwhile, many of the people on the reservation grew restless and bored, unwilling to give in to government agents' urging that they settle down and become farmers. Soon, white settlers realized that the land used by the Indians for grazing their horses was prime wheat-growing land. They decided they wanted it, and the U.S. government obliged them by passing the Slater Act in 1885, which established an allotment system for reservation land.

Lands are allotted

Under allotment, reservation land was divided into 160-acre plots that were "given" to individual Indians. Any land left over was opened up to white settlement. By the end of the allotment period, the 250,000 acres in the Umatilla reservation had shrunk to 82,742 acres for 1,118 Indians.

Allotment affected the Indians in many ways. Owning plots of land went against traditional Indian values of using land in common. Conflicts arose when Indians who owned large herds of horses could no longer graze them on land now used for farming. People whose families had lived in an area for as long as anyone could remember were told that they no longer could live there because someone else had title to the land.

Twentieth-century successes

The Indians continued to find it hard to adjust to reservation life, and many left, moving to urban areas to look for work. Those who remained behind faced unrelenting poverty. Conditions only began to improve in the 1960s, when money from land claims and from new federal government programs allowed the tribe to begin development projects. The land claim issue was raised in 1951, when the Umatilla filed lawsuits against the United States, demanding payment for 4 million acres of land taken in the 1855 treaty. In 1965 they were finally awarded more than $2 million. The Umatilla won other claims for the loss of fishing rights when fishing sites were destroyed by the construction of a dam.

The Confederated Tribes of the Umatilla Indian Reservation took advantage of these funds and other monies from the government to improve their living conditions and to develop an economic base. In the 1980s, the government agreed to allow gambling on reservations. Gambling casinos were built, and more money flowed into the reservation. The Confederated Tribes are using the money wisely, and have adopted many ambitious programs to revive their culture.

RELIGION

Like many tribes of the West, the Umatilla did not believe in one supreme being. They believed in guardian spirits, who gave each person the specific power required to make it through life. By way of a ceremony called a vision quest, an individual got in touch with his or her guardian spirit. People could not control the type of powers received from the spirits. They might receive the power to cure illnesses or the power to be successful in the hunt or war. Songs and drumming were the way they communicated with their guardian spirits. Individual Umatilla "owned" rhythmic and hypnotic personal songs that were their most important possesions.

The most powerful guardian spirits were the heavenly ones: the Sun, Moon, and stars. Other spirits came from animals, thunder, wind, and other forces of nature. Umatilla who received powers from these spirits were directly connected to nature and could hear the whispers and songs of the trees and the messages of beasts of all kinds.

The Umatilla's religious feelings were expressed through a ritual called the Washat Dance. The dance marked changes in the seasons and rites of passage, and it featured male and female dancers, seven drummers, and feasts of salmon and roots. The Washat Dance religion flourished in ancient times, went through changes under the influence of Christian missionaries in the mid-1800s, and then was restored to its original meaning by Dream Prophets in the late 1800s. Umatilla Dream Prophets named Luls and Pinapuyuset helped people in the Columbia Plateau stay in touch with their old religion when it was under attack by Christian missionaries. The Washat Dance religion remains a major form of religions expression in the Northwest.

LANGUAGE

The Umatilla version of the Northern Sahap-
tian language is related to the languages spoken
by the Yakima, Palouse, and Walla Walla, among
others. After the establishment of the reservation
in the late nineteenth century, all the people there
adopted the language of the Nez Perce. By the
1990s, only a handful of people could speak or
even understand the languages of the Umatilla,
Walla Walla, and Cayuse Indians. Furthermore,
the languages formerly spoken by the people on
the reservation had never even been written
down.

Today, tribal elders realize that unless they
write their languages down and teach them to
young people, they will be lost forever. Tribal
elder Edith McCloud, who teaches the Walla
Walla language, explained why she was at first
unwilling to pass on her knowledge of the language. "When I first started, I would have preferred never to have the language written down,
never documented. What our elders used to say
was that the white man is taking everything from us except our language. We didn't want to give it away. But today, in today's world, children are conditioned to learn from documents, tape recorders and
now computers. If we keep the language to ourselves and try to teach
it only verbally it really is going to get lost."

McCloud is only one of several tribal elders who are now teaching weekly classes in the Umatilla, Walla Walla, and other languages.
This is part of an ambitious program to revive and preserve the
ancient languages; it is being funded by profits received from tribal
gambling operations.

Hoo-Sis-Mox-Mox, a Umatilla
chief, 1900.

GOVERNMENT

Each Umatilla group who shared a winter camp had its own chief
or headman. Long ago the position was hereditary (passed down from
father to son), but when they began to hunt buffalo, the Umatilla
adopted the Plains custom of electing chiefs because of their skills.
The primary duty of a chief was to keep the peace and to promote
good behavior among the people; he could not force people to obey
him but rather had to convince them his way was best. The chief

represented his group in meetings with other chiefs. Because a chief's authority was so limited, many people were extremely upset that, when only a few chiefs signed the 1855 treaty with the U.S. government, all Indians were forced to move to the reservation. However, they soon gave in to the reality that if they did not move to a reservation, they would be destroyed.

When the Umatilla, Cayuse, and Walla Walla were on the reservation, they came under the control of government agents, who paid people of their own choosing to be chiefs. In 1949, the Confederated Tribes of the Umatilla Indian Reservation formed their own government. Now decisions about life on the reservation are made by a nine-member board of trustees that is elected by the general council (consisting of all tribal members age eighteen and older).

ECONOMY

The Umatilla economy depended on fishing before the tribe acquired horses in the early 1700s. Then the economy expanded to include buffalo hunting as well as fishing. Every year during the fishing season, tribes from all over the Northwest and as far away as the Great Plains came to the Columbia River to trade buffalo meat for dried fish.

The early days on the reservation were very hard. Indians were not allowed to leave without a permit, so they could not gather their traditional foods. They came to depend on government handouts, and grew so dispirited and hopeless that observers predicted the culture would perish. After allotment went into effect (see "History"), most Indians found they could not afford to farm their land and they leased or sold it to white farmers. Some people continued to fish in the old way but often found their fishing spots flooded and no longer usable after the building of dams on the Columbia River in the early and mid-1900s.

After suffering years of struggle and limited opportunities, the Umatilla people are experiencing a stunning turnaround. The tribal economy that once depended heavily on farming and forestry has expanded, and today the Confederated Tribes are a major economic force in northeastern Oregon. The tribal government employs a staff of more than 800 people in departments such as administration, the tribal court, economic and community development, education, finance, and fire and police protection. Tribal businesses include several that appeal to tourists, such as the extremely successful Wildhorse Casino Resort and a new cultural center.

DAILY LIFE

Families

In traditional times, extended Umatilla families—parents, children, aunts, uncles, cousins, and grandparents—all lived together in small groups called bands. Families were large, and everyone had an assigned job; they knew if they failed to do their job, the family might starve or freeze when winter came. The grandmother's job was to stay in the camp and watch the children while their mothers were out digging roots.

Education

Children began their training in adult skills at age ten. Boys watched as older men hunted and fished but were not allowed to participate until they were teens because an untrained person was an insult to his prey. Girls helped out with household chores. From ages twelve to sixteen, girls lived together in a separate house where they were closely guarded and kept away from boys. There were taught by older women how to cook and how to make baskets and clothing. They also learned about personal hygiene.

A Cayuse mother and child.

Christian missionaries began their work in Oregon as early as 1836, introducing their concept of formal education. In addition to gaining converts, the missionaries intended to guide the Indians in becoming like white Americans, and the best way to do that was to begin with the education of children. The Presbyterian missionary Dr. Marcus Whitman and others taught American-style domestic skills to Indian children. As the Indians saw it, Whitman was turning their children into servants for whites. This was one of the misunderstandings that led up to the terrible moment when Mr. Whitman had a Cayuse tomahawk buried in his skull. The Cayuse War (1847-50) followed soon after.

Roman Catholic missionaries set up a school on the reservation in the 1870s, and the Presbyterians opened their school in 1871. Some children were educated at those schools, while others were sent away to a government-run boarding school in Forest Grove, Oregon. This style of education led to a weakening of the traditional Native culture and language.

Today, reservation children attend Head Start classes on the reservation; then they usually go on to attend public schools in Pendleton. The Confederated Tribes uses money won in land claims cases to fund scholarships, and proceeds from gambling also go to fund scholarships, as well as language and tutoring programs and adult education programs.

Buildings

The Umatilla favored winter homes called longhouses, which they built along the Columbia River. The homes, sometimes as long as eighty feet, were made of dried mats arranged over a pole frame. Winter lodges could house many families, and a village might contain five or six of them.

The Umatilla devised portable mat tepees to take along on gathering and buffalo hunting trips. They did not use buffalo skins for tepees because their supply of buffalo skins was not as large as that of the Plains tribes. Today they use tepees covered with canvas for celebrations and for camping in the mountains.

Food

The Umatilla ate fish as their main food source, mainly salmon, steelhead trout, eel, and sturgeon. The tribes of the region gathered along the Columbia River in spring and fall for the salmon runs. In late summer the men hunted wild game such as deer, elk, mountain sheep, bear, antelope, wolf, fox, and cougar. In later years, the Umatilla also hunted buffalo on expeditions to the Great Plains.

While the men hunted and fished, women gathered camas roots, onions, potatoes, carrots, acorns, and a variety of nuts and berries. One type of root, called biscuitroot, was mashed and shaped into small biscuits that were dried in the sun and stored for later use. Black moss from pine and fir trees was baked to form a cheese-like food.

Today, because of dams on the Columbia River, salmon is no longer as plentiful, but it is still caught. The people on the reservation continue to rely on salmon and other traditional foods like roots, berries, deer, and elk.

Clothing and adornment

Umatilla dressed in robes, vests, and aprons, all made from skins and furs. Women wore basket-shaped hats woven from dried leaves. After they began to hunt buffalo, their clothing styles changed to resemble the leggings and dresses of the Plains Indians.

Healing practices

The Umatilla used herbal remedies to treat a variety of physical maladies. Conditions caused by evil spirits required a medicine man, or shaman (pronounced *SHAY-mun*), to cast them out. The shaman either expelled the evil spirits or filled the afflicted person with a powerful spirit to drive out the sickness. Most healing rituals involved singing, chanting, and drumming, and could get very loud. Shamans used rattles, smoke, and face-painting as part of the healing ritual. The shaman's job was a dangerous one, because those who failed to cure the patient were often killed.

ARTS

Oral literature

Tribal elders say their oral tradition dates back 10,000 years. Men and women were encouraged to display their oral skills by reciting tribal myths and tales, especially during the winter when cold weather kept everyone inside at night. A favorite character in their stories was Coyote, who sometimes played a fool and sometimes was a wise man. An often-told tale describes how Coyote made the world safe for the first Indians by ridding the world of dangerous monsters.

Decorative arts

Women were known for their beadwork; they still decorate bags, baskets, and children's dancing costumes with beautiful geometric designs. Men painted their robes and war shields with pictures of their brave deeds. Basket twining, beadwork, and regalia sewing (regalia is fancy clothing or other symbols of high rank) are some of the local arts that are being revived at Crow's Shadow Institute on the Umatilla Indian Reservation. The institute brings artists, teachers, and arts professionals from around the world to the reservation to help local artists develop careers in the arts.

The work of artists affiliated with Crow's Shadow Institute and other local artists is on display at the Tamastslikt Cultural Institute, which opened in 1998. The institute has displays that tell the story of the Cayuse, Umatilla, and Walla Walla tribes. Special exhibits entitled We Were, We Are, and We Will Be feature the work of established artists as well as children.

CUSTOMS

Rites of passage

When a boy felt he was ready to be called a man, he might go through a period of training to test his strength, courage, and endurance. The boy was sent to a spot far from the village, which was marked by a special stone. This spot was located close to tribal enemies; the boy was required to spend a day and a night there without being detected.

There was no ceremony to mark a girl's first menstruation. She simply remained in a separate hut for the duration of her period, then bathed, put on fresh clothes, and resumed her daily chores.

Courtship and marriage

Because girls were so closely watched, boys had to seize opportunities to catch them alone. A boy might court a girl by singing to her from the shadows, or waylaying her on the way to a water source. At about age sixteen, boys and girls were ready for marriage. The boy's parents sent a relative to speak to the parents of his girl of choice. If they agreed, the boys parents presented the family with horses. Much feasting and gift exchanging followed, in which the givers competed to present the best gifts; then the couple was considered married. They usually moved in with the groom's parents for a while before establishing their own home.

Babies

Pregnant women hoped to keep their babies small by swimming frequently. They avoided unpleasantness that might upset them and affect the child. Newborns were bound tightly to boards so the back of their heads would grow flat; this was considered an attractive feature, but the custom was given up after whites came and called it ugly.

War rituals

Entire tribes seldom fought together as a unit. Instead, warriors were recruited from other tribes who lived nearby. This is how the Umatilla came to participate in the Cayuse War. Horse-stealing raids were considered a form of warfare, a manly pursuit, and a way to demonstrate bravery. Raiding parties usually consisted of only five or six people.

War parties attacked in the early morning and took women and children as slaves. Sometimes slain enemy warriors were scalped or their hearts were eaten (to ingest the strength of the fallen warrior). Warriors who were taken captive were tortured by having their fingers, wrists, and limbs cut off. Upon returning to the village, successful warriors held a scalp dance, then purified themselves in a sweatbath.

Festivals and ceremonies

Ceremonies were held before raiders or war parties set off and to welcome them back home again. But the most important ceremonies concerned food, which was considered a sacred substance. In a custom known as "first food observances," the first salmon of the season or the first roots were thanked before being consumed.

Drumming and singing have always been an important part of the culture, and every important occasion featured performances that took years to learn.

Today, many tribal festivities take place on the July Grounds on the reservation. In the late 1800s the federal government tried to discourage traditional Indian celebrations. The Confederated Tribes would gather at the July Grounds and pretend to celebrate Independence Day (July 4). Actually, they were celebrating their own heritage through horse and foot races, spear throwing, dancing, singing, and drumming.

Burial

The Umatilla wrapped their dead in animal skins and buried them in shallow graves in rocky ledges. Graves were enclosed by cedar poles and stones. Often horses were killed and the corpses left near the grave. Mourners stopped eating for a while and cut off their hair to show their grief. Those who touched the body purified themselves in the sweat lodge.

Early observers among the Walla Walla claimed that death by suicide was quite common and often came about after a person's feelings had been hurt. Sometimes grieving relatives decided to be buried alive with their loved ones. A memorial feast was held five days after the burial. The dead person was praised, then his or her name was never mentioned again so their souls could rest.

CURRENT TRIBAL ISSUES

Two major tribal issues in the 1990s deal with the reburial of the remains of the individual known as Kennewick Man and the issue of salmon recovery in the Columbia River.

WALLA WALLA REGALE LEWIS & CLARK

In 1806 explorers Meriwether Lewis and William Clark visited a Walla Walla village on the return trip of their expedition. Walla Walla Chief Yellept was delighted to see them, presenting them with gifts of firewood, fish, and "a very eligant white horse." Yellept received Clark's sword in exchange for his generosity. One of the white men brought out his fiddle, and the Walla Walla villagers and their Yakima guests were treated to an hour of dancing by the white party. Lewis reported that in turn, 550 Indian men, women, and children then "sung and danced at the same time," and were pleased to have some of the white men join in the dance with them. Lewis later recorded in his journal: "I think we can justly affirm to the honor of these people that they are the most hospitable, honest, and sincere people that we have met with in our voyage."

The 1995 discovery of a 9,300-year-old skeleton near Kennewick, Washington, ignited a controversy that still raged in 1998. Kennewick Man is the oldest skeleton ever found in the Pacific Northwest. Scientists wanted to study it, while the tribe contends their religious and cultural beliefs require the immediate reburial of the remains of what is likely one of their ancestors.

In 1998 the Confederated Tribes of the Umatilla Indian Reservation announced a new campaign to restore natural salmon runs in the Columbia River Basin. The campaign is called *Waykaanashmiyay Nishaycht* ("Home for the Salmon"). The tribe and its supporters claim that dams on Columbia and Snake river tributaries are threatening the extinction of all wild salmon runs on the rivers. The Campaign Mission Statement declares: "We believe that a Pacific Northwest without salmon is unacceptable. For our children, we must again make the Columbia River and all of its tributaries Home for the Salmon."

FURTHER READING

Ballantine, Betty, and Ian Ballantine. *The Native Americans: An Illustrated History*. Atlanta: Turner Publishing, 1993.

Confederated Tribes of the Umatilla Indian Reservation Homepage. [Online] http://www.umatilla.nsn.us/main.html

"Q: Should scientists be allowed to 'study' the skeletons of ancient American Indians?" (Symposium). U.S. Representative Doc Hastings; Confederated Tribes of the Umatilla Indian Reservation Spokesman Donald Sampson. *Insight on the News,* December 22, 1997, vol. 13, no. 47, p. 24.

Ruby, Robert H., and John A. Brown. *The Cayuse Indians*. Norman: University of Oklahoma Press, 1972.

Yenne, Bill. "Umatilla." *The Encyclopedia of North American Indian Tribes*. New York: Crescent Books, 1986.

Bibliography

Books

Abrams, George H. J. *The Seneca People*. Phoenix, AZ: Indian Tribal Series, 1976.

The AFN Report on the Status of Alaska Natives: A Call for Action. Anchorage: Alaska Federation of Natives, 1989.

American Indian Reservations and Trust Areas. Washington, DC: U.S. Department of Commerce, 1996.

The American Indians: Algonquians of the East Coast. New York: Time-Life Books, 1995.

The American Indians: Hunters of the Northern Forest. New York: Time-Life Books, 1995.

Anderson, Gary Clayton. *Kinsmen of Another Kind: Dakota-White Relations in the Upper Mississippi Valley, 1650–1862*. Lincoln: University of Nebraska Press, 1984.

Anderson, Gary Clayton. *Little Crow: Spokesman for the Sioux*. St. Paul: Minnesota Historical Society Press, 1986.

Anderson, Gary Clayton. *Through Dakota Eyes: Narrative Accounts of the Minnesota Indian War of 1862*. St. Paul: Minnesota Historical Society Press, 1988.

Apess, William. *On Our Own Ground: The Complete Writings of William Apess, A Pequot*. Ed. Barry O'Connell. Amherst: University of Massachusetts Press, 1992.

Axtell, James. *The European and the Indian: Essays in the Ethnohistory of Colonial North America*. New York: Oxford University Press, 1981.

Ayer, Eleanor H. *The Anasazi*. New York: Walker Publishing, 1993.

Azelrod, Alan. *Chronicle of the Indian Wars*. New York: Prentice Hall, 1993.

Bahti, Tom. *Southwestern Indian Tribes*. Las Vegas: KC Publications, 1994.

Ballantine, Betty and Ian Ballantine, eds. *The Native Americans: An Illustrated History*. Atlanta: Turner Publishing, 1993.

Bamforth, Douglas B. *Ecology and Human Organization on the Great Plains*. New York: Plenum Press, 1988.

A Basic Call to Consciousness. Rooseveltown, NY: Akwesasne Notes, 1978.

Bataille, Gretchen M. *Native American Women: A Biographical Dictionary*. New York: Garland Publishing, 1993.

Beals, Ralph L. *Material Culture of the Pima, Papago, and Western Apache*. Berkeley, CA: Department of the Interior, National Park Service, 1934.

Bean, Lowell John. *Mukat's People: The Cahuilla Indians of Southern California*. Berkeley: University of California Press, 1972.

Beauchamp, William M. "Notes on Onondaga Dances." *An Iroquois Source Book,* Volume 2. Ed. Elisabeth Tooker. New York: Garland Publishing, 1985.

Beck, W. and Ynez Haas. *Historical Atlas of California*. Norman: University of Oklahoma Press, 1974.

Beckham, Stephen Dow. *Requiem for a People: The Rogue Indians and the Frontiersman*. Norman: University of Oklahoma Press, 1971.

Beckham, Stephen Dow, Kathryn Anne Toepel, and Rick Minor. *Native American Religious Practices and Uses in Western Oregon*. Eugene: University of Oregon Anthropological Papers, 1984.

Benson, Henry C. *Life Among the Choctaw Indians, and Sketches of the Southwest*. Cincinnati, OH: R. P. Thompson, 1860.

Berlainder, Jean Louis. *The Indians of Texas in 1830*. Washington, DC: Smithsonian Institution, 1969.

Berthrong, Donald J. *The Cheyenne and Arapaho Ordeal: Reservation and Agency Life in the Indian Territory*. Norman: University of Oklahoma Press, 1976.

Berthrong, Donald J. *The Southern Cheyennes*. Norman: University of Oklahoma Press, 1963.

Bieder, Robert E. *Native American Communities in Wisconsin, 1600–1960: A Study of Tradition and Change*. Madison: University of Wisconsin Press, 1995.

Biographical Dictionary of Indians of the Americas. Newport Beach, CA: American Indian Publishers, 1991.

Birket-Smith, Kaj and Frederica De Laguna. *The Eyak Indians of the Copper River Delta.* Copenhagen: Levin & Munksgaard, 1938.

Bischoff, William N. *The Indian War Diary of Plympton J. Kelly 1855–1856.* Tacoma: Washington State History Society, 1976.

Blaine, Martha Royce. *Pawnee Passage, 1870–1875.* Norman: University of Oklahoma Press, 1990.

Blaine, Martha Royce. *The Pawnees: A Critical Bibliography.* Bloomington: Indiana University Press for the Newberry Library, 1980.

Boas, Franz. *Chinook Texts.* Washington, DC: Bureau of American Ethnology Bulletin No. 20, 1894.

Boas, Franz. *Kwakiutl Ethnography.* Ed. Helen Codere. Chicago: University of Chicago Press, 1966.

Boas, Franz, ed. *Publications of the American Ethnological Society,* Vol. 1: *Fox Text,* by William Jones. Leyden: E. J. Brill, 1907.

Boas, Franz. *The Social Organization and the Secret Societies of the Kwakiutl Indians.* New York: Johnson Reprint Corporation, 1970.

Bolton, Herbert Eugene. *The Hasinais: Southern Caddoans As Seen by the Earliest Europeans.* Norman: University of Oklahoma Press, 1987.

Bourne, Russell. *Red King's Rebellion: Racial Politics in New England, 1675–1678.* New York: Atheneum Press, 1990.

Boyd, Maurice. *Kiowas Voices,* Vol. 1: *Ceremonial Dance, Ritual and Song.* Fort Worth: Texas Christian University Press, 1981.

Boyd, Maurice. *Kiowas Voices,* Vol. 2: *Myths, Legends, and Folktales.* Fort Worth: Texas Christian University Press, 1983.

Boyd, Robert. *People of the Dalles: The Indians of Wascopam Mission.* Lincoln: University of Nebraska Press, 1996.

Braund, Kathryn E. Holland. *Deerskins & Duffels: The Creek Indian Trade with Anglo-America, 1685–1815.* Lincoln: University of Nebraska Press, 1993.

Bray, Tamara L. and Thomas W. Killion. *Reckoning with the Dead: The Larsen Bay Repatriation and the Smithsonian Institution.* Washington, DC: Smithsonian Institution, 1994.

Brescia, William, Jr. "Choctaw Oral Tradition Relating to Tribal Origin." *The Choctaw Before Removal.* Ed. Carolyn Keller Reeves. Jackson: University Press of Mississippi, 1985.

Bringle, Mary. *Eskimos.* New York: Franklin Watts, 1973.

Brinton, Daniel G. *The Lenape and their Legends.* Philadelphia, 1884. Reprint. St. Clair Shores, MI: Scholarly Press, 1972.

Brown, Mark. *The Flight of the Nez Perce.* Lincoln: University of Nebraska Press, 1967.

Brown, Vinson. "Sioux, Eastern." *Dictionary of Indian Tribes of the Americas,* Vol. 3. Newport Beach, CA: American Indian Publishers, 1980.

Bruchac, Joseph. *New Voices from the Longhouse: An Anthology of Contemporary Iroquois Writing.* Greenfield Center, NY: Greenfield Review Press, 1989.

Bunte, Pamela A. and Robert J. Franklin. *From the Sands to the Mountain: Change and Persistence in a Southern Paiute Community.* Lincoln: University of Nebraska Press, 1987.

Burch, Ernest S. *The Eskimos.* Norman: University of Oklahoma Press, 1988.

Burnham, Dorothy K. *To Please the Caribou: Painted Caribou-skin Coats Worn by the Naskapi, Montagnais, and Cree Hunters of the Quebec Labrador Peninsula.* Toronto: Royal Ontario Museum, 1992.

Bushnell, David I., Jr. "The Choctaw of Bayou Lacomb, St. Tammany Parish, Louisiana (1909)." *A Choctaw Source Book. New York: Garland Publishing, 1985: pp. 1–37.*

Buskirk, Winfred. *The Western Apache.* Norman: University of Oklahoma Press, 1986.

Caduto, Michael J. *Keepers of the Earth.* Golden, CO: Fulcrum, 1988.

Cahokia. Lincoln: University of Nebraska Press, 1997.

Calloway, Colin G. *The Abenaki.* New York: Chelsea House Publishers, 1989.

Calloway, Colin G., ed. *Dawnland Encounters: Indians and Europeans in Northern New England.* Hanover, NH: University Press of New England, 1991.

Calloway, Colin G. *The World Turned Upside Down: Indian Voices from Early America.* Boston: St. Martin's Press, 1994.

Campisi, Jack. *The Mashpee Indians: Tribe on Trial.* Syracuse, NY: Syracuse University Press, 1991.

Carlisle, Richard. *The Illustrated Encyclopedia of Mankind.* New York: Marshall Cavendish, 1984.

Carlo, Poldine. *Nulato: An Indian Life on the Yukon.* Caldwell, ID: Caxton Printers, 1983.

Carlson, Richard G., ed. *Rooted Like the Ash Trees: New England Indians and the Land.* Naugatuck, CT: Eagle Wing Press, 1987.

Carter, Cecile Elkins. *Caddo Indians: Where We Come From.* Norman: University of Oklahoma Press, 1995.

Carter, Sarah. "Chapter 19—'We Must Farm to Enable Us to Live': The Plains Cree and Agriculture to 1900." *Native Peoples: The Canadian Experience.* Toronto: McClellan & Stewart, 1986.

Case, David S. *Alaska Natives and American Laws.* University of Alaska Press, 1984.

Cash, Joseph H. and Gerald W. Wolff. *The Comanche People.* Phoenix, AZ: Indian Tribal Series, 1974.

Castille, George Pierre, ed. *The Indians of Puget Sound.* Seattle: University of Washington Press, 1985.

Castillo, Edward D. and R. Jackson. *Indians, Franciscans, and Spanish Colonization: The Impact of the Mission System on California Indians.* Albuquerque: University of New Mexico Press, 1995.

Catlin, George. *Letters and Notes on the Manners, Customs, and Conditions of North American Indians.* Volume 2 (unabridged republication of the fourth [1844] edition). New York: Dover Publications, 1973.

Catlin, George. *North American Indians.* New York: Viking Press, 1989.

Chamberlain, Von Del. *When Stars Came Down to Earth: Cosmology of the Skidi Pawnee Indians of North America.* Los Altos, CA: Ballena Press and College Park: Center for Archaeoastronomy, University of Maryland, 1982.

Chalfant, William Y. *Without Quarter: The Wichita Expedition and the Fight on Crooked Creek.* Norman: University of Oklahoma Press, 1991.

Champagne, Duane, ed. *Chronology of Native North American History: From Pre-Columbian Times to the Present.* Detroit: Gale Research, 1994.

Champagne, Duane, ed. *Native America: Portrait of the Peoples.* Detroit: Visible Ink Press, 1994.

Champagne, Duane, ed. *The Native North American Almanac.* Detroit: Gale Research Inc., 1994.

Charlebois, Peter. *The Life of Louis Riel.* Toronto: New Canada Press, 1978.

Childers, Robert and Mary Kancewick. "The Gwich'in (Kutchin): Conservation and Cultural Protection in the Arctic Borderlands." Anchorage: Gwich'in Steering Committee, n.d.

Cleland, Charles E. *Rites of Conquest: The History and Culture of Michigan's Native Americans.* Ann Arbor: University of Michigan Press, 1992.

Clifton, James A. *The Prairie People: Continuity and Change in Potawatomi Indian Culture 1665–1965.* Lawrence: The Regents Press of Kansas, 1977.

Clifton, James A., *Star Woman and Other Shawnee Tales.* Lanham, MD: University Press of America, 1984.

Clifton, James A., George L. Cornell, and James M. McClurken. *People of the Three Fires: The Ottawa, Potawatomi and Ojibway of Michigan.* Grand Rapids, MI: Grand Rapids Inter-Tribal Council, 1986.

Cole, D. C. *The Chiricahua Apache 1846–1876: From War to Reservation.* Albuquerque: University of New Mexico Press, 1988.

Cole, Douglas. *Captured Heritage: The Scramble for Northwest Coast Artifacts.* Seattle: University of Washington Press, 1985.

Cook, Sherburne F. *The Conflict between the California Indian and White Civilization.* Berkeley: University of California Press, 1967.

Cordere, Helen, ed. *Kwakiutl Ethnography.* Chicago: University of Chicago Press, 1966.

Corkran, David H. *The Creek Frontier: 1540–1783.* Norman: University of Oklahoma Press, 1967.

Cotterill, R. S. *The Southern Indians: The Story of the Civilized Tribes Before Removal.* Norman: University of Oklahoma Press, 1954.

Covington, James W. *The Seminoles of Florida.* Gainsville: University of Florida Press, 1993.

Cox, Bruce Alden, ed. *Native People, Native Lands: Canadian Indians, Inuit and Métis.* Ottawa: Carleton University Press, 1987.

Crane, Verner W. *The Southern Frontier,* Greenwood, CT: Greenwood Press, 1969.

Crowder, David L. *Tendoy, Chief of the Lemhis.* Caldwell, ID: Caxton Publishers, 1969.

Crum, Steven J. *The Road On Which We Came.* Salt Lake City: University of Utah Press, 1994.

Curtis, Edward S. *The North American Indian.* Reprint. New York: Johnson Reprint Corporation, 1970.

Cushman, H. B. *History of the Choctaw, Chickasaw, and Natchez Indians.* New York: Russell & Russell, 1972.

Cvpvkke, Holátte (C. B. Clark). "'Drove Off Like Dogs'—Creek Removal." *Indians of the Lower South: Past and Present.* Ed. John K. Mahon. Pensacola, FL: Gulf Coast History and Humanities Conference, 1975.

D'Azevedo, Warren L., ed. *The Handbook of North American Indians,* Vol. 11: *Great Basin.* Washington, DC: Smithsonian Institution, 1986.

Dahl, Jens. *Indigenous Peoples of the Arctic.* Copenhagen: The Nordic Council, 1993.

Dauenhauer, Nora Marks and Richard Dauenhauer. *Haa Kusteeyí, Our Culture: Tlingit Life Stories.* Seattle: University of Washington Press; and Juneau, AK: Sealaska Heritage Foundation, 1994.

Dauenhauer, Nora Marks and Richard Dauenhauer. *Haa Tuwunáagu Yís, for Healing Our Spirit: Tlingit Oratory.* Seattle: University of Washington Press; and Juneau, AK: Sealaska Heritage Foundation, 1990.

Davis, Mary B., ed. *Native America in the Twentieth Century: An Encyclopedia.* New York: Garland Publishing, 1994.

Dawson, Dawn P. and Harvey Markowitz, eds. *Ready Reference: American Indians.* Pasadena, CA: Salem Press, 1995.

Deacon, Belle. *Engithidong Xugixudhoy: Their Stories of Long Ago: Told in Deg Hit'an Athabaskan by Belle Deacon.* Fairbanks: Alaska Native Language Center, 1987.

Deans, James. *Tales from the Totems of the Hidery,* Volume 2. Chicago: Archives of the International Folk-Lore Association, 1899.

Debo, Angie. *A History of the Indians of the United States.* Norman: University of Oklahoma Press, 1970.

Debo, Angie. *The Rise and Fall of the Choctaw Republic,* Second edition. Norman: University of Oklahoma Press, 1961.

Denig, Edwin Thompson. *Five Indian Tribes of the Upper Missouri: Sioux, Arikaras, Assiniboines, Crees, Crows.* Ed. John C. Ewers. Norman: University of Oklahoma Press, 1961.

Densmore, Frances. *Chippewa Customs.* St. Paul: Minnesota Historical Society Press, 1929; reprinted, 1979.

Densmore, Frances. *Choctaw Music* (Bulletin 136 of the Bureau of American Ethnology). DaCapo Press, 1936, reprint 1972.

Densmore, Francis. *Papago Music.* New York: Da Capo Press, 1972.

DeRosier, Arthur H. Jr. *The Removal of the Choctaw Indians.* Knoxville: University of Tennessee Press, 1970.

DeWald, Terry. *The Papago Indians and Their Basketry.* Tucson, AZ: DeWald, c. 1979.

Diedrich, Mark, *Dakota Oratory.* Rochester, MN: Coyote Books, 1989.

Dobyns, Henry F. *The Papago People.* Phoenix, Indian Tribal Series, c. 1972.

Dobyns, Henry F. *Papagos in the Cotton Fields, 1950.* Tucson, AZ: University of Arizona, Department of Anthropology, 1951.

Dockstader, Frederick J. *Great Native American Indians, Profiles in Life, and Leadership.* New York: Van Nostrand Runhold, Co., 1977.

Doherty, Robert. *Disputed Waters: Native Americans and the Great Lakes Fishery.* Lexington: University Press of Kentucky, 1990.

Doig, Ivan. *Winter Brothers.* New York: Harcourt Brace Jovanovich, 1980.

Driben, Paul. *We Are Métis.* New York: AMS Press, 1985.

Drucker, Philip and Robert F. Heizer. *To Make My Name Good: A Reexamination of the Southern Kwakiutl Potlatch.* Berkeley: University of California Press, 1967.

Duke, Philip. *Points in Time: Structure and Event in a Late Northern Plains Hunting Society.* Niwot: University Press of Colorado, 1991.

Dutton, Bertha P. *American Indians of the Southwest*. Albuquerque: University of New Mexico Press, 1983.

Dutton, Bertha P. *Indians of the American Southwest*. Englewood Cliffs, NJ: Prentice-Hall, 1975.

Eagle/Walking Turtle (Gary McLain). *Indian America: A Traveler's Companion,* Third edition. Santa Fe, NM: John Muir Publications, 1993.

Eastman, Charles A. *Old Indian Days*. Lincoln: University of Nebraska Press, 1991.

Eastman, Charles A. and Elaine Goodale Eastman. *Wigwam Evenings: Sioux Folk Tales Retold*. Lincoln: University of Nebraska Press, 1990.

Eckert, Allan W., *A Sorrow in Our Heart: The Life of Tecumseh*. New York: Bantam, 1992.

Edmunds, R. David. *The Potawatomi: Keepers of the Fire*. Norman: University of Oklahoma Press, 1978.

Edwards, R. David and Joseph L. Peyser. *The Fox Wars: The Mesquakie Challenge to New France*. Norman: University of Oklahoma Press, 1993.

Eells, Myron. *The Indians of Puget Sound: The Notebooks of Myron Eells*. Ed. George B. Castile. Seattle: University of Washington Press, 1985.

Eggan Fred. *The American Indian: Perspectives for the Study of Social Change*. New York: University of Cambridge Press, 1966.

Elliot, Michael L. *New Mexico State Monument: Jemez*. Santa Fe: Museum of New Mexico Press, 1993.

Elmendorf, W. W. *The Structure of Twana Culture*. Pullman: Washington State University, 1960.

Elmendorf, W. W. *Twana Narratives: Native Historical Accounts of a Coast Salish Culture*. Seattle: University of Washington Press, 1993.

Emmons, George Thornton. *The Tlingit Indians*. Seattle: University of Washington Press, 1991.

Erdoes, Richard. *The Rain Dance People*. New York: Alfred A. Knopf, 1976.

Ewers, John C. *Plains Indian History and Culture*. Norman: University of Oklahoma Press, 1997.

Fairbanks, Charles H. *The Florida Seminole People*. Phoenix: Intertribal Series, 1973.

Fehrenbach, T. R. *Comanches: Destruction of a People*. New York: Alfred A. Knopf, 1974.

Feit, Harvey A. "Chapter 8—Hunting and the Quest for Power: The James Bay Cree and Whitemen in the Twentieth Century." *Native Peoples: The Canadian Experience*. Toronto: McClellan & Stewart, 1986.

Fejes, Claire. *Villagers: Athabaskan Indian Life Along the Yukon*. New York: Random House, 1981.

The First Americans. Richmond, Virginia: Time-Life Books, 1992.

Fitting, James E. *The Archaeology of Michigan: A Guide to the Prehistory of the Great Lakes Region*. New York: Natural History Press for the American Museum of Natural History, 1969.

Fixico, Donald. "Tribal Leaders and the Demand for Natural Energy Resources on Reservation Lands." *The Plains Indians of the Twentieth Century. Ed. Peter Iverson. Norman: University of Oklahoma Press, 1985.*

Fontana, Bernard L. and John Paul Schaefer. *Of Earth and Little Rain: The Papago Indians*. Flagstaff, AZ: Northland Press, c. 1981.

Forbes, Jack D. *Apache, Navajo, and Spaniard*. Norman: University of Oklahoma Press, 1969, 1994.

Ford, Richard, R. *An Ecological Analysis Involving the Population of San Juan Pueblo, New Mexico*. New York: Garland Publishing, 1992.

Foreman, Grant. *The Five Civilized Tribes*. Norman: University of Oklahoma, 1934.

Fowler, Loretta. *Shared Symbols, Contested Meanings: Gros Ventre Culture and History, 1778–1984*. Ithaca, NY: Cornell University Press, 1987.

Franklin, Robert J. and Pamela A. Bunte. *The Paiute*. New York: Chelsea House, 1990.

Fredenberg, Ralph. "Indian Self-Determination." *Hearings before the Committee on Indian Affairs,* United States Senate. 73d Congress, 2d Session. On S. 2755 and S. 3645, Part 2: pp. 110–13, 1934.

Frey, Rodney. *The World of the Crow Indians: As Driftwood Lodges*. Norman: University of Oklahoma Press, 1987.

Fried, Jacob. "Aboriginal Population of Western Washington State." *Coast Salish and Western Washington Indians III.* Ed. David Agee Horr. New York: Garland Publishing, 1974.

Friesen, Gerald. *The Canadian Prairies: A History.* Lincoln: University of Nebraska Press, 1984.

Galens, Judy, Anna Sheets, and Robyn V. Young, editors. *Gale Encyclopedia of Multicultural America.* Detroit: Gale Research, 1995.

Gardener, Lion. "Lieft Lion Gardener: His Relation of the Pequot Warres (1660)." *Massachusetts Historical Society Collections,* third series, Vol. 3 (1833): pp. 131–60.

Garfield, Viola E. and Linn A. Forrest. *The Wolf and The Raven: Totem Poles of Southeastern Alaska.* Seattle: University of Washington Press, 1993.

Gibbs, George. *Indian Tribes of Washington Territory.* Fairfield, WA: Ye Galleon Press, 1972.

Gibson, Arrell M. *The Chickasaws.* Norman: University of Oklahoma, 1971.

Gifford, E. W. "Californian Kinship Terminologies." *University of California Publications in American Archaeology and Ethnology.* Vol. 18, No. 1. Reprint of Berkeley: University of California Press, 1922.

Gill, Sam D. and Irene F. Sullivan. *Dictionary of Native American Mythology.* London: Oxford University Press, 1992.

Giraud, Marcel. *The Métis in the Canadian West.* Translated by George Woodcock. Lincoln: University of Nebraska Press, 1986.

Goc, Michael J. *Land Rich Enough: An Illustrated History of Oshkosh and Winnebago County.* Northbridge, CA: Windsor Publications/Winnebago County Historical and Archaeological Society, 1988.

Goddard, Pliny Earle. "Life and Culture of the Hupa." *American Archaeology and Ethnology,* Vol. 3. Ed. Frederic Ward Putnam. Berkeley: University of California Publications, 1905. Reprint. New York: Kraus Reprint Corporation, 1964.

Goddard, Pliny Earle. "The Morphology of the Hupa Language." *American Archaeology and Ethnology,* Vol. 1. Ed. Frederic Ward Putnam. Berkeley: University of California Publications, 1903–1904. Reprint. New York: Kraus Reprint Corporation, 1964.

Goldman, Irving. *The Mouth of Heaven: An Introduction to Kwakiutl Religious Thought*. New York: John Wiley & Sons, 1975.

Goldschmidt, Walter R. and Harold E. Driver. "The Hupa White Deerskin Dance." *American Archaeology and Ethnology,* Vol. 35. Ed. A. L. Kroeber, et al. Berkeley: University of California Publications, 1943. Reprint. New York: Kraus Reprint Corporation, 1965.

Gonen, Amiram. *The Encyclopedia of the People of the World*. New York: Henry Holt and Company, 1993.

Goodwin, Glenville. *Myths and Tales of the White Mountain Apache*. New York: American Folk-lore Society, 1939.

Goodwin, Glenville. *The Social Organization of the Western Apache*. Chicago: University of Chicago Press, 1942.

Goodwin, Glenville. *Western Apache Raiding and Warfare*. Tucson: University of Arizona Press, 1971.

Grant, Bruce. *American Indians: Yesterday and Today*. New York: Dutton, 1960.

Green, Donald Edward. *The Creek People*. Phoenix: Indian Tribal Series, 1973.

Green, Michael D. *The Politics of Indian Removal*. Lincoln: University of Nebraska Press, 1982.

Gregory, H. F., ed. *The Southern Caddo: An Anthology*. New York: Garland Publishing, 1986.

Grinnell, George Bird. *Pawnee, Blackfoot and Cheyenne: History and Folklore of the Plains*. New York: Charles Scribner's Sons, 1961.

Grumet, Robert Steven. *Native Americans of the Northwest Coast: A Critical Bibliography*. Bloomington: Indiana University Press, 1979.

Haeberlin, Hermann and Erna Gunther. *The Indians of Puget Sound*. Seattle: University of Washington, 1967.

Hagan, Walter T. *The Sac and Fox Indians*. Norman: University of Oklahoma Press, 1958.

Hahn, Elizabeth. *The Creek*. Vero Beach, FL: Rourke Publications, 1992.

Hahn, Elizabeth. *The Pawnee*. Vero Beach, FL: Rourke Publications, 1992.

Haines, Francis. *The Nez Perces*. Norman: University of Oklahoma Press, 1955.

Haines, Francis. *The Plains Indians: Their Origins, Migrations, and Cultural Development*. New York: Thomas Y. Crowell Company, 1976.

Halbert, Henry S. "Courtship and Marriage Among the Choctaws of Mississippi (1882)." *A Choctaw Source Book*. New York: Garland Publishing, 1985.

Hale, Duane K. *Turtle Tales: Oral Traditions of the Delaware Tribe of Western Oklahoma*. Delaware Tribe of Oklahoma Press, 1984.

Harlow, Neal. *California Conquered: War and Peace on the Pacific, 1846–1850*. Berkeley: University of California Press, 1982.

Harrington, M. R. *Religion and Ceremonies of the Lenape*. New York: Museum of the American Indian Heye Foundation, 1921

Harrison, Julia D. *Métis, People Between Two Worlds*. Vancouver: Glenbow-Alberta Institute, 1985.

Harrod, Howard L. *Becoming and Remaining a People: Native American Religions on the Northern Plains*. Tucson: University of Arizona Press, 1995.

Haugh, Solanus. *Papago, the Desert People*. Washington, DC: Bureau of Catholic Indian Missions, 1958.

Hauptman, Laurence M. *Tribes and Tribulations: Misconceptions About American Indians and Their Histories*. Albuquerque: University of New Mexico Press, 1995.

Hauptman, Laurence M. and James D. Wherry, eds. *The Pequots in Southern New England: The Fall and Rise of an American Indian Nation*. Norman: University of Oklahoma Press, 1990.

Haviland, William A. and Marjory W. Power. *The Original Vermonters: Native Inhabitants, Past and Present*. Hanover, NH: University Press of New England, 1981.

Heath, D. B., ed. *Mourt's Relation: A Journal of the Pilgrims at Plymouth* (1622). Reprint. Cambridge, MA: Applewood Books, 1986.

Heckewelder, John. *History, Manner, and Customs of the Indian Nations Who Once Inhabited Pennsylvania and the Neighbouring States*. Philadelphia: Historical Society of Pennsylvania, 1876.

Heizer, R. F. and M. A. Whipple, *The California Indians: A Source Book*. Berkeley: University of California Press, 1951.

Heizer, R. F. and T. Kroeber, eds. *Ishi the Last Yahi: A Documentary History*. Berkeley: University of California Press, 1979.

Heizer, Robert F., ed. *The Handbook of North American Indians,* Vol. 8: *California.* Washington, DC: Smithsonian Institution, 1978.

Helm, June, ed. *The Handbook of North American Indians,* Vol. 6: *Subarctic.* Washington, DC: Smithsonian Institution, 1981.

Hickerson, Harold. *The Chippewa and Their Neighbors: A Study in Ethnohistory.* New York: Holt, Rinehart and Winston, 1970.

Hines, Donald M. *Magic in the Mountains, the Yakima Shaman: Power & Practice.* Issaquah, WA: Great Eagle Publishing, 1993.

Hippler, Arthur E. and John R. Wood. *The Subarctic Athabascans.* Fairbanks: University of Alaska, 1974.

Hodge, Frederick Webb. *Handbook of American Indians North of Mexico.* New York: Pageant Books, 1959.

Hoig, Stan. *Tribal Wars of the Southern Plains.* Norman: University of Oklahoma Press, 1993.

Hoijer, Harry. *Apachean Culture History and Ethnology.* Eds. Keith H. Basso and Morris E. Opler. Tucson: University of Arizona Press, 1971.

Hoijer, Harry. *Chiricahua and Mescalero Apache Texts.* Chicago: University of Chicago Press, 1938.

Holt, Ronald L. *Beneath These Red Cliffs: An Ethnohistory of the Utah Paiutes.* Albuquerque: University of New Mexico Press, 1992.

Hoover, Herbert T. *The Yankton Sioux.* New York: Chelsea House, 1988.

Hornung, Rick. *One Nation Under the Gun: Inside the Mohawk Civil War.* New York: Pantheon Books, 1992.

Hothem, Lar. *Treasures of the Mound Builders: Adena and Hopewell Artifacts of Ohio.* Lancaster, Ohio: Hothem House Books, 1989.

Howard, James H., *Shawnee! The Ceremonialism of a Native American Tribe and Its Cultural Background.* Athens: Ohio University Press, 1981.

Hoxie, Frederick E. *The Crow.* New York: Chelsea House, 1989.

Hoxie, Frederick E., ed. *Encyclopedia of North American Indians.* Boston: Houghton Mifflin Company, 1996.

Hoyt, Anne Kelley. *The Bibliography of the Chickasaw.* Metuchen, New Jersey: The Scarecrow Press, 1987.

Hrdlicka, Ales. *Physical Anthropology of the Lenape or Delawares, and of the Eastern Indians in General.* Washington, DC: U.S. Government Printing Office, 1916.

Hudson, Charles. *The Southeastern Indians.* Knoxville: University of Tennessee Press, 1976.

Hudson, Peter J. "Choctaw Indian Dishes (1939)." *A Choctaw Source Book.* New York: Garland Publishing, 1985: pp. 333–35.

Hudson, Travis and Ernest Underhay. *Crystals in the Sky: An Intellectual Odyssey Involving Chumash Astronomy, Cosmology and Rock Art.* Socorro, NM: Ballena Press, 1978.

Hyde, George E. *Indians of the Woodlands: From Prehistoric Times to 1725.* Norman: University of Oklahoma Press, 1962.

Ignacio, Amera. "Her Remark Offended Me." *Native Heritage: Personal Accounts by American Indians, 1790 to the Present.* Ed. Arlene Hirschfelder. New York: Macmillan, 1995.

Indian America; A Traveler's Companion. Santa Fe: John Muir Publications, 1989.

Indian Reservations: A State and Federal Handbook. Jefferson, NC: McFarland & Co., 1974.

Iverson, Peter. *The Plains Indians of the Twentieth Century.* Norman: University of Oklahoma Press, 1986.

Ives, John, W. *A Theory of Northern Athapaskan Prehistory.* Boulder, CO: Westview Press, 1990.

Jennings, Francis. *The Invasion of America: Indians, Colonization, and the Cant of Conquest.* Chapel Hill: University of North Carolina Press, 1975.

Joe, Rita and Lynn Henry. *Song of Rita Joe: Autobiography of a Mi'kmaq Poet.* Lincoln: University of Nebraska Press, 1996.

Johansen, Bruce E. *Life and Death in Mohawk Country.* Golden, CO: North American Press, 1993.

Johnson, Elias. *Legends, Traditions and Laws of the Iroquois, or Six Nations, and History of the Tuscarora Indians* (1881). Reprint. New York: AMS Press, 1978.

Johnson, John F. C., ed. *Eyak Legends: Stories and Photographs.* Anchorage: Chugach Heritage Foundation, n.d.

Johnson, Michael G. *The Native Tribes of North America: A Concise Encyclopedia.* New York: Macmillan, 1994.

Johnston, Basil H. *Tales the Elders Told: Ojibway Legends.* Toronto: Royal Ontario Museum, 1981.

Jonaitis, Aldona. *Art of the Northern Tlingit.* Seattle, Washington: University of Washington Press, 1986.

Jonaitis, Aldona, ed. *Chiefly Feasts: The Enduring Kwakiutl Potlatch.* New York: American Museum of Natural History, 1991.

Jorgensen, Joseph G. *Salish Language and Culture.* Bloomington: Indiana University Publications, 1969.

Jorgensen, Joseph G. *The Sun Dance Religion: Power for the Powerless.* Chicago: University of Chicago Press, 1972.

Joseph, Alice, Jane Chesky, and Rosamond B. Spicer. *The Desert People: A Study of the Papago Indians.* Chicago, IL: University of Chicago Press, 1974.

Josephy, Alvin M. Jr. *500 Nations: An Illustrated History of North American Indians.* New York: Alfred A. Knopf, 1994.

Josephy, Alvin M. Jr. *The Indian Heritage of America.* New York: Alfred A. Knopf, 1968.

Josephy, Alvin M. Jr. *The Nez Perce Indians and the Opening of the Northwest.* New Haven, CT: Yale University Press, 1965.

Josephy, Alvin M. Jr. *Now That the Buffalo's Gone: A Study of Today's American Indians.* New York: Alfred A. Knopf, 1982.

Kalifornsky, Peter. *A Dena'ina Legacy: K'tl'egh'i Sukdu: The Collected Writings of Peter Kalifornsky.* Eds. James Kari and Alan Boraas. Fairbanks: Alaska Native Language Center, 1991.

Kappler, Charles J. *Indian Affairs, Laws, and Treaties,* four volumes. Washington, DC: U.S. Government Printing Office, 1929.

Kari, James, ed. *Athabaskan Stories from Anvik: Rev. John W. Chapman's "Ten'a Texts and Tales."* Fairbanks: Alaska Native Language Center, 1981.

Kari, James, translator and editor. "When They Were Killed at 'Lake That Has an Arm' (Kluane Lake)." *Tatl'ahwt'aenn Nenn': The Headwaters Peoples Country: Narratives of the Upper Ahtna Athabaskans.* Fairbanks: Alaska Native Language Center, 1985.

Kasner, Leone Leston. *Siletz: Survival for an Artifact.* Dallas OR: Itemizer-Observer, 1977.

Kennedy, Roger G. *Hidden Cities: The Discovery and Loss of Ancient American Civilization.* New York: Macmillan, 1994.

Kenner, Charles L. *A History of New Mexican-Plains Indian Relations.* Norman: University of Oklahoma Press, 1969, 1994.

Kent, Zachary, *Tecumseh.* Chicago, IL: Children's Press, 1992.

Kidwell, Clara Sue and Charles Roberts. *The Choctaws: A Critical Bibliography.* Bloomington: Indiana University Press for the Newberry Library, 1980.

Kirk, Ruth and Richard D. Daugherty. *Hunter of the Whale.* New York: William Morrow, 1974.

Klein, Barry T. *Reference Encyclopedia of the American Indian,* Seventh edition. West Nyack, NY: Todd Publications, 1995.

Klein, Laura F. and Lillian A. Ackerman. *Women and Power in Native North America.* Norman: University of Oklahoma, 1995.

Kluckhohn, Clyde and Dorothea Leighton. *The Navaho.* 1946. Revised edition. Cambridge, MA: Harvard University Press, 1974.

Korp, Maureen. *The Sacred Geography of the American Mound Builders.* New York: Edwin Mellen Press, 1990.

Kraft, Herbert C. *The Lenape: Archaeology, History, and Ethnography.* Newark: New Jersey Historical Society, 1986.

Kraft, Herbert C. *The Lenape Indians of New Jersey.* South Orange, NJ: Seton Hall University Museum, 1987.

Krech, Shepard III, ed. *Indians, Animals and the Fur Trade.* Athens: University of Georgia Press, 1981.

Kroeber, Alfred L. "The Achomawi and Atsugewi," "The Chilula.," "The Luiseño: Elements of Civilization," "The Luiseño: Organization of Civilization," "The Miwok," and "The Pomo." *Handbook of the Indians of California.* Washington, DC: U.S. Government Printing Office, 1925.

Krupp, E. C. *Beyond the Blue Horizon: Myths & Legends of the Sun, Moon, Stars, & Planets.* New York: Oxford University Press, 1991.

Lacey, Theresa Jensen. *The Pawnee.* New York: Chelsea House Publishers, 1996.

Ladd, Edmund J. "Zuñi Religion and Philosophy." *Zuñi & El Morro.* Santa Fe: SAR Press, 1983.

Langdon, Steve J. *The Native People of Alaska*. Anchorage: Greatland Graphics, 1993.

Laubin, Reginald and Gladys Laubin. *Indian Dances of North America: Their Importance to Indian Life*. Norman: University of Oklahoma Press, 1976.

Laughlin, William S. "The Aleut-Eskimo Community." *The North American Indians: A Sourcebook*. Ed. Roger C. Owen. New York: Macmillan, 1967.

Leach, Douglas E. *Flintlock and Tomahawk: New England in King Philip's War*. New York: Macmillan, 1959.

Leitch, Barbara A. *A Concise Dictionary of Indian Tribes of North America*. Algonac, MI: Reference Publications, 1979.

Lewis, Anna. *Chief Pushmataha, American Patriot: The Story of the Choctaws' Struggle for Survival*. New York: Exposition Press, 1959.

Lewis, David Rich. *Neither Wolf Nor Dog: American Indians, Environment, and Agrarian Change*. Oxford: Oxford University Press, 1994.

Liptak, Karen. *North American Indian Ceremonies*. New York: Franklin Watts, 1992.

Lowie, Robert H. *The Crow Indians*. Lincoln: University of Nebraska Press, 1983.

Lowie, Robert H. *Indians of the Plains*. Garden City, NY: Natural History Press, 1963.

Lucius, William A. and David A. Breternitz. *Northern Anasazi Ceramic Styles: A Fieldguide for Identification*. Center for Indigenous Studies in the Americas Publications in Anthropology, 1992.

Lund, Annabel. *Heartbeat: World Eskimo Indian Olympics: Alaska Native Sport and Dance Traditions*. Juneau: Fairweather Press, 1986.

Lurie, Nancy Oestreich. "Weetamoo, 1638–1676." *North American Indian Lives*. Milwaukee: Milwaukee Public Library, 1985.

MacEwan, Grant. *Métis Makers of History*. Saskatoon: Western Producer Prairie Books, 1981.

Madsen, Brigham D. *The Shoshoni Frontier and the Bear River Massacre*. Salt Lake City: University of Utah Press, 1985.

Mahon, John K. *History of the Second Seminole War 1835–1842*. Gainsville: University of Florida Press, 1967.

Maillard, Antoine Simon and Joseph M. Bellenger. *Grammaire de la Langue Mikmaque*. English translation published as *Grammar of the Mikmaque Language*. New York: AMS Press, 1970.

Mails, Thomas E. *The Cherokee People: The Story of the Cherokees from Earliest Origins to Contemporary Times*. Tulsa, OK: Council Oak Books, 1992.

Mails, Thomas E. *The Mystic Warriors of the Plains: The Culture, Arts, Crafts and Religion of the Plains Indians*. Tulsa: Council Oaks Books, 1991.

Mails, Thomas E. *Peoples of the Plains*. Tulsa, OK: Council Oak Books, 1997.

Mails, Thomas E. *The Pueblo Children of the Earth Mother.* Vol. 2. Garden City, NY: Doubleday, 1983.

Malinowksi, Sharon, ed. *Notable Native Americans*. Detroit: Gale Research, 1995.

Malinowski, Sharon and Simon Glickman, eds. *Native North American Biography*. Detroit: U•X•L, 1996.

Malone, Patrick M. *The Skulking Way of War: Technology and Tactics Among the New England Indians*. Lanham, MA: Madison Books, 1991.

Mandelbaum, David G. *The Plains Cree: An Ethnographic, Historical, and Comparative Study*. Regina, Saskatchewan: Canadian Plains Research Center, 1979.

Markowitz, Harvey, ed. *American Indians,* Pasadena, CA: Salem Press, 1995.

Marquis, Arnold. *A Guide to America's Indians: Ceremonials, Reservations, and Museums*. Norman: University of Oklahoma Press, 1974.

Marriott, Alice L. *The Ten Grandmothers*. Norman: University of Oklahoma Press, 1945.

Marriott, Alice and Carol K. Rachlin. *Plains Indian Mythology*. New York: Thomas Y. Crowell, 1975.

Martin, Calvin. *Keepers of the Game: Indian-Animal Relationships and the Fur Trade*. Berkeley: University of California Press, 1978.

Matthiessen, Peter. *In the Spirit of Crazy Horse*. New York: Viking Penguin, 1980.

Maxwell, James A., ed. *America's Fascinating Indian Heritage*. New York: The Reader's Digest Association, 1978.

Mayhall, Mildred P. *The Kiowas*. Norman: University of Oklahoma Press, 1962.

Mays, Buddy. *Indian Villages of the Southwest*. San Francisco: Chronicle Books, 1985.

McBride, Bunny. *Molly Spotted Elk: A Penobscot in Paris*. Norman and London: University of Oklahoma Press, 1995.

McFadden, Steven. *Profiles in Wisdom: Native Elders Speak About the Earth*. Sante Fe: Bear & Co., 1991.

McFee, Malcolm. *Modern Blackfeet: Montanans on a Reservation*. New York: Holt, Rinehart and Winston, 1972.

McGinnis, Anthony. *Counting Coup and Cutting Horses: Intertribal Warfare on the Northern Plains 1738–1889*. Evergreen, CO: Cordillera Press, 1990.

McKee, Jesse O. and Jon A. Schlenker. *The Choctaws: Cultural Evolution of a Native American Tribe*. Jackson: University Press of Mississippi, 1980.

McKennan, Robert, A. "The Upper Tanana Indians." *Yale University Publications in Anthropology: 55*. New Haven, CT: Yale University, 1959.

Melody, Michael E. *The Apaches: A Critical Bibliography*. Bloomington: Indiana University Press, 1977.

Merriam, C. Hart. "The Luiseño: Observations on Mission Indians." *Studies of California Indians*. Edited by the Staff of the Department of Anthropology of the University of California. Berkeley: University of California Press, 1962.

Meyer, Roy W. *History of the Santee Sioux: United States Indian Policy on Trial*. Lincoln: University of Nebraska Press, 1993.

Miller, Bruce W. *Chumash: A Picture of Their World*. Los Osos, CA: Sand River Press, 1988.

Miller, Jay. *The Delaware*. Chicago: Childrens Press, 1994.

Milliken, Randall. *A Time of Little Choice: The Disintegration of Tribal Culture in the San Francisco Bay Area, 1769–1810*. Menlo Park, CA: Ballena Press, 1995.

Milloy, John S. *The Plains Cree: Trade, Diplomacy and War, 1790 to 1870*. Winnipeg: University of Manitoba Press, 1988.

Minge, Ward Alan. *Acoma: Pueblo in the Sky*. Albuquerque: University of New Mexico Press, 1976.

Minority Rights Group. *Polar Peoples: Self Determination and Development*. London: Minority Rights Publications, 1994.

Mississippian Communities and Households. Tuscaloosa: University of Alabama Press, 1995.

Momaday, N. Scott. *The Way to Rainy Mountain*. Albuquerque: University of New Mexico Press, 1969.

Moore, John H. *The Cheyenne Nation: A Social and Demographic History*. Lincoln: University of Nebraska Press, 1987.

Moorhead, Max L. *The Apache Frontier: Jacobo Ugarte and Spanish-Indian Relations in Northern New Spain, 1769–1791*. Norman: University of Oklahoma Press, 1968.

Moquin, Wayne, ed. *Great Documents in American Indian History*. New York: Da Capo Press, 1973.

Morgan, Lewis H. *League of the Ho-de-no-sau-nee or Iroquois*. New Haven, CT: Human Relations Area Files, 1954: p. 243.

Morrison, R. Bruce and C. Roderick Wilson, eds. *Native Peoples: The Canadian Experience*. Toronto: McClellan & Stewart, 1986.

Murie, James R. *Ceremonies of the Pawnee*. Smithsonian Contributions to Anthropology, No. 27. Washington, DC: Smithsonian Institution, 1981. Reprint. Lincoln: University of Nebraska Press for the American Indian Studies Research Institute, 1989.

Murphy, Robert F. and Yolanda Murphy. "Shoshone-Bannock Subsistence and Society." *Anthropological Records*. 16:7. Berkeley: University of California Press, 1960.

Myers, Arthur. *The Pawnee*. New York: F. Watts, 1993.

Myers, William Starr, ed. *The Story of New Jersey,* Volume 1. Ed. New York: Lewis Historical Publishing Company, 1945.

Mysteries of the Ancient Americas: The New World Before Columbus. Pleasantville, NY: The Reader's Digest Association, 1986.

Nabakov, Peter and Robert Easton. *Native American Architecture.* New York: Oxford University Press, 1989.

Nairne, Thomas. *Nairne's Mushogean Journals: The 1708 Expedition to the Mississippi River.* Jackson: University Press of Mississippi, 1988.

Native Cultures in Alaska. Anchorage: Alaska Geographic Society, 1996.

Newcomb, W. W. Jr. *The Indians of Texas: From Prehistoric to Modern Times.* Austin: University of Texas Press, 1961.

Newkumet, Vynola Beaver and Howard L. Meredith. *Hasinai: A Traditional History of the Caddo Confederacy.* College Station: Texas A & M University Press, 1988.

Noble, David Grant. *Pueblos, Villages, Forts & Trails: A Guide to New Mexico's Past.* Albuquerque: University of New Mexico Press, 1994.

Northway, Walter. *Walter Northway.* Fairbanks: Alaska Native Language Center, 1987.

Norton, Jack. *Genocide in Northwestern California: When Our Worlds Cried.* San Francisco: Indian Historian Press, 1979.

O'Brien, Sharon. *American Indian Tribal Governments.* Norman: University of Oklahoma Press, 1989.

Olmsted, D. L. *Achumawi Dictionary.* Berkeley: University of California Press, 1966.

Olson, Ronald L. *The Quinault Indians.* Seattle: University of Washington Press, 1967.

O'Neill, Laurie A. *The Shawnees: People of the Eastern Woodlands.* Brookfield, CT: The Millbrook Press, 1995.

Opler, Morris Edward. *An Apache Life-Way.* New York: Cooper Square Publishers, 1965.

Orr, Charles, ed. *History of the Pequot War.* Cleveland: Helman-Taylor, 1897.

Ortiz, Alfonso, ed. *The Handbook of North American Indians,* Vol. 10: *Southwest.* Washington, DC: Smithsonian Institution, 1983.

Ortiz, Alfonso. *The Pueblo.* New York: Chelsea House Publishers, 1992.

Osgood, Cornelius. "Ingalik Mental Culture." *Yale University Publications in Anthropology: 56.* New Haven, CT: Yale University, 1959.

Oswalt, Wendell H. "The Crow: Plains Warriors and Bison Hunters." *This Land Was Theirs: A Study of North American Indians.* Mountain View, CA: Mayfield Publishing, 1988.

Owen, Roger C., James J. F. Deetz, and Anthony D. Fisher, eds. *A Guide to Indian Tribes of the Pacific Northwest.* Norman: University of Oklahoma Press, 1986.

Owen, Roger C., James J. F. Deetz, and Anthony D. Fisher, eds. *Indians of the Pacific Northwest: A History.* Norman: University of Oklahoma Press, 1981.

Owen, Roger C., James J. F. Deetz, and Anthony D. Fisher, eds. *The North American Indians: A Sourcebook.* New York: MacMillan, 1967.

Parsons, Elsie Clews. "Notes on the Caddo." *Memoirs of the American Anthropological Association,* No. 57. Menasha, WI: American Anthropological Association, 1941.

Parsons, Elsie Clews. *Pueblo Mothers and Children.* Ed. Barbara A. Babcock. Santa Fe: Ancient City Press, 1991.

Parsons, Elsie Clews. *The Social Organization of the Tewa of New Mexico.* American Anthropological Association Memoirs, Nos. 36–39. Reprint. New York: Kraus, 1964.

Patencio, Francisco. *Stories and Legends of the Palm Springs Indians As Told to Margaret Boynton.* Los Angeles: Times-Mirror Press, 1943.

Paterek, Josephine. *Encyclopedia of American Indian Costume.* Santa Barbara: ABC-CLIO, 1994.

Pauketat, Timothy R. *Temples for Cahokia Lords.* Ann Arbor: University of Michigan, Museum of Anthropology, 1993.

Peat, F. David. *Lighting the Seventh Fire: The Spiritual Ways, Healing, and Science of the Native American.* NY: Carol Publishing Group, 1994.

Penney, David W. *Art of the American Indian Frontier: The Chandler-Pohrt Collection.* Seattle: University of Washington Press, 1992.

Perdue, Theda. *The Cherokee.* New York: Chelsea House Publishers, 1989.

Peroff, N. C. *Menominee Drums: Tribal Termination and Restoration, 1954–1974.* Norman: University of Oklahoma Press, 1982.

Perry, Richard J. *Apache Reservation: Indigenous Peoples and the American State.* Austin: University of Texas Press, 1993.

Perry, Richard J. *Western Apache Heritage: People of the Mountain Corridor.* Austin: University of Texas Press, 1991.

Perttula, Timothy K. "The Caddo Nation." *Archeological and Ethnohistoric Perspectives.* Austin: University of Texas Press, 1992.

Phillips, G.H. *Indians and Indian Agents: The Origins of the Reservation System in California, 1849–1852.* Norman: University of Oklahoma Press, 1997.

Place, Ann Marie. "Putting a Face on Colonization: Factionalism and Gender Politics in the Life History of Awashunkes, the 'Squaw Sachem' of Saconet." *Northeastern Indians Lives.* Ed. Robert S. Grumet. Amherst: University of Massachusetts Press, 1996.

Pond, Samuel. *The Dakota People or Sioux in Minnesota as They Were in 1834.* St. Paul: Minnesota Historical Society Press, 1986.

Pope, Saxton T. "The Medical History of Ishi." *University of California Publications in American Archaeology and Ethnology.* Vol. 13, No. 5. Berkeley: University of California Press, 1920.

Pope, Saxton T. "Yahi Archery." *University of California Publications in American Archaeology and Ethnology,* Vol. 13, No. 3. Berkeley: University of California Press, 1923.

Porter, Frank W. III. *The Coast Salish Peoples.* New York: Chelsea House Publishers, 1989.

Powers, Stephen. "The Achomawi." *Tribes of California.* Berkeley: University of California Press, 1976. Reprinted from *Contributions to North American Ethnology,* Vol. 3. Washington, DC: U.S. Government Printing Office, 1877.

Preacher, Stephen. *Anasazi Sunrise: The Mystery of Sacrifice Rock.* El Cajon, CA: The Rugged Individualist, 1992.

Press, Margaret L. "Chemehuevi: A Grammar and Lexicon." *Linguistics,* Vol. 92. Berkeley: University of California Press, 1979.

Rand, Silas Tertius. *Dictionary of the Language of the Micmac Indians, Who Reside in Nova Scotia, New Brunswick, Prince Edward Island, Cape Breton, and Newfoundland.* Halifax, Nova Scotia: Nova Scotia Print Co., 1888. Reprint. New York, Johnson Reprint Corp., 1972.

Ray, Arthur J. *Indians in the Fur Trade: Their Role as Trappers, Hunters & Middle Man in the Lands Southwest of Hudson Bay, 1660–1860.* Toronto: University of Toronto Press, 1974.

Reddy, Marlita A. *Statistical Record of Native North Americans.* Detroit: Gale Research, 1996.

Rice, Julian, ed. *Deer Women and Elk Men: The Lakota Narratives of Ella Deloria.* Albuquerque: University of New Mexico Press, 1992.

Richardson, Rupert Norval. *The Comanche Barrier to the South Plains Settlement.* Glendale, CA: Arthur H. Clarke, 1955.

Roberts, David. *In Search of the Old Ones.* New York: Simon & Schuster, 1996.

Rockwell, Wilson. *The Utes: A Forgotten People.* Denver, CO: Alan Swallow, 1956.

Rohner, Ronald P. and Evelyn C. Rohner. *The Kwakiutl: Indians of British Columbia.* New York: Holt, Rinehart and Winston, 1970.

Rollings, Willard H. *The Osage: An Ethnohistorical Study of Hegemony on the Prairie-Plains.* Columbia: University of Missouri Press, 1992.

Rountree, Helen C., ed. *Pocahontas's People: The Powhatan Indians of Virginia through Four Centuries.* Norman: University of Oklahoma Press, 1990.

Rountree, Helen C., ed. *Powhatan Foreign Relations, 1500–1722.* Charlottesville: University Press of Virginia, 1993.

Rountree, Helen C., ed. *The Powhatan Indians of Virginia: Their Native Culture.* Norman: University of Oklahoma Press, 1989.

Ruby, Robert H. *The Chinook Indians: Traders of the Lower Columbia River.* Norman: University of Oklahoma Press, 1976.

Ruby, Robert H. and John A. Brown. *A Guide to Indian Tribes of the Pacific Northwest.* Norman: University of Oklahoma Press, 1986.

Russell, Frank. *The Pima Indians.* Tucson: University of Arizona Press, 1975.

Salisbury, Richard F. *A Homeland for the Cree: Regional Development in James Bay 1971–1981.* Kingston & Montreal: McGill-Queen's University Press, 1986.

Salzmann, Zdenek. *The Arapaho Indians: A Research Guide and Bibliography.* New York: Greenwood Press, 1988.

Samuel, Cheryl. *The Chilkat Dancing Blanket*. Seattle: Pacific Search Press, 1982.

Sando, Joe S. *Pueblo Nations: Eight Centuries of Pueblo Indian History*. Santa Fe: Clear Light Publishers, 1992.

Sauter, John and Bruce Johnson. *Tillamook Indians of the Oregon Coast*. Portland OR: Binfords and Mort, 1974.

Sawchuck, Joe. *The Métis of Manitoba: Reformulation of an Ethnic Identity*. Toronto: Peter Martin Associates, 1978.

Schlesier, Karl H. "Introduction," and "Commentary: A History of Ethnic Groups in the Great Plains A.D. 500–1550." *Plains Indians, A.D. 500–1500: The Archaeological Past of Historic Groups*. Ed. Karl H. Schlesier. Norman: University of Oklahoma Press, 1994.

Schultz, Willard James. *Blackfeet and Buffalo: Memories of Life among the Indians*. Norman: University of Oklahoma Press, 1962.

Schuster, Helen. *The Yakimas: A Critical Bibliography*. Bloomington: Indiana University Press, 1982.

Segal, Charles M. and David C. Stineback, eds. *Puritans, Indians and Manifest Destiny*. New York: Putnam, 1977.

Seger, John H. *Early Days among the Cheyenne and Arapaho Indians*. Ed. Stanley Vestal. Norman: University of Oklahoma Press, 1956.

Seiler, Hansjakob. *Cahuilla Texts with an Introduction*. Bloomington: Indiana University, 1970.

Shaffer, Lynda Norene. *Native Americans Before 1492: The Moundbuilding Centers of the Eastern Woodlands*. New York: M. E. Sharpe, 1992.

Shames, Deborah, ed. *Freedom with Reservation: The Menominee Struggle to Save Their Land and People*. Madison: National Committee to Save the Menominee People and Forests/Wisconsin Indian Legal Services, 1972.

Shawano, Marlene Miller. *Native Dress of the Stockbridge Munsee Band Mohican Indians*. Stockbridge Munsee Reservation Library, n.d.

Shipek, Florence. *Pushed into the Rocks: Southern California Indian Land Tenure, 1769–1986*. Lincoln: University of Nebraska Press, 1990.

Silverberg, Robert. *The Mound Builders*. Greenwich, CT: New York Graphic Society, Ltd., 1970.

Siy, Alexandra, *The Eeyou: People of Eastern James Bay*. New York: Dillon Press, 1993.

Slickpoo, Allen P. and Deward E. Walker Jr. *Noon Nee-Me-Poo: We, the Nez Perces*. Lapwai: Nez Perce Tribe of Idaho, 1973.

Smelcer, John. "Dotson'Sa, Great Raven Makes the World." *The Raven and the Totem: Traditional Alaska Native Myths and Tales*. Anchorage: Salmon Run, 1992: pp. 124–25.

Smith, Anne M., ed. *Shoshone Tales*. Salt Lake City: University of Utah Press, 1993.

Smith, F. Todd. *The Caddo Indians: Tribes at the Convergence of Empires, 1542–1854*. College Station: University of Texas A&M Press, 1995.

Smith, Marian W. *Indians of the Urban Northwest*. New York: AMS Press, 1949.

Smith, Marian W. *The Puyallup-Nisqually*. New York: Columbia University Press, 1940.

Snow, Dean R. *The Iroquois*. Cambridge, MA: Blackwell Publishers, 1994.

Speck, Frank G. *Penobscot Man: The Life History of a Forest Tribe in Maine*. Philadelphia: University of Pennsylvania Press, 1940.

Speck, Frank G. *A Study of the Indian Big House Ceremony*. Harrisburg: Pennsylvania Historical Commission, 1931.

Spector, Janet D. *What This Awl Means: Feminist Archaeology at a Wahpeton Dakota Village*. St. Paul: Minnesota Historical Society Press, 1993.

Spicer, Edward H. *Cycles of Conquest: The Impact of Spain, Mexico, and the United States on the Indians of the Southwest, 1533–1960*. Tucson, AZ: University of Arizona Press, 1962.

Spindler, George and Louise Spindler. *Dreamers With Power: The Menomini Indians*. New York: Holt, Rinehart & Winston, 1971.

Spittal, W. G., ed. *Iroquois Women: An Anthology*. Ohsweken, Ontario: Iroqrafts Ltd., 1990.

Spradley, James P. *Guests Never Leave Hungry: The Autobiography of James Sewid, A Kwakiutl Indian*. New Haven: Yale University Press, 1969.

Statistical Data for Planning Stockbridge Munsee Reservation. Billings, MT: U.S. Department of the Interior, Bureau of Indian Affairs, 1975.

Steele, Ian K. *Warpaths: Invasions of North America.* New York: Oxford University Press, 1994.

Steward, Julian H. *Basin-Plateau Aboriginal Sociopolitical Groups.* Washington, DC: Smithsonian Institution. *The Bureau of American Ethnology Bulletin,* No. 120. Washington, DC: U.S. Government Printing Office, 1938.

Stewart, Omer C. *Peyote Religion: A History.* Norman: University of Oklahoma, 1987.

Stevens, Susan McCullough. "Passamaquoddy Economic Development in Cultural and Historical Perspective." *World Anthropology: American Indian Economic Development.* Ed. Sam Stanley. The Hague: Mouton Publishers, 1978.

Stockel, H. Henrietta. "Ceremonies and Celebrations." *Women Of the Apache Nation: Voices of Truth.* Reno: University of Nevada Press, 1991.

Subarctic. Ed. June Helm. Washington, DC: Smithsonian Institution, 1981.

Suttles, Wayne, ed. *The Handbook of North American Indians,* Vol. 7: *Northwest Coast.* Washington, DC: Smithsonian Institution, 1990.

Swanson, Earl H, ed. *Languages and Culture of Western North America.* Pocatello: Idaho State University Press, 1970.

Swanton, John Reed. *Indian Tribes of the Lower Mississippi Valley and Adjacent Coast of the Gulf of Mexico.* Washington, DC: U.S. Government Printing Office, 1911.

Swanton, John Reed. *The Indian Tribes of North America,* Vol. 1: *Northeast.* Washington, DC: Smithsonian Institution. Reprinted from: *The Bureau of American Ethnology Bulletin,* No. 145. Washington, DC: U.S. Government Printing Office, 1953.

Swanton, John Reed. *Source Material for the Social and Ceremonial Life of the Choctaw Indians.* Bulletin No. 103. Washington, DC: U.S. Government Printing Office, 1931.

Symington, Fraser. *The Canadian Indian: The Illustrated History of the Great Tribes of Canada.* Toronto: McClelland & Stewart, 1969.

Tanner, Helen H., ed. *Atlas of Great Lakes Indian History.* Norman: University of Oklahoma Press, 1987.

Tantaquidgeon, Gladys. *Folk Medicine of the Delaware and Related Algonkian Indians.* Harrisburg: Pennsylvania Historical and Museum Commission, Anthropological Series 3, 1972.

Tantaquidgeon, Gladys. *A Study of Delaware Indian Medicine Practice and Folk Beliefs.* Harrisburg: Pennsylvania Historical Commission, 1942.

Teit, James A. "The Salishan Tribes of the Western Plateaus." *Bureau of American Ethnology Annual Report.* No. 45. Ed. Franz Boas. 1927–1928.

Tennberg, Monica, ed. *Unity and Diversity in Arctic Societies.* Rovaniemi, Finland: International Arctic Social Sciences Association, 1996.

Terrell, John Upton. *American Indian Almanac.* New York: World Publishing, 1971.

Thomas, Cyrus. *Report on the Mound Explorations of the Bureau of Ethnology.* Washington, DC: Smithsonian Institution, 1894.

Thomas, David Hurst, ed. *A Great Basin Shoshonean Source Book.* New York: Garland Publishing, 1986.

Thompson, Chad. *Athabaskan Languages and the Schools: A Handbook for Teachers.* Juneau: Alaska Department of Education, 1984.

Thompson, Judy. *From the Land: Two Hundred Years of Dene Clothing.* Hull, Quebec: Canadian Museum of Civilization, 1994.

Through Indian Eyes: The Untold Story of Native American Peoples. Pleasantville, NY: Reader's Digest Association, 1995.

Tilton, Robert S. *Pocahontas: The Evolution of an American Narrative.* New York: Cambridge University Press, 1994.

Tohono O'Odham: History of the Desert People. Arizona: Papago Tribe, c1985.

Tooker, Elisabeth, ed. *An Iroquois Source Book,* Volumes 1 and 2. New York: Garland Publishing, 1985.

"Traditional and Contemporary Ceremonies, Rituals, Festivals, Music, and Dance." *Native America: Portrait of the Peoples.* Ed. Duane Champagne. Detroit: Gale Research, 1994.

Trafzer, Clifford E. *The Chinook.* New York: Chelsea House, 1990.

Trafzer, Clifford E. *Yakima, Palouse, Cayuse, Umatilla, Walla Walla, and Wanapum Indians.* Metuchen, New Jersey: Scarecrow Press, 1992.

Trigger, Bruce G., ed. *The Handbook of North American Indians, Vol. 15: Northeast.* Washington, DC: Smithsonian Institution, 1978.

Trigger, Bruce G. *Natives and Newcomers: Canada's "Heroic Age" Reconsidered.* Manchester: McGill-Queen's University Press, 1985.

Trimble, Stephen. *The People: Indians of the American Southwest.* Santa Fe: NM: Sar Press, 1993.

Tyson, Carl N. *The Pawnee People.* Phoenix: Indian Tribal Series, 1976.

Underhill, Ruth. *The Autobiography of a Papago Woman.* Menasha, WI: American Anthropological Memoirs #48, 1936.

Underhill, Ruth. *Life in the Pueblos.* Santa Fe: Ancient City Press, 1991.

Underhill, Ruth. *Singing for Power.* Tucson: University of Arizona Press, 1979.

United American Indians of New England. "National Day of Mourning." *Literature of the American Indian.* Ed. Thomas E. Sanders and Walter W. Peek. Abridged edition. Beverly Hills, CA: Glencoe Press, 1976.

The Vinland Sagas: The Norse Discovery of America. Translated by Magnus Magnusson and Hermann Palsson. Baltimore: Penguin, 1965.

Vogel, Virgil J. *American Indian Medicine.* Norman: University of Oklahoma Press, 1970.

The Wabanakis of Maine and the Maritimes: A Resource Book About Penobscot, Passamaquoddy, Maliseet, Micmac, and Abenaki Indians. Philadelphia: American Friends Service Committee (AFSC), 1989.

Waldman, Carl. *Atlas of the North American Indian.* New York: Facts On File, 1985.

Waldman, Carl. *Encyclopedia of Native American Tribes.* New York: Facts on File, 1988.

Waldman, Carl. *Who Was Who in Native American History: Indians and NonIndians From Early Contacts Through 1900.* New York: Facts on File, 1990.

Waldman, Harry, ed. "Caddo." *Encyclopedia of Indians of the Americas.* St. Clair Shores, MI: Scholarly Press, 1974.

Walens, Stanley. *Feasting with Cannibals: An Essay on Kwakiutl Cosmology*. Princeton, NJ: Princeton University Press, 1981.

Wallace, Anthony F. C. *The Death and Rebirth of the Seneca: The History and Culture of the Great Iroquois Nation, Their Destruction and Demoralization, and Their Cultural Revival at the Hands of the Indian Visionary, Handsome Lake*. New York: Knopf, 1969.

Wallace, Anthony F. C. *King of the Delawares: Teedyuscung 1700–1763*. Philadelphia: University of Pennsylvania Press, 1949.

Walthall, John A. *Moundville: An Introduction to the Archaeology of a Mississippian Chiefdom*. Tuscaloosa: University of Alabama, Alabama Museum of Natural History, 1977.

Warren, William W. *History of the Ojibway People*. St. Paul: Minnesota Historical Society Press, 1885, reprint 1984.

Waterman, Thomas T. "The Yana Indians." *University of California Publications in American Archaeology and Ethnology*, Vol. 13, No. 2. Berkeley: University of California Press, 1918.

Weatherford, Jack. *Native Roots, How the Indians Enriched America*. New York: Ballantine Books, 1991.

Wedel, Waldo R. *An Introduction to Pawnee Archeology*. Bulletin of the Smithsonian Institution, Bureau of American Ethnology, No. 112. Washington, DC: U.S. Government Printing Office, 1936. Reprint. Lincoln, NE: J & L Reprint, 1977.

Wedel, Waldo R. *Prehistoric Man on the Great Plains*. Norman: University of Oklahoma Press, 1961.

Wells, Samuel J. and Roseanna Tubby, eds. *After Removal: The Choctaw in Mississippi*. Jackson: University Press of Mississippi, 1986.

Weltfish, Gene. *The Lost Universe: Pawnee Life and Culture*. Lincoln: University of Nebraska Press, 1977.

Weslager, Clinton A. *The Delaware Indian Westward Migration*. Wallingford, PA: Middle Atlantic Press, 1978.

Weslager, Clinton A. *The Delaware Indians: A History*. New Brunswick, NJ: Rutgers University Press, 1972.

White, Leslie A. *The Acoma Indians, People of the Sky City*. Originally published in *47th Annual Report of the Bureau of American Ethnology*. Washington, DC: Smithsonian Institution, 1932; Glorieta, NM: The Rio Grande Press, 1973.

White, Raymond. "Religion and Its Role Among the Luiseño." *Native Californians: A Theoretical Retrospective.* Eds. Lowell J. Bean and Thomas C. Blackburn. Socorro, NM: Ballena Press, 1976.

White, Richard. *Land Use, Environment, and Social Change.* Seattle: University of Washington Press, 1992.

Wilbur, C. Keith. *The New England Indians.* Old Saybrook, CT: Globe Pequot Press, 1978.

Wilker, Josh. *The Lenape.* New York: Chelsea House Publishers, 1994.

Wilson, Terry P. *The Underground Reservation: Osage Oil.* Lincoln: University of Nebraska Press, 1985.

Wissler, Clark. *Indians of the United States.* New York: Doubleday, 1940.

Witherspoon, Gary. *Language and Art in the Navajo Universe.* Ann Arbor: University of Michigan Press, 1977.

Wolcott, Harry F. *A Kwakiutl Village and School.* Prospect Heights, IL: Waveland Press, 1984.

Wood, Peter H., Gregory A. Waselkov, and M. Thomas Hatley, eds. *Powhatan's Mantle: Indians in the Colonial Southeast.* Lincoln: University of Nebraska Press, 1989.

Wood, W. Raymond. "Plains Trade in Prehistoric and Protohistoric Intertribal Relations." *Anthropology on the Great Plains.* Eds. Raymond Wood and Margot Liberty. Lincoln: University of Nebraska Press, 1980.

Woodward, Grace Steele. *Pocahontas.* Norman: University of Oklahoma Press, 1969.

Woodward, Susan L. and Jerry N. McDonald. *Indian Mounds of the Middle Ohio Valley: A Guide to Adena and Ohio Hopewell Sites.* Newark, OH: McDonald & Woodward Publishing Co., 1986.

Worcester, Donald E. *The Apache.* Norman: University of Oklahoma Press, 1979.

The World of the American Indians. Washington, DC: National Geographic Society, 1974.

Wright, Muriel H. *A Guide to the Indian Tribes of Oklahoma.* Norman: University of Oklahoma Press, 1951, 1986.

Yenne, Bill. *The Encyclopedia of North American Indian Tribes.* New York: Crescent Books, 1986.

Yenne, Bill and Susan Garratt. *North American Indians.* Secaucus, NJ: Chartwell Books, 1984.

Young, Mary Elizabeth. *Redskins, Ruffleshirts, and Rednecks.* Norman: University of Oklahoma Press, 1961.

Periodicals

Alexander, Don. "A First Nation Elder's Perspective on the Environment" (interview with Haida Nation activist Lavina White). *Alternatives* (March/April 1994): p. 12.

Angulo, Jaime de. "The Achumawi Life Force" (Extract, "La psychologie religieuse des Achumawi." *Anthropos* 23, 1928). *Journal of California Anthropology* 2, No. 1 (1974): pp. 60–63.

Arden, Harvey. "Living Iroquois Confederacy." *National Geographic,* Vol. 172, No. 3 (September 1987): pp. 370–403.

Barrett, Samuel A. "The Ethnogeography of the Pomo and Neighboring Indians." *University of California Publications in American Archaeology and Ethnology* 6:1 (1908): pp. 1–332.

Barrett, Samuel A., and Edward W. Gifford. "Miwok Material Culture." *Public Museum of the City of Milwaukee Bulletin* 2:4 (1933): pp. 117–376.

Capron, Lewis. "Florida's Emerging Seminoles." *National Geographic,* Vol. 136, No. 5 (November 1969): pp. 716–34.

Carlson, Paul H. "Indian Agriculture, Changing Subsistence Patterns, and the Environment on the Southern Great Plains." *Agricultural History* 66, No. 2 (1992): pp. 52–60.

Carney, Jim. "Drinking Cut Short Sockalexis' Pro Career." *Beacon Journal* (October 13, 1995).

Crisp, David. "Tribes Make Manufacturing Push: Advocates Use Network to Expand Reach." *Billings Gazette* (February 11, 1996).

Dixon, Roland B. "Achomawi and Atsugewi Tales." *Journal of American Folk-Lore* 21, No. 80 (1908): pp. 159–77.

Dixon, Roland B. "Notes on the Achomawi and Atsugewi Indians of Northern California." *American Anthropologist* 10, No. 2 (1908): pp. 208–20.

DuBois, Constance Goddard. "The Religion of the Luiseño Indians of Southern California." *University of California Publications in American Archaeology and Ethnology* 8, No. 3 (1908): pp. 69–186.

Durham, Michael S. "Mound Country." *American Heritage,* Vol. 46, No. 2 (April 1995): p. 118.

Egan, Timothy. "Tribe Stops Study of Bones That Challenges Its History." *New York Times* (September 30, 1996): A1, A10.

Euler, Robert C. "Southern Paiute Ethnohistory." *Anthropological Papers.* 78:28. University of Utah (April 1966).

Fagan, Brian. "Bison Hunters of the Northern Plains." *Archaeology* 47, No. 3 (1994): pp. 37–41.

Farrell, John Aloysius. "Cheyenne Know Cost, Perils Tied to Energy Development." *Denver Post* (November 21, 1983).

Fischman, Joshua. "California Social Climbers: Low Water Prompts High Status." *Science,* Vol. 272 (May 10, 1996): pp. 811–12.

Fontana, Bernard L. "Restoring San Xavier del Bac, 'Our Church': Tohono O'odham Work to Restore the 200-Year-Old Church Built by Their Ancestors." *Native Peoples* (Summer 1995): pp. 28–35.

French, Bob. "Seminoles: A Collision of Cultures, Independent Indians' Lifestyle Faces Scrutiny," *Sun-Sentinel* (December 24 , 1995).

Garth, Thomas R. "Atsugewi Ethnography." *Anthropological Records* 14, No. 2 (1953): pp. 129–212.

Garth, Thomas R. "Emphasis on Industriousness among the Atsugewi." *American Anthropologist* 47, No. 4 (1945): pp. 554–66.

Gifford, E. W. "Notes on Central Pomo and Northern Yana Society." *American Anthropologist* 30, No. 4 (1928): pp. 675–84.

Gifford, E. W. and A. L. Kroeber. "Culture Element Distributions, IV: Pomo." *University of California Publications in American Archaeology and Ethnology* 37(4): pp. 117–254.

Gildart, Bert. "The Mississippi Band of Choctaw: in the Shadow of Naniw Waiya." *Native Peoples* (Summer 1996): pp. 44–50.

Goddard, Pliny Earle. "Chilula Texts." *University of California Publications in American Archaeology and Ethnology* 10, No. 7 (1914): pp. 289–379.

Halbert, Henry S. "The Choctaw Creation Legend," *Publications of the Mississippi Historical Society* 2 (1901): pp. 223–34.

Halbert, Henry S. "A Choctaw Migration Legend." *American Antiquarian and Oriental Journal,* 16 (1894): pp. 215–26.

Halbert, Henry S. "Nanih Waiya, the Sacred Mound of the Choctaws," *Publications of the Mississippi Historical Society* 2 (1899): pp. 223–34.

Hanks, Christopher C. and David Pokotylo. "The Mackenzie Basin: An Alternative Approach to Dene and Metis Archaeology." *Arctic,* Vol. 42, No. 2 (1989): pp. 139–47.

Heizer, R. F. "Impact of Colonization on Native California Societies." *Journal of San Diego History,* 24:1 (1978): pp. 121–39.

Heizer, R. F. and T. Kroeber, eds. "Indians Myths of South Central California." *University of California Publications in American Archaeology and Ethnology* 4, No. 4 (1907): pp. 167–250.

Hooper, Lucile. "The Cahuilla Indians." *University of California Publications in Archaeology and Ethnology,* 16, No. 6 (April 10, 1920): pp. 315–80

Horn, Patricia. "Polluting Sacred Ground." *Dollars and Sense* (October 1992): pp. 15–18.

"Incinerator Planned Near Pipe Spring." *National Parks* (July/August 1990).

"Indian Roots of American Democracy." *Northeast Indian Quarterly* (Winter/Spring 1987/1988).

Johnson, Kirk. "An Indian Tribe's Wealth Leads to the Expansion of Tribal Law." *New York Times* (May 22, 1994): p. 1.

Keegan, John. "Warfare on the Plains." *Yale Review 84,* No. 1 (1996): pp. 1–48.

Kelly, Isabel T. "Southern Paiute Ethnography." *Anthropological Papers.* 69:21. University of Utah (May 1964). Reprint. New York: Johnson Reprint Corporation, 1971.

Kniffen, Fred B. "Achomawi Geography." *University of California Publications in American Archaeology and Ethnology* 23, No. 5 (1928): pp. 297–332.

Koppel, Tom. "The Spirit of Haida Gwai." *Canadian Geographic* (March/April 1996): p. 2.

LaDuke, Winona. "Like Tributaries to a River," *Sierra* 81, No. 6 (November/December 1996): pp. 38–45.

LaFrance, Joan. "Essay Review." *Harvard Educational Review* (Fall 1992): pp. 388–95.

Lekson, Stephen H. "Pueblos of the Mesa Verde." *Archaeology,* Vol. 48, No. 5 (September/October 1995): pp. 56–57.

Lepper, Bradley T. "Tracking Ohio's Great Hopewell Road." *Archaeology,* Vol. 48, No. 6 (November–December 1995): p. 52.

Lincecum, Gideon. "Life of Apushimataha." *Publications of the Mississippi Historical Society* 9 (1905–06): pp. 415–85.

Linden, Eugene. "Bury My Heart at James Bay: the World's Most Extensive Hydropower Project Has Disrupted Rivers, Wildlife, and the Traditions of the Quebec Indians. Is It Really Needed?" *Time* Vol. 138, No. 2 (July 15, 1991): p. 60.

Lindgren, Kristy. "Sgt. David H. Mace Shot Wampanoag David Hendricks Eleven Times and Is Still a Free Man." *News From Indian Country,* 7, No. 4 (1993): pp. 1–2.

"Makah Tribe's Net Snares Gray Whale." *Oregonian* (July 18, 1995).

"The Makah's Case for Whale Hunting." *Seattle-Post Intelligencer* (June 8, 1995).

"Menominee Honored at UN Ceremony for Forest Practices." *News From Indian Country,* IX, No. 9 (Mid-May 1995): p. 3.

Menominee Indian Tribe of Wisconsin. "Land of the Menominee" (brochure), c. 1994.

"The Menominee Nation and Its Treaty Rights." *News From Indian Country,* IX, No. 11 (Mid-June 1995): p. 2.

Menominee Nation Treaty Rights, Mining Impact, and Communications Offices. "Protect Menominee Nation Treaty Rights." *News From Indian Country,* X, No. 10 (Late-May 1996): p. 14A.

Millin, Peggy Tabor. "Passing the Torch: Technology Saves a Culture." *Native Peoples,* 9, No. 3 (1996): pp. 48–54.

Momatiuk, Yva and John Eastcott. "*Nunavut* Means Our Land." *Native Peoples* 9, No. 1 (Fall/Winter 1995): p. 42.

Mooney, James. "Calendar History of the Kiowa Indians." *Seventeenth Annual Report of the Bureau of American Ethnology.* Washington, DC: U.S. Government Printing Office, 1898.

Morrison, Joan. "Protect the Earth Gathering Focuses Mining Opposition." *News From Indian Country,* X, No. 5 (Mid-March 1996): p. 2.

Newman, Peter C. "The Beaching of a Great Whale." *Maclean's*. (Vol. 104, No. 37): p. 38.

Norman, Geoffrey. "The Cherokee: Two Nations, One People." *National Geographic* (May 1995): pp. 72–97.

"1,000 Gather to Oppose Exxon." *News From Indian Country*, X, No. 10 (Late-May 1996): pp. 1A, 5A.

Peterson, Lindsay. "Living History: Ruby Tiger Osceola, a 100-Year-Old Seminole Indian, Is Both a Link to the Past and a Leader for the Future." *The Tampa Tribune* (March 12, 1996).

Petit, Charles. "Ishi May Not Have Been the Last Yahi Indian." *San Francisco Chronicle* (February 6, 1996).

Plungis, Jeff. "Administering Environmental Justice." *Empire State Report* (January 1995): pp. 61+.

Roberts, Chris. "Schemitzun: The Pequot People's Feast of Green Corn and Dance." *Native Peoples*, Vol. 7, No. 4 (Summer 1994): pp. 66–70.

Rossiter, William. "CSI Opposes Whaling by the Makah." *Cetacean Society International*. Vol. 5, No. 1 (January, 1996).

Sapir, Edward. "Yana Texts." *University of California Publications in American Archaeology and Ethnology* 9, No. 1 (1910): pp. 1–235.

Sapir, Edward. "The Position of Yana in the Hokan Stock." *University of California Publications in American Archaeology and Ethnology* 13, No. 1 (1917): pp. 1–34.

Sapir, Edward and Leslie Spier. "Notes on the Culture of the Yana." *Anthropological Records* 3, No. 3 (1943): pp. 239–98.

Shaw, Christopher. "A Theft of Spirit?" *New Age Journal* (July/August 1995): pp. 84+.

Sparkman, Philip Stedman. "The Culture of the Luiseño Indians." *University of California Publications in American Archaeology and Ethnology* 8, No. 4 (1908): pp. 187–234.

Spier, Leslie. "The Sun Dance of the Plains Indians: Its Development and Diffusion." *Anthropological Papers of the American Museum of Natural History* 16, No. VII (1921): pp. 459–525.

Stirling, Matthew W. "Indians of the Far West." *National Geographic* (February 1948): pp. 175–200.

Strong, W. D. "The Plains Culture in the Light of Archaeology." *American Anthropologist* 35, No. 2 (1933): pp. 271–87.

Stuart, George E, "Etowah: A Southeast Village in 1491." *National Geographic,* 180, No. 4 (October 1991): pp. 54–67.

Theimer, Sharon. "Menominee Nation Lawsuit Wins Over Motion to Dismiss." *News From Indian Country,* X, No. 5 (Mid-March 1996): p. 3A.

Thompson, Ian. "The Search for Settlements on the Great Sage Plain." *Archaeology,* Vol. 48, No. 5 (September/October 1995): pp. 57–63.

Thurston, Harry and Stephen Homer. "Power in a Land of Remembrance: Their Rivers, Lands." *Audubon.* (Vol. 93, No. 6): p. 52.

Tobias, John L. "Canada's Subjugation of the Plains Cree, 1879–1885." *Canadian Historical Review,* Vol. 64 (December 1983): p. 519.

Todhunter, Andrew. "Digging Into History." *Washington Post Book World* (May 26, 1996): pp. 9, 13.

Turner, Steve and Todd Nachowitz. "The Damming of Native Lands." *Nation,* Vol. 253, No. 13 (October 21, 1991): p. 6.

Van Natta, Don Jr. "Tribe Saw a Promise, but Party Saw a Pledge." *New York Times* (August 12, 1997): A1, C20.

"The Water Famine." *Indigenous Peoples' Literature* (January 7, 1996).

Wedel, Waldo R. "Some Aspects of Human Ecology in the Central Plains." *American Anthropologist* 55, No. 4 (1953): pp. 499–514.

"Welcome to the Land of the Menominee-Forest." *News From Indian Country,* IX, No. 14 (Late-July 1995): p. 6.

White, Raymond. "Luiseño Social Organization." *University of California Publications in American Archaeology and Ethnology* 48, No. 2 (1963): pp. 91–194.

White, Raymond. "The Luiseño Theory of 'Knowledge.'" *American Anthropologist* 59, No. 2 (1957): pp. 1–19.

White, Raymond. "Two Surviving Luiseño Indian Ceremonies." *American Anthropologist* 55, No. 4 (1953): pp. 569–78.

Williams, Lee. "Medicine Man." *New Mexico Magazine* 62 (May 1984): pp. 62–71.

Web Sites

Beckman, Tad. "The Yurok and Hupa of the Northern Coast." [Online] http://www4.hmc.edu:8001/humanities/indian/ca/ch10.htm (accessed on April 22, 1999).

The Cheyenne Indians. [Online] http://www.uwgb.edu/~galta/mrr/cheyenne (accessed on April 21, 1999).

Lawrence, Elizabeth Atwood, "The Symbolic Role of Animals in the Plains Indian Sun Dance." [Online] http://envirolink.org/arrs/psyeta/sa/sa.1/lawrence.html (accessed on April 21, 1999).

Magagnini, Stephen. "Indians find 'new buffalo' in casinos." *The Modesto Bee Online.* [Online] http://www.modbee.com/metro/story/0,1113,4447,00.html (accessed on April 22, 1999).

Powersource Consultants. *Important Dates in Cherokee History.* [Online] http://www.powersource.com:80/nation/dates.html (accessed on April 21, 1999).

Stockbridge-Munsee Home Page. [Online] http://www.pressenter.com/org/tribes/munsee.htm (accessed on April 21, 1999).

CD-ROMs

"Cherokee Language." *Microsoft Encarta 96 Encyclopedia.* Redmond, WA: Microsoft, 1993–95.

Kappler, Charles, ed. *Treaties of American Indians and the United States. Treaties with the Menominees, 1817, 1831 (February 8 and February 17), 1832, 1836, 1848, 1854, 1856. Treaty with the Chippewa, 1833. Treaty with the Stockbridge and Munsee, 1839,* version 1.00. Indianapolis: Objective Computing, 1994.

Schoolcraft, Henry R. "Archives of Aboriginal Knowledge" and "Thirty Years with the Indian Tribes," on *The Indian Question,* version 1.00. Indianapolis: Objective Computing, 1994.

Other Sources

Klasky, Philip M. "An Extreme and Solemn Relationship: Native American Perspectives: Ward Valley Nuclear Dump." A thesis submitted to the faculty of San Francisco State University in partial fulfillment of the requirements of the degree Master of Arts in Geography, May 1997.

Low, Sam. *The Ancient World* (television documentary). QED Communications, Inc./Pennsylvania State University, 1992.

Mashantucket Pequot Nation. "The Fox People." (Leaflet), c. 1994.

Mashantucket Pequot Nation. "The Mashantucket Pequots: A Proud Tradition" and "Foxwoods Resort Casino." (brochures), n.d.

Acknowledgments

Grateful acknowledgment is made to the following sources whose works appear in this volume. Every effort has been made to trace copyright, but if omissions have been made, please contact the publisher.

"Blueberry Pudding." Marx, Pamela. From *Travel-the-World Cookbook* by Pamela A. Marx. Copyright © 1996 by Pamela A. Marx. Reproduced by permission of Addison-Wesley Educational Publishers, Inc.

"The Bluebird and Coyote." *American Indian Myths and Legends* edited by Richard Erdoes and Alfonso Ortiz. Copyright © 1984 by Richard Erdoes and Alfonso Ortiz. Reproduced by permission of Pantheon Books, a division of Random House, Inc.

"Ceremony and Song." Ruoff, A. LaVonne Brown, ed. *Literatures of the American Indian.* Chelsea House Publishers, 1991. Copyright © by Chelsea House Publishers, a division of Main Line Book Co. All rights reserved. Reproduced by permission.

"Cheyenne Bread." Cox, Beverly, and Martin Jacobs. From *Spirit of the Harvest.*" Copyright © 1991 Stewart, Tabori & Chang. Reproduced by permission.

"Chippewa Wild Rice." Copyright © 1965 by Yeffe Kimball and Jean Anderson. From *The Art of American Indian Cooking* published by Doubleday. Reproduced by permission of McIntosh & Otis, Inc.

"Choctaw Acorn Biscuits." Cox, Beverly, and Martin Jacobs. From *Spirit of the Harvest.* Copyright © 1991 Stewart, Tabori & Chang. Reproduced by permission.

"Comanche Chickasaw Plum Bars." Kavasch, E. Barrie. From *Enduring Harvests: Native American Foods and Festivals for Every Season.* Copyright © 1995 Globe Pequot Press. Reproduced by permission.

"Coyote in the Cedar Tree." Ramsey, Jarold. From *Coyote Was Going There: Indian Literature in the Oregon Country.* Copyright © 1977 University of Washington Press. Reproduced by permission.

"Coyote Wants To Be Chief." Premo, Anna. From *Shoshone Tales*. Edited by Anne M. Smith. University of Utah Press, 1993. © 1993 by the University of Utah Press. All rights reserved. Reproduced by permission.

"The Death of Wiyót, the Creator." Curtis, Edward S. From *The North American Indian." Edited by Frederick Webb Hodge. Copyright © 1970 Johnson Reprint Corporation.*

"The Emergence." Tithla, Bane. From *Myths and Tales of the White Mountain Apache*. Copyright © 1939 American Folklore Society. Reproduced by permission.

"An Encounter with the Tamciye." Garth, Thomas R. From *Atsugewi Ethnography*. Copyright © 1953 Anthropological Records.

"The Girl and the Devil." Bushnell, David I. From *Choctaw Myths and Legends*. Copyright © 1985 Garland Publishing. Reproduced by permission.

"Glacial Mists Cooler." Kavasch, E. Barrie. From *Enduring Harvests: Native American Foods and Festivals for Every Season*. Copyright © 1995 Globe Pequot Press. Reproduced by permission.

"Of Glooskap and the Sinful Serpent." Leland, Charles G. From *The Alogonquin Legends of New England: or Myths and Folklore of the Micmac, Passamaquoddy, and Penobscot Tribes*. Copyright © 1884 Houghton, Mifflen. Reproduced by permission.

"High Plains Pemmican." Kavasch, E. Barrie. From *Enduring Harvests: Native American Foods and Festivals for Every Season*. Copyright © 1995 Globe Pequot Press. Reproduced by permission.

"The Horrible Bear." Jewell, Donald P. From *Indians of the Feather River: Tales and Legends of Concow Maidu of California*. Copyright © 1987 Ballena Press. Reproduced by permission.

"How the Chumash Came To Be." Blackburn, Thomas C. From *December's Child: A Book of Chumash Oral Narratives*. Copyright © 1975 Berkeley: University of California Press. Reproduced by permission.

"How the Clans Came To Be." From *Creek Lifestyles, Customs and Legends*. Ryal Public School. Reproduced by permission. [Online] http://www.edumaster.net/schools/ryal/creek.html (18 September 1998).

"How the Moon Was Made." Clay, Charles. From *Swampy Cree Legends*. The Macmillan Company of Canada Limited, 1938. Copyright, Canada 1938 by The Macmillan Company of Canada Limited. All rights reserved.

"How Youth Are Instructed by Tribal Elders." Spindler, George, and Louise Spindler. From *Dreamers with Power: The Menomini Indians.* Copyright © 1971 Holt, Rinehart & Winston. Reproduced by permission.

"Jerky." Frank, Lois Ellen. From *Native American Cooking: Foods of the Southwest Indian Nations* by Lois Ellen Frank. Copyright © 1991 by Lois Ellen Frank. Reproduced by permission of Clarkson N. Potter, a division of Crown Publishers, Inc.

"King Philip's Prophecy." William Apess. Reprinted from Barry O'Connell, ed., *On Our Own Ground: The Complete Writings of William Apess, a Pequot.* (Amherst: University of Massachusetts Press, 1992). Copyright © 1992 by the University of Massachusetts Press.

"Mary O'Brien's Apricot Blueberry Cookies." Kavasch, E. Barrie. From *Enduring Harvests: Native American Foods and Festivals for Every Season.* Copyright © 1995 Globe Pequot Press. Reproduced by permission.

"Mohawk Baked Squash." Wolfson, Evelyn. From *The Iroquois: People of the Northeast.* Copyright © 1992 The Millbrook Press. Reproduced by permission.

"The Morning Star." Lacey, Theresa Jensen. From *The Pawnee.* Chelsea House Publishers, 1995. Copyright © 1996 by Chelsea House Publishers, a division of Main Line Book Co. All rights reserved. Reproduced by permission.

"Nanabozho and Winter-Maker." Coleman, Sister Bernard, Ellen Frogner, and Estelle Eich. From *Ojibwa Myths and Legends.* Copyright © 1962 Ross and Haines.

"Navajo Peach Pudding." Frank, Lois Ellen. From *Native American Cooking: Foods of the Southwest Indian Nations* by Lois Ellen Frank. Copyright © 1991 by Lois Ellen Frank. Reproduced by permission of Clarkson N. Potter, a division of Crown Publishers, Inc.

"Pawnee Ground Roast Pound Meat with Pecans." Kavasch, E. Barrie. From *Enduring Harvests: Native American Foods and Festivals for Every Season.* Copyright © 1995 Globe Pequot Press. Reproduced by permission.

"Powhatan Hazelnut Soup" Copyright © 1965 by Yeffe Kimball and Jean Anderson. From *The Art of American Indian Cooking* published by Doubleday. Reproduced by permission of McIntosh & Otis, Inc.

The photographs and illustrations appearing in U•X•L Encyclopedia of Native American Tribes were received from the following sources:

Covers Volume 1: tepee, **Library of Congress;** Seminole thatched houses, **P & F Communications. David Phillips, photographer;** Volume 2: Rocky Mountains from Ute Reservation, **North Wind Picture Archives. Reproduced by permission;** Taos Pueblo scene, **Library of Congress;** Volume 3: Inuit mother and child, **National Archives and Records Administration;** Young man at Sioux pow-wow, **Sygma Photo News. Photograph by F. Paolini. Reproduced by permission;** Volume 4: Ramona Lugu, Cahuilla in front of home, **Los Angeles Central Library. Reproduced by permission;** Tlingit longhouse with totem poles, **Corbis. Photograph by Tom Bean. Reproduced by permission.**

© **1998 North Wind Picture Archives. Reproduced by permission.** pp. 3, 133, 405; **National Anthropological Archives. Reproduced by permission:** pp. 15, 1066, 1071; **Print by M. J. Burns. North Wind Picture Archives. Reproduced by permission:** p. 21; **University of Pennsylvania Museum. Reproduced by permission:** pp. 23, 1040, 1192; **Photograph by Frank C. Wotm. Library of Congress:** pp. 24, 25; **North Wind Picture Archives. Reproduced by permission:** pp. 32, 42, 51, 90, 109, 121, 141, 160, 172, 246, 247, 290, 317, 319, 329, 346, 373, 379, 381, 400, 418, 419, 443, 463, 468, 476, 498, 527, 534, 599, 637, 687, 693, 722, 756, 766, 785, 792, 796, 814, 827, 884, 897, 975, 1140; **Library of Congress:** pp. 36, 91, 146, 166, 219, 313, 416, 582, 615, 676, 732, 769, 778, 824, 848, 856, 908, 963, 965, 1087, 1117, 1162, 1173; **Bettmann. Reproduced by permission:** pp. 39, 45, 874; **AP/Wide World Photos, Inc. Reproduced by permission:** pp. 53, 84, 118, 138, 271, 305, 424, 458, 503, 750, 841, 1009, 1246; © **1997 N. Carter/North Wind Picture Archives. Reproduced by permission:** pp. 62, 92, 497, 499; **Photograph by Bruce M. Fritz.** *The Capital Times.* **Reproduced by permission:** p. 63; **CORBIS/Bettmann. Reproduced by permission:** pp. 67, 108, 188, 356, 533, 828, 832, 877, 925; **Photograph by W. H. Wessa. Library of Congress:** p. 68; **Archive Photos. Reproduced by permission:** pp. 148, 153, 192, 358, 482, 485, 526, 578, 1048; **National Archives and Records Administration:** pp. 152, 178, 296, 348, 436, 464, 538, 546, 592, 635, 641, 643, 645, 748, 793, 810, 960, 1165, 1217, 1235; **Photograph by C. M. Bell. National Archives:** p. 176; © **1977 North Wind Picture Archives. Reproduced by permission:** p. 202; © **1994 North Wind Picture Archives. Reproduced by permission:** p. 209; **National Archives:**

pp. 234, 807, 935; **Granger Collection. New York. Reproduced by permission:** p. 249; © **1995. North Wind Picture Archives. Reproduced by permission:** pp. 388, 465, 492, 553, 601, 892; © **1993 North Wind Pictures Archives:** p. 391; **Mesa Verde National Park/National Park Service. Reproduced by permission:** p. 402; **Painting by Waldo Mootzka. Photograph by Seth Rothman. Dick Howard Collection. Reproduced by permission:** p. 460; **Southwest Museum. Reproduced by permission:** pp. 477, 479, 480, 979, 991, 1050; **Photograph by Edward S. Curtis. The Library of Congress:** pp. 512, 567, 694, 1116, 1256, 1259; **Photograph by Edward S. Curtis. CORBIS. Reproduced by permission:** pp. 517, 547; **CORBIS/Arne Hodalic. Reproduced by permission:** p. 519; © **1991 N. Carter/North Wind Picture Archives. Reproduced by permission:** p. 535; **CORBIS/E. O. Hoppe. Reproduced by permission:** p. 550; **Photograph by T. Harmon Parkhurst. Courtesy Museum of New Mexico, negative number 7454:** p. 559; **Photograph by Bluford W. Muir. CORBIS. Reproduced by permission:** p. 579; **Photograph by Orville L. Snider. CORBIS. Reproduced by permission:** p. 581; **CORBIS/Adam Woolfit. Reproduced by permission:** p. 585; **CORBIS/David G. Houser. Reproduced by permission:** pp. 606, 950; **CORBIS/Tom Bean. Reproduced by permission:** p. 610, 1269; **CORBIS. Reproduced by permission:** pp. 670, 672, 768, 922; **CORBIS/Joel Bennett. Reproduced by permission:** p. 675; **Provincial Archives of Manitoba. Reproduced by permission:** p. 714; **Photograph by Wiliam S. Soule. National Archives and Records Administration:** p. 736; **CORBIS/ Brian Vikander. Reproduced by permission:** p. 773; **Photgraph by Alexander Gardner. CORBIS. Reproduced by permission:** pp. 782, 784; **Photograph by William S. Soule. The Library of Congress:** p. 783; **Photograph by William H. Jackson. National Archives and Records Administration:** p. 840; **Buffalo Bill Historical Center, Cody, WY. Gift of Mrs. Cornelius Vanderbilt Whitney. Reproduced by permission:** p. 883; **Photograph by Eadweard Muybridge. National Archives and Records Administration:** p. 934; **Photograph by Larry Philllips. Institute of American Indian Arts Museum, Santa Fe:** p. 952; **Los Angeles Public Library. Reproduced by permission:** p. 992; **California History Section, California State Library. Reproduced by permission:** p. 1018; **CORBIS/David Muench. Reproduced by permission:** p. 1021; **Smithsonian Insititution, Bureau of American Ethnology. Reproduced by permission:** pp. 105, 1036; **CORBIS/Ed Young. Reproduced by permission:** p. 1081; **American Museum of Natural History. Reproduced by permission:** p. 1126; **CORBIS/**

Natalie Fobes. Reproduced by permission: pp. 1142, 1221, 1224; Photograph by Blankenburg Photo. CORBIS/PEMCO—Webster Stevens Collection; Museum of History & Industry, Seattle. Reproduced by permission: p. 1144; Photograph © Thomas Hoepker. Reproduced by permission of Joe Manfredini: p. 1177; Photograph by William McLennan. University of British Columbia Museum of Anthropology. Reproduced by permission: p. 1179; KWA-Gulth Arts Ltd. Reproduced by permission of Richard Hunt: p. 1194; Photograph by Edward S. Curtis. Univerversity of Pennsylvania Museum. Reproduced by permission: p. 1198; Photograph by Anthony Bolante. Reuters/Archive Photos. Reproduced by permission: p. 1207; CORBIS/Museum of History and Industry, Seattle. Reproduced by permission: p. 1210; CORBIS/Seattle Post–Intelligencer Collection. Museum of History and Industry, Seattle. Reproduced by permission: p. 1254; Courtesy Dept. of Library Services American Museum of Natural History, Neg. No. 41184. Reproduced by permission: p. 1268; Reproduced by permission of Preston Singletary: p. 1271; Photograph by Jeff Greenberg. Archive Photos. Reproduced by permission: p. 1272; Photograph by Winter and Pont. CORBIS. Reproduced by permission: p. 1274.

Index

Italic type indicates volume numbers; boldface type indicates entries and their page numbers; (ill.) indicates illustration.

Allegheny Mountains *1:* 186

Allen, Elsie *4:* 1120

Allotment *1:* 115, 226, 270, 283, 314; *3:* 765, 875, 876, 914; *4:* 980

Allotment Act. *See* General Allotment Act

Alta California *4:* 972

Alutiiq *3:* 624

Alutiit *3:* 624

Alvarado, Hernando de *2:* 545

Ambrosia Lake Mine *2:* 548

American Civil War *1:* 62, 195, 250; *2:* 458; *3:* 726

American Indian Movement (AIM) *1:* 85, 115, 126; *2:* 367; *3:* 866, 876

American Indian Religious Freedom Act *4:* 1146

American Revolutionary War (1775–83) *1:* 7, 14, 17, 33, 50-51, 58, 61, 79, 114, 146, 183, 187, 245, 267, 281, 295

Amiotee, Arthur *3:* 883

Anasazi *2:* 369, 386, 387, **397-410,** 398 (map), 405 (ill.), 523, 532, 575, 589

Anderson, Ethan *4:* 1111

Androscoggin *1:* 11

Angakok *3:* 648

Anglican Church *3:* 695

Animal population *3:* 913

Animism *4:* 1140

Anishinabeg 1: 111, 116; *3:* 654, 656, 660

Anne, Queen *1:* 161

Annual Menominee Nation Contest Powwow *1:* 72

Annuities *2:* 331

Antap *4:* 1003

Antonio, Juan *4:* 996

Anza, Juan Bautista de *4:* 987

Apache *2:* 329, 386, 389, 390, 393-394, **411-454,** 412 (map), 416 (ill.), 418 (ill.), 424 (ill.), 489, 491, 496, 509, 511-512, 515, 527, 546, 556, 567, 575-576, 591-592; *2:* 607; *3:* 656

Apache Dance for the Mountain Spirits *2:* 437

Apache Gold Casino *2:* 446

Apache Mission of the Reformed Church *2:* 434

Apache Survival Coalition *2:* 444

Apache Wars *2:* 393, 430

Apache War Women *2:* 438

Apalachicolas *1:* 309

Apess, William *1:* 135, 141, 210

Appalachian Mountains *1:* 218, 245

Appamattuck *1:* 157

Aquash, Anna Mae *1:* 85

Arapaho *2:* 359; *3:* 722, 727, **729-742,** 730 (map), 733, 736 (ill.), 764, 765

Arapooish, Chief *3:* 791

Aravaipa Apache *2:* 607

Arctic 3: 620-630, 622 (map), 641, 643

Arctic Circle *3:* 631, 654

Arctic National Wildlife Refuge *3:* 627, 663

Arguello, Luis *4:* 1122

Arikara *1:* 221; *3:* 723

Arizona *2:* 397, 491, 523, 525

Arkansas *1:* 246, 250, 262

Arkansas River *3:* 763

Arkansaw Indians *1:* 222

Arlington National Cemetery *3:* 802

Aroostook Band of Micmac Indians *1:* 75-76, 79-81, 84

Aroostook Band of Micmacs Settlement Act *1:* 81

Arrohatek *1:* 157

Arthur, Chester A. *2:* 457-458

Asah, Spencer *3:* 813

Asi *1:* 323

Assimilation *1:* 8, 34, 66; *2:* 332, 394; *3:* 807; *4:* 1065

Assiniboin *3:* 683, 722, 724-725, 745

Association of Aroostook Indians (AAI) *1:* 79

Astor, John Jacob *4:* 1149

Athabaskan *2:* 441, 449, 496; *3:* 621, 624, 654, 683; *4:* 1029, 1030

Athabaskan Old-Time Fiddling Festival *3:* 663

Athabaskan speakers *2:* 386, 389; *3:* 722; *4:* 1136

Atlatl 2: 406, 408

Atsugewi *4:* 1093-1106

Attaquin, Helen *1:* 204, 212

Auchiah, James *3:* 813

Auk *4:* 1263

Awatovi *2:* 458

Aztec *2:* 388-389, 404

Aztlán *2:* 388-389

B

Baca, Lorenzo *2:* 426

Baffin Island *3:* 631

Baker Massacre *3:* 747

"The Ballad of Ira Hayes" (song) *2:* 522

Banks, Dennis *1:* 115, 126; *3:* 876

Bannock *2:* 330, 334, 339, 342, 357, 359; *3:* 945

Baptists *1:* 35, 189, 225, 234, 271

Barboncito *2:* 507

Basketmakers *2:* 398

Basketry *1:* 18, 25, 137, 239, 258, 260; *2:* 336, 349, 407, 446, 447, 561, 613; *4:* 1004, 1010, 1025, 1039, 1055, 1165, 1179, 1189, 1194, 1205, 1210

Batoche, battle of *3:* 708

(DRUMS) *1:* 64, 67, 73

De Vaca, Cabeza *2:* 389

De Velasco, Don Luis *1:* 159

Developmental Pueblo period
  2: 400

Devil's Lake Reservation *3:* 855

Diabetes *2:* 349, 616

Diné Community College *2:* 502

Diné (Navajo) *2:* 392;

Dinjii Zhuh (Gwich'in or Locheux)
  3: 660

Diseases *1:* 33, 71, 103, 131, 115,
  161, 201, 217; *2:* 330; *3:* 622,
  724, 913; *4:* 974, 1138

Ditidaht *4:* 1136

Dodge, Henry Chee *2:* 507; *3:* 901

Dog sleds *3:* 644, 647

Dog Soldiers *3:* 773

Donaghey, Richard *1:* 241

Donation Land Law of 1851 *3:* 960

Dotson'Sa (The Great Raven)
  3: 655

Dover Indian Trading Post *1:* 106

Doyon, Limited *3:* 663

Dozier, Edward P. *2:* 542

Drake, Francis *4:* 1078, 1108

Dream Dance *1:* 149

Dream guessing *1:* 41

Dream Prophets *3:* 962

Dreamer religion *3:* 948

Drum (or Dream) Dance Religion
  1: 64, 239

Dukepoo, Frank C. *2:* 471, 542

Dull Knife, battle of *3:* 874

Dull Knife Memorial College
  3: 771

Dummer's War *1:* 16

Dumont, Gabriel *3:* 710, 717

Dust Bowl, 1930s *3:* 810

Duwamish *4:* **1159-1168,**
  1160 (map)

Dylan, Bob *2:* 522

E

Eagle *4:* 1002, 1003, 1176, 1178

Earth Lodge Cult *4:* 1126

Earthen mounds *1:* 87-100

Eastern Abenaki *1:* 22

Eastern Algonquian languages
  1: 80

Eastern Band of Cherokee, North
  Carolina *1:* 244-245, 251-252,
  254-255, 259, 261-262

Eastern Niantic *1:* 129

Eastern Paucatuck Pequot
  Reservation *1:* 129-130

Eastern Shawnee *1:* 183, 190-191,
  193-194

Eastern Shoshone *2:* 355, 360, 361

Eastman, Charles A. *3:* 865

Echohawk, John E. *3:* 849

Echo-Hawk, Walter R. *3:* 849

Echota Cherokee Tribe of Alabama
  1: 244

Ecology *1:* 8, 57, 67, 73; *2:* 335

Eda'nsa *4:* 1183

Edenshaw, Charles *4:* 1184

Edmonds, Dayton *1:* 241

Effigies *1:* 88-90; *2:* 594

Ellal, Martha Langevin *1:* 135, 141

El Paso, Texas *2:* 523

Embroidery *3:* 714

The Enemyway *2:* 504

Epidemics *1:* 4, 201, 202 (ill.);
  2: 391, 458; *3:* 635, 686, 915;
  4: 1031, 1110, 1149, 1173,
  1188, 1204, 1265

Eriksson, Leif *1:* 76

Eric the Red *3:* 633

Eskimo. *See* Inuit.

Eskimo languages *3:* 624

Esteban *2:* 591

Estevanicio *2:* 591

Etowah Cherokee Nation,
  Tennessee *1:* 244

Etowah, Georgia *1:* 310

Evans, Minnie *1:* 155

Even Start program *1:* 151

Everglades (Florida) *1:* 313, 315,
  316, 321, 325

Everglades Agricultural Area *1:* 316

Evil Manito 3: 689

Eyak *3:* 656, 659

F

Fallen Timbers, battle of *1:* 187

"Fall line" *1:* 218

False Faces *1:* 41

Farmer, Gary Dale *1:* 47

Feast Day at Acoma (ill.) *2:* 547

Feast of San Geronimo *2:* 584

Feather Dance *1:* 43

Federal Acknowledgment Program
  4: 1150

Federal Bureau of Investigation
  (FBI) *3:* 825

Federal court system *2:* 337

Federal Proclamation of 1783 *1:* 7

Federal recognition of tribes *1:*
  155, 168, 227; *4:* 1023

Fetishes *2:* 594, 595

Fiddle music *3:* 662

Fire *1:* 239

Fire Keeper School *1:* 151

First Amendment *4:* 1205

First Mesa *2:* 455

First Nations Dance Company
  1: 241

First Powhatan War *1:* 161

First Riel Rebellion *3:* 707

First Salmon Ceremony
  4: 1041, 1141

First Seminole War *1:* 311

First Thanksgiving *1:* 201, 212

Fish curing *4:* 1189

Inuvialuk 3: 624

Iowa 3: 723

Iroquoian languages 1: 37, 221, 253

Iroquois Confederacy 1: 2, 13, 14, **29-48**, 30 (map), 32 (ill.), 40 (ill.), 43 (ill.), 49-50, 77, 145, 171, 183, 218, 221, 243, 265

Iroquois passports 1: 34

Irretaba 2: 476

Irving, Washington 3: 821

Isadowa 3: 905

Ishi 4: 1124-1125, 1126 (ill.), 1127-1132, 1134

Ishi, the Last Yahi 4: 1125

Ishi in Two Worlds 4: 1127, 1128

Ishi Wilderness 4: 1122

Ishtaboli 1: 290

Isleta Pueblo 2: 523, 579

J

Jackie Beard Pow Wow 3: 772

Jackson, Andrew 1: 223-224, 248, 282, 284, 308, 312

Jackson, Helen Hunt 4: 988, 1049

James Bay Hydroelectric Project 3: 627, 685, 689-690

James Bay and Northern Quebec Agreement 3: 627, 689

James, Frank Wamsutta 1: 212

James I 1: 161

James, Overton 1: 273

Jamestown Colony 1: 5, 160-161

Japan 2: 494

Japanese Americans, internment of 2: 477

Jefferson, Thomas 1: 90; 3: 869, 891, 912

Jeffords, Thomas 2: 430

Jemez Pueblo 2: 523, 527, **555-564** 559 (ill.)

Jemez River 2: 555, 556, 562

Jicarilla Apache 2: 417, 529, 555, 565

Job-training programs 1: 155; 2: 337

Johnson, Lyndon Baines 2: 602

Joint Use Area, Hopi-Navajo (JUA) 2: 394-395, 494

Joseph, Chief 3: 944-946, 954

Joseph, Old Chief 3: 946, 954

Judith River 3: 791

Jumper, Betty Mae Tiger 1: 325

Jurisdictional Act of 1928 4: 981

K

Kabotie, Fred 2: 471

Kachina 2: 403, 459, 460 (ill.), 461, 466, 467, 469, 529, 530

Kadohadacho 1: 229, 236

Kahnawake Mohawk 1: 53

Kaibab Reservation, Arizona 2: 351

Kalispel 3: 913, 916, 921

Kanesataké Mohawks 1: 53

Kanesatake, Quebec 1: 53

Kansa 1: 222; 3: 723

Kansas 1: 195, 222, 250; 2: 526

Karmat 3: 643

Kashaya Pomo 4: 1109

K'ashot'ine (Hareskin) 3: 660

Kaska 3: 659

Kaskalla, Rod 2: 601

Kathlamet 4: 1147

Kawaiisu 2: 330, 334

Kayaks 3: 644

Kayenta, Arizona 2: 397

Kecoughtan 1: 157

"Keetowah faction" (Cherokee) 1: 224, 225

Kegg, Maude 1: 123

Kelsey, Henry 3: 724

Kenai Peninsula 3: 624

Kennebec 1: 11

Kenojuak 3: 652

Kentucky 1: 186, 222, 243

Keokuk 1: 182

Keres 2: 390

Keresan 2: 523, 530, 548

Kerr Dam 3: 916

Keshena 1: 58

Kettle Falls 3: 921

A Key into the Language of America 1: 105

Ki 2: 516

Kialegee Tribal Town 1: 299

Kichai 3: 906

Kickapoo 1: 148-150, 172, 174, 183

Kicking Bear 3: 878

Kiehtan 1: 204

King George's War 1: 16

King Philip (Metacomet) 1: 203, 210

King Philip's Prophecy 1: 209

King Philip's War 1: 14, 103, 105, 109, 203-206, 209, 212

King William's War (1689–1697) 1: 14

Kingdom of Acu 2: 545

Kingdom of Quivira 3: 903

Kino, Eusebio Francisco 2: 605, 609

Kiowa 2: 393; 3: 722, **803-818**, 806 (map)

Kiowa Apache 2: 418; 3: 722, 803

Kiowa Nation Culture Museum 3: 811

Kiowa Tanoan language family 3: 722

Kiowa Tribal Complex, Carnegie, Oklahoma 3: 811

Kishpoko 1: 194

Maidu 4: 1061-1076, 1062 (map), 1066 (ill.), 1071 (ill.), 1121, 1126

Maidu Indian World Maker Route 4: 1066

Main Poche 1: 156

Maine 1: 11

Makah 4: 1136, 1201-1214, 1202 (map), 1207 (ill.), 1210 (ill.)

Makah Cultural and Research Center 4: 1205, 1209

Makah Reservation 4: 1201, 1205, 1209

Maliseet 1: 17, 19, 22

Malki Museum, Morongo Reservation 4: 995

Mandan 3: 722, 723, 727, 731

Mangas Coloradas 2: 430

Manhattan Island (ill.) 1: 32

Manhattan Purchase 4: 1133

Manifest Destiny 4: 1161, 1203, 1229

Manissean 1: 101

Manitoba 3: 683

Manitoba Act of 1870 3: 708, 711

Manitoba Métis Federation 3: 711

Manitou 1: 204

Manittoo 1: 104

Mankiller, Wilma 1: 220, 263

Manuelito 2: 506

Maricopa 2: 476, 509, 512, 514

Marin 4: 1090

Marine Mammal Protection Act of 1972 3: 625

Martha's Vineyard 1: 199, 206

Martin, Mungo 4: 1198

Martin, Philip 1: 292

Mary O'Brien's Apricot Blueberry Cookies (recipe) 1: 258

Masaw 2: 466

Mashantucket (Western Pequot) 1: 129-130, 134-136, 138, 140-141

Mashantucket Pequot Indian Land Claims Settlement Act (1983) 1: 135

Mashantucket Pequot Museum and Research Center 1: 138

Mashapaug 1: 101

Mashpee 1: 205

Mashpee Manufacturing Company 1: 206

Mashpee Wampanoag Indians 1: 200, 206

Masked Dancers (Pueblo) 2: 530

Masks (ills.) 1: 42; 4: 1179, 1194

Maskwas, John (ill.) 1: 148

Mason, Charlie 2: 401

Mason-Dixon line 1: 216

Massachusett 1: 101, 105

Massachusett language 1: 205

Massachusetts 1: 11, 19, 258

Massachusetts Bay Colony 1: 103

Massacre at Wounded Knee 3: 868, 875

Massasoit 1: 201-203, 212

Masset Indian Reserve 4: 1169, 1175

Mastahmo 2: 477, 486

Mathews, Alex , Pawnee chief (ill.) 3: 841

Mathews, John Joseph 3: 835

Matrilineal kinship system 1: 2194: 1136

Mattaponi 1: 157, 167

Mayan 1: 295; 2: 404

McCartys, New Mexico 2: 549

McGillivray, Alexander 1: 223

McKay, Mabel 4: 1120

McKinley Country Fair 2: 598

Means, Russell 3: 876, 887

Meares, John 4: 1202

Measles and mumps 1: 4

Medicine bundle 1: 148; 3: 724, 740, 786, 799

Medicine Creek Treaty 4: 1229

Medicine Lodge Religion (Midewiwin) 1: 64

Medicine Lodge Society 1: 116

Medicine Lodge Treaty of 1867 3: 765

Medicine Man School 2: 502

Medicine Rocks 4: 1245

Medicine Society 1: 148

Meeker massacre 2: 374

Meeker, Nathan 2: 373

Mekoche 1: 194

Membertou, Henri 1: 77, 85

Memphis, Tennessee 1: 221

Mendocino Reservation 4: 1111

Mennonites 3: 767

Menominee 1: 59-74, 60 (map), 62 (ill.), 67 (ill.), 265

Menominee Indian Tribe of Wisconsin 1: 59-60

Menominee Restoration Act 1: 64, 66

Mesas 2: 397, 571

Mesa Verde, Colorado 2: 381, 397, 399, 409

Mescalero Apache 2: 417, 420 (ill.), 433-435, 427, 529

Mesquakie (Fox) Indian Settlement 1: 169, 170, 173, 179

Metacomet (King Philip) 1: 202-203, 210, 212

Methodists 1: 35, 226, 272; 4: 1178

Métis 3: 654, 656, 660, 662, 683, 685, 687, 703-719, 704 (map), 714 (ill.)

Métis Association of Saskatchewan 3: 711

Métis National Council 3: 711

Métis provisional government 3: 707

Metoac 1: 129, 134

Metoaka 1: 168

Mexican American War 2: 330, 389, 392, 393, 413, 511, 528, 547, 558, 567; 4: 977, 1080

Railroads *1*: 250, 282; *2*: 476, 506, 547, 593; *3*: 727; *4*: 1230

Rainforests *3*: 654

Ramah Reservation *2*: 493

Ramirez, Alex *4*: 1027

Ramona 4: 988

Rancheria *2*: 336; *4*: 981, 1065, 1082, 1090, 1096, 1111

Rancheria Act of 1958 *4*: 1081-1082

Rappahannock *1*: 156, 160

Raven *3*: 655; *4*: 1140, 1174, 1176, 1180

Raven Father *3*: 650

Raw meat *3*: 646

Reagan, Ronald *2*: 494

Red Cloud *3*: 872, 874 (ill.), 875, 880, 887

Red Cloud's War *3*: 873

Red Jacket *1*: 47

Red Power Movement *1*: 115; *3*: 876

Red River *1*: 224

Red River carts *3*: 713

Red River Settlement *3*: 706

Red River War *3*: 779

Red Stick War *1*: 295

Red Tomahawk *3*: 899

Redcorn, Buddy *3*: 835

Redthunder, Soy *3*: 954

Redwood Creek *4*: 1029, 1030, 1032, 1035, 1037, 1038

Regional corporations of Alaska *3*: 663

Reid, Bill *4*: 1180, 1184

Reifel, Ben *3*: 887

Religious freedom *1*: 226

Relocation programs *1*: 296 *2*: 332

Removal Act. *See* Indian Removal Act

Renewal of Traditions *1*: 277

Renville, Gabriel *3*: 865

Reservation *1*: 8, 30, 35, 38, 117; *2*: 331, 336; *3*: 663, 727, 914-915; *4*: 1132

Reservations in New Mexico *2*: 393

Reservations in Oklahoma *1*: 222

Reservation police force *1*: 137

The Revolt of 1847 *2*: 577

Revolutionary War. *See* American Revolutionary War

Rhode Island *1*: 104-105

Ribbon Dance *1*: 305

Ridge, John *1*: 249

Ridge, Major *1*: 249

Riel , Louis David, Jr. *3*: 662, 707 (ill.), 708-709

Rio Chama *2*: 565

Rio Grande Pueblo *2*: 401

Rio Grande River *2*: 458, 466, 523, 565

Rio Pueblo *2*: 581

Risling, David *4*: 1043

Rite of Personal Chant *1*: 43

River Crow *3*: 791

Roads *2*: 399; *3*: 677

Roanoke Island *1*: 159

Roberts, Hollis E. *1*: 283, 292

Robinson, Rose *2*: 471

Rock art *2*: 349

Rocky Boy's Reservation *3*: 683, 688

Rocky Mountains *2*: 328, 340, 354, 489; *3*: 745, 790, 791

Rogers, Robert *1*: 16

Rogue River Indians *4*: 1243

Rogue River Wars *4*: 1243, 1244

Rolfe, John *1*: 160

Roman Catholic church *1*: 65, 77, 80, 158, *2*. 444, 491, 496, 535; *4*: 1229, 1231

Roosevelt Dam *2*: 513

Roosevelt, Franklin D. *1*: 18

Rose, Wendy *2*: 471; *4*: 1091

Ross, John *1*: 223, 246-248, 250

"Ross Party" of Cherokee *1*: 246

Rough Rock, Arizona *2*: 502

Round Dance *2*: 350, 364

Round Valley Reservation *4*: 1111, 1123

Royal Canadian Mounted Police *3*: 636

Royal Presidio Chapel, Monterey, California (ill.) *4*: 1021

Royal Proclamation of 1763 *1*: 186

Rumsen *4*: 1017

Running *2*: 474, 486, 488, 562, 887

Running Brave 3: 887

Running Strong for Native American Youth *3*: 887

Russia *3*: 621, 622, 624, 626, 661, 669-670; *4*: 1109, 1138

Russian America (Alaska) *4*: 1138

Russian American Company *3*: 621, 634

Russian missionaries *3*: 672

Russian Orthodox church *3*: 621, 671; *4*: 1138, 1171, 1267

S

Sa, Kai *2*: 601

Sac *1*: 169-182

Sac and Fox *1*: 59, **169-182,** 170 (map), 172 (ill.), 173 (map), 178 (ill.)

Sac and Fox Gallery *1*: 179

Sac and Fox Nation of Missouri *1*: 172

Sac and Fox of the Mississippi in Iowa *1*: 173

Sac and Fox Reservation, Stroud, Oklahoma *1*: 172, 179-180

Sacajawea *2*: 354, 355, 368

Sachems *1*: 105, 136

Sacred Arrow ceremony *3*: 772